Information Systems for Competitive Advantage

Information Systems for Competitive Advantage

"Look, I'm here ... and early!" Felix remarks, sitting at the table as Tara, Jan, Kelly, and Neil enter the room.

Tara, offering peace with Felix, exclaims, "Yes, Felix, you are!"

"I could come to a lot more 'meetings' once we stopped trying to meet in person and all at once. It was just such a drag to get everyone together at the same time."

"I'll say. Kelly, this is the first time we've met in person in a month, and we're doing it now just so we can show you and Neil what we've got so far." As Jan makes this statement, she's thinking about the time and money she saved not having to arrange for child care for multiple meetings.

"Great. What have you got?" Kelly asks, excited to hear what the team has developed.

"Well," Tara says, clearly struggling with her words, "well, we found that we really didn't know who we are ... No, that's not right. I mean, we know who we are, but we had trouble expressing it in words."

Felix jumps in, "Kelly, it's like this. We think we succeed because we offer the best workout in the city. But, what does *best* really mean? It isn't because of our great juice bar, even though it is great. We decided we're best because of our *intensity*. People come here, it's all business, we get to it and provide a fast-paced, to-the-max cardio workout. People leave here pumped and upbeat!"

"OK, that makes sense to me. Go on."

"So, in an effort to reduce costs, we can't lose that," Felix says, wistfully.

Tara jumps back into the conversation. "So, in our discussion board, we wrote about ways to reduce costs. We had a long thread going and we weren't getting very far until Jan pointed out that the size of the class doesn't seem to impact intensity . . . in fact, packing her spinning classes actually adds to the intensity."

"Yeah, I did," admits Jan. "But I'm not crazy about where this goes. Because, if we pack our classes more, well, we'll save FlexTime money, but . . . well, I may as well say it, fewer classes means less money to us. If we're not teaching we're not getting paid . . ."

An awkward pause fills the room.

Felix jumps in, "We love FlexTime and we're willing to take a hit in the short run. But, how much of a hit will it be? And for how long? We don't know. And we're worried, too."

"Maybe I can help there." Neil speaks for the first time. Everyone turns to listen. "I've got a couple of thoughts. But, first, thanks for taking this so seriously and for bringing this issue to light. As you know, we record all of our class registration data into our database. We've got records going back several years. I can look at that data and see how many classes might be affected. We can look for classes that have lower enrollments, but also at the differences between average class size and maximum class size."

"And then what?" Kelly looks at Neil . . . wondering where he's going with this.

"That will tell us how many classes we might want to cancel, what the benefit would be. And, if there is substantial cost savings to be had, it will help to answer Felix's question about how much of a hit we'll have to take."

Later, Kelly and Neil are talking alone in Neil's office.

"This is risky, Neil. If we start cancelling classes, it will look like we're in trouble. We don't want the staff to start communicating that to our customers."

"Yeah, you're right. And we might lose some staff. But, we haven't decided anything yet. I need to look at the data and see the impact. It's not worth doing if it doesn't help our bottom line, and I'm not sure it will."

"Neil, isn't it great that they get what makes Flex-Time special? I was really proud of them for coming up with this idea. These jobs mean a lot to them."

"If we do make classes larger, maybe I can come up with some bonus program . . . maybe we take the average maximum number of students for each class in each time slot and then provide a bonus for each student they enroll over that number . . . or . . . " Neil looks over Kelly's shoulder, deep in thought.

"I don't mean to be negative, but this sounds complicated. Anyway, I've got a class to teach."

"OK, Kelly, I'll get back to you with what I find out." ▧

Study Questions

Q1 How does organizational strategy determine information systems structure?

Q2 What five forces determine industry structure?

Q3 How does analysis of industry structure determine competitive strategy?

Q4 How does competitive strategy determine value chain structure?

Q5 How do business processes generate value?

Q6 How does competitive strategy determine business processes and the structure of information systems?

Q7 How do information systems provide competitive advantages?

Q8 2021?

MIS is the development and use of information systems that enable organizations to achieve their goals and objectives. This chapter focuses on how information systems support competitive strategy and how IS can create competitive advantages. As you will learn in your organizational behavior classes, a body of knowledge exists to help organizations analyze their industry, select a competitive strategy, and develop business processes. In the first part of this chapter, we will survey that knowledge and show how to use it, via several steps, to structure information systems. Then, in the last section, we will discuss how companies use information systems to gain a competitive advantage.

Q1 How Does Organizational Strategy Determine Information Systems Structure?

According to the definition of MIS, information systems exist to help organizations achieve their goals and objectives. As you will learn in your business strategy class, an organization's goals and objectives are determined by its *competitive strategy*. Thus, ultimately, competitive strategy determines the structure, features, and functions of every information system.

Figure 1 summarizes this situation. In short, organizations examine the structure of their industry and determine a competitive strategy. That strategy determines value chains, which, in turn, determine business processes. The structure of business processes determines the design of supporting information systems.

Michael Porter, one of the key researchers and thinkers in competitive analysis, developed three different models that can help you understand the elements of Figure 1. We begin with his five forces model.

Q2 What Five Forces Determine Industry Structure?

Organizational strategy begins with an assessment of the fundamental characteristics and structure of an industry. One model used to assess an industry structure is Porter's **five forces model**,[1] summarized in Figure 2. According to this model, five competitive forces determine industry profitability: bargaining power of

Figure 1
Organizational Strategy Determines Information Systems

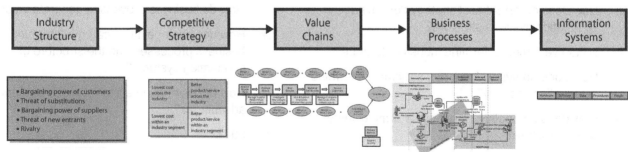

---

[1]Michael Porter, *Competitive Strategy: Techniques for Analyzing Industries and Competitors* (New York: Free Press, 1980).

- Bargaining power of customers
- Threat of substitutions
- Bargaining power of suppliers
- Threat of new entrants
- Rivalry

Figure 2
Porter's Five Forces Model of Industry Structure

Source: Based on Michael E. Porter, *Competitive Advantage: Creating and Sustaining Superior Performance* (The Free Press, a Division of Simon & Schuster Adult Publishing Group). Copyright © 1985, 1998 by Michael E. Porter.

Force	Example of Strong Force	Example of Weak Force
Bargaining power of customers	Toyota's purchase of auto paint	Your power over the procedures and policies of your university
Threat of substitutions	Frequent-traveler's choice of auto rental	Patients using the only drug effective for their type of cancer
Bargaining power of suppliers	Students purchasing gasoline	Grain farmers in a surplus year
Threat of new entrants	Corner latte stand	Professional football team
Rivalry	Used car dealers	Internal Revenue Service

Figure 3
Examples of Five Forces

customers, threat of substitutions, bargaining power of suppliers, threat of new entrants, and rivalry among existing firms. The intensity of each of the five forces determines the characteristics of the industry, how profitable it is, and how sustainable that profitability will be.

To understand this model, consider the strong and weak examples for each of the forces in Figure 3. A good check on your understanding is to see if you can think of different forces of each category in Figure 3. Also, take a particular industry—say, auto repair—and consider how these five forces determine the competitive landscape of that industry.

Figure 4 illustrates FlexTime's analysis of these five forces. The two most serious threats are from their landlord (their location is critical to their clientele and FlexTime

Force	FlexTime Example	Force Strength	FlexTime's Response
Bargaining power of customers	"I want to pay less for my trainer."	Weak	Explain value delivered
Threat of substitutions	"I think I'll join a softball league."	Medium	Emphasize importance of cardio health and fitness to lifestyle
Bargaining power of suppliers	"We're raising your rent."	High	Acquire its own building
Threat of new entrants	"There's a hot new club across the street."	Medium	Superior product
Rivalry	"I'm going to the club on 12th Street."	High	Superior product

Figure 4
Five Forces at FlexTime

is in year 4 of a 5-year lease) and from rivalry. Its response to the rivalry threat is superior product. As you will see, information systems cannot help FlexTime with the landlord problem, but they can provide considerable help in creating a superior product.

Like FlexTime, organizations examine these five forces and determine how they intend to respond to them. That examination leads to competitive strategy.

Q3 How Does Analysis of Industry Structure Determine Competitive Strategy?

See the Ethics Guide later in the chapter to learn how a change in management can greatly affect a company's competitive strategy.

An organization responds to the structure of its industry by choosing a **competitive strategy**. Porter followed his five forces model with the model of four competitive strategies, shown in Figure 5.[2] According to Porter, firms engage in one of these four strategies. An organization can focus on being the cost leader, or it can focus on differentiating its products from those of the competition. Further, the organization can employ the cost or differentiation strategy across an industry, or it can focus its strategy on a particular industry segment.

Consider the car rental industry, for example. According to the first column of Figure 5, a car rental company can strive to provide the lowest-cost car rentals across the industry, or it can seek to provide the lowest-cost car rentals to an industry segment—say, U.S. domestic business travelers.

As shown in the second column, a car rental company can seek to differentiate its products from the competition. It can do so in various ways—for example, by providing a wide range of high-quality cars, by providing the best reservation system, by having the cleanest cars or the fastest check-in, or by some other means. The company can strive to provide product differentiation across the industry or within particular segments of the industry, such as U.S. domestic business travelers.

According to Porter, to be effective, the organization's goals, objectives, culture, and activities must be consistent with the organization's strategy. To those in the MIS field, this means that all information systems in the organization must reflect and facilitate the organization's competitive strategy.

FlexTime has chosen a focused differentiation strategy. Its focus is on downtown, urban, city workers. The environment is sophisticated and adults-only. As stated by FlexTime's staff at the start of this chapter, it differentiates by providing a superior product—an intense, to-the-max workout that leaves clients pumped and excited.

Figure 5
Porter's Four Competitive Strategies

	Cost	Differentiation
Industry-wide	Lowest cost across the industry	Better product/service across the industry
Focus	Lowest cost within an industry segment	Better product/service within an industry segment

[2]Based on Michael Porter, *Competitive Strategy* (New York: Free Press, 1985).

Q4 How Does Competitive Strategy Determine Value Chain Structure?

Organizations analyze the structure of their industry, and, using that analysis, they formulate a competitive strategy. They then need to organize and structure the organization to implement that strategy. If, for example, the competitive strategy is to be *cost leader*, then business activities need to be developed to provide essential functions at the lowest possible cost.

A business that selects a *differentiation* strategy would not necessarily structure itself around least-cost activities. Instead, such a business might choose to develop more costly systems, but it would do so only if those systems provided benefits that outweighed their risks. Porter defined **value** as the amount of money that a customer is willing to pay for a resource, product, or service. The difference between the value that an activity generates and the cost of the activity is called the **margin**. A business with a differentiation strategy will add cost to an activity only as long as the activity has a positive margin.

A **value chain** is a network of value-creating activities. That generic chain consists of five **primary activities** and four **support activities**.

Primary Activities in the Value Chain

To understand the essence of the value chain, consider a small manufacturer—say, a bicycle maker (see Figure 6). First, the manufacturer acquires raw materials using the inbound logistics activity. This activity concerns the receiving and handling of raw materials and other inputs. The accumulation of those materials adds value in the sense that even a pile of unassembled parts is worth something to some customer. A collection of the parts needed to build a bicycle is worth more than an empty space on a shelf. The value is not only the parts themselves, but also the time required to contact vendors for those parts, to maintain business relationships with those vendors, to order the parts, to receive the shipment, and so forth.

In the operations activity, the bicycle maker transforms raw materials into a finished bicycle, a process that adds more value. Next, the company uses the outbound logistics activity to deliver the finished bicycle to a customer. Of course, there is no customer to send the bicycle to without the marketing and sales value activity. Finally, the service activity provides customer support to the bicycle users.

Figure 6
Bicycle Maker's Value Chain

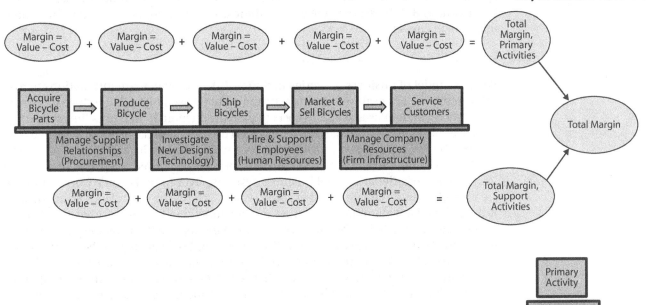

Figure 7

Task Descriptions for Primary Activities of the Value Chain

Source: Based on Michael E. Porter, *Competitive Advantage: Creating and Sustaining Superior Performance* (The Free Press, a Division of Simon & Schuster Adult Publishing Group) Copyright © 1985, 1998 by Michael E. Porter.

Primary Activity	Description
Inbound Logistics	Receiving, storing, and disseminating inputs to the product
Operations/Manufacturing	Transforming inputs into the final product
Outbound Logistics	Collecting, storing, and physically distributing the product to buyers
Sales and Marketing	Inducing buyers to purchase the product and providing a means for them to do so
Customer Service	Assisting customer's use of the product and thus maintaining and enhancing the product's value

Each stage of this generic chain accumulates costs and adds value to the product. The net result is the total margin of the chain, which is the difference between the total value added and the total costs incurred. Figure 7 summarizes the primary activities of the value chain.

Support Activities in the Value Chain

The support activities in the generic value chain contribute indirectly to the production, sale, and service of the product. They include procurement, which consists of the processes of finding vendors, setting up contractual arrangements, and negotiating prices. (This differs from inbound logistics, which is concerned with ordering and receiving in accordance with agreements set up by procurement.)

Porter defined technology broadly. It includes research and development, but it also includes other activities within the firm for developing new techniques, methods, and procedures. He defined human resources as recruiting, compensation, evaluation, and training of full-time and part-time employees. Finally, firm infrastructure includes general management, finance, accounting, legal, and government affairs.

Supporting functions add value, albeit indirectly, and they also have costs. Hence, as shown in Figure 6, supporting activities contribute to a margin. In the case of supporting activities, it would be difficult to calculate the margin because the specific value added of, say, the manufacturer's lobbyists in Washington, D.C., is difficult to know. But there is a value added, there are costs, and there is a margin, even if it is only in concept.

Value Chain Linkages

Porter's model of business activities includes **linkages**, which are interactions across value activities. For example, manufacturing systems use linkages to reduce inventory costs. Such a system uses sales forecasts to plan production; it then uses the production plan to determine raw materials needs and then uses the material needs to schedule purchases. The end result is just-in-time inventory, which reduces inventory sizes and costs.

By describing value chains and their linkages, Porter started a movement to create integrated, cross-departmental business systems. Over time, Porter's work led to the creation of a new discipline called *business process design*. The central idea is that organizations should not automate or improve existing functional systems. Rather, they should create new, more efficient business processes that integrate the activities of all departments involved in a value chain. You will see an example of a linkage in the next section.

Value chain analysis has a direct application to manufacturing businesses like the bicycle manufacturer. However, value chains also exist in service-oriented companies like FlexTime. The difference is that most of the value in a service company is generated by the operations, marketing and sales, and service activities. Inbound and outbound logistics are not typically as important. You will have a chance to reflect on these differences in Using Your Knowledge Question 1 at the end of the chapter.

Using MIS InClass   *A Group Exercise*

Industry Structure → Competitive Strategy → Value Chains → Business Processes → Information Systems

Superstock Royalty Free

As shown in Figure 1, information systems are a logical consequence of an organization's analysis of industry structure via the chain of models shown in the title of this feature. Consequently, you should be able to combine your knowledge of an organization's market, together with observations of the structure and content of its Web storefront, to infer the organization's competitive strategy and possibly make inferences about its value chains and business processes. The process you use here can be useful in preparing for job interviews, as well.

Form a three-person team (or as directed by your professor) and perform the following exercises. Divide work as appropriate, but create common answers for the team.

1. The following pairs of Web storefronts have market segments that overlap in some way. Briefly visit each site of each pair:

   - *www.sportsauthority.com* vs. *www.soccer.com*
   - *www.target.com* vs. *www.sephora.com*
   - *www.woot.com* vs. *www.amazon.com*
   - *www.petco.com* vs. *www.healthyfoodforpets.com*
   - *www.llbean.com* vs. *www.rei.com*

2. Select two pairs from the list. For each pair of companies, answer the following questions:
   a. How do the companies' market segments differ?
   b. How do their competitive pressures differ?
   c. How do their competitive strategies differ?
   d. How is the "feel" of the content of their Web sites different?
   e. How is the "feel" of the user interface of their Web sites different?
   f. How could either company change its Web site to better accomplish its competitive strategy?
   g. Would the change you recommended in step f necessitate a change in one or more of the company's value chains? Explain.

3. Use your answers in step 2 to explain the following statement: "The structure of an organization's information system (here a Web storefront) is determined by its competitive strategy." Structure your answer so that you could use it in a job interview to demonstrate your overall knowledge of business planning.

4. Present your team's answers to the rest of the class.

Q5 How Do Business Processes Generate Value?

A **business process** is a network of activities that generate value by transforming inputs into outputs. The **cost** of the business process is the cost of the inputs plus the cost of the activities. The margin of the business process is the value of the outputs minus the cost.

A business process is a network of activities. Each **activity** is a business function that receives inputs and produces outputs. An activity can be performed by a human,

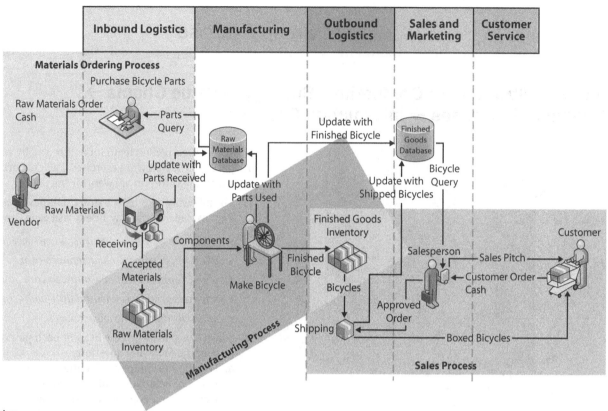

Figure 8
Three Examples
of Business Processes

by a computer system, or by both. The inputs and outputs can be physical, like bicycle parts, or they can be data, such as a Purchase Order. A **repository** is a collection of something; a database is a repository of data and a raw material repository is an inventory of raw materials.

Consider the three business processes for a bicycle manufacturer shown in Figure 8. The materials ordering process transforms cash[3] into a raw materials inventory. The manufacturing process transforms raw materials into finished goods. The sales process transforms finished goods into cash. Notice that the business processes span the value chain activities. The sales process involves sales and marketing as well as outbound logistics activities, as you would expect. Note, too, that while none of these three processes involve a customer-service activity, customer service plays a role in other business processes.

Also notice that activities get and put data resources from and to databases. For example, the purchase-bicycle-parts activity queries the raw materials database to determine the materials to order. The receiving activity updates the raw materials database to indicate the arrival of materials. The make-bicycle activity updates the raw materials database to indicate the consumption of materials. Similar actions are taken in the sales process against the finished goods database.

Business processes vary in cost and effectiveness. In fact, the streamlining of business processes to increase margin (add value, reduce costs, or both) is key to competitive advantage. To get a flavor of process design, however, consider Figure 9, which shows an alternate process for the bicycle manufacturer. Here, the

---

[3]For simplicity, the flow of cash is abbreviated in this diagram. Business processes for authorizing, controlling, making payments, and receiving revenue are, of course, vital.

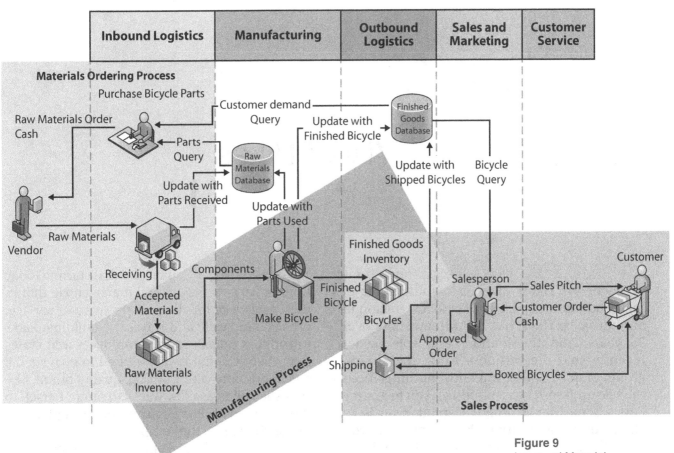

Figure 9
Improved Material
Ordering Process

purchase-bicycle-parts activity not only queries the raw materials inventory database, it also queries the finished goods inventory database. Querying both databases allows the purchasing department to make decisions not just on raw materials quantities, but also on customer demand. By using this data, purchasing can reduce the size of raw materials inventory, reducing production costs and thus adding margin to the value chain. This is an example of using a linkage across business processes to improve process margin.

As you will learn, however, changing business processes is not easy to do. Most process design requires people to work in new ways, to follow different procedures, and employees often resist such change. In Figure 9, the employees who perform the purchase-bicycle-parts activity need to learn to adjust their ordering processes to use customer purchase patterns. Another complication is that data stored in the finished goods database likely will need to be redesigned to keep track of customer demand data. That redesign effort will require that some application programs be changed as well.

Q6 How Does Competitive Strategy Determine Business Processes and the Structure of Information Systems?

Figure 10 shows a business process for renting bicycles. The value-generating activities are shown in the top of the table and the implementation of those activities for two companies with different competitive strategies is shown in the rows below.

The first company has chosen a competitive strategy of low-cost rentals to students. Accordingly, this business implements business processes to minimize costs.

Ethics Guide

Yikes! Bikes

Suppose you are an operations manager for Yikes! Bikes, a manufacturer of high-end mountain bicycles with $20 million in annual sales. Yikes! has been in business over 25 years, and the founder and sole owner recently sold the business to an investment group, Major Capital. You know nothing about the sale until your boss introduces you to Andrea Parks, a partner at Major Capital, who is in charge of the acquisition. Parks explains to you that Yikes! has been sold to Major Capital and that she will be the temporary general manager. She explains that the new owners see great potential in you, and they want to enlist your cooperation during the transition. She hints that if your potential is what she thinks it is, you will be made general manager of Yikes!

Parks explains that the new owners decided there are too many players in the high-end mountain bike business, and they plan to change the competitive strategy of Yikes! from high-end differentiation to lowest-cost vendor. Accordingly, they will eliminate local manufacturing, fire most of the manufacturing department, and import bikes from China. Further, Major Capital sees a need to reduce expenses and plans a 10 percent across-the-board staff reduction and a cut of two-thirds of the customer support department. The new bikes will be of lesser quality than current Yikes! bikes, but the price will be substantially less. The new ownership group believes it will take a few years for the market to realize that Yikes! bikes are not the same quality as they were. Finally, Parks asks you to attend an all-employee meeting with the founder and her.

At the meeting, the founder explains that due to his age and personal situation, he decided to sell Yikes! to Major Capital and that starting today Andrea Parks is the general manager. He thanks the employees for their many years of service, wishes them well, and leaves the building. Parks introduces herself to the employees and states that Major Capital is very excited to own such a great company with a strong, quality brand. She says she will take a few weeks to orient herself to the business and its environment and plans no major changes to the company.

You are reeling from all this news when Parks calls you into her office and explains that she needs you to prepare two reports. In one, she wants a list of all the employees in the manufacturing department, sorted by their salary (or wage for hourly employees). She explains that she intends to cut the most costly employees first. "I don't want to be inflexible about this, though," she says. "If there is someone whom you think we should keep, let me know, and we can talk about it."

She also wants a list of the employees in the customer support department, sorted by the average amount of time each support rep spends with customers. She explains, "I'm not so concerned with payroll expense in customer support. It's not how much we're paying someone; it's how much time they're wasting with customers. We're going to have a bare-bones support department, and we want to get rid of the gabby chatters first."

You are, understandably, shocked and surprised . . . not only at the speed with which the transition has occurred, but also because you wouldn't think the founder would do this to the employees. You call him at home and tell him what is going on.

"Look," he explains, "when I sold the company, I asked them to be sure to take care of the employees. They said they would. I'll call Andrea, but there's really nothing I can do at this point; they own the show."

In a black mood of depression, you realize you don't want to work for Yikes! anymore, but your wife is 6 months' pregnant with your first child. You need medical insurance for her at least until the baby is born. But what miserable tasks are you going to be asked to do before then? And you suspect that if you balk at any task, Parks won't hesitate to fire you, too.

As you leave that night you run into Lori, the most popular customer support representative and one of your favorite employees. "Hey," Lori asks you, "what did you think of that meeting? Do you believe Andrea? Do you think they'll let us continue to make great bikes?" ■

Discussion Questions

1. In your opinion, did the new owners take any illegal action? Is there evidence of a crime in this scenario?

2. Was the statement that Parks made to all of the employees unethical? Why or why not? If you questioned her about the ethics of her statement, how do you think she would justify herself?

3. What do you think Parks will tell the founder if he calls as a result of your conversation with him? Does he have any legal recourse? Is Major Capital's behavior toward him unethical? Why or why not?

4. Parks is going to use information to perform staff cuts. What do you think about her rationale? Ethically, should she consider other factors, such as number of years of service, past employee reviews, or other criteria?

5. How do you respond to Lori? What are the consequences if you tell her what you know? What are the consequences of lying to her? What are the consequences of saying something noncommittal?

6. If you actually were in this situation, would you leave the company? Why or why not?

7. In business school, we talk of principles like competitive strategy as interesting academic topics. But, as you can see from the Yikes! case, competitive strategy decisions have human consequences. How do you plan to resolve conflicts between human needs and tough business decisions?

8. How do you define *job security*?

	Value-Generating Activity	Greet Customer	Determine Needs	Rent Bike	Return Bike & Pay
Low-cost rental to students	**Message that implements competitive strategy**	"You wanna bike?"	"Bikes are over there. Help yourself."	"Fill out this form, and bring it to me over here when you're done."	"Show me the bike." "OK, you owe $23.50. Pay up."
	Supporting business process	None.	Physical controls and procedures to prevent bike theft.	Printed forms and a shoe box to store them in.	Shoe box with rental form. Minimal credit card and cash receipt system.
High-service rental to business executives at conference resort	**Message that implements competitive strategy**	"Hello, Ms. Henry. Wonderful to see you again. Would you like to rent the WonderBike 4.5 that you rented last time?"	"You know, I think the WonderBike Supreme would be a better choice for you. It has …"	"Let me just scan the bike's number into our system, and then I'll adjust the seat for you."	"How was your ride?" "Here, let me help you. I'll just scan the bike's tag again and have your paperwork in just a second." "Would you like a beverage?" "Would you like me to put this on your hotel bill, or would you prefer to pay now?"
	Supporting business process	Customer tracking and past sales activity system.	Employee training and information system to match customer and bikes, biased to "up-sell" customer.	Automated inventory system to check bike out of inventory.	Automated inventory system to place bike back in inventory. Prepare payment documents. Integrate with resort's billing system.

Figure 10
Operations Value Chains
for Bicycle Rental Companies

The second company has chosen a differentiation strategy. It provides "best-of-breed" rentals to executives at a high-end conference resort. Notice that this business has designed its business processes to ensure superb service. To achieve a positive margin, it must ensure that the value added will exceed the costs of providing the service.

Now, consider the information systems required for these business processes. The student rental business uses a shoe box for its data facility. The only computer/software/data component in its business is the machine provided by its bank for processing credit card transactions.

The high-service business, however, makes extensive use of information systems, as shown in Figure 11. It has a CRM database that tracks past customer rental activity, and an inventory database that is used to select and up-sell bicycle rentals as well as to control bicycle inventory with a minimum of fuss to its high-end customers.

So the bottom line is this: Organizations analyze their industry and choose a competitive strategy. Given that strategy, they design business processes that span value-generating activities. Those processes determine the scope and requirements of each organization's information systems. Given this background, we will now examine how information systems generate a competitive advantage.

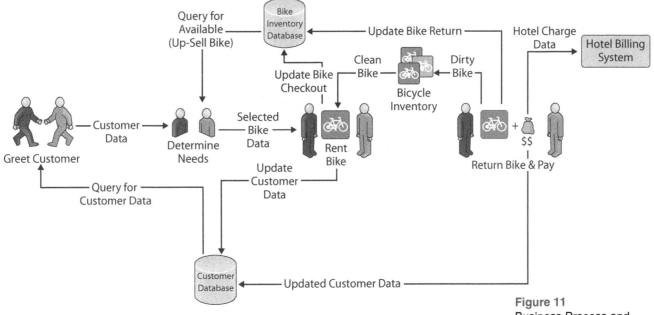

Figure 11
Business Process and Information Systems for High-Service Bike Rental

Q7 How Do Information Systems Provide Competitive Advantages?

In your business strategy class, you will study the Porter models in greater detail than we have discussed here. When you do so, you will learn numerous ways that organizations respond to the five competitive forces. For our purposes, we can distill those ways into the list of principles shown in Figure 12. Keep in mind that we are applying these principles in the context of the organization's competitive strategy.

You can also apply these principles to your personal competitive advantage, as discussed in the Guide later in the chapter.

Some of these competitive techniques are created via products and services, and some are created via the development of business processes. Consider each.

Competitive Advantage via Products

The first three principles in Figure 12 concern products or services. Organizations gain a competitive advantage by creating *new* products or services, by *enhancing* existing products or services, and by *differentiating* their products and services from those of their competitors. FlexTime differentiates on the basis of quality of workout.

Information systems create competitive advantages either as part of a product or by providing support to a product. Consider, for example, a car rental agency like Hertz or Avis. An information system that produces information about the car's location and provides driving instructions to destinations is part of the car rental and thus is part of the product itself (see Figure 13a). In contrast, an information system that schedules car maintenance is not part of the product, but instead supports the

Figure 12
Principles of Competitive Advantage

> **Product Implementations**
> 1. Create a new product or service
> 2. Enhance products or services
> 3. Differentiate products or services
>
> **Process Implementations**
> 4. Lock in customers and buyers
> 5. Lock in suppliers
> 6. Raise barriers to market entry
> 7. Establish alliances
> 8. Reduce costs

Figure 13
Two Roles for Information
Systems Regarding Products

a. Information System as Part of a Car Rental Product

b. Information System That Supports a Car Rental Product

Daily Service Schedule — November 17, 2010

StationID   22
StationName   Lubrication

ServiceDate	ServiceTime	VehicleID	Make	Model	Mileage	ServiceDescription
11/17/2010	12:00 AM	155890	Ford	Explorer	2244	Std. Lube
11/17/2010	11:00 AM	12448	Toyota	Tacoma	7558	Std. Lube

StationID   26
StationName   Alignment

ServiceDate	ServiceTime	VehicleID	Make	Model	Mileage	ServiceDescription
11/17/2010	9:00 AM	12448	Toyota	Tacoma	7558	Front end alignment inspect

StationID   28
StationName   Transmission

ServiceDate	ServiceTime	VehicleID	Make	Model	Mileage	ServiceDescription
11/17/2010	11:00 AM	155890	Ford	Explorer	2244	Transmission oil change

product (see Figure 13b). Either way, information systems can help achieve the first three principles in Figure 12.

The remaining five principles in Figure 12 concern competitive advantage created by the implementation of business processes.

Competitive Advantage via Business Processes

Organizations can *lock in customers* by making it difficult or expensive for customers to switch to another product. This strategy is sometimes called establishing high **switching costs**. Organizations can *lock in suppliers* by making it difficult to switch to another organization, or, stated positively, by making it easy to connect to and work with the organization. Finally, competitive advantage can be gained by *creating entry barriers* that make it difficult and expensive for new competition to enter the market.

Another means to gain competitive advantage is to *establish alliances* with other organizations. Such alliances establish standards, promote product awareness and needs, develop market size, reduce purchasing costs, and provide other benefits. Finally, organizations can gain competitive advantage by *reducing costs*. Such reductions enable the organization to reduce prices and/or to increase profitability. Increased profitability means not just greater shareholder value, but also more cash, which can fund further infrastructure development for even greater competitive advantage.

All of these principles of competitive advantage make sense, but the question you may be asking is, "How do information systems help to create competitive advantage?" To answer that question, consider a sample information system.

How Does an Actual Company Use IS to Create Competitive Advantages?

ABC, Inc.,[4] is a worldwide shipper with sales well in excess of $1 billion. From its inception, ABC invested heavily in information technology and led the shipping industry in the application of information systems for competitive advantage. Here we consider one example of an information system that illustrates how ABC successfully uses information technology to gain competitive advantage.

---

[4]The information system described here is used by a major transportation company that did not want its name published in this textbook.

ABC maintains customer account data that include not only the customer's name, address, and billing information, but also data about the people, organizations, and locations to which the customer ships. Figure 14 shows a Web form that an ABC customer is using to schedule a shipment. When the ABC system creates the form, it fills the Company name drop-down list with the names of companies that the customer has shipped to in the past. Here, the user is selecting Prentice Hall.

When the user clicks the Company name, the underlying ABC information system reads the customer's contact data from a database. The data consist of names, addresses, and phone numbers of recipients from past shipments. The user then selects a Contact name, and the system inserts that contact's address and other data into the form using data from the database, as shown in Figure 15. Thus, the system saves customers from having to reenter data for people to whom they have shipped in the past. Providing the data in this way also reduces data-entry errors.

Figure 16 shows another feature of this system. On the right-hand side of this form, the customer can request that ABC send email messages to the sender (the customer), the recipient, and others as well. The customer can choose for ABC to send an email when the shipment is created and when it has been delivered. In Figure 16, the user has provided three email addresses. The customer wants all three addresses

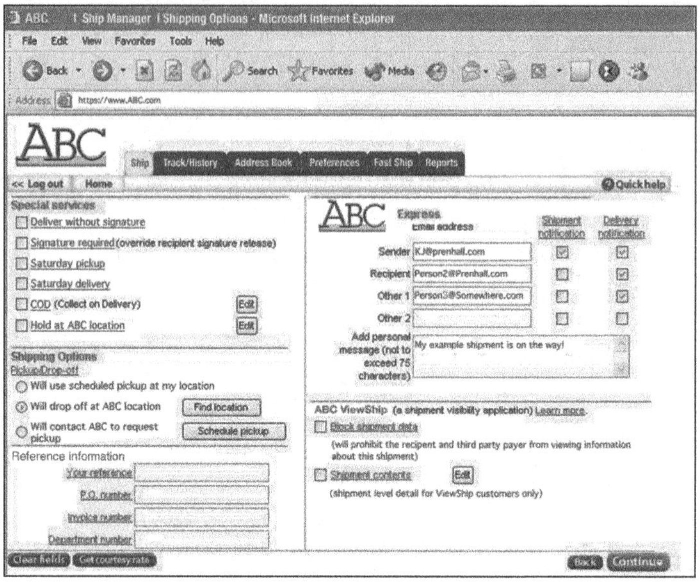

Figure 16
ABC, Inc., Web Page to
Specify Email Notification

to receive delivery notification, but only the sender will receive shipment notification. The customer can add a personal message as well. By adding this capability to the shipment scheduling system, ABC has extended its product from a package-delivery service to a package- *and* information-delivery service.

Figure 17 shows one other capability of this information system. It has generated a shipping label, complete with bar code, for the user to print. By doing this, the company not only reduces errors in the preparation of shipping labels, but it also causes the customer to provide the paper and ink for document printing! Millions of such documents are printed every day, resulting in a considerable savings to the company.

How Does This System Create a Competitive Advantage?

Now consider the ABC shipping information system in light of the competitive advantage factors in Figure 12. This information system *enhances* an existing service because it eases the effort of creating a shipment to the customer while reducing errors. The information system also helps to *differentiate* the ABC package delivery service from competitors that do not have a similar system. Further, the generation of email messages when ABC picks up and delivers a package could be considered to be a *new* service.

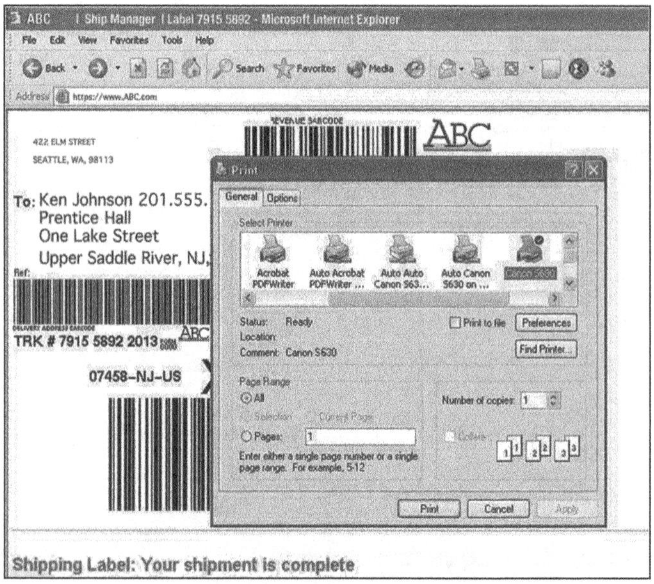

Only customers who have access to the Internet can use this shipping system. Do organizations have an ethical obligation to provide equivalent services to those who do not have access? The Guide later in the chapter explores this question.

Figure 17
ABC, Inc., Web Page
to Print a Shipping Label

Because this information system captures and stores data about recipients, it reduces the amount of customer work when scheduling a shipment. Customers will be *locked in* by this system: If a customer wants to change to a different shipper, he or she will need to rekey recipient data for that new shipper. The disadvantage of rekeying data may well outweigh any advantage of switching to another shipper.

This system achieves a competitive advantage in two other ways as well: First, it raises the barriers to market entry. If another company wants to develop a shipping service, it will not only have to be able to ship packages, but it will also need to have a similar information system. In addition, the system reduces costs. It reduces errors in shipping documents, and it saves ABC paper, ink, and printing costs.

Of course, to determine if this system delivers a *net savings* in costs, the cost of developing and operating the information system will need to be offset against the gains in reduced errors and paper, ink, and printing costs. It may be that the system costs more than the savings. Even still, it may be a sound investment if the value of intangible benefits, such as locking in customers and raising entry barriers, exceeds the net cost.

Before continuing, review Figure 12. Make sure that you understand each of the principles of competitive advantage and how information systems can help achieve them. In fact, the list in Figure 12 probably is important enough to memorize, because you can also use it for non-IS applications. You can consider any business project or initiative in light of competitive advantage.

Q8 2021?

What does FlexTime look like in 2021? Put on your rose-colored glasses and assume that FlexTime overcomes the current downturn, revenue picks up, and FlexTime addresses the threat of its landlord by buying its own, four-story, ultra-hip building . . . a former warehouse that oozes urban charm. What kinds of communications facilities does it put into the new building? What data connectivity do clients want? It depends on what systems FlexTime decides to implement.

Assume that FlexTime keeps pace with emerging research on optimal workout schedules (see *www.angelfire.com/wa3/loserschallenge/cardio.html* and *www.sportsci.org/jour/0101/cf.htm*). Given this research and that developed between now and 2021, FlexTime could develop information systems that track client workouts and their intensity and relate that data to net cardiovascular benefits. It could also correlate workout data with dietary data and relate all of that to client weight loss or gain. Maybe FlexTime provides this data to medical insurers and helps its active clients to obtain reductions in their medical insurance premiums.

But notice the word *could*. Should it? Is it worthwhile for FlexTime to develop such systems? This chapter provides a framework for deciding. Would such capability increase FlexTime's ability to meet its competitive strategy? Or, perhaps in light of these technologies, FlexTime will reevaluate the five forces and adjust its competitive strategy and then assess whether such systems are needed in that new competitive environment.

Now put on your dark-colored glasses. Suppose the economic downturn proves too much for FlexTime and it is forced to reconfigure into a shadow of its former self. Maybe FlexTime is no longer a single business entity. Maybe it becomes a federation of trainers, workout spaces, dieticians, and recreational sports leagues. Maybe that federation uses free data storage, data communication, emerging collaboration tools and systems to appear as a virtual organization to clients, but one that is composed of independently owned and operated small business entities.

Who knows? But you can be the beneficiary of this story, regardless of how it turns out. You can, if you attain marketable skills that include the ability to access, evaluate, and integrate emerging technology into business as it dynamically unfolds.

Guide

Limiting Access to Those Who Have Access

An adage of investing is that it's easier for the rich to get richer. Someone who has $10 million invested at 5 percent earns $500,000 per year. Another investor with $10,000 invested at that same 5 percent earns $500 per year. Every year, the disparity increases as the first investor pulls farther and farther ahead of the second.

This same adage applies to intellectual wealth as well. It's easier for those with considerable knowledge and expertise to gain even more knowledge and expertise. Someone who knows how to search the Internet can learn more readily than someone who does not. And every year, the person with greater knowledge pulls farther and farther ahead. Intellectual capital grows in just the same way that financial capital grows.

Searching the Internet is not just a matter of knowledge, however. It's also a matter of access. The increasing reliance on the Web for information and commerce has created a **digital divide** between those who have Internet access and those who do not. This divide continues to deepen as those who are connected pull farther ahead of those who are not.

Various groups have addressed this problem by making Internet access available in public places, such as libraries, community centers, and retirement homes. As of 2007, The Bill and Melinda Gates Foundation has given more than $262 million to public libraries for the purchase of personal computers and Internet access. Total donations since then are not published, but their foundation continues to give more support to libraries, particularly with matching funds to support computer maintenance and faster Internet connectivity (see *www.gatesfoundation. org/topics/Pages/libraries.aspx#*).

Such gifts help, but not everyone can be served this way, and even with such access, there's a big convenience difference between going to the library and walking across your bedroom to access the Internet—and you don't have to stand in line.

The advantages accrue to everyone with access, every day. For the connected, it is the primary means of learning, well, anything. Directions to your friend's house? Movies at local theaters? Want to buy music, books, or tools? Want convenient access to your checking account? Want to decide whether to refinance your condo? Want to know what TCP/IP means? Use the Internet, if you have it.

All of this intellectual capital resides on the Internet because businesses benefit by putting it there. It's much cheaper to provide product support information over the Internet than on printed documents. The savings include not only the costs of printing, but also the costs of warehousing and mailing. Further, when product specifications change, the organization just changes the Web site. There is no obsolete material to dispose of and no costs for printing and distributing the revised material. Those who have Internet access gain current information faster than those who do not.

What happens to those who do not have Internet access? They fall farther and farther behind. The digital divide segregates the haves from the have-nots, creating new class structures. Such segregation is subtle, but it is segregation, nonetheless.

Do organizations have a responsibility to address this matter? If 98 percent of a company's market segment has Internet access, does the company have a responsibility to provide non-Internet materials to that other 2 percent? On what basis does that responsibility lie? Does a government agency have a responsibility to provide equal information to those who have Internet access and those who do not? When those who are connected can obtain information nearly instantaneously, 24/7, is it even possible to provide equal information to the connected and the unconnected?

It's a worldwide problem. Connected societies and countries pull farther and farther ahead. How can any economy that relies on traditional mail compete with an Internet-based economy?

If you're taking MIS, you're already connected; you're already one of the haves, and you're already pulling ahead of the have-nots. The more you learn about information systems and their use in commerce, the faster you'll pull ahead. The digital divide increases. ■

Discussion Questions

1. Do you see evidence of a digital divide on your campus? In your hometown? Among your relatives? Describe personal experiences you've had regarding the digital divide.

2. Do organizations have a legal responsibility to provide the same information for nonconnected customers that they do for connected customers? If not, should laws be passed requiring organizations to do so?

3. Even if there is no current legal requirement for organizations to provide equal information to nonconnected customers, do they have an ethical responsibility to do so?

4. Are your answers to questions 2 and 3 different for government agencies than they are for commercial organizations?

5. Because it may be impossible to provide equal information, another approach for reducing the digital divide is for the government to enable nonconnected citizens to acquire Internet access via subsidies and tax incentives. Do you favor such a program? Why or why not?

6. Suppose that nothing is done to reduce the digital divide and that it is allowed to grow wider and wider. What are the consequences? How will society change? Are these consequences acceptable?

SECURITY

Guide

Your Personal Competitive Advantage

Consider the following possibility: You work hard, earning your degree in business, and you graduate, only to discover that you cannot find a job in your area of study. You look for 6 weeks or so, but then you run out of money. In desperation, you take a job waiting tables at a local restaurant. Two years go by, the economy picks up, and the jobs you had been looking for become available. Unfortunately, your degree is now 2 years old; you are competing with students who have just graduated with fresh degrees (and fresh knowledge). Two years of waiting tables, good as you are at it, does not appear to be good experience for the job you want. You're stuck in a nightmare—one that will be hard to get out of, and one that you cannot allow to happen.

Examine Figure 12 again, but this time consider those elements of competitive advantage as they apply to you personally. As an employee, the skills and abilities you offer are your personal product. Examine the first three items in the list, and ask yourself, "How can I use my time in school—and in this MIS class, in particular—to create new skills, to enhance those I already have, and to differentiate my skills from the competition?" (By the way, you will enter a national/international market. Your competition is not just the students in your class; it's also students in classes in Ohio, California, British Columbia, Florida, New York, and every place else they're teaching MIS today.)

Suppose you are interested in a sales job. Perhaps you want to sell in the pharmaceutical industry. What skills can you learn from your MIS class that will make you more competitive as a future salesperson? Ask yourself, "How does the pharmaceutical industry use MIS to gain competitive advantage?" Get on the Internet and find examples of the use of information systems in the pharmaceutical industry. How does Pfizer, for example, use a customer information system to sell to doctors? How can your knowledge of such systems differentiate you from your competition for a job there? How does Pfizer use a knowledge management system? How does the firm keep track of drugs that have an adverse effect on each other?

The fourth and fifth items in Figure 12 concern locking in customers, buyers, and suppliers. How can you interpret those elements in terms of your personal competitive advantage? Well, to lock in, you first have to have a relationship to lock in. So do you have an internship? If not, can you get one? And once you have an internship, how can you use your knowledge of MIS to lock in your job so that you get a job offer? Does the company you are interning for have a CRM system (or any other information system that is important to the company)? If users are happy with the system, what characteristics make it worthwhile? Can you lock in a job by becoming an expert user of this system? Becoming an expert user not only locks you into your job, but it also raises barriers to entry for others who might be competing for the job. Also, can you suggest ways to improve the system, thus using your knowledge of the company and the system to lock in an extension of your job?

Human resources personnel say that networking is one of the most effective ways of finding a job. How can you use this class to establish alliances with other students? Is there an email list server for the students in your class? What about Facebook? LinkedIn? Twitter? How can you use those facilities to develop job-seeking alliances with other students? Who in your class already has a job or an internship? Can any of those people provide hints or opportunities for finding a job?

Don't restrict your job search to your local area. Are there regions of your country where jobs are more plentiful? How can you find out about student organizations in those regions? Search the Web for MIS classes in other cities, and make contact with students there. Find out what the hot opportunities are in other cities.

Finally, as you study MIS, think about how the knowledge you gain can help you save costs for your employers. Even more, see if you can build a case that an employer would actually save money by hiring you. The line of reasoning might be that because of your knowledge of IS you will be able to facilitate cost savings that more than compensate for your salary.

In truth, few of the ideas that you generate for a potential employer will be feasible or pragmatically useful. The fact that you are thinking creatively, however, will indicate to a potential employer that you have initiative and are grappling with the problems that real businesses have. As this course progresses, keep thinking about competitive advantage, and strive to understand how the topics you study can help you to accomplish, personally, one or more of the principles in Figure 12. ■

Discussion Questions

1. Summarize the efforts you have taken thus far to build an employment record that will lead to job offers after graduation.

2. Considering the first three principles in Figure 12, describe one way in which you have a competitive advantage over your classmates. If you do not have such competitive advantage, describe actions you can take to obtain one.

3. In order to build your network, you can use your status as a student to approach business professionals. Namely, you can contact them for help with an assignment or for career guidance. For example, suppose you want to work in banking and you know that your local bank has a customer information system. You could call the manager of that bank and ask him or her how that system creates a competitive advantage for the bank. You also could ask to interview other employees and go armed with the list in Figure 12. Describe two specific ways in which you can use your status as a student and the list in Figure 12 to build your network in this way.

4. Describe two ways that you can use student alliances to obtain a job. How can you use information systems to build, maintain, and operate such alliances?

Sourabh/Shutterstock

Active Review

Use this Active Review to verify that you understand the ideas and concepts that answer the chapter's study questions.

Q1 How does organizational strategy determine information systems structure?

Diagram and explain the relationship of industry structure, competitive strategy, value chains, business processes, and information systems. Working from industry structure to IS, explain how the knowledge you've gained in these first three chapters pertains to that diagram.

Q2 What five forces determine industry structure?

Name and briefly describe the five forces. Give your own examples of both strong and weak forces of each type, similar to those in Figure 3.

Q3 How does analysis of industry structure determine competitive strategy?

Describe four different strategies as defined by Porter. Give an example of four different companies that have implemented each of the strategies.

Q4 How does competitive strategy determine value chain structure?

Define the terms *value*, *margin*, and *value chain*. Explain why organizations that choose a differentiation strategy can use value to determine a limit on the amount of extra cost to pay for differentiation. Name the primary and support activities in the value chain and explain the purpose of each. Explain the concept of linkages.

Q5 How do business processes generate value?

Define *business process*, *cost*, and *margin* as they pertain to business processes. Explain the purpose of an activity and describe types of repository. Explain the importance of business process redesign and describe the difference between the business processes in Figure 8 and those in Figure 9.

Q6 How does competitive strategy determine business processes and the structure of information systems?

In your own words, explain how competitive strategy determines the structure of business processes. Use the examples of a clothing store that caters to struggling students and a clothing store that caters to professional businesspeople in a high-end neighborhood. List the activities in the business process for the two companies and create a chart like that in Figure 9. Explain how the information systems requirements differ between the two stores.

Q7 How do information systems provide competitive advantages?

List and briefly describe eight principles of competitive advantage. Consider your college bookstore. List one application of each of the eight principles. Strive to include examples that involve information systems.

Q8 2021?

Assume that FlexTime overcomes the current revenue challenge and buys a new building. Describe the new information systems that FlexTime could create by 2021. Summarize how FlexTime should go about deciding which systems to implement. In contrast, describe what is likely to happen if FlexTime fails and becomes a shadow of its former self. Explain how technology could help its remnants merge with others to become a virtual company.

▰ Key Terms and Concepts

Activity	Digital divide	Repository
Business process	Five forces model	Support activities
Business process management	Linkages	Switching costs
Competitive strategy	Margin [of a business	Value
Cost [of a business	process]	Value chain
process]	Primary activities	

▰ Using Your Knowledge

1. Apply the value chain model to FlexTime. FlexTime does have some inventory, principally fruit and soft drinks, energy bars, and other health food that it sells at its juice bar. But, fundamentally, FlexTime is a service business. It provides facilities, equipment, and skilled personnel to teach classes and provide personal training to clients. It also provides towels, soap, shampoo, and showers for clients to use after working out.

   a. Describe how each of the primary value chain activities pertains to FlexTime. Rank the importance of that activity to FlexTime's success on a scale of 1 (low) to 5 (high). Justify your ranking.

   b. Describe how each support value chain activity pertains to FlexTime. Rank the importance of that activity to FlexTime's success on a scale of 1 (low) to 5 (high). Justify your ranking.

   c. Diagram two business processes that support the primary activities you identified as most important in part a. Use Figures 8 and 9 as a guide.

   d. Explain how each of the business processes in your answer to part c adds value to FlexTime. How does the business process need to be designed to support FlexTime's competitive strategy of a high-intensity workout? How would the value chain be different if FlexTime wanted to be the lowest-cost provider of healthcare services?

   e. Describe an information system that would support the business process you identified in your answer to part d. How would that information system differ for a company with FlexTime's competitive strategy, as compared to a company with a lowest-cost competitive strategy?

2. Apply the value chain model to a mail-order company such as L.L.Bean (*www.llbean.com*). What is its competitive strategy? Describe the tasks L.L.Bean must accomplish for each of the primary value chain activities. How does L.L.Bean's competitive strategy and the nature of its business influence the general characteristics of its information systems?

3. Suppose you decide to start a business that recruits students for summer jobs. You will match available students with available jobs. You need to learn what positions are available and what students are available for filling those positions. In starting your business, you know you will be competing with local newspapers, Craigslist (*www.craigslist.org*), and with your college. You will probably have other local competitors as well.

   a. Analyze the structure of this industry according to Porter's five forces model.

   b. Given your analysis in part a, recommend a competitive strategy.

   c. Describe the primary value chain activities as they apply to this business.

   d. Describe a business process for recruiting students.

   e. Describe information systems that could be used to support the business process in part d.

   f. Explain how the process you describe in part d and the system you describe in part e reflect your competitive strategy.

4. Consider the two different bike rental companies in Figure 10. Think about the bikes that they rent. Clearly, the student bikes will be just about anything that can be ridden out of the shop. The bikes for the business executives, however, must be new, shiny, clean, and in tip-top shape.

   a. Compare and contrast the operations value chains of these two businesses as they pertain to the management of bicycles.

   b. Describe a business process for maintaining bicycles for both businesses.

   c. Describe a business process for acquiring bicycles for both businesses.

   d. Describe a business process for disposing of bicycles for both businesses.

   e. What roles do you see for information systems in your answers to the earlier questions? The information systems can be those you develop within your company or they can be those developed by others, such as Craigslist.

5. Samantha Green owns and operates Twigs Tree Trimming Service. Samantha graduated from the forestry program of a nearby university and worked for a large landscape design firm, performing tree trimming and

removal. After several years of experience, she bought her own truck, stump grinder, and other equipment and opened her own business in St. Louis, Missouri.

Although many of her jobs are one-time operations to remove a tree or stump, others are recurring, such as trimming a tree or groups of trees every year or every other year. When business is slow, she calls former clients to remind them of her services and of the need to trim their trees on a regular basis.

Samantha has never heard of Michael Porter or any of his theories. She operates her business "by the seat of her pants."

a. Explain how an analysis of the five competitive forces could help Samantha.
b. Do you think Samantha has a competitive strategy? What competitive strategy would seem to make sense for her?
c. How would knowledge of her competitive strategy help her sales and marketing efforts?
d. Describe, in general terms, the kind of information system that she needs to support sales and marketing efforts.

6. FiredUp, Inc., is a small business owned by Curt and Julie Robards. Based in Brisbane, Australia,

FiredUp manufactures and sells a lightweight camping stove called the Fired Now. Curt, who previously worked as an aerospace engineer, invented and patented a burning nozzle that enables the stove to stay lit in very high winds—up to 90 miles per hour. Julie, an industrial designer by training, developed an elegant folding design that is small, lightweight, easy to set up, and very stable. Curt and Julie manufacture the stove in their garage, and they sell it directly to their customers over the Internet and via phone.

a. Explain how an analysis of the five competitive forces could help FiredUp.
b. What does FiredUp's competitive strategy seem to be?
c. Briefly summarize how the primary value chain activities pertain to FiredUp. How should the company design these value chains to conform to its competitive strategy?
d. Describe business processes that FiredUp needs in order to implement its marketing and sales and also its service value chain activities.
e. Describe, in general terms, information systems to support your answer to part d.

Collaboration Exercise

Collaborate with students on the following exercise. In particular, consider using Google Docs, Windows Live SkyDrive, Microsoft SharePoint, or some other collaboration tool.

Singing Valley Resort is a top-end 50-unit resort located high in the Colorado mountains. Rooms rent for $400 to $4,500 per night, depending on the season and the type of accommodations. Singing Valley's clientele are well-to-do; many are famous entertainers, sports figures, and business executives. They are accustomed to, and demand, superior service.

Singing Valley resides in a gorgeous mountain valley and is situated a few hundred yards from a serene mountain lake. It prides itself on superior accommodations; tip-top service; delicious, healthful, organic meals; and exceptional wines. Because it has been so successful, Singing Valley is 90 percent occupied except during the "shoulder seasons" (November, after the leaves change and before the snow arrives, and late April, when winter sports are finished but the snow is still on the ground.)

Singing Valley's owners want to increase revenue, but because the resort is nearly always full and because its rates are already at the top of the scale it cannot do so via

occupancy revenue. Thus, over the past several years it has focused on up-selling to its clientele activities such as fly-fishing, river rafting, cross-country skiing, snow-shoeing, art lessons, yoga and other exercise classes, spa services, and the like.

To increase the sales of these optional activities, Singing Valley prepared in-room marketing materials to advertise their availability. Additionally, it trained all registration personnel on techniques of casually and appropriately suggesting such activities to guests on arrival.

The response to these promotions was only mediocre, so Singing Valley's management stepped up its promotions. The first step was to send email to its clientele advising them of the activities available during their stay. An automated system produced emails personalized with names and personal data.

Unfortunately, the automated email system backfired. Immediately upon its execution, Singing Valley management received numerous complaints. One long-term customer objected that she had been coming to Singing Valley for 7 years and asked if they had yet noticed that she was confined to a wheelchair. If they had noticed, she said, why did they send her a personalized invitation for a hiking trip? The agent of another famous client complained that the personalized email was sent to her client and her husband, when anyone who had turned on a TV in the past 6 months knew the two of them were involved in an exceedingly acrimonious divorce. Yet another customer complained that, indeed, he and his wife had vacationed at Singing Valley 3 years ago, but he had not been there since. To his knowledge, his wife had not been there, either, so he was puzzled as to why the email referred to their visit last winter. He wanted to know if, indeed, his wife had recently been to the resort, without him. Of course, Singing Valley had no way of knowing about customers it had insulted who never complained.

During the time the automated email system was operational sales of extra activities were up 15 percent. However, the strong customer complaints conflicted with its competitive strategy so, in spite of the extra revenue, Singing Valley stopped the automated email system, sacked the vendor who had developed it, and demoted the Singing Valley employee who had brokered the system. Singing Valley was left with the problem of how to increase its revenue.

Your team's task is to develop two innovative ideas for solving Singing Valley's problem. At the minimum, include the following in your response:

a. An analysis of the five forces of the Singing Valley market. Make and justify any necessary assumptions about their market.

b. A statement of Singing Valley's competitive strategy.

c. A statement of the problem. A problem is a perceived difference between what is and what ought to be. If the members of your group have different perceptions of the problem, all the better. Use a collaborative process to obtain the best possible problem description to which all can agree.

d. Document in a general way (like the top row of Figure 10), the process of up-selling an activity.

e. Develop two innovative ideas for solving the Singing Valley problem. For each idea, provide:
 * A brief description of the idea
 * A process diagram (like Figure 11) of the idea. Figure 11 was produced using Microsoft Visio; if you have access to that product, you'll save time and have a better result if you also use it.
 * A description of the information system needed to implement the idea

f. Compare the advantages and disadvantages of your alternatives in part e and recommend one of them for implementation.

▬ Case Study

Bosu Balance Trainer

The Bosu balance trainer is a device for developing balance, strength, and aerobic conditioning. Invented in 1999, Bosu has become popular in leading health clubs, in athletic departments, and in homes. Bosu stands for "both sides up," because either side of the equipment can be used for training. Figure 18 shows a Bosu in use.

Bosu is not only a new training device, but it also reflects a new philosophy in athletic conditioning that focuses on balance. According to the Bosu inventor, David Weck, "The Bosu Balance Trainer was born of passion to improve my balance. In my lifelong pursuit of enhanced athleticism, I have come to understand that balance is the foundation on which all other performance components are built." In order to obtain broad market acceptance both for his philosophy as well as for the Bosu product, Weck licensed the sales and marketing of Bosu to FitnessQuest in 2001.

Bosu devices have been very successful and that success attracted copycat products. FitnessQuest successfully defeated such products using a number of techniques, but primarily by leveraging its alliances with professional trainers.

According to Dustin Schnabel, Bosu product manager,

"We have developed strong and effective relationships with more than 10,000 professional trainers. We do all we can to make sure those trainers succeed with Bosu and they in turn encourage their clients to purchase our product rather than some cheap imitation.

"It's all about quality. We build a quality product, we create quality relationships with the trainers, and we make sure those trainers have everything they need from us to provide a quality experience to their clients."

That strategy worked well. In the fall of 2004, Fitness Quest had a serious challenge to Bosu from a large sports equipment vendor who had preexisting alliances with major chains such as Target and Wal-Mart. The competitor introduced a Bosu copycat at a slightly lower price. Within a few months, in an effort to gain sales, they reduced their price, eventually several times, until it was less than half the price of the Bosu. Today, that copycat product is not to be seen. According to Schnabel, "They couldn't give that product away. Why? Because customers were coming in the store to buy the Bosu product that their trainers recommended."

Figure 18

Figure 19

Sources: Bosu, *www.bosu.com* (accessed June 2009); IndoRow, *www.indorow.com* (accessed June 2009); and Conversation with Dustin Schnabel, July 2009.

Questions

1. Review the principles of competitive advantage in Figure 12. Which types of competitive advantage has Bosu used to defeat copycat products?

2. What role did information systems play in your answer to question 1?

3. What additional information systems could Fitness Quest develop to create barriers to entry to the competition and to lock in customers?

4. In 2004, FitnessQuest had alliances with trainers and their competitor had alliances with major retailers. Thus, both companies were competing on the basis of their alliances. Why do you think FitnessQuest won this competition? To what extent did their success leveraging relationships with trainers depend on information systems? On other factors?

5. The case does not state all of the uses that FitnessQuest makes of its trainer database. List five applications of that database that would increase FitnessQuest's competitive position.

6. Describe major differences between the Bosu product and the IndoRow product. Consider product use, product price, customer resistance, competition, competitive threats, and other factors related to market acceptance.

7. Describe information systems that FitnessQuest could use to strengthen its strategy for bringing IndoRow to market. Consider the factors you identified in your answer to question 6 in your response.

Fitness Quest maintains a database of trainer data. They use that database for email and postal correspondence, as well as for other marketing purposes. For example, after a marketing message has been sent, Schnabel and others watch the database for changes in trainer registration. Registrations increase after a well-received message and they fall off when messages are off-target.

Fitness Quest and Schnabel are in the process of introducing new cardio training class equipment called Indo-Row (shown in Figure 19), for which they intend to use the same marketing strategy. First, they will leverage their relationships with trainers to obtain trainer buy-in for the new concept. Then, when that buy-in occurs, they will use it to sell Indo-Row to individuals.

Go to *www.IndoRow.com* and watch the video. As you'll see, IndoRow competes directly with other equipment-based forms of group exercise like Spinning®. Schnabel states that many clubs and workout studios are looking for a new, fun, and innovative group training medium, and Indo-Row offers a solution to that need.

You can learn more about Bosu devices at *www.bosu.com*, more about IndoRow at *www.IndoRow.com*, and more about FitnessQuest at *www.FitnessQuest.com*.

Application Exercises

1. Figure AE-1 shows an Excel spreadsheet that the resort bicycle rental business uses to value and analyze its bicycle inventory. Examine this figure to understand the meaning of the data. Now use Excel to create a similar spreadsheet. Note the following:

    - The top heading is in 20-point Calibri font. It is centered in the spreadsheet. Cells A1 through H1 have been merged.
    - The second heading, Bicycle Inventory Valuation, is in 18-point Calibri, italics. It is centered in Cells A2 through H2, which have been merged.
    - The column headings are set in 11-point Calibri, bold. They are centered in their cells, and the text wraps in the cells.

    a. Make the first two rows of your spreadsheet similar to that in Figure AE-1. Choose your own colors for background and type, however.
    b. Place the current date so that it is centered in cells C3, C4, and C5, which must be merged.
    c. Outline the cells as shown in the figure.
    d. Figure AE-1 uses the following formulas:

    Cost of Current Inventory = Bike Cost × Number on Hand

    Revenue per Bike = Total Rental Revenue/Number on Hand

    Revenue as a Percent of Cost of Inventory = Total Rental Revenue/Cost of Current Inventory

    Please use these formulas in your spreadsheet, as shown in Figure AE-1.
    e. Format the cells in the columns, as shown.
    f. Give three examples of decisions that management of the bike rental agency might make from this data.
    g. What other calculation could you make from this data that would be useful to the bike rental management? Create a second version of this spreadsheet in your worksheet document that has this calculation.

2. In this exercise, you will learn how to create a query based on data that a user enters and how to use that query to create a data entry form.

    a. Download the Microsoft Access file **Ch03Ex02**. Open the file and familiarize yourself with the data in the Customer table.
    b. Click *Create* in the Access ribbon. On the far right, select *Query Design*. Select the Customer table as the basis for the query. Drag Customer Name, Customer Email, Date Of Last Rental, Bike Last Rented, Total Number Of Rentals, and Total Rental Revenue into the columns of the query results pane (the table at the bottom of the query design window).

Figure AE-1

	Make of Bike	Bike Cost	Number on Hand	Cost of Current Inventory	Number of Rentals	Total Rental Revenue	Revenue per Bike	Revenue as Percent of Cost of Inventory
1				Resort Bicycle Rental				
2				Bicycle Inventory Valuation				
3			Wednesday, October 27, 2010					
5	Wonder Bike	$325	12	$3,900	85	$6,375	$531	163.5%
6	Wonder Bike II	$385	4	$1,540	34	$4,570	$1,143	296.8%
7	Wonder Bike Supreme	$475	8	$3,800	44	$5,200	$650	136.8%
8	LiteLift Pro	$655	8	$5,240	25	$2,480	$310	47.3%
9	LiteLift Ladies	$655	4	$2,620	40	$6,710	$1,678	256.1%
10	LiteLift Racer	$795	3	$2,385	37	$5,900	$1,967	247.4%

c. In the CustomerName column, in the row labeled Criteria, place the following text:

[Enter Name of Customer:]

Type this exactly as shown, including the square brackets. This notation tells Access to ask you for a customer name to query.

d. In the ribbon, click the red exclamation mark labeled *Run*. Access will display a dialog box with the text "Enter Name of Customer:" (the text you entered in the query Criteria row). Enter the value *Scott, Rex* and click OK.

e. Save your query with the name *Parameter Query.*

f. Click the Home tab on the ribbon and click the Design View (upper left-hand button on the Home ribbon). Replace the text in the Criteria column of the CustomerName column with the following text. Type it exactly as shown:

Like "*" & [Enter part of Customer Name to search by:] & "*"

g. Run the query by clicking Run in the ribbon. Enter *Scott* when prompted *Enter part of Customer Name to search by*. Notice that the two customers who have the name Scott are displayed. If you have any problems, ensure that you have typed the phrase above *exactly* as shown into the Criteria row of the CustomerName column of your query.

h. Save your query again under the name *Parameter Query.* Close the query window.

i. Click *Create* in the Access ribbon. Under the Forms group, select the down arrow to the right of More Forms. Choose *Form Wizard.* In the dialog that opens, in the Tables/Queries box, click the down arrow. Select *Parameter Query.* Click the double chevron (>>) symbol and all of the columns in the query will move to the Selected Fields area.

j. Click *Next* three times. In the box under *What title do you want for your form?* enter *Customer Query Form* and click *Finish.*

k. Enter *Scott* in the dialog box that appears. Access will open a form with the values for Scott, Rex. At the bottom of the form, click the right-facing arrow and the data for Scott, Bryan will appear.

l. Close the form. Select *Object Type* and *Forms* in the Access Navigation Pane. Double-click the Customer Query Form and enter the value *James*. Access will display data for all six customers having the value James in their name.

Information Technology Opener

Information Technology

This part addresses the technology that underlies information systems. You may think that such technology is unimportant to you as a business professional. However, as you will see at FlexTime, today's managers and business professionals work with information technology all the time, as consumers, if not in a more involved way.

We will discuss hardware and software and define basic terms and fundamental computing concepts. You will see that Neil and Kelly have important decisions to make about the next version of software that they will use to run their business.

We will also address the data component of information technology by describing database processing. You will learn essential database terminology and be introduced to techniques for processing databases. We will also introduce data modeling, because you may be required to evaluate data models for databases that others develop

for you. At FlexTime, Neil will use a database to analyze the cost-saving alternatives.

Next, we continue the discussion of computing devices and describe data communications and Internet technologies. FlexTime is responding to the threat of its landlord (a supplier) by buying its own building. FlexTime needs to save costs, but it also needs to wire the building for data communications in the next 10 years. What capabilities does FlexTime need?

The purpose of this part is to teach you technology sufficient for you to be an effective IT consumer, like Neil at FlexTime. You will learn basic terms, fundamental concepts, and useful frameworks so that you will have the knowledge to ask good questions and make appropriate requests of the information systems professionals who will serve you. Those concepts and frameworks will be far more useful to you than the latest technology trend, which may be outdated by the time you graduate!

Alamy Images

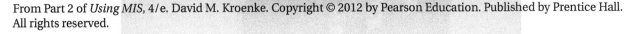

From Part 2 of *Using MIS*, 4/e. David M. Kroenke. Copyright © 2012 by Pearson Education. Published by Prentice Hall.

Chapter 2 (original Chapter 4 of "Using MIS, 4/e")

Hardware and Software

From Chapter 4 of *Using MIS*, 4/e. David M. Kroenke. Copyright © 2012 by Pearson Education. Published by Prentice Hall. All rights reserved.

Hardware and Software

"Neil, I hate to interrupt our night out together, but I'm confused about the software problem at work. Why didn't you upgrade the program?"

"Let me back up, Kelly. Four years ago, we paid $35,000 for Version 2 of the Studio Management software."

"OK, I've got that."

"Since then, we've paid a support fee of $5,000 a year. That fee enables us to call their tech support when something goes wrong, like when we installed the three new printers last year. They help us in other ways, too."

"So, Neil, that means we've paid them $55,000 so far?"

"Right. Now, 2 years ago they came out with Version 3 of their software. I looked at it and didn't see any reason to upgrade, and they wanted another $25,000 license fee. So, I passed on it."

"OK, that seems logical. So what's the problem?"

"When I was at Siebel, we called it *strangle and cram.* Actually, I think the term came from IBM in the 1960s, but it doesn't matter. The idea is that you cut off support to an older version of the product (that's the *strangle*) and tell your customers that to get support, they have to upgrade to the new version (that's the *cram*)."

"Wow. Can we sue them or something?"

"Do we want to mess up our lives with a lawsuit?"

"No."

"Besides, the contracts say they can do this."

"So we upgrade?"

"Maybe, Kelly. The thing is, though, their architecture is old. Even with the new version they're still using thick clients and I just don't think we want to stay there."

"Neil, I have absolutely no idea what you're talking about. And I'm hungry. Let's order."

They order.

"Kelly, you know that computer that sits in the corner of my office? That's our server. It's a computer that receives requests from the other computers and processes them. All the other computers at FlexTime are client computers; they call the server to do things like store data in our database. But, to make that work, we had to install a special computer program on each client."

"So what are you telling me?"

"Thick clients are out; they're based on 1980s' technology. The new way is to use Internet technology and substitute a browser for the thick client. Lots of reasons to do that, but one is that nobody needs a special program installed on their computer to access our systems. They can do it from a browser. So, I don't have to keep installing and uninstalling software on our trainers' computers. People can also access the system from their iPhones, or whatever they're using. They just use their browsers."

"So this upgrade that they're cramming is based on older technology?"

"Right. I've been looking at other options. Problem is we'd have to train everyone to use the new system . . . and that would be ugly. . . and costly."

"Well, if we have to do it, we have to do it."

"Yeah. We could wait until we have the new building, but I hate to put that much change on everyone at once."

"OK, so what's holding you back?"

"Cost. They want $65,000 up front and 10 percent, $6,500, a year for support."

"Ouch."

"There's another option: open source. There's a group that's created a version that might do the job, and it's free."

"How can it be free?"

"Well, I should say license free. We won't have to pay the up-front cost but we would pay the company that supports it."

"But why no up-front cost?"

"Because the programmers who build it are unpaid volunteers."

"Neil, are you saying we're going to run our business on a program created by a bunch of amateurs?"

"No, not amateurs. Think Wikipedia. It's done by volunteers, and the quality of the information there is high. The Wikipedia community sees to that. It's the same for good open source software. Linux was built that way."

"Linux? Oh no, another term. That's enough. Let's eat."

"How do other small businesses do it? I mean you spent all those years selling software, you know the game. How does the average club owner make these decisions?"

"They waste a lot of money."

"And time." ■

Study Questions

Q1 What do business professionals need to know about computer hardware?

Q2 What do business professionals need to know about software?

Q3 Is open source software a viable alternative?

Q4 How can you use this knowledge?

Q5 2021?

Like Neil, you might go into the computer industry and then transition to some other business. If so, you'll know "how the game is played," as Kelly says. However, you might not. You might become a department manager, or own your own small business, or be appointed to your law firm's technology committee. Whatever direction your career takes, you don't want to be one of those professionals who "waste a lot of money . . . and time." The knowledge from this chapter can help.

You don't need to be an expert. You don't need to be a hardware engineer or a computer programmer. You do need to know enough, however, to be an effective consumer. You need the knowledge and skills to ask important, relevant questions and understand the answers. We begin with basic hardware and software concepts. Then we will discuss how you can use your knowledge to prepare a computer budget for your department and then we wrap up by forecasting trends in hardware and software in 2021.

Q1 What Do Business Professionals Need to Know About Computer Hardware?

Hardware consists of electronic components and related gadgetry that input, process, output, and store data according to instructions encoded in computer programs or software. Figure 1 shows the components of a generic computer. Notice that the basic hardware categories are input, process, output, and storage.

Basic Components

As shown in Figure 1, typical **input hardware** devices are the keyboard, mouse, document scanners, and bar-code (Universal Product Code) scanners like those used in grocery stores. Microphones also are input devices; with tablet PCs, human handwriting can be input as well. Older input devices include magnetic ink readers (used for reading the ink on the bottom of checks) and scanners such as the Scantron test scanner.

Processing devices include the **central processing unit (CPU)**, which is sometimes called "the brain" of the computer. Although the design of the CPU has nothing in common with the anatomy of animal brains, this description is helpful, because the CPU does have the "smarts" of the machine. The CPU selects instructions, processes

Figure 1
Input, Process, Output,
and Storage Hardware

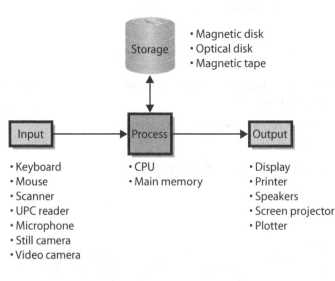

Storage
- Magnetic disk
- Optical disk
- Magnetic tape

Input
- Keyboard
- Mouse
- Scanner
- UPC reader
- Microphone
- Still camera
- Video camera

Process
- CPU
- Main memory

Output
- Display
- Printer
- Speakers
- Screen projector
- Plotter

Figure 2
USB Connector

Source: Shutterstock.

them, performs arithmetic and logical comparisons, and stores results of operations in memory. Some computers have two or more CPUs. A computer with two CPUs is called a **dual-processor** computer. **Quad-processor** computers have four CPUs. Some high-end computers have 16 or more CPUs.

CPUs vary in speed, function, and cost. Hardware vendors such as Intel, Advanced Micro Devices, and National Semiconductor continually improve CPU speed and capabilities while reducing CPU costs. Whether you or your department needs the latest, greatest CPU depends on the nature of your work, as you will learn.

The CPU works in conjunction with **main memory**. The CPU reads data and instructions from memory, and it stores results of computations in main memory. We will describe the relationship between the CPU and main memory later in the chapter. Main memory is sometimes called **RAM**, for random access memory.

Output hardware consists of video displays, printers, audio speakers, overhead projectors, and other special-purpose devices, such as large flatbed plotters.

Storage hardware saves data and programs. Magnetic disk is by far the most common storage device, although optical disks such as CDs and DVDs also are popular. Thumb drives are small, portable magnetic storage devices that can be used to backup data and to transfer it from one computer to another. In large corporate data centers, data is sometimes stored on magnetic tape.

In the past, many different plug receptacles were required to connect keyboards, mice, printers, cameras, and so on. Starting in 2000, all of these were replaced with **Universal Serial Bus (USB)** connectors like that shown in Figure 2. USB connectors simplified the connection of peripheral gear to computers for both manufacturers and users and are widely used.

Computer Data

Before we can further describe hardware, we need to define several important terms. We begin with binary digits.

Binary Digits

Computers represent data using **binary digits**, called **bits**. A bit is either a zero or a one. Bits are used for computer data because they are easy to represent electronically, as illustrated in Figure 3. A switch can be either closed or open. A computer can be designed so that an open switch represents zero and a closed switch represents one. Or the orientation of a magnetic field can represent a bit; magnetism in one direction represents a zero, magnetism in the opposite direction represents a one. Or, for optical media, small pits are burned onto the surface of the disk so that they will reflect light. In a given spot, a reflection means a one; no reflection means a zero.

Figure 3
Bits Are Easy to Represent
Physically

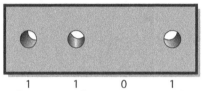

A. Light switches representing 1101   B. Direction of magnetism representing 1101

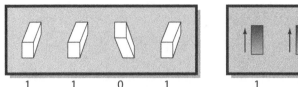

C. Reflection/no reflection representing 1101

Sizing Computer Data

All computer data are represented by bits. The data can be numbers, characters, currency amounts, photos, recordings, or whatever. All are simply a string of bits.

For reasons that interest many but are irrelevant for future managers, bits are grouped into 8-bit chunks called **bytes**. For character data, such as the letters in a person's name, one character will fit into one byte. Thus, when you read a specification that a computing device has 100 million bytes of memory, you know that the device can hold up to 100 million characters.

Bytes are used to measure sizes of noncharacter data as well. Someone might say, for example, that a given picture is 100,000 bytes in size. This statement means the length of the bit string that represents the picture is 100,000 bytes or 800,000 bits (because there are 8 bits per byte).

The specifications for the size of main memory, disk, and other computer devices are expressed in bytes. Figure 4 shows the set of abbreviations that are used to represent data-storage capacity. A **kilobyte**, abbreviated **K**, is a collection of 1,024 bytes. A **megabyte**, or **MB**, is 1,024 kilobytes. A **gigabyte**, or **GB**, is 1,024 megabytes, and a **terabyte**, or **TB**, is 1,024 gigabytes.

Sometimes you will see these definitions simplified as 1K equals 1,000 bytes and 1MB equals 1,000K. Such simplifications are incorrect, but they do ease the math. Also, disk and computer manufacturers have an incentive to propagate this misconception. If a disk maker defines 1MB to be 1 million bytes—and not the correct 1,024K—the manufacturer can use its own definition of MB when specifying drive capacities. A buyer may think that a disk advertised as 100MB has space for $100 \times 1,024K$ bytes, but in truth the drive will have space for only $100 \times 1,000,000$ bytes. Normally, the distinction is not too important, but be aware of the two possible interpretations of these abbreviations.

Figure 4
Important Storage-Capacity
Terminology

Term	Definition	Abbreviation
Byte	Number of bits to represent one character	
Kilobyte	1,024 bytes	K
Megabyte	1,024 K = 1,048,576 bytes	MB
Gigabyte	1,024 MB = 1,073,741,824 bytes	GB
Terabyte	1,024 GB = 1,099,511,627,776 bytes	TB

In Fewer Than 300 Words, How Does a Computer Work?

Figure 5 shows a snapshot of a computer in use. The CPU is the major actor. To run a program or process data, the computer first transfers the program or data from disk to *main memory*. Then, to execute an instruction, it moves the instruction from main memory into the CPU via the **data channel** or **bus**. The CPU has a small amount of very fast memory called a **cache**. The CPU keeps frequently used instructions in the cache. Having a large cache makes the computer faster, but cache is expensive.

Main memory of the computer in Figure 5 contains program instructions for Microsoft Excel, Adobe Acrobat, and a browser (Microsoft Internet Explorer or Mozilla Firefox). It also contains a block of data and instructions for the **operating system (OS)**, which is a program that controls the computer's resources.

Main memory is too small to hold all of the programs and data that a user might want to process. For example, no personal computer has enough memory to hold all of the code in Microsoft Word, Excel, and Access. Consequently, the CPU loads programs into memory in chunks. In Figure 5, one portion of Excel was loaded into memory. When the user requested additional processing (say, to sort the spreadsheet), the CPU loaded another piece of Excel.

If the user opens another program (say, Word) or needs to load more data (say, a picture), the operating system will direct the CPU to attempt to place the new program or data into unused memory. If there is not enough memory, it will remove something, perhaps the block of memory labeled More Excel, and then it will place the just-requested program or data into the vacated space. This process is called **memory swapping**.

Why Does a Manager Care How a Computer Works?

You can order computers with varying sizes of main memory. An employee who runs only one program at a time and who processes small amounts of data requires very little memory—1GB will be adequate. However, an employee who processes many programs at the same time (say, Word, Excel, Firefox, Access, Acrobat, and other programs) or an employee who processes very large files (pictures, movies, or sound files) needs lots of main memory, perhaps 3GB or more. If that employee's computer

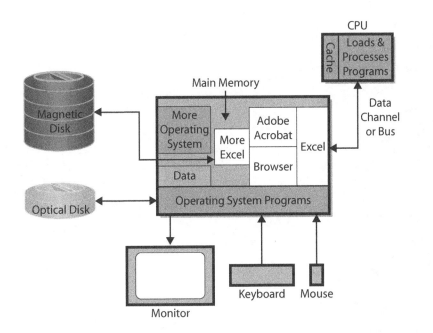

Figure 5
Computer Components, in Use

has too little memory, then the computer will constantly be swapping memory, and it will be slow. (This means, by the way, that if your computer is slow and if you have many programs open, you likely can improve performance by closing one or more programs. Depending on your computer and the amount of memory it has, you might also improve performance by adding more memory.)

The Ethics Guide in this chapter poses questions about computer hardware and software that offer more than most users need.

You can also order computers with CPUs of different speeds. CPU speed is expressed in cycles called *hertz*. In 2011, a slow personal computer has a speed of 1.5 Gigahertz. A fast personal computer has a speed of 3+ Gigahertz, with dual processing. As predicted by Moore's Law, CPU speeds continually increase.

Additionally, CPUs today are classified as **32-bit** or **64-bit**. Without delving into the particulars, a 32-bit is less capable and cheaper than a 64-bit CPU. The latter can address more main memory; you need a 64-bit processor to effectively utilize more than 4GB of memory. 64-bit processors have other advantages as well, but they are more expensive than 32-bit processors.

An employee who does only simple tasks such as word processing does not need a fast CPU; a 32-bit, 1.5 Gigahertz CPU will be fine. However, an employee who processes large, complicated spreadsheets or who manipulates large database files or edits large picture, sound, or movie files needs a fast computer like a 64-bit, dual processor with 3.5 Gigahertz or more.

One last comment: The cache and main memory are **volatile**, meaning their contents are lost when power is off. Magnetic and optical disks are **nonvolatile**, meaning their contents survive when power is off. If you suddenly lose power, the contents of unsaved memory—say, documents that have been altered—will be lost. Therefore, get into the habit of frequently (every few minutes or so) saving documents or files that you are changing. Save your documents before your roommate trips over the power cord.

What Is the Difference Between a Client and a Server?

Before we can discuss computer software, you need to understand the difference between a client and a server. Figure 6 shows the computing environment of the typical user. Users employ **client** computers for word processing, spreadsheets, database access, and so forth. Most client computers also have software that enables them to connect to a network. It could be a private network at their company or school, or it

Figure 6
Client and Server Computers

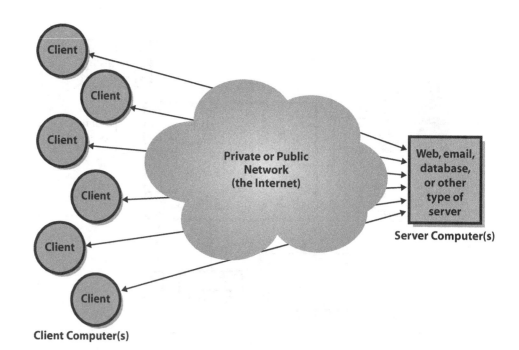

Private or Public Network (the Internet)

Web, email, database, or other type of server

Server Computer(s)

Client Computer(s)

Figure 7
A Server Farm

Source: © Michael Soo/Alamy.

could be the Internet, which is a public network.

Servers, as their name implies, provide some service. Some servers process email; others process Web sites; others process large, shared databases; and some provide all of these functions or other, similar functions.

A server is just a computer, but as you might expect, server computers must be fast and they usually have multiple CPUs. They need lots of main memory, at least 4GB, and they require very large disks—often a terabyte or more. Because servers are almost always accessed from another computer via a network, they have limited video displays, or even no display at all. For the same reason, many have no keyboard.

For sites with large numbers of users (e.g., Amazon.com), servers are organized into a collection of servers called a **server farm** like the one shown in Figure 7. Servers in a farm coordinate their activities in an incredibly sophisticated and fascinating technology dance. They receive and process hundreds, possibly thousands, of service requests per minute. For example, in December 2009 Amazon.com processed an average of 110 order items per second for 24 hours straight.[1] In this dance, computers hand off partially processed requests to each other while keeping track of the current status of each request. They can pick up the pieces when a computer in the farm fails. All of this is done in the blink of an eye, with the user never knowing any part of the miracle underway. It is absolutely gorgeous engineering!

You may hear two new terms that have become popular with regard to server computers: grid and cloud. A **grid** is a network of computers that operates as an integrated whole; the grid appears to be a single computer. The grid may operate to support a server farm, or it may support some other computing need. Organizations lease time on a grid from other organizations that create, support, and manage that grid.

Cloud Computing

Cloud computing is a form of hardware/software leasing in which organizations obtain server resources from vendors that specialize in server processing.[2] The amount of server time and the resources leased is flexible and can change dynamically (and dramatically). Customers pay only for resources used. Major companies that offer cloud computing products include Amazon.com, IBM, Microsoft, and Oracle.

---

[1]*http://phx.corporate-ir.net/phoenix.zhtml?c=176060&p=irol-newsArticle&ID=1369429&highlight=.*
[2]See, for example, *www-03.ibm.com/cloud.*

Ethics Guide

Churn and Burn

An anonymous source, whom we'll call Janet, made the following statements about computing devices:

"I never upgrade my system. At least, I try not to. Look, I don't do anything at work but write memos and access email. I use Microsoft Word, but I don't use any features that weren't available in Word 3.0, 25 years ago. This whole industry is based on 'churn and burn': They churn their products so we'll burn our cash.

"All this hype about 64-bit processors and 500GB disks—who needs them? I'm sure I don't. And if Microsoft hadn't put so much junk into Windows, we could all be happy on an Intel 486 processor like the one I had in 1993. We're suckers for falling into the 'you gotta have this' trap.

"Frankly, I think there's a conspiracy between hardware and software vendors. They both want to sell new products, so the hardware people come up with these incredibly fast and huge computers. Then, given all that power, the software types develop monster products bloated with features and functions that nobody uses. It would take me months to learn all of the features in Word, only to find out that I don't need those features.

"To see what I mean, open Microsoft Word, click on View, then select Toolbars. In my version of Word, there are 19 toolbars to select, plus one more to customize my own toolbar. Now what in the world do I need with 19 toolbars? I write all the time, and I have two selected: Standard and Formatting. Two out of 19! Could I pay Microsoft 2/19 of the price of Word, because that's all I want or use?

"Here's how they get you, though. Because we live in a connected world, they don't have to get all of us to use those 19 toolbars, just one of us. Take Bridgette, over in Legal, for example. Bridgette likes to use the redlining features, and she likes me to use them when I change draft contracts she sends me. So if I want to work on her documents, I have to turn on the Reviewing toolbar. You get the idea; just get someone to use a feature and, because it is a connected world, then all of us have to have that feature.

"Viruses are one of their best ploys. They say you better buy the latest and greatest in software—and then apply all the patches that follow so that you'll be protected from the latest zinger from the computer 'bad guys.' Think about that for a minute. If vendors had built the products correctly the first time, then there would be no holes for the baddies to find, would there? So they have a defect in their products that they turn to a sales advantage. You see, they get us to focus on the virus and not on the hole in their product. In truth, they should be saying, 'Buy our latest product to protect yourself from the defective junk we sold you last year.' But truth in advertising hasn't come that far.

"Besides that, users are their own worst enemies as far as viruses are concerned. If I'm down on 17th Street at 4 in the morning, half drunk and with a bundle of cash hanging out of my pocket, what's likely to happen to me? I'm gonna get mugged. So if I'm out in some weirdo chat room—you know, out where you get pictures of weird sex acts and whatnot—and download and run a file, then of course I'm gonna get a virus. Viruses are brought on by user stupidity, that's all.

"One of these days, users are going to rise up and say, 'That's enough. I don't need any more. I'll stay with what I have, thank you very much.' In fact, maybe that's happening right now. Maybe that's why software sales aren't growing like they were. Maybe people have finally said, 'No more toolbars!'" ■

Discussion Questions

1. Summarize Janet's view of the computer industry. Is there merit to her argument? Why or why not?

2. What holes do you see in the logic of her argument?

3. Someone could take the position that these statements are just empty rantings—that Janet can say all she wants, but the computer industry is going to keep on doing as it has been. Is there any point in Janet sharing her criticisms?

4. Comment on Janet's statement—"Viruses are brought on by user stupidity, that's all."

5. All software products ship with known problems. Microsoft, Adobe, and Apple all ship software that they know has failures. Is it unethical for them to do so? Do software vendors have an ethical responsibility to openly publish the problems in their software? How do these organizations protect themselves from lawsuits for damages caused by known problems in software?

6. Suppose a vendor licenses and ships a software product that has both known and unknown failures. As the vendor learns of the unknown failures, does it have an ethical responsibility to inform the users about them? Does the vendor have an ethical responsibility to fix the problems? Is it ethical for the vendor to require users to pay an upgrade fee for a new version of software that fixes problems in an existing version?

iStockphoto.com

Your university is a prime candidate to use cloud computing for systems like class registration. If you are on a semester program, registration occurs only three times a year, so servers that are dedicated solely to registration will be idle most of the year. With cloud computing, your university could lease server resources when it needs them from a cloud vendor like IBM. Your university will use substantial computing resources to support registration in August, January, and June, but nearly none in other months. It will pay just for the services that it uses.

Cloud computing allows multiple organizations to utilize the same computing infrastructure. Tax preparation firms can use the same IBM computers in April that your university uses in August, January, and June. In a sense, cloud computing is a form of CPU-cycle inventory consolidation.

Q2 What Do Business Professionals Need to Know About Software?

As a future manager or business professional, you need to know the essential terminology and software concepts that will enable you to be an intelligent software consumer. To begin, consider the basic categories of software shown in Figure 8.

Every computer has an *operating system,* which is a program that controls that computer's resources. Some of the functions of an operating system are to read and write data, allocate main memory, perform memory swapping, start and stop programs, respond to error conditions, and facilitate backup and recovery. In addition, the operating system creates and manages the user interface, including the display, keyboard, mouse, and other devices.

Although the operating system makes the computer usable, it does little application-specific work. If you want to write a document or query a customer database, you need *application programs* such as Microsoft Word or Oracle Customer Relationship Management (CRM). These programs must be licensed in addition to the operating system.

Both client and server computers need an operating system, though they need not be the same. Further, both clients and servers can process application programs. The application's design determines whether the client, the server, or both, process it.

You need to understand two important software constraints. First, a particular version of an operating system is written for a particular type of hardware. For example, Microsoft Windows works only on processors from Intel and companies that make processors that conform to the Intel **instruction set** (the commands that a CPU can process). Furthermore, the 32-bit version of Windows runs only on Intel computers with 32-bit CPUs and the 64-bit version of Windows runs only on Intel computers with 64-bit CPUs. In other cases, such as Linux, many versions exist for many different instruction sets and for both 32- and 64-bit computers.

Second, application programs are written to use a particular operating system. Microsoft Access, for example, will run only on the Windows operating system. Some applications come in multiple versions. There are, for example, Windows and

Figure 8
Categories of Computer Software

	Operating System	Application Programs
Client	Programs that control the client computer's resources	Applications that are processed on client computers
Server	Programs that control the server computer's resources	Applications that are processed on server computers

Macintosh versions of Microsoft Word. But unless informed otherwise, assume that a particular application runs on just one operating system.

We will next consider the operating system and application program categories of software.

What Are the Four Major Operating Systems?

Every computer system has an operating system. All client server computers have an operating system, as well as your iPhone, iPad, Kindle, and smart phone. Here we will be concerned only with four operating systems that you might choose, or be influenced by (see Figure 9). These systems are used on both client and server computers.

Windows

For business users, the most important operating system is Microsoft **Windows**. Some version of Windows resides on more than 85 percent of the world's desktops, and, considering just business users, the figure is more than 95 percent. Many different versions of Windows are available: Windows 7, Windows Vista, and Windows XP run on user computers. Windows Server is a version of Windows designed for servers. As stated, Windows runs the Intel instruction set on both 32- and 64-bit computers.

Mac OS

Apple Computer, Inc., developed its own operating system for the Macintosh, **Mac OS**. The current version is Mac OS X. Macintosh computers are used primarily by graphic artists and workers in the arts community. Mac OS was designed originally to run the line of CPU processors from Motorola. In 1994, Mac OS switched to the PowerPC processor line from IBM. As of 2006, Macintosh computers are available for both PowerPC and Intel CPUs. A Macintosh with an Intel processor is able to run both Windows and the Mac OS.

Figure 9
What a Manager Needs to Know About Software

Category	Operating System (OS)	Instruction Set	Common Applications	Typical User
Client	Windows	Intel	Microsoft Office: Word, Excel, Access, PowerPoint, many other applications	Business Home
	Mac OS (pre–2006)	Power PC	Macintosh applications plus Word and Excel	Graphic artists Arts community
	Mac OS (post–2006)	Intel	Macintosh applications plus Word and Excel Can also run Windows on Macintosh hardware	Graphic artists Arts community
	Unix	Sun and others	Engineering, computer-assisted design, architecture	Difficult for the typical client, but popular with some engineers and computer scientists
	Linux	Just about anything	Open Office (Microsoft Office look-alike)	Rare—used where budget is very limited
Server	Windows Server	Intel	Windows server-type applications	Business with commitment to Microsoft
	Unix	Sun and others	Unix server applications	Fading . . . Linux taking its market
	Linux	Just about anything	Linux & Unix server applications	Very popular—promulgated by IBM

Most people would agree that Apple has led the way in developing easy-to-use interfaces. Certainly, many innovative ideas have first appeared in a Macintosh and then later been added, in one form or another, to Windows.

Unix

Unix is an operating system that was developed at Bell Labs in the 1970s. It has been the workhorse of the scientific and engineering communities since then. Unix is generally regarded as being more difficult to use than either Windows or the Macintosh. Many Unix users know and employ an arcane language for manipulating files and data. However, once they surmount the rather steep learning curve most Unix users become fanatic supporters of the system. Sun Microsystems and other vendors of computers for scientific and engineering applications are the major proponents of Unix. In general, Unix is not for the business user.

Linux

Linux is a version of Unix that was developed by the **open source community** (see Q3). This community is a loosely coupled group of programmers who mostly volunteer their time to contribute code to develop and maintain Linux. The open source community owns Linux, and there is no fee to use it. Linux can run on client computers, but it is most frequently used for servers, particularly Web servers.

IBM is the primary proponent of Linux. Although IBM does not own Linux, IBM has developed many business systems solutions that use Linux. By using Linux, IBM does not have to pay a license fee to Microsoft or another OS vendor.

Own Versus License

When you buy a computer program, you are not actually buying that program. Instead, you are buying a **license** to use that program. For example, when you buy a Windows license, Microsoft is selling you the right to use Windows. Microsoft continues to own the Windows program. Large organizations do not buy a license for each computer user. Instead, they negotiate a **site license**, which is a flat fee that authorizes the company to install the product (operating system or application) on all of that company's computers or on all of the computers at a specific site.

In the case of Linux, no company can sell you a license to use it. It is owned by the open source community, which states that Linux has no license fee (with certain reasonable restrictions). Large companies such as IBM and smaller companies such as RedHat can make money by supporting Linux, but no company makes money selling Linux licenses.

Virtualization

Cloud computing is feasible because cloud vendors harness the power of virtualization. **Virtualization** is the process by which one computer hosts the appearance of many computers. One operating system, called the **host operating system** runs one or more operating systems as applications. Those hosted operating systems are called **virtual machines (vm)**. Each virtual machine has disk space and other resources allocated to it. The virtual machine operates as if it has exclusive control over those resources, just as if they were installed on their own computer. The host operating system controls the activities of the virtual machines it hosts to prevent them from interfering with one another.

Three types of virtualization exist:

- PC virtualization
- Server virtualization
- Desktop virtualization

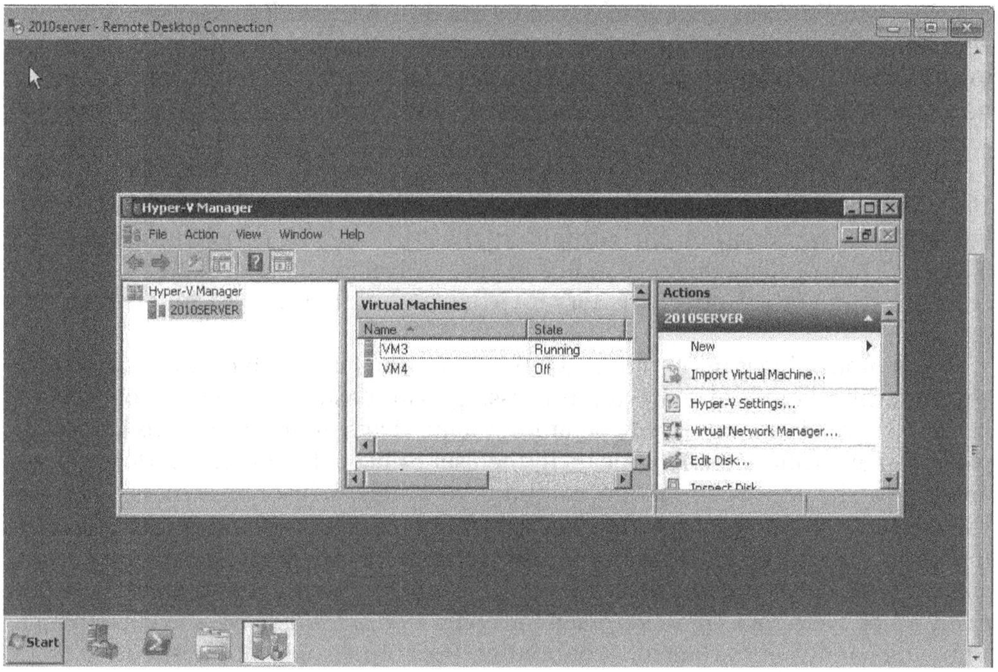

Figure 10
Windows Server Computer
Hosting Two Virtual Machines

With **PC virtualization**, a personal computer, such as a desktop or portable computer, hosts several different operating systems. Say a user needs, for some reason, to have both Windows Vista and Windows 7 running on his or her computer. In that circumstance, the user can install a virtual host operating system and then both Vista and Windows 7 on top of it. In that way, the user can have both systems on the same hardware.

With **server virtualization**, a server computer hosts one or more, other server computers. In Figure 10, a Windows Server computer is hosting two virtual machines. Users can log onto either of those virtual machines and they will appear as normal servers. Figure 11 shows how virtual machine VM3 appears to a user of that server. Notice that a user of VM3 is running a browser that is accessing SharePoint.

Figure 11
Virtual Machine

Now, why does any organization want to do this? Because it is very easy to set up a virtual machine and configure it in a specific way. Virtualization allows cloud vendors to add and remove instances of servers very quickly and cheaply. If your university needs another 100 servers in August, IBM need only create 100 virtual machines on its server computers. It can do this with automation, involving almost no human labor.

If two days later your school needs another 100 instances, IBM allocates another 100 instances. Behind the scenes, IBM is likely moving these instances among servers, balancing its workload on the computers that run the virtual machine operating systems. None of that activity is visible to your university or to the students who are registering for class. Hence, it is server virtualization that makes cloud computing feasible.

Such processing is important and interesting, but it is possible that desktop virtualization will revolutionize desktop processing. With **desktop virtualization**, a server hosts many versions of desktop operating systems. Each of those desktops has a complete user environment and appears to the user to be just another PC. However, the desktop can be accessed from any computer to which the user has access. Thus, you could be at an airport and go to an airport computer and access your virtualized desktop. To you, it appears as if that airport computer is you own personal computer. Later, you could do the same to a utility computer sitting in your hotel room. Meanwhile, many other users could have accessed the computer in the airport, and each thought he or she had his or her personal computer. Desktop virtualization is in its infancy, but it will have major impact during the early years of your career, as discussed in Q5, 2021.

What Types of Applications Exist, and How Do Organizations Obtain Them?

Application software performs a service or function. Some application programs are general purpose, such as Microsoft Excel or Word. Other application programs provide specific functions. QuickBooks, for example, is an application program that provides general ledger and other accounting functions. We begin by describing categories of application programs and then describe sources for them.

What Categories of Application Programs Exist?

Horizontal-market application software provides capabilities common across all organizations and industries. Word processors, graphics programs, spreadsheets, and presentation programs are all horizontal-market application software.

Examples of such software are Microsoft Word, Excel, and PowerPoint. Examples from other vendors are Adobe's Acrobat, Photoshop, and PageMaker and Jasc Corporation's Paint Shop Pro. These applications are used in a wide variety of businesses, across all industries. They are purchased off-the-shelf, and little customization of features is necessary (or possible).

Vertical-market application software serves the needs of a specific industry. Examples of such programs are those used by dental offices to schedule appointments and bill patients, those used by auto mechanics to keep track of customer data and customers' automobile repairs, and those used by parts warehouses to track inventory, purchases, and sales.

Vertical applications usually can be altered or customized. Typically, the company that sold the application software will provide such services or offer referrals to qualified consultants who can provide this service.

One-of-a-kind application software is developed for a specific, unique need. The IRS develops such software, for example, because it has needs that no other organization has.

How Do Organizations Acquire Application Software?

You can acquire application software in exactly the same ways that you can buy a new suit. The quickest and least risky option is to buy your suit off-the-rack. With this method, you get your suit immediately, and you know exactly what it will cost. You may not, however, get a good fit. Alternately, you can buy your suit off-the-rack and have it altered. This will take more time, it may cost more, and there's some possibility that the alteration will result in a poor fit. Most likely, however, an altered suit will fit better than an off-the-rack one.

Finally, you can hire a tailor to make a custom suit. In this case, you will have to describe what you want, be available for multiple fittings, and be willing to pay considerably more. Although there is an excellent chance of a great fit, there is also the possibility of a disaster. Still, if you want a yellow and orange polka-dot silk suit with a hissing rattlesnake on the back, tailor-made is the only way to go. You can buy computer software in exactly the same ways: **off-the-shelf software**, **off-the-shelf with alterations software**, or tailor-made. Tailor-made software is called **custom-developed software**.

Organizations develop custom application software themselves or hire a development vendor. Like buying the yellow and orange polka-dot suit, such development is done in situations in which the needs of the organization are so unique that no horizontal or vertical applications are available. By developing custom software, the organization can tailor its application to fit its requirements.

Custom development is difficult and risky. Staffing and managing teams of software developers is challenging. Managing software projects can be daunting. Many organizations have embarked on application development projects only to find that the projects take twice as long—or longer—to finish as planned. Cost overruns of 200 and 300 percent are not uncommon.

In addition, every application program needs to be adapted to changing needs and changing technologies. The adaptation costs of horizontal and vertical software are amortized over all of the users of that software, perhaps thousands or millions of customers. For custom software developed in-house, however, the developing company must pay all of the adaptation costs itself. Over time, this cost burden is heavy.

Because of the risk and expense, in-house development is the last-choice alternative and is used only when there is no other option. Figure 12 summarizes software sources and types.

What Is Firmware?

Firmware is computer software that is installed into devices such as printers, print servers, and various types of communication devices. The software is coded just like other software, but it is installed into special, read-only memory of the printer or other device. In this way, the program becomes part of the device's memory; it is as if the

Software Source

		Off-the-shelf	Off-the-shelf and then customized	Custom-developed
Software Type	Horizontal applications			
	Vertical applications			
	One-of-a-kind applications			

Figure 12
Software Sources and Types

program's logic is designed into the device's circuitry. Users do not need to load firmware into the device's memory.

Firmware can be changed or upgraded, but this is normally a task for IS professionals. The task is easy, but it requires knowledge of special programs and techniques that most business users choose not to learn.

Why Are Thin Clients Preferred to Thick Clients?

When you use client applications such as Word, Excel, or Acrobat, those programs run only on your computer. You need not be connected to the Internet or any other network for them to run.

Other applications, called **client-server applications**, require code on both the client and the server. Email is a good example. When you send email, you run a client program such as Microsoft Outlook that has been installed on your computer. Outlook then connects over the Internet or a private network to mail server software on a server. Similarly, when you access a Web site, you run a browser (client software) on your computer that connects over a network to Web server software on a server.

A client-server application that requires nothing more than a browser is called a **thin client**. An application such as Microsoft Outlook that requires programs other than a browser on the user's computer is called a **thick client**. The terms *thin* and *thick* refer to the amount of code that must run on the client computer. All other things being equal, thin-client applications are preferred to thick-client applications because they require only a browser; no special client software needs to be installed. Additionally, thin (browser-only) clients make it easier for people to access systems from remote locations and from special-purpose devices such as cell phones or iPads.

As stated, client and server computers can run different operating systems. Many organizations have standardized on Windows for their clients but use Windows Server or Linux for their servers. Figure 13 shows an example. Two

Figure 13
Thin and Thick Clients

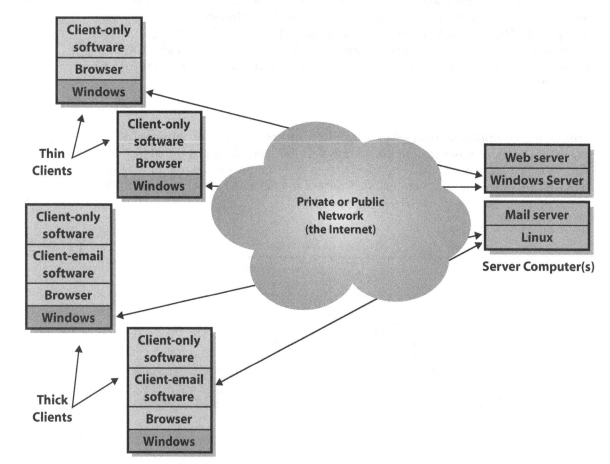

thin clients are connecting via browsers to a Web server that is running Windows Server. Two thick clients are connecting via an email client to an email server that is running Linux. Those two clients are thick because they have client email software installed.

Q3 Is Open Source Software a Viable Alternative?

To answer this question, you first need to know a bit about the open source movement and process. Most computer historians would agree that Richard Matthew Stallman is the father of the movement. In 1983, he developed a set of tools called **GNU** (a self-referential acronym meaning *GNU Not Unix*) for creating a free Unix-like operating system. Stallman made many other contributions to open source, including the **GNU general public license (GPL) agreement**, one of the standard license agreements for open source software. Stallman was unable to attract enough developers to finish the free Unix system, but continued making other contributions to the open source movement.

In 1991, Linus Torvalds, working in Helsinki, began work on another version of Unix, using some of Stallman's tools. That version eventually became Linux, the high-quality and very popular operating system discussed previously.

The Internet proved to be a great asset for open source, and many open source projects became successful, including:

* Open Office (a Microsoft Office look-alike)
* Firefox (a browser)
* MySQL (a DBMS)
* Apache (a Web server)
* Ubuntu (a Windows-like desktop operating system)
* Android (a mobile-device operating system)

Why Do Programmers Volunteer Their Services?

To anyone who has never enjoyed writing computer programs, it is difficult to understand why anyone would donate their time and skills to contribute to open source projects. Programming is, however, an intense combination of art and logic, and designing and writing a complicated computer program is exceedingly pleasurable (and addictive). Like many programmers, at times in my life I have gleefully devoted 16 hours a day to writing computer programs—day after day—and the days would fly by. If you have an artistic and logical mind, you ought to try it.

Anyway, the first reason that people contribute to open source is that it is great fun! Additionally, some people contribute to open source because it gives them the freedom to choose the projects upon which they work. They may have a programming day job that is not terribly interesting, say, writing a program to manage a computer printer. Their job pays the bills, but it's not fulfilling.

In the 1950s, Hollywood studio musicians suffered as they recorded the same style of music over and over for a long string of uninteresting movies. To keep their sanity, those musicians would gather on Sundays to play jazz, and a number of high-quality jazz clubs resulted. That's what open source is to programmers. A place where they can exercise their creativity while working on projects they find interesting and fulfilling.

Another reason for contributing to open source is to exhibit one's skill, both for pride as well as to find a job or consulting employment. A final reason is to start a business selling services to support an open source product.

Using MIS InClass   *A Group Exercise*

Choosing a Computer

Newscom

In this exercise, you and a team of students will be asked to compete with other student groups to identify the most appropriate computer for three different scenarios. For each scenario, you need to determine the hardware and software needs that you think are appropriate. Needs include the size and type of computer, the processor speed, the sizes of main memory and disk, the operating system, application programs, maintenance and support agreements, and any other factors you deem appropriate. Given those needs, you will search the Web for the best system and price that you can find. You are competing with other student groups, so think and search carefully!

The following Web sites may be useful in your deliberations:

www.dell.com

www.hp.com

www.lenovo.com

www.cnet.com

Do not constrain yourselves to this list, however.

The scenarios are as follows:

1. Your roommate, a political science major, asks you to help her purchase a new laptop computer. She wants to use the computer for email, Internet access, and for note-taking in class. She wants to spend less than $1,000.

   a. What CPU, memory, and disk specifications would you recommend?
   b. What software does she need?
   c. Shop for the best computer deal for her.
   d. Which computer would you recommend, and why?
   e. Present your answer to the rest of the class. May the best group win!

2. Your father asks you to help him purchase a new computer. He wants to use his computer for email, Internet access, downloading pictures from his digital camera, uploading those pictures to a shared photo service, and writing documents for members of his antique auto club.

   a. What CPU, memory, and disk specifications would you recommend?
   b. What software does he need?
   c. Shop for the best computer deal.
   d. Which computer would you recommend, and why?
   e. Present your answer to the rest of the class. May the best group win!

3. Due to a budget reduction, your campus newspaper lost its university funding, and you and a group of five students have decided to replace it with your own newspaper. To do so, your group decides that it needs three computers; at least two of them need to be laptops. One can be either a laptop or a desktop.

   The university offers to sell you three Dell laptops for $2,100. Each laptop has 3GB of main memory, a 250GB disk, and a dual 1.7 MHz, 32-bit CPU. The laptops include Windows Vista and Office 2007 Ultimate (Access, Excel, Groove, InfoPath, OneNote, PowerPoint, Publisher, and Word).

   a. What CPU, memory, and disk specifications do you need?
   b. What software do you need?
   c. Shop for the best deal you can find.
   d. Should you buy the university's computers? Explain.
   e. Present your answer to the rest of the class. May the best group win!

How Does Open Source Work?

The term *open source* means that the source code of the program is available to the public. **Source code** is computer code as written by humans and that is understandable by humans. Figure 14 shows a portion of the computer code that I wrote for the Web site *www.LearningMIS.com*. Source code is compiled into **machine code** that is processed by a computer. Machine code is, in general, not understandable by humans and cannot be modified. When you access *www.LearningMIS.com,* the machine code version of the program in Figure 14 runs on your computer. We do not show machine code in a figure because it would look like this:

110100101001011111100111011110010001110000011111101110111100111 . . .

In a **closed source** project, say Microsoft Office, the source code is highly protected and only available to trusted employees and carefully vetted contractors. The source code is protected like gold in a vault. Only those trusted programmers can make changes to a closed source project.

With open source, anyone can obtain the source code from the open source project's Web site. Programmers alter or add to this code depending on their interests and goals. In most cases, programmers can incorporate code they find into their own projects. They may be able to resell those projects depending on the type of license agreement the project uses.

Open source succeeds because of collaboration. A programmer examines the source code and identifies a need or project that seems interesting. He or she then creates a new feature, redesigns or reprograms an existing feature, or fixes a known problem. That code is then sent to others in the open source project who then evaluate the quality and merits of the work and add it to the product, if appropriate.

Typically, there is a lot of give and take. Or, there are many cycles of iteration and feedback. Because of this iteration, a well-managed project with strong peer reviews can result in very high-quality code, like that in Linux.

```
#region Dependency Properties

public static readonly DependencyProperty
    LessonIDProperty = DependencyProperty.Register(
        "LessonID",
        typeof(int),
        typeof(Lesson),
        new PropertyMetadata(new PropertyChangedCallback(Lesson.OnLessonDataChanged)));

public int LessonID
{
    get { return (int)GetValue(LessonIDProperty); }
    set { SetValue(LessonIDProperty, value); }
}

private static void OnLessonDataChanged(DependencyObject d, DependencyPropertyChangedEventArgs e)
{

    // reload the stage for the new TopicID property
    Lesson thisLesson = d as Lesson;

    lessonObject = thisLesson; // there is only one lesson object ... this is a static ref to it

    thisLesson.LoadLessonData(); // get data from xml file on server
    //call to thisLesson.CreateLessonForm(); must be done after load b/c of asynchronous read
}

#endregion
```

Figure 14
Source Code Sample

So, Is Open Source Viable?

The answer depends on to whom and for what. Open source has certainly become legitimate. According to *The Economist,* "It is now generally accepted that the future will involve a blend of both proprietary and open-source software."[3] During your career, open source will likely take a greater and greater role in software. However, whether open source works for a particular situation depends on the requirements and constraints of that situation.

In some cases, companies choose open source software because it is "free." It turns out that this advantage may be less important than you'd think, because in many cases, support and operational costs swamp the initial licensing fee.

Q4 How Can You Use This Knowledge?

Over the course of your career, application software, hardware, and firmware will change, sometimes rapidly. The Guide later in the chapter challenges you to choose a strategy for addressing this change.

As a future business professional, you will need basic knowledge of hardware and software for two major reasons. First, you will need it to make some decisions about which products you use. Second, as a manager, you will be involved in creating or approving hardware budgets. Consider each.

What Buying Decisions Do You Make?

In general, most business professionals have some role in the specification of the client hardware and software they use. Business managers also play a role in the specification of client hardware and software for employees whom they manage. The particular role depends on the policy of the manager's organization. Large organizations will have an IS department that is likely to set standards for client hardware and software.

In medium to small organizations, policies are often less formal, and managers will need to take an active role in setting the specifications for their own and their employees' computers. Figure 15 summarizes sources of costs and Figure 16 lists the major criteria for selecting both hardware and software. The goal, of course, is to select the hardware and software that will meet requirements at the minimum total system cost.

Figure 15
Sources of System Costs

	Development	**Operational**
Hardware	Hardware purchases	Hardware maintenance fees
Software	Software licenses Project costs for custom software	Software maintenance and support fees and costs
Data	Data conversion costs	Data acquisition costs
Procedures	Design, development, and documentation	Procedure maintenance costs
People	Initial training costs	Labor costs of using system

---

[3] "Unlocking the Cloud," *The Economist,* May 28, 2009. Available at *www.economist.com/opinion/displaystory.cfm?story_id=13740181* (accessed June 2009).

Category	Hardware	Software
Client	Specify: • CPU speed • Size of main memory • Size of magnetic disk • CD or DVD and type • Monitor type and size	Specify: • Windows, Mac, or Linux OS. May be dictated by organizational standard. • PC applications such as Microsoft Office, Adobe Acrobat, Photoshop, Paint Shop Pro. May be dictated by organizational standard. • Browser such as Internet Explorer, FireFox, or Netscape Navigator. • Requirements for the client side of client-server applications. • Need for thin or thick client.
Server	In most cases, a business manager has no role in the specification of server hardware (except possibly a budgetary one).	• Specify requirements for the server side of client-server applications. • Work with technical personnel to test and accept software.

Figure 16
A Business Manager's Role in Hardware and Software Specifications

Except in rare circumstances, medium to small organizations will usually standardize on a single client operating system because the costs of supporting more than one are unjustifiable. Most organizations choose Microsoft Windows clients. Some arts and design businesses standardize on the Macintosh, and some engineering firms standardize on Unix. Organizations that have limited budgets might choose to use Linux with Ubuntu and Open Office on the clients, but this is rare.

Managers and their employees might have a role in specifying horizontal application software, such as Microsoft Office, or other software appropriate for their operating systems. They will also have an important role in specifying requirements for vertical market or custom applications.

Concerning the server, a business manager typically has no role in the specification of server hardware, other than possibly approving the budget. Instead, technical personnel make such decisions. A business manager and those who will be the clients of a client-server application specify the requirements for vertical and custom-server software. They will also work with technical personnel to test and accept that software.

What Process Should You Use to Establish a Computer Budget?

The steps for preparing a departmental hardware budget are summarized in Figure 17. You need first to determine the base requirements. This involves assessing the work your employees perform, creating job categories, and determining the computer workload requirements for each category.

In accounts payable, for example, you might determine that you have three categories of workers: administrators, accounts payable specialists, and managers. You further determine that the administrators need hardware and software to access the company's Web portal, to email, and to perform minimal word processing. The accounts payable specialists need the same capabilities as the administrators, but they also need access to the organization's accounts payable system. Finally, you and other managers need to be able to perform the same work as the specialists, plus you need to process large spreadsheets for preparing budgets. You also need to access the company's payroll and human resources systems.

Figure 17
A Process for Preparing a
Departmental IT Budget

Determine base requirements:
• The types of workload your employees perform
• The hardware requirements for each type
• The software requirements for each type

Forecast requirement changes during the budget period:
• Changes in the number of employees
• Changes in workload—new job tasks or information systems
• Mandatory changes in hardware or software

Prepare the budget:
• Using guidance from the IT department and accounting,
  price the hardware and software
• Determine if your department will be charged for networks,
  servers, communications, or other overhead expenses
• Add overhead charges as necessary

Assess results:
• Consider budget in context of competitive strategy
• If substantial increases in budget size, prepare justification
• Consider budget in context of prior year's budget
• Determine sources of significant difference and explain
• Modify budget as appropriate

Document results:
• Prepare for justification
• Save documents and notes for preparation of next year's IT budget

Once you have identified the job categories and the computer workload requirements for each, you can apply the knowledge from this chapter to determine hardware and software requirements for each type. You can also use past departmental experience as a guide. If employees complain about computer performance with the equipment they have, you can determine if more is needed. If there are no bottlenecks or performance problems, you know the current equipment will do.

Establishing a computer budget involves knowing the right questions to ask. The Guide later in the chapter discusses the importance of improving your ability to ask intelligent questions.

Given the base requirements, the next step is to forecast changes. Will you be adding or losing employees during the year? Will the workload change? Will your department be given new tasks that will necessitate additional hardware or software? Finally, during the year will your organization mandate changes in hardware or software? Will you be required to upgrade your operating system or applications software? If so, will your budget be charged for those upgrades?

Once you have the base requirements and your change forecasts, you can prepare the budget. The first task is to price the hardware and software. Your IT department will most likely have established standards for hardware and software from which you will select. They will probably have negotiated prices on your behalf. If not, the accounting department can probably help you estimate costs based on their prior experience. You can also learn from the past experience of your own department.

Your organization may have a policy of charging the department's overhead fees for networks, servers, and communications. If so, you will need to add those charges to the budget as well.

When you have finished the preparation of the budget, you should assess it for feasibility and reasonableness. First, consider your organization's competitive

56

strategy. If your organization is a cost leader, any increases in your budget will be carefully scrutinized, and you should be prepared with strong justifications. If your organization uses a differentiation strategy, then be certain that any increases in your budget relate directly to the ways in which your company differentiates. Before submitting your budget, prepare justifications for any such increases.

You can expect that your budget will be reviewed in the context of prior years' budgets. If you are proposing substantial changes to your budget, anticipate that you will be asked to justify them. Reasons that you may need more equipment include:

- Substantial change in your departmental head count
- Important new departmental functions or responsibilities
- Upgrading to major new versions of operating system or other software
- Implementation of new systems that require additional hardware
- Change in the way overhead expenses are allocated to your department

If you find it difficult to justify budgetary increases, you may need to review and revise your budget. Perhaps you can do with refurbished equipment, or maybe you can delay the upgrade of all of your computers to the new operating system, or maybe you can find ways of reallocating hardware among the employees in your department that will save costs. Even if none of these options are workable, you can document that you investigated them in your budget justification or mention them in any budgetary review meetings.

Finally, document your results. You can use such documentation not only to justify your budget this year but also to help you prepare next year's budget. Keep any spreadsheets as well as notes and documents used to prepare and justify your budget.

Q5 2021?

The year 2010 was a watershed year for computer hardware. In 2010, the market voted and the results came in: Apple 10, Microsoft 0.

Why? In the future computing devices won't look like computers. Microsoft knew this, but blundered along, assuming that whatever the new devices looked like they would still carry some version of Windows.

Not so, said the buyers of iPhones and iPads. Not so. In 2010, Microsoft brought out its disastrous Kin phone. After investing more than $2 billion into its development, it pulled Kin from the market after selling 500 phones in the first 6 weeks, and meanwhile continued to build its Windows 7 Series phone operating system for the 2010 Christmas season. Will it fare any better? It seems doubtful.

Microsoft bases its marketing campaign on claims that users want access to networks and applications on their "three screens," which to Microsoft means computer screen, phone screen, and television screen. Microsoft encourages those who build applications with its development tools to construct their applications to function well on all three screens.

But Apple didn't buy into that idea. Instead, Apple invested in completely new computing devices with touch screens and useful, natural-feeling interface innovations. The iPod, iPhone, and iPad all broke new ground. Amazon.com did something similar, though less spectacular, with its Kindle devices. None of these devices fit into the three-screen model, nor do any of them run Windows.

And how did the market vote? iPhone sales were up 5,000% in 2009. While Kin sold 500 units, customers stood in line for hours to buy the iPad, and early sales of the iPhone 4 were 10 times projections. Apparently, people prefer new devices that don't fit into the established three-screen categories.

Figure 18
A PC Mule at the Airport

Source: Photolibrary.com.

So, where will this take us by 2021? Today, everyone takes their PC or other device wherever they go. Every day, business professionals, working like **PC mules**, work their way through airport security, unpacking and packing their computer loads. (See Figure 18.)

By 2021, PC mules will be rarer than pack mules. Users will carry their phones, their iPads, and whatever iSomethings come along. They'll do so because they're small and powerful.

But what about large-screen access? Maybe some PC mules will survive, but more likely is that large-screen computing/connectivity devices will be available everywhere, like pay telephones once were. Instead of carrying your computer, you'll simply use a public device and connect to your data in the cloud. You won't need your desktop Office applications because you'll be using Web apps in your browser. You won't need your local data files because all those files will be in the cloud.

This trend will accelerate with thin-client versions of all applications. If any computer will provide access to those applications and your data, why carry a computer? We PC mules will be the first to agree.

But there is a limitation. My personal computer provides more than just data and thick-client applications. It has my personal organization. It has my screensaver, it has my desktop picture and icons, it has my files arranged just the way I want them. I need my computer to provide my personal world in a familiar way.

Enter desktop virtualization. By 2021, any cost performance issues of desktop virtualization will be gone, and you will access any public computer, connect to your personal virtual desktop, and, voilá, be running what you now think to be your computer. In fact, it is your computer, except that it is running on a public machine that is connected to your virtual desktop in the cloud.

If that is the case, why haul any hardware anywhere? At least why haul any hardware that weighs more than a few ounces? In this world, your hotel room comes with a computer; your airplane seat comes with a computer, your bus seat comes with a computer, your convention center is full of computers. With all of these devices, you need only access your virtual client, somewhere in the cloud, and you are up and running on "your machine."

This mode of access solves another aggravating problem. Many professionals use several different computers and have different sets of data on each. This situation creates data synchronization problems. If you work on your computer at home, when you get to work you have to synchronize (or **synch**) your computer at work with any changes you've made on the computer you took home. But, if your machine is a virtual client in the cloud, everything is always synchronized, because there's only one version.

So, where does that leave Microsoft? Or Google? Or Apple? It's the Wild West all over again. Who knows? Everything depends on how those companies respond, which ultimately comes down to you and your classmates. The next decade will bring enormous change in hardware/software technologies, companies, industries, and users. You will be in the vanguard of consumers who decide. And a small percentage of you will have the great good fortune to work in the IT industry during this raucous time, cowboy hats and all!

Guide

Keeping Up to Speed

Have you ever been to a cafeteria where you put your lunch tray on a conveyor belt that carries the dirty dishes into the kitchen? That conveyor belt reminds me of technology. Like the conveyor, technology just moves along, and all of us run on top of the technology conveyor, trying to keep up. We hope to keep up with the relentless change of technology for an entire career without ending up in the techno-trash.

Technology change is a fact, and the only appropriate question is, "What am I going to do about it?" One strategy you can take is to bury your head in the sand: "Look, I'm not a technology person. I'll leave it to the pros. As long as I can send email and use the Internet, I'm happy. If I have a problem, I'll call someone to fix it."

That strategy is fine, as far as it goes, and many businesspeople use it. Following that strategy won't give you a competitive advantage over anyone, and it will give someone else a competitive advantage over you, but as long as you develop your advantage elsewhere, you'll be OK—at least for yourself.

What about your department, though? If an expert says, "Every computer needs a 500GB disk," are you going to nod your head and say, "Great. Sell 'em to me!" Or are you going to know enough to realize that's a big disk (by 2011 standards, anyway) and ask why everyone needs such a large amount of storage? Maybe then you'll be told, "Well, it's only another $150 per machine from the 120GB disk." At that point, you can make a decision, using your own decision-making skills, and not rely solely on the IS expert. Thus, the prudent business professional in the twenty-first century has a number of reasons not to bury his or her head in the technology sand.

At the other end of the spectrum are those who love technology. You'll find them everywhere—they may be accountants, marketing professionals, or production-line supervisors who not only know their field, but also enjoy information technology. Maybe they were IS majors or had double majors that combined IS with another area of expertise (e.g., IS with accounting). These people read CNET News and ZDNet most days, and they can tell you the latest on desktop virtualization. Those people are sprinting along the technology conveyor belt; they will never end up in the techno-trash, and they will use their knowledge of IT to gain competitive advantage throughout their careers.

Many business professionals fall in between these extremes. They don't want to bury their heads, but they don't have the desire or interest to become technophiles (lovers of technology) either. What to do? There are a couple of strategies. For one, don't allow yourself to ignore technology. When you see a technology article in the *Wall Street Journal*, read it. Don't just skip it because it's about technology. Read the technology ads, too. Many vendors invest heavily in ads that instruct without seeming to. Another option is to take a seminar or pay attention to professional events that combine your specialty with technology. For example, when you go to the banker's convention, attend a session or two on "Technology Trends for Bankers." There are always sessions like that, and you might make a contact with similar problems and concerns in another company.

Probably the best option, if you have the time for it, is to get involved as a user representative in technology committees in your organization. If your company is doing a review of its CRM system, for instance, see if you can get on the review committee. When there's a need for a representative from your department to discuss needs for the next-generation help-line system, sign up. Or, later in your career, become a member of the business practice technology committee, or whatever they call it at your organization.

Just working with such groups will add to your knowledge of technology. Presentations made to such groups, discussions about uses of technology, and ideas about using IT for competitive advantage will all add to your IT knowledge. You'll gain important contacts and exposure to leaders in your organization as well.

It's up to you. You get to choose how you relate to technology. But be sure you choose; don't let your head fall into the sand without thinking about it. ■

Discussion Questions

1. Do you agree that the change of technology is relentless? What do you think that means to most business professionals? To most organizations?

2. Think about the three postures toward technology presented here. Which camp will you join? Why?

3. Write a two-paragraph memo to yourself justifying your choice in question 2. If you chose to ignore technology, explain how you will compensate for the loss of competitive advantage. If you're going to join one of the other two groups, explain why, and describe how you're going to accomplish your goal.

4. Given your answer to question 2, assume that you're in a job interview and the interviewer asks about your knowledge of technology. Write a three-sentence response to the interviewer's question.

Guide

Questioning Your Questions

Many school experiences mislead you to believe that answering a question is the important part of learning. In fact, answering a question is the easy part. For most problems in the business world, the difficult and creative acts are generating the questions—and formulating a strategy for getting the answers. Once the questions and strategy are set, the rest is simply legwork.

As a future consumer of information technology and services, you will benefit from being able to ask good questions and effectively obtain answers to them. It is probably the single most important behavior you can learn. Because of the rapid change of technology, you will constantly be required to learn about new IS alternatives and how you can apply them in your business.

Perhaps you've heard that "there is no such thing as a bad question." This statement is nonsense. There are billions of bad questions, and you will be better off if you learn not to ask them.

Questions can be bad in three ways: They can be irrelevant, dead, or asked of the wrong source. Consider the first way. If you know the subject and if you're paying attention, you can avoid asking irrelevant questions. One of the goals of this text is to teach you about IT and IS so that you can avoid asking irrelevant technology questions.

A dead question is one that leads to nowhere—it provides no insight into the subject. Here's an example of a dead question: "Is the material on How a Computer Works going to be on the test?" The answer will tell you whether

It is not possible to become a good thinker and be a poor questioner. Thinking is not driven by answers, but rather, by questions.[4]

you need to study that topic for the exam, but it won't tell you why. The answer will help you in school, but it won't help you use MIS on the job.

Instead, ask questions like, "What is the purpose of the section on how a computer works?" "Why are we studying it?" or "How will it help me use MIS in my career?" These are good questions because they go somewhere. Your professor may respond, "From that discussion you'll learn how to save money because you'll know whether to buy your staff more memory or a faster CPU." Possibly, you won't understand that answer; in that case, you can ask more questions that will lead you to understand how it pertains to your use of MIS.

Or, your professor may say, "Well, I think that section is a waste of time, and I told the author that in a recent email." From there, you can ask your professor why she thinks it's a waste of time, and you can wonder why the author would write something that is a waste of time. Maybe the author and your professor have different points of view. Such musings are excellent because they lead you to more learning.

The third way questions can be bad is that they are asked of the wrong source. Information technology questions fall into three types: "What is it?" "How can I use it?" and "Is it the best choice?" The first type asks for a simple definition. You can easily Google or Bing the answers to such questions. Hence, you ought not to ask "What is it?" questions of valuable or expensive sources; you are wasting your money and their time if you

---

[4]Richard Paul and Linda Elder, *Critical Thinking* (Upper Saddle River, NJ: Prentice Hall, 2001), p. 113.

do. And, when you ask such a question, you appear unprepared because you didn't take the time to find the easy answer.

The next type of question, "How can I use it?" is harder. Answering that question requires knowledge of both technology and your business. Although you can research that question over the Internet, you need knowledge to relate it to your present circumstance. In a few years, this is the sort of question that you will be expected to answer for your organization. It's also the type of question you might ask an expert.

Finally, the most difficult type of question is, "Is it the best choice for our company or situation?" Answering this type of question requires the ability to judge among alternatives according to appropriate criteria. These are the kinds of questions you probably do want to ask an expensive source.

Notice, too, that only "What is it?" questions have a verifiably correct answer. The next two types are questions of judgment. No answer can be shown to be correct, but some answers are better than others. As you progress in your educational career, you should be learning how to discern the quality of judgment and evaluative answers. Learn to question your questions. ■

Discussion Questions

Suppose you are interviewing an expert about how she thinks Microsoft will respond to the challenge of open source. Using that as an example, answer questions 1 through 7.

1. Using your own words, what is the difference between a good question and a bad one?

2. What types of questions waste time?

3. What types of questions are appropriate to ask your professor?

4. How do you know when you have a good answer to a question? Consider the three types of questions described here in your answer.

5. Under what circumstances would you ask a question to which you already know the answer?

6. Suppose you have 15 minutes with your boss's boss's boss. What kinds of questions are appropriate in such an interview? Even though you don't pay money to meet with this person, explain how this is an expensive source.

7. Evaluate the quality of questions 1 through 5. Which are the best questions? What makes one better than the other? If you can, think of better ways of asking these questions, or even better questions.

Active Review

Use this Active Review to verify that you understand the ideas and concepts that answer the chapter's study questions.

Q1 What do business professionals need to know about computer hardware?

List categories of hardware and explain the purpose of each. Define *bit* and *byte*. Explain why bits are used to represent computer data. Define the units of bytes used to size memory. In general terms, explain how a computer works. Explain how a manager can use this knowledge. Explain why you should save your work from time to time while you are using your computer.

Q2 What do business professionals need to know about software?

Review Figure 9 and explain the meaning of each cell in this table. Describe three kinds of virtualization, and explain the use of each. Explain the difference between software ownership and software licenses. Explain the differences among horizontal-market, vertical-market, and one-of-a-kind applications. Describe the three ways that organizations can acquire software.

Q3 Is open source software a viable alternative?

Define *GNU* and *GPL*. Name three successful open source projects. Describe four reasons programmers contribute to open source projects. Define *open source, closed source, source code,* and *machine code*. In your own words, explain why open source is a legitimate alternative but may or may not be appropriate for a given application.

Q4 How can you use this knowledge?

Describe the two major reasons you need the knowledge of this chapter. Review Figure 16 and explain each cell of this table. Summarize the process you should use to develop a computer budget.

Q5 2021?

Describe the ways in which the market voted in 2010. Explain how this trend in computing devices will eliminate PC mules. Describe the role and value of desktop virtualization. Explain how you will access your computer in 2021 and why you will not need to synch. Summarize what we can say about the impact of these trends on Microsoft, Google, Apple, and you.

Key Terms and Concepts

32-bit processor	Closed source	Grid
64-bit processor	Cloud computing	Hardware
Application software	Custom-developed software	Horizontal-market application
Binary digit	Data channel	Host operating system
Bits	Desktop virtualization	Input hardware
Bus	Dual processor	Instruction set
Bytes	Firmware	Kilobyte (K)
Cache	Gigabyte (GB)	License
Central processing unit (CPU)	GNU	Linux
Client	GNU General Public License	Mac OS
Client-server applications	(GPL) agreement	Machine code

Main memory
Megabyte (MB)
Memory swapping
Nonvolatile
Off-the-shelf software
Off-the-shelf with alterations
  software
One-of-a-kind application
Open source community
Operating system (OS)
Output hardware

PC virtualization
PC mules
Quad processor
RAM
Server farm
Servers
Server virtualization
Site license
Source code
Storage hardware
Synch

Terabyte (TB)
Thick client
Thin client
Universal Serial Bus (USB)
Unix
Vertical-market application
Virtualization
Virtual machines (vm)
Volatile
Windows

Using Your Knowledge

1. Suppose that your roommate, a political science major, asks you to help her purchase a new laptop computer. She wants to use the computer for email, Internet access, and for note-taking in class. She wants to spend less than $1,000.

  a. What CPU, memory, and disk specifications would you recommend?

  b. What software does she need?

  c. Shop *www.dell.com*, *www.hp.com*, and *www. lenovo.com* for the best computer deal.

  d. Which computer would you recommend, and why?

2. Suppose that your father asks you to help him purchase a new computer. He wants to use his computer for email, Internet access, downloading pictures from his digital camera, uploading those pictures to a shared photo service, and writing documents to members of his antique auto club.

  a. What CPU, memory, and disk specifications would you recommend?

  b. What software does he need?

  c. Shop *www.dell.com*, *www.hp.com*, and *www. lenovo.com* for the best computer deal.

  d. Which computer would you recommend, and why?

3. Microsoft offers free licenses of certain software products to students at colleges and universities that participate in the Microsoft Developer Network (MSDN) Academic Alliance (AA). If your college or university participates in this program, you have the opportunity to obtain hundreds of dollars of software, for free. Here is a partial list of the software you can obtain:

  * Microsoft Access 2010
  * OneNote 2010
  * Expression Studio 4
  * Windows 2008 Server
  * Microsoft Project 2010
  * Visual Studio Developer
  * SQL Server 2008
  * Visio 2010

  a. Search *www.microsoft.com*, *www.google.com*, or *www.bing.com* and determine the function of each of these software products.

  b. Which of these software products are operating systems and which are application programs?

  c. Which of these programs are DBMS products (the subject of the next chapter)?

  d. Which of these programs should you download and install tonight?

  e. Either (1) download and install the programs in your answer to part d, or (2) explain why you would not choose to do so.

  f. Does the MSDN AA provide an unfair advantage to Microsoft? Why or why not?

4. Suppose you work at FlexTime and Neil has asked you to help analyze the software situation. He wants to compute the total costs of three alternatives: (1) upgrading to Version 3 of the current software, (2) licensing the open source software, and (3) licensing another vendor's thin-client software. He has asked you to identify all of the costs that should be considered. Note that he is not asking you to determine those costs, nor even to know how to determine those costs. He simply wants a list of costs to consider.

  a. Using Figure 15 as a guide, identify potential costs for each component for development and operation of the new system.

  b. Using your intuition, do you think the list of costs that you identified in part a is likely to swamp the costs of the software license fee? Why or why not?

Collaboration Exercise

Collaborate with students on the following exercise. In particular, consider using Google Docs, Windows Live SkyDrive, Microsoft SharePoint, or some other collaboration tool.

Suppose you manage the sales and marketing department at a company that generates $100 million in sales—say, a manufacturer of fireplace inserts and related equipment. Assume you just started the job and that at the end of your second day the corporate operations officer (COO) sticks her head into your office and announces, "I'm in a rush and have to go, but I wanted to let you know that I put $80,000 in the budget for computers for your department next year. Is that OK? Unfortunately, I've got to know by the day after tomorrow. Thanks."

How do you respond? You have 2 days to decide. If you agree to the $80,000 and it turns out to be insufficient, then sometime next year your department will lack computing resources and you'll have a management problem. If that happens, you may have to spend over your budget. You know that cost control is important to your new employer, so you dread overspending. However, if you ask for more than $80,000, you need to justify why you need it. You will need to document the computer equipment and software your department needs, explain why you need it, and estimate how much it will cost.

Given the short time frame, and given that as a new employee you probably have already scheduled the next 2 days full of meetings, you will need to delegate at least part of this problem to someone. You might delegate it to a computer salesperson, but that is akin to inviting the fox to babysit the chickens. Or, you could delegate it to some of your employees, but as a new employee you

do not yet know who has the capability to answer this question. You could also ask the IS department at your organization to help you.

In any case, whether you find the time to answer this question yourself, assign it to your employees, or ask for help from the IS department, you will need knowledge of computer hardware and software capabilities and costs in order to assess the quality of the answer you have.

To respond to this request, assume you have been given the following list of data about the department and its information needs:

* You will upgrade all of your department's computers to Windows 7 and Office 2010 in the next year. Your company has negotiated a site license for these products, and the IS department allocates that license cost to each computer. For your department, you will pay $100 for each computer that uses Office 2010 and another $75 for each computer that uses Windows 7. You are not required nor allowed to buy any software for new computers. If the computer comes with software, that software will be destroyed by the IS department's standard installation process.
* You have identified three classes of computer users in your department. The main memory, RAM, and disk storage requirements for each class of user are shown in Figure 19. This figure shows the specifications of existing computers as well as the hardware requirements for each class after the upgrade.

Figure 19
Hardware Specifications for Three Classes of Computers

Class of Computer	Current Hardware Specification (Main Memory, Processor, Disk)	Hardware Required After Upgrade (Main Memory, Processor, Disk)
A	256MB, 0.5GHz, 30GB	1GB, 1GHz, 80GB
B	512MB, 1GHz, 80GB	2GB, 2GHz, 150GB
C	1GB, 2GHz, 2 x 125GB	4GB, 2GHz—dual, 2 x 250GB

Job Title	Number of Employees	Computer System Required	Computer Type
Product manager	8	B	Laptop
Telesales	12	A	Desktop
Department administrator	2	A	Desktop
Marketing communications manager	4	B	Laptop
Marketing analyst	4	C (desktop) B (laptop)	Both, a desktop and laptop for each analyst
Marketing programs manager	6	B	Desktop
You	1	???	???

Figure 20
Department Employees and Computer Requirements

● Figure 20 shows the job titles of employees in your department, the number of employees of each type, the class of computer they require, and whether they use a desktop or a laptop. (You are a new employee, do not yet have a computer, and can specify your own requirements.)

● A computer can be reassigned to other employees as long as the computer meets the minimum processing requirements. A laptop can substitute for a desktop if a display, keyboard, and mouse are purchased to go with it.

● The IS department assesses each computer an annual $1,200 fee for network, server, and other overhead costs.

● Assume that telesales personnel will grow by 10 percent in the next year but there will be no other changes in the number of personnel in your department.

● Ten of the existing class B computers have a maximum main memory of 1GB. The rest of the class B computers have a maximum main memory of 512MB. All of the existing class C computers have a maximum main memory of 4GB.

a. Given this data, is $80,000 enough? If not, how much money should be allocated in your department?

b. Explain how you will meet the computer needs of the employees in your department. Assume you are required to buy new computers and equipment from Dell, HP, or Lenovo.

c. Describe how you will modify and reallocate existing computers (e.g., upgrading an existing class B computer and assigning it to an employee who next year needs a class A computer).

67

Case Study

Dell Leverages the Internet, Directly, but for How Long?

When Michael Dell started Dell Computer in 1984, personal computers were sold only in retail stores. Manufacturers shipped to wholesalers, who shipped to retail stores, which sold to end users. Companies maintained expensive inventories at each stage of this supply chain. Dell thought that he could eliminate the retail channel by selling computers directly to consumers:

> I was inspired by how I saw computers being sold. It seemed to me that it was very expensive and it was inefficient. A computer cost at the time about $3,000 but there were only about $600 worth of parts inside the computer. And so I figured, hey, what if you sold the computer for $800? You don't need to sell it for $3,000. And so we changed the whole way computers were being sold by lowering the cost of distribution and sales and taking out this extra cost that was inefficient.
>
> Now, what I didn't know was that the Internet would come along and now people can go on the Internet and they can go to *Dell.com* and buy a computer and that makes it a lot easier.
>
> I'd say the most important thing we did was listen very carefully to our customers. We asked, what do they want, what do they need and how can we meet their needs and provide something that's really valuable to them? Because if we could take care of our customers, they'll want to buy more products from us, and they have.[5]

Eliminating retail stores not only reduced costs, but it also brought Dell closer to the customer, enabling it to listen better than the competition. It also eliminated sales channel inventories, which allowed Dell to rapidly bring new computers with new technology to the customer. This eliminates the need to recycle or sell off existing pipeline inventory whenever a new model is announced.

Additionally, Dell focused on its suppliers and now has one of the most efficient supply chains in the industry. Dell pays close attention to its suppliers and shares information with them on product quality, inventory, and related subjects via its secure Web site *http://valuechain.dell.com*. According to its Web site, the first two qualities Dell looks for in suppliers are (1) cost competitiveness and (2) an understanding of Dell's business.

In addition to computer hardware, Dell provides a variety of services. It provides basic technical support with every computer, and customers can upgrade this basic support by purchasing one of four higher levels of support. Additionally, Dell offers deployment services to organizations to configure and deploy Dell systems, both hardware and preinstalled software, into customers' user environments. Dell offers additional services to maintain and manage Dell systems once they have been deployed.

Dell enjoyed unprecedented success until the recent economic downturn. In May 2009, Dell reported that first-quarter earnings had fallen 63 percent compared to a year earlier, and sales had dropped 23 percent. This report was on top of the prior quarter in which earnings dropped 48 percent from the same quarter a year before.

The problem is not only Dell's however. Sales were down in 2009 for other hardware vendors as well. The economy is responsible for some of this decline, and some of it is also due to the fact that customers were waiting to buy PCs after Windows 7 came out in late 2010.

However, another financial result had to have been troubling to Dell. In that year, Intel reported that sales were returning to "normal patterns," and Cisco (maker of routers and other communication devices) reported that sales seemed to have bottomed out. So, the components of PCs seem to be selling, but not PCs themselves. What might this mean?

In September 2009, Dell tipped its hand as to how it views the future. On September 21 of that year, it bought Perot Systems for $3.9 billion. Perot was a provider of information systems services to health care and government customers. Clearly, Dell plans some change in its corporate strategy.

Sources: © 2005 Dell Inc. All Rights Reserved. "Dell: No Relief in Sight," *BusinessWeek*, May 28, 2009. Available at *www.businessweek.com/technology/content/may2009/tc20090528_130058.htm* (accessed June 2009).

---

[5]Michael Dell, speech before the Miami Springs Middle School, September 1, 2004. Retrieved from *www.dell.com*, under Michael/Speeches (accessed January 2005).

Questions

1. Explain how selling direct has given Dell a competitive advantage.
2. What information systems does Dell need to have to sell directly to the consumer? Visit *http://dell.com* for inspiration and ideas.
3. Besides selling direct, what other programs has Dell created that give it a competitive advantage?
4. Consider Dell's recent financial troubles.

   a. What are the implications of the company's tactics when revenue falls 63 percent but sales fall only 23 percent?

   b. Intel sells CPUs and memory, and its sales have stabilized. Dell and HP make computers, and their sales continue to decline. Assume the sales of other PC manufacturers are similar to those for Dell and HP. What do you conclude?

   c. Go to *http://news.cnet.com/8301-1001_3-10357598-92.html.* Summarize what you believe the Perot purchase means about Dell's future direction. Is this a smart move for Dell? Why or why not?

Application Exercises

1. Read the Collaboration Exercise for this chapter. Create an Excel spreadsheet to compute the cost of new computers for the $80,000 problem. Use the spreadsheet in Figure AE-2 as an example.

   Construct your spreadsheet so that you can change prices, charges, and job title employee count and Excel will update the Total Cost for Category as well as Total Cost. As stated in the note in the spreadsheet, the costs shown here are only examples, as is the choice of computer for the manager (you).

2. Sometimes you will have data in one Office application and want to move it to another Office application without rekeying it. Often this occurs when data was created for one purpose but then is used for a second purpose. For example, Figure AE-3 presents a portion of an Excel spreadsheet that shows the assignment of computers to employees. Neil, at FlexTime, might use such a spreadsheet to track who has which equipment.

   Suppose that you (or Neil) want to use this data to help you assess how to upgrade computers. Let's say, for example, that you want to upgrade all of the computers' operating systems to Windows 7. Furthermore, you want to first upgrade the computers that most need upgrading, but suppose you have a limited budget. To address this situation, you would like to query the data in Figure AE-3, find all computers that do not have Windows 7, and then select those with slower CPUs or smaller memory as candidates for upgrading. To do this, you need to move the data from Excel into Access.

   Once you have analyzed the data and determined the computers to upgrade, you want to produce a report. In that case, you may want to move the data from Access back to Excel, or perhaps into Word. In this exercise, you will learn how to perform these tasks.

   a. To begin, download the Excel file **Ch04Ex02** from this text's Web site into one of your directories. We will import the data in this file into Access, but before

---

Figure AE-2
New-Hardware Cost Calculator

Source: Microsoft product screenshot reprinted with permission from Microsoft Corporation.

	A	B	C	D	E	F	G
2				New–Hardware Cost Calculator			
3							
4		Laptop	Desktop				
5	Price of Class A Computer	$1,500	$1,000		Note for teams answering the $80,000		
6	Price of Class B Computer	$2,000	$1,500		collaboration project: Prices shown are		
7	Price of Class C Computer	$2,500	$2,000		just examples. Actual prices will likely be		
8					different. Also, the choice of Laptop B for		
9	Vista Software Charge	$75	$75		the manager is only for example. Another		
10	Office 2007 Software Charge	$100	$100		choice may make more sense.		
11	Network and Server Charge	$1,200	$1,200				
12							
13							
14							
15	Job Title	Number of Employees	Computer System Required	Computer Type	Hardware and Software Cost	Total Cost for Category	
16	Product manager	8	B	Laptop	$3,375	$27,000	
17	Telesales	12	A	Desktop	$2,375	$28,500	
18	Department Admin	2	A	Desktop	$2,375	$4,750	
19	Marketing Communications Manager	4	B	Laptop	$3,375	$13,500	
20	Marketing Analyst	4	C (desktop)	Both, a desktop and	$3,375	$13,500	
21			B (laptop)	laptop for each analyst	$2,575	$10,300	
22	Marketing Programs Manager	6	B	Desktop	$1,375	$8,250	
23	Manager (You)	1	B	Laptop	$3,375	$3,375	
24							
25					Total Cost	$109,175	

Figure AE-3
Sample Excel Data for Import

Source: Microsoft product screenshot reprinted with permission from Microsoft Corporation.

we do so familiarize yourself with the data by opening it in Excel. Notice that there are three worksheets in this workbook. Close the Excel file.

b. Create a blank Access database. Name the database *Ch04Ex02_Answer*. Place it in some directory; it may be the same directory into which you have placed the Excel file, but it need not be. Close the default table that Access creates and delete it.

c. Now, we will import the data from the three worksheets in the Excel file **Ch04Ex02** into a single table in your Access database. In the ribbon, select *External Data* and *Import from Excel*. Start the import. For the first worksheet (Denver), you should select *Import the source data into a new table in the current database*. Be sure to click *First Row Contains Column Headings* when Access presents your data. You can use the default Field types and let Access add the primary key. Name your table *Employees* and click *Finish*. There is no need to save your import script.

   For the second and third worksheets, again click *External Data, Import Excel*, but this time select *Append a copy of the records to the table Employees*. Import all data.

d. Open the *Employee* table and examine the data. Notice that Access has erroneously imported a blank line and the *Primary Contact* data into rows at the end of each data set. This data is not part of the employee records, and you should delete it (in three places—once for each worksheet). The *Employee* table should have a total of 40 records.

e. Now, create a parameterized query on this data. Place all of the columns except *ID* into the query. In the *OS* column, set the criteria to select rows for which the value is not *Windows 7*. In the *CPU* (GHz) column, enter the criterion: <=[Enter cutoff value for CPU] and in the *Memory* (GB) column, enter the criterion: <=[Enter cutoff value for Memory]. Test your query. For example, run your query and enter a value of *2* for both CPU and memory. Verify that the correct rows are produced.

f. Use your query to find values of CPU and memory that give you as close to a maximum of 15 computers to upgrade as possible.

g. When you have found values of CPU and memory that give you 15, or nearly 15, computers to upgrade, leave your query open. Now, click *External data, Word*, and create a Word document that contains the results of your query. Adjust the column widths of the created table so that it fits on the page. Write a memo around this table explaining that these are the computers that you believe should be upgraded.

3. Assume you have been asked to create a spreadsheet to help make a buy-versus-lease decision for the servers on your organization's Web farm. Assume that you are considering the servers for a 5-year period, but you do not know exactly how many servers you will need. Initially, you know you will need 5 servers, but you might need as many as 50, depending on the success of your organization's e-commerce activity.

a. For the buy-alternative calculations, set up your spreadsheet so that you can enter the base price of the server hardware, the price of all software, and a maintenance expense that is some percentage of the hardware price. Assume that the percent you enter covers both hardware and software maintenance. Also assume that each server has a 3-year life, after which it has no value. Assume straight-line depreciation for computers used less than 3 years, and that at the end of the 5 years you can sell the computers you have used for less than 3 years for their depreciated value. Also assume that your organization pays 2 percent interest on capital expenses. Assume the servers cost $5,000 each, and the needed software costs $750. Assume that the maintenance expense varies from 2 to 7 percent.

b. For the lease-alternative calculations, assume that the leasing vendor will lease the same computer hardware as you can purchase. The lease includes all the software you need as well as all maintenance. Set up your spreadsheet so that you can enter various lease costs, which vary according to the number of years of the lease (1, 2, or 3). Assume the cost of a 3-year lease is $285 per machine per month, a 2-year lease is $335 per machine per month, and a 1-year lease is $415 per machine per month. Also, the lessor offers a 5 percent discount if you lease from 20 to 30 computers and a 10 percent discount if you lease from 31 to 50 computers.

c. Using your spreadsheet, compare the costs of buy versus lease under the following situations. (Assume you either buy or lease. You cannot lease some and buy some.) Make assumptions as necessary and state those assumptions.

   (1) Your organization requires 20 servers for 5 years.
   (2) Your organization requires 20 servers for the first 2 years and 40 servers for the next 3 years.
   (3) Your organization requires 20 servers for the first 2 years, 40 servers for the next 2 years, and 50 servers for the last year.
   (4) Your organization requires 10 servers the first year, 20 servers the second year, 30 servers the third year, 40 servers the fourth year, and 50 servers the last year.
   (5) For the previous case, does the cheaper alternative change if the cost of the servers is $4,000? If it is $8,000?

Chapter 3 (original Chapter 5 of "Using MIS, 4/e")

Database Processing

From Chapter 5 of *Using MIS*, 4/e. David M. Kroenke. Copyright © 2012 by Pearson Education. Published by Prentice Hall.

Database Processing

"Nope. It doesn't make any sense. I looked at the data and found we can't pack customers into classes. We don't have enough capacity."

"But, Neil, look at that Sunday night spinning class . . . it's half full. We could put another 25 people into that class."

"It's not what it seems. I queried the database, and at first glance you'd think we have plenty of opportunity to fill unoccupied seats. According to our database, we have a 9.7 percent vacancy rate in our classes."

"That's a lot."

"Yes, but looking more closely, I found that all of those empty seats occur in awkward time slots. The database shows that all of Monday–Saturday primetime class slots are full—99.8 percent occupancy."

"Wow."

"It's the Sunday and the mid-day classes that have the vacancies."

"Well, let's try to consolidate those classes."

"Not a good idea . . . for two reasons. One, we'd only be able to cancel two, maybe three classes, and that doesn't save us much. But, the stronger reason it won't work is that people are inflexible in the time slots they chose."

"How do you know that?"

"Felix I was amazed . . . but 93 percent of our customers always take a class on the same day and time. Even if they change classes, they always change to the same date and time."

"I guess that makes sense, Neil. They've got their lives set up to come here at a particular time on particular days and, well, they don't want to change that."

"That's true for more than 9 out of 10 customers."

"Hey, Neil, it's great that our software lets you query the data like that."

"Actually, it's not so flexible. I have about 25 standard queries that I can make against the database, selecting customers who've taken particular classes, etc. Those standard queries don't give me all the data I need. If I were a programmer type, I could write my own queries against the database, but I'm not."

"So what do you do?"

"Felix, I'm a whiz at Excel! I run a database query that's as close as possible to what I want and then bring the results into Excel. I move and sort and sum and average the data around in Excel until I get the information I want."

"That seems like a pain."

"Yeah, maybe, but it works."

"Neil, that leaves us where we started, doesn't it? If we can't save money by packing customers into classes, what are we going to do?"

"I'm looking at the juice bar right now. Seems like our inventory costs are too high and we may need to reduce its operating hours. But don't say anything to anyone about that. I haven't looked at the data yet."

"The trainers will be glad we aren't cancelling classes."

"Yes, why don't you tell them on your team site? And not cancelling classes saves us possible public relations problems with our customers. Anyway, we avoided a train wreck on this one. Hey, I'm gonna go for a run. Cheers!" ■

Study Questions

Q1 What is the purpose of a database?

Q2 What is a database?

Q3 What are the components of a database application system?

Q4 How do database applications make databases more useful?

Q5 How are data models used for database development?

Q6 How is a data model transformed into a database design?

Q7 What is the users' role in the development of databases?

Q8 2021?

Chapter Preview

Businesses of every size organize data records into collections called *databases*. At one extreme, small businesses use databases to keep track of customers; at the other extreme, huge corporations such as Dell and Amazon.com use databases to support complex sales, marketing, and operations activities. In between, we have businesses like FlexTime that use databases as a crucial part of their operations, but they don't have a trained and experienced staff to manage and support the databases. To obtain answers to the one-of-a-kind queries he needs, Neil needs to be creative and adaptable in the way that he accesses and uses his database.

This chapter discusses the why, what, and how of database processing. We begin by describing the purpose of databases and then explain the important components of database systems. We then overview the process of creating a database system and summarize your role as a future user of such systems.

Users have a crucial role in the development of database applications. Specifically, the structure and content of the database depends entirely on how users view their business activity. To build the database, the developers will create a model of that view using a tool called the entity-relationship model. You need to understand how to interpret such models, because the development team might ask you to validate the correctness of such a model when building a system for your use. Finally, we describe the various database administration tasks.

This chapter focuses on database technology. Here we consider the basic components of a database and their functions.

Q1 What Is the Purpose of a Database?

The purpose of a database is to keep track of things. When most students learn that, they wonder why we need a special technology for such a simple task. Why not just use a list? If the list is long, put it into a spreadsheet.

In fact, many professionals do keep track of things using spreadsheets. If the structure of the list is simple enough, there is no need to use database technology. The list of student grades in Figure 1, for example, works perfectly well in a spreadsheet.

Suppose, however, that the professor wants to track more than just grades. Say that the professor wants to record email messages as well. Or, perhaps the professor wants to record both email messages and office visits. There is no place in Figure 1

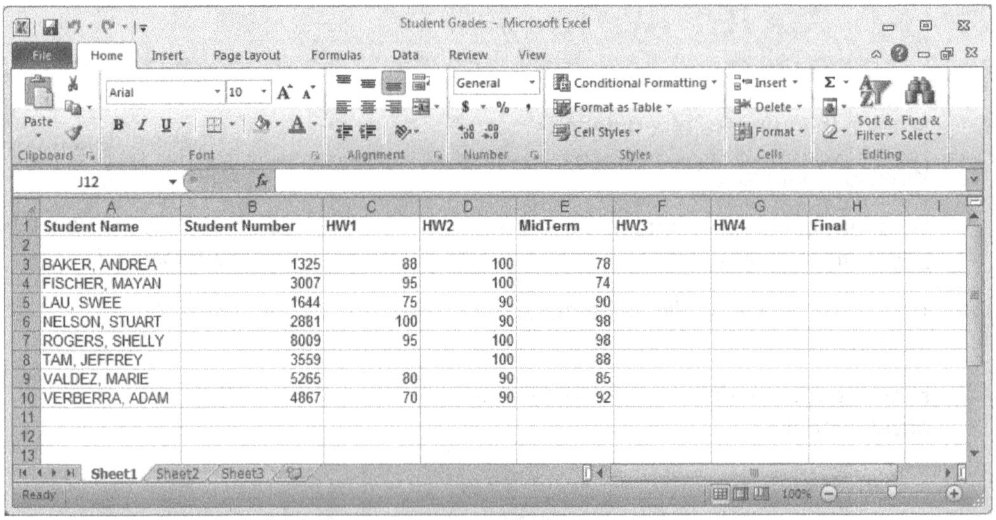

Student Name	Student Number	HW1	HW2	MidTerm	HW3	HW4	Final
BAKER, ANDREA	1325	88	100	78			
FISCHER, MAYAN	3007	95	100	74			
LAU, SWEE	1644	75	90	90			
NELSON, STUART	2881	100	90	98			
ROGERS, SHELLY	8009	95	100	98			
TAM, JEFFREY	3559		100	88			
VALDEZ, MARIE	5265	80	90	85			
VERBERRA, ADAM	4867	70	90	92			

Figure 1
A List of Student Grades, Presented in a Spreadsheet

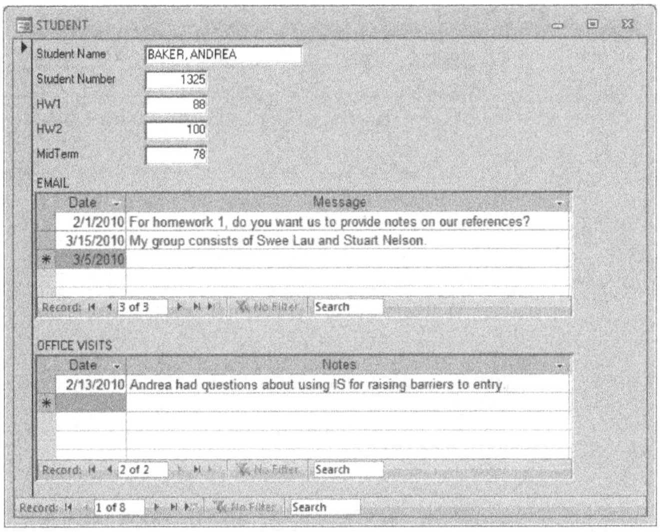

Figure 2
Student Data Shown in a Form, from a Database

to record that additional data. Of course, the professor could set up a separate spreadsheet for email messages and another one for office visits, but that awkward solution would be difficult to use because it does not provide all of the data in one place.

Instead, the professor wants a form like that in Figure 2. With it, the professor can record student grades, emails, and office visits all in one place. A form like the one in Figure 2 is difficult, if not impossible, to produce from a spreadsheet. Such a form is easily produced, however, from a database.

The key distinction between Figures 1 and 2 is that the data in Figure 1 is about a single theme or concept. It is about student grades only. The data in Figure 2 has multiple themes; it shows student grades, student emails, and student office visits. We can make a general rule from these examples: Lists of data involving a single theme can be stored in a spreadsheet; lists that involve data with multiple themes require a database. We will say more about this general rule as this chapter proceeds.

To summarize, the purpose of a database is to keep track of things that involve more than one theme.

Q2 What Is a Database?

A **database** is a self-describing collection of integrated records. To understand this definition, you first need to understand the terms illustrated in Figure 3. A **byte** is a character of data. In databases, bytes are grouped into

As you will see, databases can be more difficult to develop than spreadsheets; this difficulty causes some people to prefer to work with spreadsheets—or at least pretend to—as described in the Guide later in the chapter.

Figure 3
Student Table (also called a file)

Columns, also called fields

Student Number	Student Name	HW1	HW2	MidTerm
1325	BAKER, ANDREA	88	100	78
1644	LAU, SWEE	75	90	90
2881	NELSON, STUART	100	90	98
3007	FISCHER, MAYAN	95	100	74
3559	TAM, JEFFREY		100	88
4867	VERBERRA, ADAM	70	90	92
5265	VALDEZ, MARIE	80	90	85
8009	ROGERS, SHELLY	95	100	98

Rows, also called records

Characters, also called bytes

Figure 4
Hierarchy of Data Elements

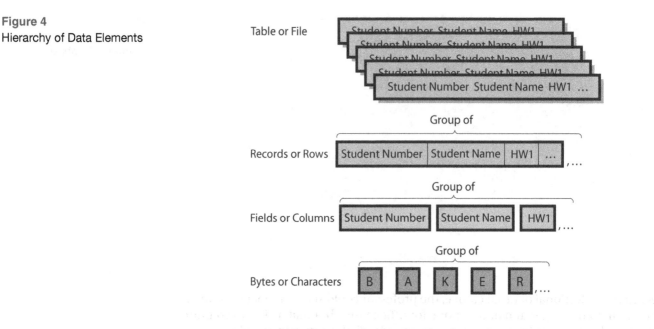

columns, such as *Student Number* and *Student Name*. Columns are also called **fields**. Columns or fields, in turn, are grouped into **rows**, which are also called **records**. In Figure 3, the collection of data for all columns (*Student Number*, *Student Name*, *HW1*, *HW2*, and *MidTerm*) is called a *row* or a *record*. Finally, a group of similar rows or records is called a **table** or a **file**. From these definitions, you can see that there is a hierarchy of data elements, as shown in Figure 4.

It is tempting to continue this grouping process by saying that a database is a group of tables or files. This statement, although true, does not go far enough. As shown in Figure 5, a database is a collection of tables *plus* relationships among the rows in those tables, *plus* special data, called *metadata*, that describes the structure of the database. By the way, the cylindrical symbol ▓ represents a computer disk drive. It is used in diagrams like that in Figure 5 because databases are normally stored on magnetic disks.

What Are Relationships Among Rows?

Consider the terms on the left-hand side of Figure 5. You know what tables are. To understand what is meant by *relationships among rows in tables*, examine Figure 6. It shows sample data from the three tables *Email*, *Student*, and *Office_Visit*. Notice the column named *Student Number* in the *Email* table. That column indicates the row in *Student* to which a row of *Email* is connected. In the first row of *Email*, the *Student Number* value is 1325. This indicates that this particular email was received from the student whose *Student Number* is 1325. If you examine the *Student* table, you will see that the row for Andrea Baker has this value. Thus, the first row of the *Email* table is related to Andrea Baker.

Now consider the last row of the *Office_Visit* table at the bottom of the figure. The value of *Student Number* in that row is 4867. This value indicates that the last row in *Office_Visit* belongs to Adam Verberra.

Figure 5
Components of a Database

Tables or Files
+
Relationships
Among
Rows in Tables   =   Database
+
Metadata

Email Table

EmailNum	Date	Message	Student Number
1	2/1/2010	For homework 1, do you want us to provide notes on our references?	1325
2	3/15/2010	My group consists of Swee Lau and Stuart Nelson.	1325
3	3/15/2010	Could you please assign me to a group?	1644

Student Table

Student Number	Student Name	HW1	HW2	MidTerm
1325	BAKER, ANDREA	88	100	78
1644	LAU, SWEE	75	90	90
2881	NELSON, STUART	100	90	98
3007	FISCHER, MAYAN	95	100	74
3559	TAM, JEFFREY		100	88
4867	VERBERRA, ADAM	70	90	92
5265	VALDEZ, MARIE	80	90	85
8009	ROGERS, SHELLY	95	100	98

Office_Visit Table

VisitID	Date	Notes	Student Number
2	2/13/2010	Andrea had questions about using IS for raising barriers to entry.	1325
3	2/17/2010	Jeffrey is considering an IS major. Wanted to talk about career opportunities.	3559
4	2/17/2010	Will miss class Friday due to job conflict.	4867

Figure 6
Example of Relationships
Among Rows

From these examples, you can see that values in one table relate rows of that table to rows in a second table. Several special terms are used to express these ideas. A **key** is a column or group of columns that identifies a unique row in a table. *Student Number* is the key of the *Student* table. Given a value of *Student Number*, you can determine one and only one row in *Student*. Only one student has the number 1325, for example.

Every table must have a key. The key of the *Email* table is *EmailNum*, and the key of the *Student_Visit* table is *VisitID*. Sometimes more than one column is needed to form a unique identifier. In a table called *City*, for example, the key would consist of the combination of columns (*City, State*), because a given city name can appear in more than one state.

Student Number is not the key of the *Email* or the *Office_Visit* tables. We know that about *Email* because there are two rows in *Email* that have the *Student Number* value 1325. The value 1325 does not identify a unique row, therefore *Student Number* cannot be the key of *Email*.

Nor is *Student Number* a key of *Office_Visit*, although you cannot tell that from the data in Figure 6. If you think about it, however, there is nothing to prevent a student from visiting a professor more than once. If that were to happen, there would be two rows in *Office_Visit* with the same value of *Student Number*. It just happens that no student has visited twice in the limited data in Figure 6.

Columns that fulfill a role like that of *Student Number* in the *Email* and *Office_Visit* tables are called **foreign keys**. This term is used because such columns are keys, but they are keys of a different (foreign) table than the one in which they reside.

Before we go on, databases that carry their data in the form of tables and that represent relationships using foreign keys are called **relational databases**. (The term *relational* is used because another, more formal name for a table is **relation**.) In the past, there were databases that were not relational in format, but such databases have nearly disappeared. Chances are you will never encounter one, and we will not consider them further.[1]

Metadata

Recall the definition of database: A database is a self-describing collection of integrated records. The records are integrated because, as you just learned, relationships among rows are represented in the database. But what does *self-describing* mean?

It means that a database contains, within itself, a description of its contents. Think of a library. A library is a self-describing collection of books and other materials. It is self-describing because the library contains a catalog that describes the library's contents. The same idea also pertains to a database. Databases are self-describing because they contain not only data, but also data about the data in the database.

Metadata are data that describe data. Figure 7 shows metadata for the *Email* table. The format of metadata depends on the software product that is processing the database. Figure 7 shows the metadata as they appear in Microsoft Access. Each row of the top part of this form describes a column of the *Email* table. The columns of these descriptions are *Field Name*, *Data Type*, and *Description*. *Field Name* contains the name of the column, *Data Type* shows the type of data the column may hold, and *Description* contains notes that explain the source or use of the column. As you can see, there is one row of metadata for each of the four columns of the *Email* table: *EmailNum*, *Date*, *Message*, and *Student Number*.

Figure 7
Sample Metadata (in Access)

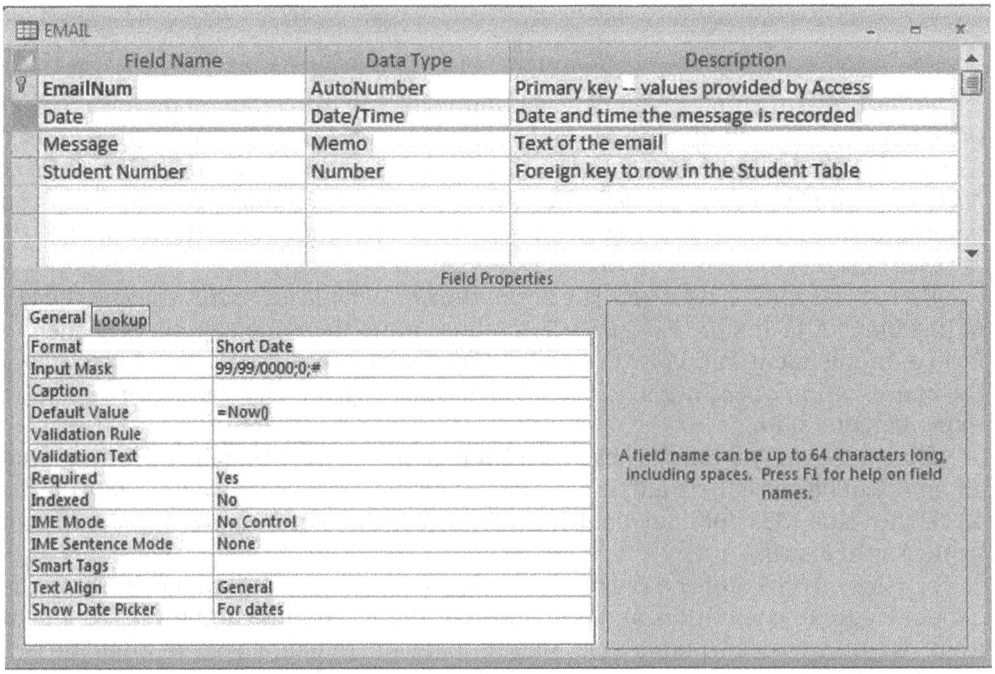

---

[1]Another type of database, the **object-relational database**, is rarely used in commercial applications. Search the Web if you are interested in learning more about object-relational databases. In this book, we will describe only relational databases.

Using MIS InClass *A Group Exercise*

How Much Is a Database Worth?

iStockphoto.com and Superstock Royalty Free

FlexTime realizes over 15,000 person-visits, an average of 500 visits per day. We've seen how important their database is in assessing the possibility of packing more clients into classes. In fact, as you can see in the video, Neil believes the database is their single most important asset. According to Neil:

> Take away anything else—the building, the equipment, the inventory—anything else, and we'd be back in business 6 months or less. Take away our customer database, however, and we'd have to start all over. It would take us another 8 years to get back where we are.

Why is the database so crucial? It records everything the company's customers do.

If FlexTime decides to offer an early morning kickboxing class featuring a particular trainer, it can use its database to offer that class to everyone who ever took an early morning class, a kickboxing class, or a class by that trainer. Customers receive targeted solicitations for offerings they care about and,

maybe equally important, they don't receive solicitations for those they don't care about. Clearly, the FlexTime database has value and, if it wanted to, FlexTime could sell that data.

In this exercise, you and a group of your fellow students will be asked to consider the value of a database to organizations other than FlexTime.

1. Many small business owners have found it financially advantageous to purchase their own building. As one owner remarked upon his retirement, "We did well with the business, but we made our real money by buying the building." Explain why this might be so.

2. To what extent does the dynamic you identified in your answer to item 1 pertain to databases? Do you think it likely that, in 2050, some small businesspeople will retire and make statements like, "We did well with the business, but we made our real money from the database we generated?" Why or why not? In what ways is real estate different from database data? Are these differences significant to your answer?

3. Suppose you had a national database of student data. Assume your database includes the name, email address, university, grade level, and major for each student. Name five companies that would find that data valuable, and explain how they might use it. (For example, Pizza Hut could solicit orders from students during finals week.)

4. Describe a product or service that you could develop that would induce students to provide the data in item 3.

5. Considering your answers to items 1 through 4, identify two organizations in your community that could generate a database that would potentially be more valuable than the organization itself. Consider businesses, but also think about social organizations and government offices.

   For each organization, describe the content of the database and how you could entice customers or clients to provide that data. Also, explain why the data would be valuable and who might use it.

6. Prepare a 1-minute statement of what you have learned from this exercise that you could use in a job interview to illustrate your ability to innovate the use of technology in business.

7. Present your answers to items 1–6 to the rest of the class.

The bottom part of this form provides more metadata, which Access calls *Field Properties*, for each column. In Figure 7, the focus is on the *Date* column (note the light rectangle drawn around the *Date* row). Because the focus is on *Date* in the top pane, the details in the bottom pane pertain to the *Date* column. The Field Properties describe formats, a default value for Access to supply when a new row is created, and the constraint that a value is required for this column. It is not important for you to remember these details. Instead, just understand that metadata are data about data and that such metadata are always a part of a database.

The presence of metadata makes databases much more useful. Because of metadata, no one needs to guess, remember, or even record what is in the database. To find out what a database contains, we just look at the metadata inside the database.

Q3 What Are the Components of a Database Application System?

A database, all by itself, is not very useful. The tables in Figure 6 have all of the data the professor wants, but the format is unwieldy. The professor wants to see the data in a form like that in Figure 2 and also as a formatted report. Pure database data are correct, but in raw form they are not pertinent or useful.

Figure 8 shows the components of a **database application system**. Such applications make database data more accessible and useful. Users employ a database application that consists of forms (like that in Figure 2), formatted reports, queries, and application programs. Each of these, in turn, calls on the database management system (DBMS) to process the database tables. We will first describe DBMSs and then discuss database application components.

What Is a Database Management System?

A **database management system (DBMS)** is a program used to create, process, and administer a database. As with operating systems, almost no organization develops its own DBMS. Instead, companies license DBMS products from vendors such as IBM, Microsoft, Oracle, and others. Popular DBMS products are **DB2** from IBM, **Access** and **SQL Server** from Microsoft, and **Oracle** from the Oracle Corporation. Another popular DBMS is **MySQL**, an open source DBMS product that is license-free for most applications.[2] Other DBMS products are available, but these five process the great bulk of databases today.

Note that a DBMS and a database are two different things. For some reason, the trade press and even some books confuse the two. A DBMS is a software program; a database is a collection of tables, relationships, and metadata. The two are very different concepts.

Figure 8
Components of a Database Application System

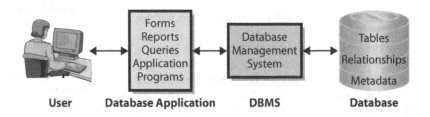

| User | Database Application | DBMS | Database |

---

[2]MySQL was supported by the MySQL company. In 2008, that company was acquired by Sun Microsystems, which was, in turn, acquired by Oracle later that year. Because MySQL is open source, Oracle does not own the source code, however. As of 2009, a rumor was circulating the Web that one of the original MySQL developers was going to start another open source project based on the current code. What an industry!

Creating the Database and Its Structures

Database developers use the DBMS to create tables, relationships, and other structures in the database. The form in Figure 7 can be used to define a new table or to modify an existing one. To create a new table, the developer just fills the new table's metadata into the form.

To modify an existing table—say, to add a new column—the developer opens the metadata form for that table and adds a new row of metadata. For example, in Figure 9 the developer has added a new column called *Response?*. This new column has the data type *Yes/No*, which means that the column can contain only one value—*Yes* or *No*. The professor will use this column to indicate whether he has responded to the student's email. A column can be removed by deleting its row in this table, though doing so will lose any existing data.

Processing the Database

The second function of the DBMS is to process the database. Applications use the DBMS for four operations: to *read, insert, modify,* or *delete* data. The applications call upon the DBMS in different ways. From a form, when the user enters new or changed data, a computer program behind the form calls the DBMS to make the necessary database changes. From an application program, the program calls the DBMS directly to make the change.

Structured Query Language (SQL) is an international standard language for processing a database. All five of the DBMS products mentioned earlier accept and process SQL (pronounced "see-quell") statements. As an example, the following SQL statement inserts a new row into the *Student* table:

```
INSERT INTO Student
([Student Number], [Student Name], HW1, HW2, MidTerm)
VALUES
(1000, 'Franklin, Benjamin', 90, 95, 100);
```

As stated, statements like this one are issued "behind the scenes" by programs that process forms. Alternatively, they can be issued directly to the DBMS by an application program.

You do not need to understand or remember SQL language syntax. Instead, just realize that SQL is an international standard for processing a database. SQL can also be used to create databases and database structures. You will learn more about SQL if you take a database management class.

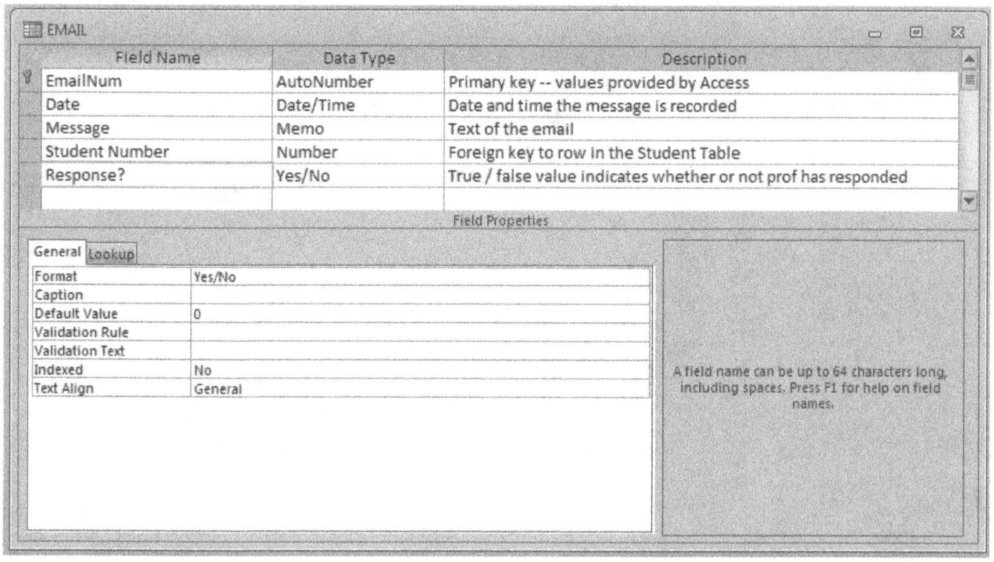

Figure 9

Adding a New Column to a Table (in Access)

Ethics Guide

Nobody Said I Shouldn't

"My name is Chris and I do systems support for our group. I configure the new computers, set up the network, make sure the servers are operating, and so forth. I also do all of the database backups. I've always liked computers. After high school, I worked odd jobs to make some money, then I got an associate degree in information technology from our local community college.

"Anyway, as I said, I make backup copies of our databases. One weekend, I didn't have much going on, so I copied one of the database backups to a DVD and took it home. I had taken a class on database processing as part of my associate degree, and we used SQL Server (our database management system) in my class. In fact, I suppose that's part of the reason I got the job. Anyway, it was easy to restore the database on my computer at home, and I did.

"Of course, as they'll tell you in your database class, one of the big advantages of database processing is that databases have metadata, or data that describe the content of the database. So, although I didn't know what tables were in our database, I did know how to access the SQL Server metadata. I just queried a table called *sysTables* to learn the names of our tables. From there it was easy to find out what columns each table had.

"I found tables with data about orders, customers, salespeople, and so forth, and, just to amuse myself, and to see how much of the query language SQL that I could remember, I started playing around with the data. I was curious to know which order entry clerk was the best, so I started querying each clerk's order data, the total number of orders, total order amounts, things like that. It was easy to do and fun.

"I know one of the order entry clerks, Jason, pretty well, so I started looking at the data for his orders. I was just curious, and it was very simple SQL. I was just playing around with the data when I noticed something odd. All of his biggest orders were with one company, Valley Appliances, and even stranger, every one of its orders had a huge discount. I thought, well, maybe that's typical. Out of curiosity, I started looking at data for the other clerks, and very few of them had an order with Valley Appliances. But, when they did, Valley didn't get a big discount. Then I looked at the rest of Jason's orders, and none of them had much in the way of discounts, either.

"The next Friday, a bunch of us went out for a beer after work. I happened to see Jason, so I asked him about Valley Appliances and made a joke about the discounts. He asked me what I meant, and then I told him that I'd been looking at the data for fun and that I saw this odd pattern. He just laughed, said he just 'did his job,' and then changed the subject.

"Well, to make a long story short, when I got to work on Monday morning, my office was cleaned out. There was nothing there except a note telling me to go see my boss. The bottom line was, I was fired. The company also threatened that if I didn't return all of its data, I'd be in court for the next 5 years . . . things like that. I was so mad I didn't even tell them about Jason. Now my problem is that I'm out of a job, and I can't exactly use my last company for a reference."

Discussion Questions

1. Where did Chris go wrong?

2. Do you think it was illegal, unethical, or neither for Chris to take the database home and query the data?

3. Does the company share culpability with Chris?

4. What do you think Chris should have done upon discovering the odd pattern in Jason's orders?

5. What should the company have done before firing Chris?

6. Is it possible that someone other than Jason is involved in the arrangement with Valley Appliances? What should Chris have done in light of that possibility?

7. What should Chris do now?

8. "Metadata make databases easy to use, for both authorized and unauthorized purposes." Explain what organizations should do in light of this fact.

Administering the Database

A third DBMS function is to provide tools to assist in the administration of the database. Database administration involves a wide variety of activities. For example, the DBMS can be used to set up a security system involving user accounts, passwords, permissions, and limits for processing the database. To provide database security, a user must sign on using a valid user account before she can process the database.

Permissions can be limited in very specific ways. In the Student database example, it is possible to limit a particular user to reading only *Student Name* from the *Student* table. A different user could be given permission to read the entire *Student* table, but limited to update only the *HW1*, *HW2*, and *MidTerm* columns. Other users can be given still other permissions.

In addition to security, DBMS administrative functions include backing up database data, adding structures to improve the performance of database applications, removing data that are no longer wanted or needed, and similar tasks.

For important databases, most organizations dedicate one or more employees to the role of **database administration**. Figure 10 summarizes the major responsibilities for this function. You will learn more about this topic if you take a database management course.

Figure 10
Summary of Database
Administration Tasks

Category	Database Administration Task	Description
Development	Create and staff DBA function	Size of DBA group depends on size and complexity of database. Groups range from one part-time person to small group.
	Form steering committee	Consists of representatives of all user groups. Forum for community-wide discussions and decisions.
	Specify requirements	Ensure that all appropriate user input is considered.
	Validate data model	Check data model for accuracy and completeness.
	Evaluate application design	Verify that all necessary forms, reports, queries, and applications are developed. Validate design and usability of application components.
Operation	Manage processing rights and responsibilities	Determine processing rights/restrictions on each table and column.
	Manage security	Add and delete users and user groups as necessary; ensure that security system works.
	Track problems and manage resolution	Develop system to record and manage resolution of problems.
	Monitor database performance	Provide expertise/solutions for performance improvements.
	Manage DBMS	Evaluate new features and functions.
Backup and Recovery	Monitor backup procedures	Verify that database backup procedures are followed.
	Conduct training	Ensure that users and operations personnel know and understand recovery procedures.
	Manage recovery	Manage recovery process.
Adaptation	Set up request tracking system	Develop system to record and prioritize requests for change.
	Manage configuration change	Manage impact of database structure changes on applications and users.

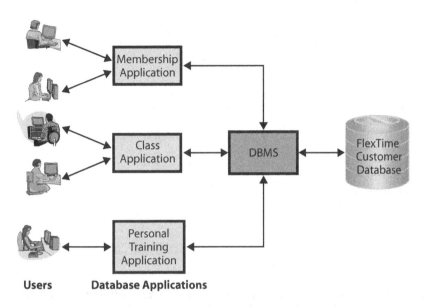

Figure 11
User of Multiple Database
Applications

Users   **Database Applications**

Q4 How Do Database Applications Make Databases More Useful?

A **database application** is a collection of forms, reports, queries, and application programs that process a database. A database may have one or more applications, and each application may have one or more users. Figure 11 shows three applications used at FlexTime. The first one is used to bill and manage FlexTime memberships; the second schedules and bills scheduled classes; and the third tracks and supports personal training sessions. These applications have different purposes, features, and functions, but they all process the same FlexTime customer database.

What Are Forms, Reports, and Queries?

Figure 2 shows a typical database application data entry **form**, and Figure 12 shows a typical **report**. Data entry forms are used to read, insert, modify, and delete data. Reports show data in a structured context.

One of the definitions of information is "data presented in a meaningful context." The structure of this report creates information because it shows the student data in a context that will be meaningful to the professor. Some reports, like the one in Figure 12, also compute values as they present the data. An example is the computation of *Mid Term Total* in Figure 12.

DBMS programs provide comprehensive and robust features for querying database data. For example, suppose the professor who uses the Student database remembers that one of the students referred to the topic *barriers to entry* in an office visit, but cannot remember which student or when. If there are hundreds of

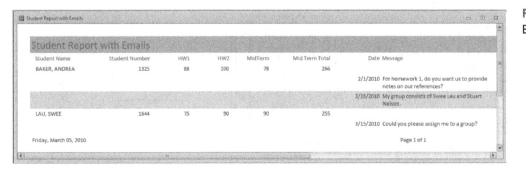

Figure 12
Example of a Student Report

Figure 13a

Sample Query Form Used
to Enter Phrase for Search

Enter Parameter Value ? ✖

Enter words or phrase for search:

barriers to entry|

OK   Cancel

Figure 13b

Sample Query Results
of Query Operation

Office Visits Keyword Query   ─ ▢ ✖

Student Name	Date	Notes
BAKER, ANDREA	2/13/2010	Andrea had questions about using IS for raising barriers to entry.
*		

Record: ◄ 1 of 1 ► ►I ►* 🗙 No Filter   Search

students and visits recorded in the database, it will take some effort and time for the professor to search through all office visit records to find that event. The DBMS, however, can find any such record quickly. Figure 13(a) shows a **query** form in which the professor types in the keyword for which she is looking. Figure 13(b) shows the results of the query.

Why Are Database Application Programs Needed?

Forms, reports, and queries work well for standard functions. However, most applications have unique requirements that a simple form, report, or query cannot meet. For example, in an order-entry application what should be done if only a portion of a customer's request can be met? If someone wants 10 widgets and we only have 3 in stock, should a backorder for 7 more be generated automatically? Or, should some other action be taken?

Application programs process logic that is specific to a given business need. In the Student database, an example application is one that assigns grades at the end of the term. If the professor grades on a curve, the application reads the breakpoints for each grade from a form, and then processes each row in the *Student* table, allocating a grade based on the break points and the total number of points earned.

Another important use of application programs is to enable database processing over the Internet. For this use, the application program serves as an intermediary between the Web server and the database. The application program responds to events, such as when a user presses a submit button; it also reads, inserts, modifies, and deletes database data.

For example, Figure 14 shows four different database application programs running on a Web server computer. Users with browsers connect to the Web

Figure 14

Four Application Programs
on a Web Server Computer

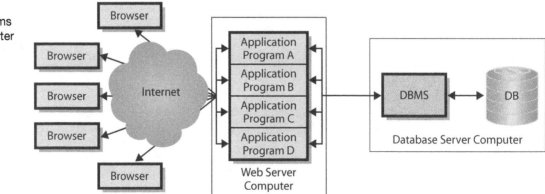

server via the Internet. The Web server directs user requests to the appropriate application program. Each program then processes the database as necessary.

Multi-User Processing

Figures 11 and 14 show multiple users processing the database. Such **multi-user processing** is common, but it does pose unique problems that you, as a future manager, should know about. To understand the nature of those problems, consider the following scenario.

Two users, Andrea and Jeffrey, are FlexTime employees using the Class application in Figure 11. Andrea is on the phone with her customer, who wants to enroll in a particular spinning class. At the same time, Jeffrey is talking with his customer, who wants to enroll in that same class. Andrea reads the database to determine how many vacancies that class has. (She unknowingly invokes the Class application when she types in her data entry form.) The DBMS returns a row showing there is one slot left in that class.

Meanwhile, just after Andrea accesses the database, Jeffrey's customer says she wants in that class, and so he also reads the database (via the Class application program) to determine how many slots are available. The DBMS returns the same row to him, indicating that one slot is left.

Andrea's customer now says that he will enroll in the class, and Andrea records this fact in her form. The application rewrites that class row back to the database, indicating that there are no slots left.

Meanwhile, Jeffrey's customer says that she will take the class. Jeffrey records this fact in his form, and the application (which still is using the row it read indicating that a slot is available) rewrites that class row to the database, indicating there are no openings left. Jeffrey's application knows nothing about Andrea's work and hence does not know that her customer has already taken the last slot.

Clearly, there is a problem. Both customers have been assigned the same last slot in the class. When they attend the class, one of them will not have a bike to ride, which will be frustrating to the customers as well as the instructor.

This problem, known as the **lost-update problem**, exemplifies one of the special characteristics of multi-user database processing. To prevent this problem, some type of locking must be used to coordinate the activities of users who know nothing about one another. Locking brings its own set of problems, however, and those problems must be addressed as well. We will not delve further into this topic here, however.

Realize from this example that converting a single-user database to a multi-user database requires more than simply connecting another computer. The logic of the underlying application processing needs to be adjusted as well.

Be aware of possible data conflicts when you manage business activities that involve multi-user processing. If you find inaccurate results that seem not to have a cause, you may be experiencing multi-user data conflicts. Contact your IS department for assistance.

Enterprise DBMS Versus Personal DBMS

DBMS products fall into two broad categories. **Enterprise DBMS** products process large organizational and workgroup databases. These products support many, possibly thousands, of users and many different database applications. Such DBMS products support 24/7 operations and can manage databases that span dozens of different magnetic disks with hundreds of gigabytes or more of data. IBM's DB2, Microsoft's SQL Server, and Oracle's Oracle are examples of enterprise DBMS products.

Personal DBMS products are designed for smaller, simpler database applications. Such products are used for personal or small workgroup applications that involve

Figure 15
Personal Database System

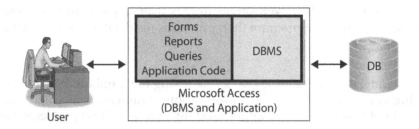

fewer than 100 users, and normally fewer than 15. In fact, the great bulk of databases in this category have only a single user. The professor's Student database is an example of a database that is processed by a personal DBMS product.

In the past, there were many personal DBMS products—Paradox, dBase, R:base, and FoxPro. Microsoft put these products out of business when they developed Access and included it in the Microsoft Office suite. Today, about the only remaining personal DBMS is Microsoft Access.

To avoid one point of confusion for you in the future, the separation of application programs and the DBMS shown in Figure 11 is true only for enterprise DBMS products. Microsoft Access includes features and functions for application processing along with the DBMS itself. For example, Access has a form generator and a report generator. Thus, as shown in Figure 15, Access is both a DBMS *and* an application development product.

Q5 How Are Data Models Used for Database Development?

Because the design of the database depends entirely on how users view their business environment, user involvement is critical for database development. Think about the Student database. What data should it contain? Possibilities are: *Students, Classes, Grades, Emails, Office_Visits, Majors, Advisers, Student_Organizations*—the list could go on and on. Further, how much detail should be included in each? Should the database include campus addresses? Home addresses? Billing addresses?

In fact, there are dozens of possibilities, and the database developers do not and cannot know what to include. They do know, however, that a database must include all the data necessary for the users to perform their jobs. Ideally, it contains that amount of data and no more. So, during database development the developers must rely on the users to tell them what to include in the database.

Database structures can be complex, in some cases very complex. So, before building the database the developers construct a logical representation of database data called a **data model**. It describes the data and relationships that will be stored in the database. It is akin to a blueprint. Just as building architects create a blueprint before they start building, so, too, database developers create a data model before they start designing the database.

For a philopsophical perspective on data models, see the Guide later in the chapter.

Figure 16 summarizes the database development process. Interviews with users lead to database requirements, which are summarized in a data model. Once the users have approved (validated) the data model, it is transformed into a database design. That design is then implemented into database structures. We will consider data modeling and database design briefly in the next two sections. Again, your goal should be to learn the process so that you can be an effective user representative for a development effort.

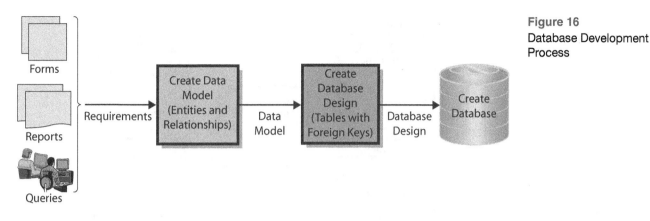

Figure 16
Database Development
Process

What Is the Entity-Relationship Data Model?

The **entity-relationship (E-R) data model** is a tool for constructing data models. Developers use it to describe the content of a data model by defining the things (*entities*) that will be stored in the database and the *relationships* among those entities. A second, less popular, tool for data modeling is the **Unified Modeling Language (UML)**. We will not describe that tool here. However, if you learn how to interpret E-R models, with a bit of study you will be able to understand UML models as well.

Entities

An **entity** is some thing that the users want to track. Examples of entities are *Order*, *Customer*, *Salesperson*, and *Item*. Some entities represent a physical object, such as *Item* or *Salesperson*; others represent a logical construct or transaction, such as *Order* or *Contract*. For reasons beyond this discussion, entity names are always singular. We use *Order*, not *Orders*; *Salesperson*, not *Salespersons*.

Entities have **attributes** that describe characteristics of the entity. Example attributes of *Order* are *OrderNumber*, *OrderDate*, *SubTotal*, *Tax*, *Total*, and so forth. Example attributes of *Salesperson* are *SalespersonName*, *Email*, *Phone*, and so forth.

Entities have an **identifier**, which is an attribute (or group of attributes) whose value is associated with one and only one entity instance. For example, *OrderNumber* is an identifier of *Order*, because only one *Order* instance has a given value of *OrderNumber*. For the same reason, *CustomerNumber* is an identifier of *Customer*. If each member of the sales staff has a unique name, then *SalespersonName* is an identifier of *Salesperson*.

Before we continue, consider that last sentence. Is the salesperson's name unique among the sales staff? Both now and in the future? Who decides the answer to such a question? Only the users know whether this is true; the database developers cannot know. This example underlines why it is important for you to be able to interpret data models, because only users like you will know for sure.

Figure 17 shows examples of entities for the Student database. Each entity is shown in a rectangle. The name of the entity is just above the rectangle, and the identifier is shown in a section at the top of the entity. Entity attributes are shown in the remainder of the rectangle. In Figure 17, the *Adviser* entity has an identifier called *AdviserName* and the attributes *Phone*, *CampusAddress*, and *EmailAddress*.

Observe that the entities *Email* and *Office_Visit* do not have an identifier. Unlike *Student* or *Adviser*, the users do not have an attribute that identifies a particular email. We *could* make one up. For example, we could say that the identifier of *Email* is *EmailNumber*, but if we do so we are not modeling how the users view their world. Instead, we are forcing something onto the users. Be aware of this possibility when you review data models about your business. Do not allow the database developers to create something in the data model that is not part of your business world.

91

Figure 17
Student Data Model Entities

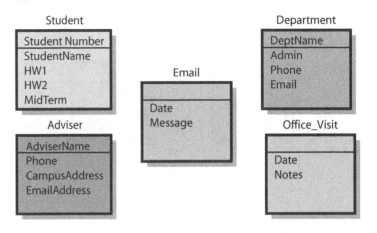

Relationships

Entities have **relationships** to each other. An *Order*, for example, has a relationship to a *Customer* entity and also to a *Salesperson* entity. In the Student database, a *Student* has a relationship to an *Adviser*, and an *Adviser* has a relationship to a *Department*.

Figure 18 shows sample *Department*, *Adviser*, and *Student* entities and their relationships. For simplicity, this figure shows just the identifier of the entities and not the other attributes. For this sample data, *Accounting* has three professors—Jones, Wu, and Lopez—and *Finance* has two professors—Smith and Greene.

The relationship between *Advisers* and *Students* is a bit more complicated, because in this example an adviser is allowed to advise many students, and a student is allowed to have many advisers. Perhaps this happens because students can have multiple majors. In any case, note that Professor Jones advises students 100 and 400 and that student 100 is advised by both Professors Jones and Smith.

Diagrams like the one in Figure 18 are too cumbersome for use in database design discussions. Instead, database designers use diagrams called **entity-relationship (E-R) diagrams**. Figure 19 shows an E-R diagram for the data in Figure 18. In this figure, all of the entities of one type are represented by a single rectangle. Thus, there are rectangles for the *Department, Adviser,* and *Student* entities. Attributes are shown as before in Figure 17.

Figure 18
Example of Department, Adviser, and Student Entities and Relationships

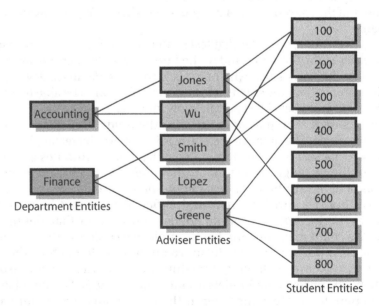

Figure 19
Sample Relationships
Version 1

Additionally, a line is used to represent a relationship between two entities. Notice the line between *Department* and *Adviser*, for example. The forked lines on the right side of that line signify that a department may have more than one adviser. The little lines, which are referred to as **crow's feet**, are shorthand for the multiple lines between *Department* and *Adviser* in Figure 18. Relationships like this one are called **1:N**, or **one-to-many relationships**, because one department can have many advisers, but an adviser has at most one department.

Now examine the line between *Adviser* and *Student*. Notice the short lines that appear at each end of the line. These lines are the crow's feet, and this notation signifies that an adviser can be related to many students and that a student can be related to many advisers, which is the situation in Figure 18. Relationships like this one are called **N:M**, or **many-to-many relationships**, because one adviser can have many students and one student can have many advisers.

Students sometimes find the notation N:M confusing. Interpret the *N* and *M* to mean that a variable number, greater than one, is allowed on each side of the relationship. Such a relationship is not written *N:N*, because that notation would imply that there are the same number of entities on each side of the relationship, which is not necessarily true. *N:M* means that more than one entity is allowed on each side of the relationship and that the number of entities on each side can be different.

Figure 20 shows the same entities with different assumptions. Here, advisers may advise in more than one department, but a student may have only one adviser, representing a policy that students may not have multiple majors.

Which, if either, of these versions is correct? Only the users know. These alternatives illustrate the kinds of questions you will need to answer when a database designer asks you to check a data model for correctness.

Figures 19 and 20 are typical examples of an entity-relationship diagram. Unfortunately, there are several different styles of entity-relationship diagrams. This one is called, not surprisingly, a **crow's-foot diagram** version. You may learn other versions if you take a database management class.

The crow's-foot notation shows the maximum number of entities that can be involved in a relationship. Accordingly, they are called the relationship's **maximum cardinality**. Common examples of maximum cardinality are 1:N, N:M, and 1:1 (not shown).

Another important question is, "What is the minimum number of entities required in the relationship?" Must an adviser have a student to advise, and must a student have an adviser? Constraints on minimum requirements are called **minimum cardinalities**.

Figure 20
Sample Relationships
Version 2

Figure 21
Sample Relationships Showing
Both Maximum and Minimum
Cardinalities

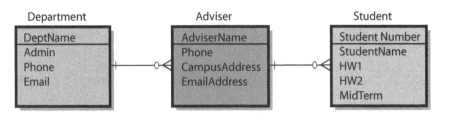

Figure 21 presents a third version of this E-R diagram that shows both maximum and minimum cardinalities. The vertical bar on a line means that at least one entity of that type is required. The small oval means that the entity is optional; the relationship *need not* have an entity of that type.

Thus, in Figure 21 a department is not required to have a relationship to any adviser, but an adviser is required to belong to a department. Similarly, an adviser is not required to have a relationship to a student, but a student is required to have a relationship to an adviser. Note, also, that the maximum cardinalities in Figure 21 have been changed so that both are 1:N.

Is the model in Figure 21 a good one? It depends on the policy of the university. Again, only the users know for sure.

Q6 How Is a Data Model Transformed into a Database Design?

Database design is the process of converting a data model into tables, relationships, and data constraints. The database design team transforms entities into tables and expresses relationships by defining foreign keys. Database design is a complicated subject; as with data modeling, it occupies weeks in a database management class. In this section, however, we will introduce two important database design concepts: normalization and the representation of two kinds of relationships. The first concept is a foundation of database design, and the second will help you understand important design considerations.

Normalization

Normalization is the process of converting a poorly structured table into two or more well-structured tables. A table is such a simple construct that you may wonder how one could possibly be poorly structured. In truth, there are many ways that tables can be malformed—so many, in fact, that researchers have published hundreds of papers on this topic alone.

Consider the *Employee* table in Figure 22(a). It lists employee names, hire dates, email addresses, and the name and number of the department in which the employee works. This table seems innocent enough. But consider what happens when the Accounting department changes its name to Accounting and Finance. Because department names are duplicated in this table, every row that has a value of "Accounting" must be changed to "Accounting and Finance."

Data Integrity Problems

Suppose the Accounting name change is correctly made in two rows, but not in the third. The result is shown in Figure 22(b). This table has what is called a **data integrity problem**: Some rows indicate that the name of Department 100 is "Accounting and Finance," and another row indicates that the name of Department 100 is "Accounting."

Employee

Name	HireDate	Email	DeptNo	DeptName
Jones	Feb 1, 2008	Jones@ourcompany.com	100	Accounting
Smith	Dec 3, 2010	Smith@ourcompany.com	200	Marketing
Chau	March 7, 2010	Chau@ourcompany.com	100	Accounting
Greene	July 17, 2009	Greene@ourcompany.com	100	Accounting

(a) Table Before Update

Employee

Name	HireDate	Email	DeptNo	DeptName
Jones	Feb 1, 2008	Jones@ourcompany.com	100	Accounting and Finance
Smith	Dec 3, 2010	Smith@ourcompany.com	200	Marketing
Chau	March 7, 2010	Chau@ourcompany.com	100	Accounting and Finance
Greene	July 17, 2009	Greene@ourcompany.com	100	Accounting

(b) Table with Incomplete Update

Figure 22
A Poorly Designed
Employee Table

This problem is easy to spot in this small table. But consider a table like the *Customer* table in the Amazon.com database or the eBay database. Those databases may have millions of rows. Once a table that large develops serious data integrity problems, months of labor will be required to remove them.

Data integrity problems are serious. A table that has data integrity problems will produce incorrect and inconsistent information. Users will lose confidence in the information, and the system will develop a poor reputation. Information systems with poor reputations become serious burdens to the organizations that use them.

Normalizing for Data Integrity

The data integrity problem can occur only if data are duplicated. Because of this, one easy way to eliminate the problem is to eliminate the duplicated data. We can do this by transforming the table in Figure 22 into two tables, as shown in Figure 23. Here, the name of the department is stored just once; therefore no data inconsistencies can occur.

Employee

Name	HireDate	Email	DeptNo
Jones	Feb 1, 2008	Jones@ourcompany.com	100
Smith	Dec 3, 2010	Smith@ourcompany.com	200
Chau	March 7, 2010	Chau@ourcompany.com	100
Greene	July 17, 2009	Greene@ourcompany.com	100

Department

DeptNo	DeptName
100	Accounting
200	Marketing
300	Information Systems

Figure 23
Two Normalized Tables

Of course, to produce an employee report that includes the department name, the two tables in Figure 23 will need to be joined back together. Because such joining of tables is common, DBMS products have been programmed to perform it efficiently, but it still requires work. From this example, you can see a trade-off in database design: Normalized tables eliminate data duplication, but they can be slower to process. Dealing with such trade-offs is an important consideration in database design.

The general goal of normalization is to construct tables such that every table has a *single* topic or theme. In good writing, every paragraph should have a single theme. This is true of databases as well; every table should have a single theme. The problem with the table in Figure 22 is that it has two independent themes: employees and departments. The way to correct the problem is to split the table into two tables, each with its own theme. In this case, we create an *Employee* table and a *Department* table, as shown in Figure 23.

As mentioned, there are dozens of ways that tables can be poorly formed. Database practitioners classify tables into various **normal forms** according to the kinds of problems they have. Transforming a table into a normal form to remove duplicated data and other problems is called *normalizing* the table.[3] Thus, when you hear a database designer say, "Those tables are not normalized," she does not mean that the tables have irregular, not-normal data. Instead, she means that the tables have a format that could cause data integrity problems.

Summary of Normalization

As a future user of databases, you do not need to know the details of normalization. Instead, understand the general principle that every normalized (well-formed) table has one and only one theme. Further, tables that are not normalized are subject to data integrity problems.

Be aware, too, that normalization is just one criterion for evaluating database designs. Because normalized designs can be slower to process, database designers sometimes choose to accept non-normalized tables. The best design depends on the users' processing requirements.

Representing Relationships

Figure 24 shows the steps involved in transforming a data model into a relational database design. First, the database designer creates a table for each entity. The identifier of the entity becomes the key of the table. Each attribute of the entity becomes a column of the table. Next, the resulting tables are normalized so that each table has a single theme. Once that has been done, the next step is to represent relationship among those tables.

Figure 24
Transforming a Data Model into a Database Design

- Represent each entity with a table
  - Entity identifier becomes table key
  - Entity attributes become table columns
- Normalize tables as necessary
- Represent relationships
  - Use foreign keys
  - Add additional tables for N:M relationships

---

[3]See David Kroenke and David Auer, *Database Processing*, 11th ed. (Upper Saddle River, NJ: Prentice Hall, 2010) for more information.

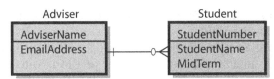

Figure 25
Representing a 1:N
Relationship

(a) 1:N Relationship Between Adviser and Student Entities

Adviser Table—Key is AdviserName

AdviserName	EmailAddress
Jones	Jones@myuniv.edu
Choi	Choi@myuniv.edu
Jackson	Jackson@myuniv.edu

Student Table—Key is StudentNumber

StudentNumber	StudentName	MidTerm
100	Lisa	90
200	Jennie	85
300	Jason	82
400	Terry	95

(b) Creating a Table for Each Entity

Adviser Table—Key is AdviserName

AdviserName	EmailAddress
Jones	Jones@myuniv.edu
Choi	Choi@myuniv.edu
Jackson	Jackson@myuniv.edu

Foreign Key Column Represents Relationship

Student—Key is StudentNumber

StudentNumber	StudentName	MidTerm	AdviserName
100	Lisa	90	Jackson
200	Jennie	85	Jackson
300	Jason	82	Choi
400	Terry	95	Jackson

(c) Using the *AdviserName* Foreign Key to Represent the 1:N Relationship

For example, consider the E-R diagram in Figure 25(a). The *Adviser* entity has a 1:N relationship to the *Student* entity. To create the database design, we construct a table for *Adviser* and a second table for *Student*, as shown in Figure 25(b). The key of the *Adviser* table is *AdviserName*, and the key of the *Student* table is *StudentNumber*.

Further, the *EmailAddress* attribute of the *Adviser* entity becomes the *EmailAddress* column of the *Adviser* table, and the *StudentName* and *MidTerm* attributes of the *Student* entity become the *StudentName* and *MidTerm* columns of the *Student* table.

The next task is to represent the relationship. Because we are using the relational model, we know that we must add a foreign key to one of the two tables. The possibilities are: (1) place the foreign key *StudentNumber* in the *Adviser* table or (2) place the foreign key *AdviserName* in the *Student* table.

The correct choice is to place *AdviserName* in the *Student* table, as shown in Figure 25(c). To determine a student's adviser, we just look into the *AdviserName* column of that student's row. To determine the adviser's students, we search the *AdviserName* column in the *Student* table to determine which rows have that adviser's name. If a student changes advisers, we simply change the value in the *AdviserName* column. Changing *Jackson* to *Jones* in the first row, for example, will assign student 100 to Professor Jones.

Figure 26
Representing an N:M Relationship

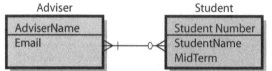

(a) N:M Relationship Between Adviser and Student

Adviser—Key is AdviserName

AdviserName	Email
Jones	Jones@myuniv.edu
Choi	Choi@myuniv.edu
Jackson	Jackson@myuniv.edu

No room to place second or third AdviserName

Student—Key is StudentNumber

StudentNumber	StudentName	MidTerm	AdviserName
100	Lisa	90	Jackson
200	Jennie	85	Jackson
300	Jason	82	Choi
400	Terry	95	Jackson

(b) Incorrect Representation of N:M Relationship

Adviser—Key is AdviserName

AdviserName	Email
Jones	Jones@myuniv.edu
Choi	Choi@myuniv.edu
Jackson	Jackson@myuniv.edu

Student—Key is StudentNumber

StudentNumber	StudentName	MidTerm
100	Lisa	90
200	Jennie	85
300	Jason	82
400	Terry	95

Adviser_Student_Intersection

AdviserName	StudentNumber
Jackson	100
Jackson	200
Choi	300
Jackson	400
Choi	100
Jones	100

Student 100 has three advisers.

(c) Adviser_Student_Intersection Table Represents the N:M Relationship

For this data model, placing *StudentNumber* in *Adviser* would be incorrect. If we were to do that, we could assign only one student to an adviser. There is no place to assign a second adviser.

This strategy for placing foreign keys will not work for N:M relationships, however. Consider the data model in Figure 26(a); here advisers and students have a many-to-many relationship. An adviser may have many students, and a student may have multiple advisers (for multiple majors).

The foreign key strategy we used for the 1:N data model will not work here. To see why, examine Figure 26(b). If student 100 has more than one adviser, there is no place to record second or subsequent advisers.

To represent an N:M relationship, we need to create a third table, as shown in Figure 26(c). The third table has two columns, *AdviserName* and *StudentNumber*. Each row of the table means that the given adviser advises the student with the given number.

As you can imagine, there is a great deal more to database design than we have presented here. Still, this section should give you an idea of the tasks that need to be accomplished to create a database. You should also realize that the database design is a direct consequence of decisions made in the data model. If the data model is wrong, the database design will be wrong as well.

Q7 What Is the Users' Role in the Development of Databases?

As stated, a database is a model of how the users view their business world. This means that the users are the final judges as to what data the database should contain and how the records in that database should be related to one another.

The easiest time to change the database structure is during the data modeling stage. Changing a relationship from one-to-many to many-to-many in a data model is simply a matter of changing the 1:N notation to N:M. However, once the database has been constructed, loaded with data, and application forms, reports, queries, and application programs have been created, changing a one-to-many relationship to many-to-many means weeks of work.

You can glean some idea of why this might be true by contrasting Figure 25(c) with Figure 26(c). Suppose that instead of having just a few rows, each table has thousands of rows; in that case, transforming the database from one format to the other involves considerable work. Even worse, however, is that someone must change application components as well. For example, if students have at most one adviser, then a single text box can be used to enter *AdviserName*. If students can have multiple advisers, then a multiple-row table will need to be used to enter *AdviserName* and a program will need to be written to store the values of *AdviserName* into the *Adviser_Student_Intersection* table. There are dozens of other consequences, consequences that will translate into wasted labor and wasted expense.

Thus, *user review of the data model is crucial.* When a database is developed for your use, you must carefully review the data model. If you do not understand any aspect of it, you should ask for clarification until you do. *Entities must contain all of the data you and your employees need to do your jobs, and relationships must accurately reflect your view of the business.* If the data model is wrong, the database will be designed incorrectly, and the applications will be difficult to use, if not worthless. Do not proceed unless the data model is accurate.

As a corollary, when asked to review a data model, take that review seriously. Devote the time necessary to perform a thorough review. Any mistakes you miss will come back to haunt you, and by then the cost of correction may be very high with regard to both time and expense. This brief introduction to data modeling shows why databases can be more difficult to develop than spreadsheets.

Q8 2021?

Investing $1,000 only makes sense if it generates more than $1,000 in value. But what if the cost is essentially zero, as with the cost of data storage and data communication? If the cost of an investment is near zero, you needn't have much value to justify the expense. One consequence of this is that by 2021 businesses will have generated and stored many more megabytes of data about you. Most of that data will find its way to data aggregators like Acxiom, which had $1.2 billion in sales in 2009 and has been described as the "biggest company you never heard of." See question 6 at the end of this chapter to delve further into Acxiom.

Data aggregators like Acxiom obtain data from public and private sources and store and process it in sophisticated ways. When you use your grocery store club card, that data is sold to a data aggregator. Credit card data, credit data, public tax records, insurance records, product warrantee card data, voter registration data, and hundreds of other types of data are sold to aggregators.

Not all of the data is identified in the same way (or, in terms of this chapter, not all of it has the same primary key). But, using a combination of phone number, address, email address, name, and other partially identifying data, such companies can integrate that disparate data into an integrated, coherent whole. They then query, report, and data mine the integrated data to form detailed descriptions about companies, communities, zip codes, households, and individuals.

Laws limit the types of data that federal and other governmental agencies can acquire and store. There are also some legal safeguards on data maintained by credit bureaus and medical facilities. However, no such laws limit data storage by most companies (nor are there laws that prohibit governmental agencies from buying results from companies like Acxiom).

So how will this change by 2021? Absent any public outcry for legislation to limit such activity, aggregator data storage will continue to grow exponentially and companies will have even more data about you, the state of your health, your wealth, your purchase habits, your family, your travel, your driving record, and, well, anything you do. Query, reporting, and data mining technology will improve, and Moore's law will make computer operations that are too slow to be practical today feasible tomorrow. The picture of you will become more and more detailed.

Why do you care? Maybe you don't, at least as long as the data is not stolen and used for criminal activity against you or as long as the data that is maintained about you is accurate. But, aside from the government, credit bureaus, and certain medical facilities, no organization is required by law to tell you the data that it stores about you and what it does with it.

So, in 2021 you call technical support for assistance with your new home entertainment center. You call an 800 number, which enables the company you call to obtain your phone number, even if it is unlisted. Behind the scenes, before anyone answers the phone, that company accesses your records and determines your age, your income, your net worth, and your buying habits. The company then allocates support services based on your data. If you're over 65 and have limited net worth, your lifetime value to that company is low (soon you'll stop buying high-end entertainment equipment), so you're placed on hold for 40 minutes and eventually speak with a rude person having 2 days of training and limited English skills.

But suppose instead that you are an up-and-coming business professional with a high net worth. In that case, you have no wait at all. You speak with someone having years of training in tech support and with the equipment you purchased. She resolves your problem in 3 minutes. In neither scenario do you know what happened.

Or, maybe you enroll in a "healthy eaters" medical insurance program, similar to "safe drivers" auto insurance. Your premiums are lower because you eat well, except that the insurance company notes from last month's data that you bought four large packages of potato chips, and your health insurance premium is increased, automatically. You have no idea why.

By 2021, the data aggregators will have 10 more years of data about you, what you've eaten, the bottles of wine you've purchased, where you've traveled, the church you attend, the clothes you've purchased, what cars you own, the speeding tickets you've received, and probably what diseases you've had. And they won't forget about those three tattoos, either.

If you don't care, they do.

Guide

No, Thanks, I'll Use a Spreadsheet

"I'm not buying all this stuff about databases. I've tried them and they're a pain—way too complicated to set up, and most of the time, a spreadsheet works just as well. We had one project at the car dealership that seemed pretty simple to me: We wanted to keep track of customers and the models of used cars they were interested in. Then, when we got a car on the lot, we could query the database to see who wanted a car of that type and generate a letter to them.

"It took forever to build that system, and it never did work right. We hired three different consultants, and the last one finally did get it to work. But it was so complicated to produce the letters. You had to query the data in Access to generate some kind of file, then open Word, then go through some mumbo jumbo using mail/merge to cause Word to find the letter and put all the Access data in the right spot. I once printed over two hundred letters and had the name in the address spot and the address in the name spot and no date. And it took me over an hour to do even that. I just wanted to do the query and push a button to get my letters generated. I gave up. Some of the salespeople are still trying to use it, but not me.

"No, unless you are getting billions in government bailouts, I wouldn't mess with a database. You have to have professional IS people to create it and keep it running. Besides, I don't really want to share my data with anyone. I work pretty hard to develop my client list. Why would I want to give it away?

"My motto is, 'Keep it simple.' I use an Excel spreadsheet with four columns: Name, Phone Number, Car Interests, and Notes. When I get a new customer, I enter the name and phone number, and then I put the make and model of cars they like in the Car Interests column. Anything else that I think is important I put in the Notes column—extra phone numbers, address data if I have it, email addresses, spouse names, last time I called them, etc. The system isn't fancy, but it works fine.

"When I want to find something, I use Excel's Data Filter. I can usually get what I need. Of course, I still can't send form letters, but it really doesn't matter. I get most of my sales using the phone, anyway." ■

Discussion Questions

1. To what extent do you agree with the opinions presented here? To what extent are the concerns expressed here justified? To what extent might they be due to other factors?

2. What problems do you see with the way that the car salesperson stores address data? What will he have to do if he ever does want to send a letter or an email to all of his customers?

3. From his comments, how many different themes are there in his data? What does this imply about his ability to keep his data in a spreadsheet?

4. Does the concern about not sharing data relate to whether or not he uses a database?

5. Apparently, management at the car dealership allows the salespeople to keep their contact data in whatever format they want. If you were management, how would you justify this policy? What disadvantages are there to this policy?

6. Suppose you manage the sales representatives, and you decide to require all of them to use a database to keep track of customers and customer car interest data. How would you sell your decision to this salesperson?

7. Given the limited information in this scenario, do you think a database or a spreadsheet is a better solution?

Guide

Immanuel Kant, Data Modeler

Only the users can say whether a data model accurately reflects their business environment. What happens when the users disagree among themselves? What if one user says orders have a single salesperson but another says that sales teams produce some orders? Who is correct?

It's tempting to say, "The correct model is the one that better represents the real world." The problem with this statement is that data models do not model "the real world." A data model is simply a model of what the data modeler perceives. This very important point can be difficult to understand; but if you do understand it, you will save many hours in data model validation meetings and be a much better data modeling team member.

The German philosopher Immanuel Kant reasoned that what we perceive as reality is based on our perceptive apparatus. That which we perceive he called phenomena. Our perceptions, such as of light and sound, are processed by our brains and made meaningful. But we do not and cannot know whether the images we create from the perceptions have anything to do with what might or might not really be.

Kant used the term *noumenal world* to refer to the essence of "things in themselves"—to whatever it is out there that gives rise to our perceptions and images. He used the term *phenomenal world* to refer to what we humans perceive and construct.

It is easy to confuse the noumenal world with the phenomenal world, because we share the phenomenal world with other humans. All of us have the same mental apparatus, and we all make the same constructions. If you ask your roommate to hand you the toothpaste, she hands you the toothpaste, not a hairbrush. But the fact that we share this mutual view does not mean that the mutual view describes in any way what is truly out there. Dogs construct a world based on smells, and orca whales construct a world based on sounds. What the "real world" is to a dog, a whale, and a human are completely different. All of this means that we cannot ever justify a data model as a "better representation of the real world." Nothing that humans can do represents the real, noumenal world. A data model, therefore, is a model of a human's model of what appears to be "out there." For example, a model of a salesperson is a model of the model that humans make of salespeople.

To return to the question that we started with, what do we do when people disagree about what should be in a data model? First, realize that anyone attempting to justify her data model as a better representation of the real world is saying, quite arrogantly, "The way I think of the world is the way that counts." Second, in times of disagreement we must ask the question, "How well does the data model fit the mental models of the people who are going to use the system?" The person who is constructing the data model may think the model under construction is a weird way of viewing the world, but that is not the point. The only valid point is whether it reflects how the users view their world. Will it enable the users to do their jobs?

Discussion Questions

1. What does a data model represent?

2. Explain why it is easy for humans to confuse the phenomenal world with the noumenal world.

3. If someone were to say to you, "My model is a better model of the real world," how would you respond?

4. In your own words, how should you proceed when two people disagree on what is to be included in a data model?

Active Review

Use this Active Review to verify that you understand the ideas and concepts that answer the chapter's study questions.

Q1 What is the purpose of a database?

State the purpose of a database. Explain the circumstances in which a database is preferred to a spreadsheet. Describe the key difference between Figures 1 and 2.

Q2 What is a database?

Define the term *database*. Explain the hierarchy of data and name three elements of a database. Define *metadata*. Using the example of *Student* and *Office_Visit* tables, show how relationships among rows are represented in a database. Define the terms *key, foreign key*, and *relational database*.

Q3 What are the components of a database application system?

Explain why a database, by itself, is not very useful to business users. Name the components of a database application system and sketch their relationship. Explain the acronym DBMS and name its functions. List five popular DBMS products. Explain the difference between a DBMS and a database. Summarize the functions of a DBMS. Define *SQL*. Describe the major functions of database administration.

Q4 How do database applications make databases more useful?

Name and describe the components of a database application. Explain the need for application programs. For multi-user processing, describe one way in which one user's work can interfere with another's. Explain why multi-user database processing involves more than just connecting another computer to the network. Define two broad categories of DBMS and explain their differences.

Q5 How are data models used for database development?

Explain why user involvement is critical during database development. Describe the function of a data model. Sketch the database development process. Define *E-R model, entity, relationship, attribute*, and *identifier*. Give an example, other than one in this text, of an E-R diagram. Define *maximum cardinality* and *minimum cardinality*. Give an example of three maximum cardinalities and two minimum cardinalities. Explain the notation in Figures 18 and 19.

Q6 How is a data model transformed into a database design?

Name the three components of a database design. Define *normalization* and explain why it is important. Define *data integrity problem* and describe its consequences. Give an example of a table with data integrity problems and show how it can be normalized into two or more tables that do not have such problems. Describe two steps in transforming a data model into a database design. Using an example not in this chapter, show how 1:N and N:M relationships are represented in a relational database.

Q7 What is the users' role in the development of databases?

Describe the users' role in the database development. Explain why it is easier and cheaper to change a data model than to change an existing database. Use the examples of Figures 25(c) and 26(c) in your answer. Describe two criteria for judging a data model. Explain why it is important to devote time to understanding a data model.

Q8 2021?

Explain why companies will store data about you. Describe a data aggregator and how data aggregators operate. Explain limits to the laws that govern data storage. Describe how the situation is likely to change by 2021. Illustrate two ways that data aggregator data might be used. Explain why you do or do not care about this issue.

Key Terms and Concepts

Access	Crow's foot	Data model
Attributes	Crow's-foot diagram	Database
Byte	Data aggregators	Database administration
Columns	Data integrity problem	Database application

Database application system	Key	Personal DBMS
Database management system (DBMS)	Lost-update problem	Query
	Many-to-many (N:M) relationships	Records
DB2		Relation
Enterprise DBMS	Maximum cardinality	Relational databases
Entity	Metadata	Relationships
Entity-relationship (E-R) data model	Minimum cardinality	Report
	Multi-user processing	Rows
Entity-relationship (E-R) diagrams	MySQL	SQL Server
	Normal forms	Structured Query Language (SQL)
Fields	Normalization	
File	Object-relational database	Table
Foreign keys	One-to-many (1:N) relationships	Unified Modeling Language (UML)
Form		
Identifier	Oracle	

▮▬ Using Your Knowledge

1. Draw an entity-relationship diagram that shows the relationships among a database, database applications, and users.
2. Consider the relationship between *Adviser* and *Student* in Figure 20. Explain what it means if the maximum cardinality of this relationship is:

   a. N:1
   b. 1:1
   c. 5:1
   d. 1:5

3. Identify two entities in the data entry form in Figure 27. What attributes are shown for each? What do you think are the identifiers?
4. Using your answer to question 3, draw an E-R diagram for the data entry form in Figure 27. Specify cardinalities. State your assumptions.

5. The partial E-R diagram in Figure 28 (next page) is for a sales order. Assume there is only one *Salesperson* per *SalesOrder*.

   a. Specify the maximum cardinalities for each relationship. State your assumptions, if necessary.
   b. Specify the minimum cardinalities for each relationship. State your assumptions, if necessary.

6. Visit *www.acxiom.com*. Navigate the site to answer the following questions.

   a. According to the Web site, what is Acxiom's privacy policy? Are you reassured by its policy? Why or why not?
   b. Navigate the Acxiom site and make a list of 10 different products that Acxiom provides.
   c. Describe Acxiom's top customers.

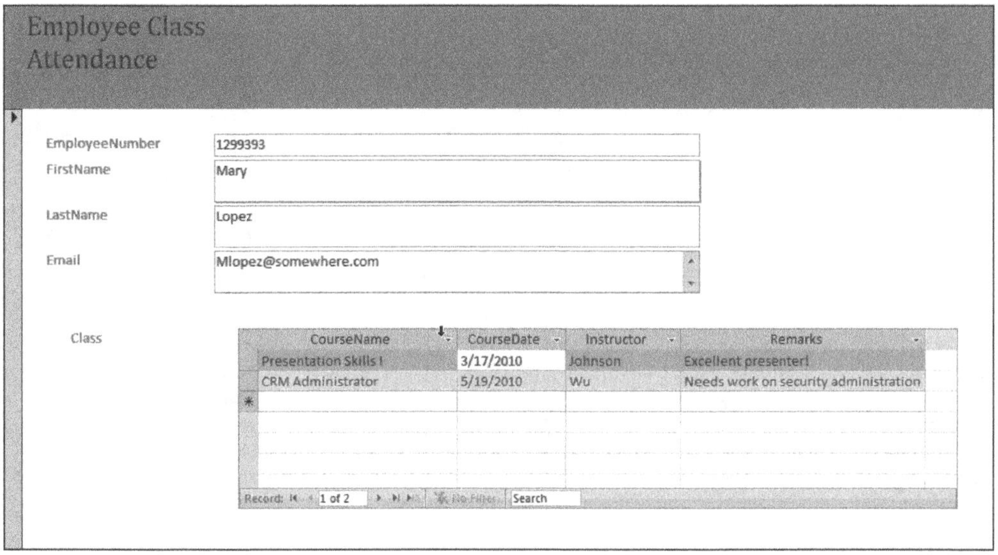

Figure 27
Sample Data Entry Form

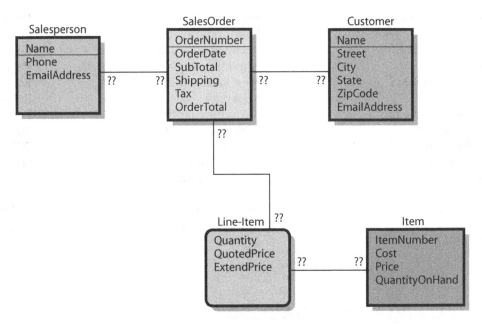

Figure 28
Partial E-R Diagram for
SalesOrder

d. Examine your answers in parts b and c and describe, in general terms, the kinds of data that Acxiom must be collecting to be able to provide those products to those customers.

e. What is the function of InfoBase?

f. What is the function of PersonicX?

g. In what ways might companies like Acxiom need to limit their marketing so as to avoid a privacy outcry from the public?

h. Should there be laws that govern companies like Acxiom? Why or why not?

i. Should there be laws that govern the types of data services that governmental agencies can buy from companies like Acxiom? Why or why not?

▬ Collaboration Exercise

Collaborate with students on the following exercise. In particular, consider using Google Docs, Windows Live SkyDrive, Microsoft SharePoint, or some other collaboration tool.

Figure 29 shows a spreadsheet that is used to track the assignment of sheet music to a choir—it could be a church choir or school or community choir. The type of choir does not matter, because the problem is universal.

Figure 29
Spreadsheet Used for
Assignment of Sheet Music

	A	B	C	D	E
1	Last Name	First Name	Email	Phone	Part
2	Ashley	Jane	JA@somewhere.com	703.555.1234	Soprano
3	Davidson	Kaye	KD@somewhere.com	703.555.2236	Soprano
4	Ching	Kam Hoong	KHC@overhere.com	703.555.2236	Soprano
5	Menstell	Lori Lee	LLM@somewhere.com	703.555.1237	Soprano
6	Corning	Sandra	SC2@overhere.com	703.555.1234	Soprano
7		B-minor mass	J.S. Bach	Soprano Copy 7	
8		Requiem	Mozart	Soprano Copy 17	
9		9th Symphony Chorus	Beethoven	Soprano Copy 9	
10	Wei	Guang	GW1@somewhere.com	703.555.9936	Soprano
11	Dixon	Eleanor	ED@thisplace.com	703.555.12379	Soprano
12		B-minor mass	J.S. Bach	Soprano Copy 11	
13	Duong	Linda	LD2@overhere.com	703.555.8736	Soprano
14		B-minor mass	J.S. Bach	Soprano Copy 7	
15		Requiem	J.S. Bach	Soprano Copy 19	
16	Lunden	Haley	HL@somewhere.com	703.555.0836	Soprano
17	Utran	Diem Thi	DTU@somewhere.com	703.555.1089	Soprano

Sheet music is expensive, choir members need to be able to take sheet music away for practice at home, and not all of the music gets back to the inventory. (Sheet music can be purchased or rented, but either way, lost music is an expense.)

Look closely at this data and you will see some data integrity problems—or at least some possible data integrity problems. For one, do Sandra Corning and Linda Duong really have the same copy of music checked out? Second, did Mozart and J. S. Bach both write a Requiem, or in row 15 should J. S. Bach actually be Mozart? Also, there is a problem with Eleanor Dixon's phone number; several phone numbers are the same as well, which seems suspicious.

Additionally, this spreadsheet is confusing and hard to use. The column labeled *First Name* includes both people names and the names of choruses. *Email* has both email addresses and composer names, and *Phone* has both phone numbers and copy identifiers. Furthermore, to record a checkout of music the user must first add a new row and then reenter the name of the work, the composer's name, and the copy to be checked out. Finally, consider what happens when the user wants to find all copies of a particular work: The user will have to examine the rows in each of four spreadsheets for the four voice parts.

In fact, a spreadsheet is ill-suited for this application. A database would be a far better tool, and situations like this are obvious candidates for innovation.

a. Analyze the spreadsheet shown in Figure 29 and list all of the problems that occur when trying to track the assignment of sheet music using this spreadsheet.

b. Figure 30(a) shows a two-entity data model for the sheet-music-tracking problem.

(1) Select identifiers for the *ChoirMember* and *Work* entities. Justify your selection.

(2) This design does not eliminate the potential for data integrity problems that occur in the spreadsheet. Explain why not.

(3) Design a database for this data model. Specify key and foreign key columns.

c. Figure 30(b) shows a second alternative data model for the sheet-music-tracking problem. This alternative shows two variations on the *Work* entity. In the second variation, an attribute named *WorkID* has been added to *Work_Version3*. This attribute is a unique identifier for the work; the DBMS will assign a unique value to *WorkID* when a new row is added to the *Work* table.

(1) Select identifiers for *ChoirMember, Work_Version2, Work_Version3*, and *Copy_Assignment*. Justify your selection.

(2) Does this design eliminate the potential for data integrity problems that occur in the spreadsheet? Why or why not?

(3) Design a database for the data model that uses *Work_Version2*. Specify key and foreign key columns.

(4) Design a database for the data models that uses *Work_Version3*. Specify key and foreign key columns.

(5) Is the design with *Work_Version2* better than the design for *Work_Version3*? Why or why not?

d. Figure 30(c) shows a third alternative data model for the sheet-music-tracking problem. In this data model, use either *Work_Version2* or *Work_Version3*, whichever you think is better.

(1) Select identifiers for each entity in your data model. Justify your selection.

(2) Summarize the differences between this data model and that in Figure 30(b). Which data model is better? Why?

(3) Design a database for this data model. Specify key and foreign key columns.

e. Which of the three data models is the best? Justify your answer.

Figure 30
Three Data-Model Alternatives

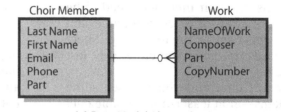

(a) Data-Model Alternative 1

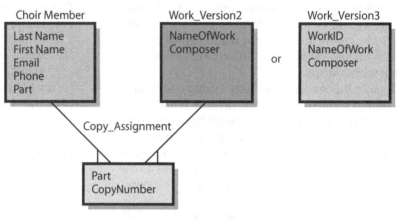

(b) Data-Model Alternative 2

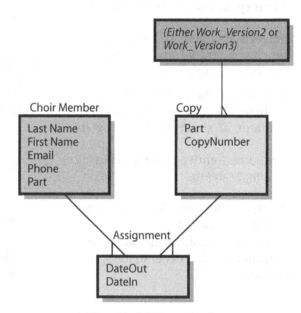

(c) Data-Model Alternative 3

Case Study

Benchmarking, Bench Marketing, or Bench Baloney

Which DBMS product is the fastest? Which product yields the lowest price/performance ratio? What computer equipment works best for each DBMS product? These reasonable questions should be easy to answer. They are not.

In fact, the deeper you dig, the more problems you find. To begin with, which product is fastest at doing what?

To have a valid comparison, all compared products must do the same work. So, vendors and third parties have defined *benchmarks*, which are descriptions of work to be done along with the data to be processed. To compare performance, analysts run competing DBMS products on the same benchmark and measure the results. Typical measures are number of transactions processed per second, number of Web pages served per second, and average response time per user.

At first, DBMS vendors set up their own benchmark tests and published those results. Of course, when vendor A used its own benchmark to claim that its product was superior to all others, no one believed the results. Clearly, vendor A had an incentive to set up the benchmark to play to its product strengths. So, third parties defined standard benchmarks. Even that led to problems, however. According to *The Benchmark Handbook*[4] (at *www.benchmarkresources.com/handbook,* accessed August 2006):

> When comparative numbers were published by third parties or competitors, the losers generally cried foul and tried to discredit the benchmark. Such events often caused benchmark wars. Benchmark wars start if someone loses an important or visible benchmark evaluation. The loser reruns it using regional specialists and gets new and winning numbers. Then the opponent reruns it using his regional specialists, and of course gets even better numbers. The loser then reruns it using some one-star gurus. This progression can continue all the way to five-star gurus.

For example, in July 2002 *PC Magazine* ran a benchmark using a standard benchmark called the *Nile benchmark.* This particular test has a mixture of database tasks that are processed via Web pages. The faster the DBMS, the more pages that can be served. The test compared five DBMS products:

* DB2 (from IBM)
* MySQL (a free, open source DBMS)
* Oracle (from Oracle Corporation)
* SQL Server (from Microsoft)
* ASE (from Sybase Corporation)

SQL Server's performance was the worst. In the magazine review, the authors stated that they believed SQL Server scored poorly because the test used a new version of a non-Microsoft driver (a program that sends requests and returns results to and from the DBMS).

As you might imagine, no sooner was this test published than the phones and email server at *PC Magazine* were inundated by objections from Microsoft. *PC Magazine* reran the tests, replacing the suspect driver with a full panoply of Microsoft products. The article doesn't say, but one can imagine the five-star Microsoft gurus who chartered the next airplane to PC Labs, where the testing was done. (You can read about both phases of the benchmark at *www.eweek. com/article2/0,4149,293,00.asp.*)

Not surprisingly when the tests were rerun with Microsoft-supporting software, SQL Server performed better than all of the other products in the first test. But that second test compares apples and oranges. The first test used standard software, and the second test used Microsoft-specific software.

When the five-star gurus from Oracle or MySQL use *their* favorite supporting products and "tune" to this particular benchmark, their re-rerun results will be superior to those for SQL Server. And round and round it will go.

Questions

1. Suppose you manage a business activity that needs a new IS with a database. The development team is divided on which DBMS you should use. One faction wants to use Oracle, a second wants to use MySQL, and a third wants to use SQL Server. They cannot decide among themselves, and so they schedule a meeting with you. The team presents all of the benchmarks shown in the article at *www.eweek.com/article2/0, 4149,293,00.asp.* How do you respond?

2. Performance is just one criterion for selecting a DBMS. Other criteria are the cost of the DBMS, hardware costs, staff knowledge, ease of use, ability to tune for extra performance, and backup and recovery capabilities. How does consideration of these other factors change your answer to question 1?

3. The Transaction Processing Council (TPC) is a nonprofit that defines transaction processing and database benchmarks and publishes vendor-neutral, verifiable performance data. Visit its Web site at *www.tpc.org.*

   a. What are TPC-C, TPC-R, and TPC-W?
   b. Suppose you work in the marketing department at Oracle. How would you use the TPC results in the TPC-C benchmark?
   c. What are the dangers to Oracle in your answer to part b?
   d. Suppose you work in the marketing department for DB2 at IBM. How would you use the TPC results in the TPC-C benchmark?
   e. Do the results for TPC-C change your answer to question 1?
   f. If you are a DBMS vendor, can you ignore benchmarks?

4. Reflect on your answers to questions 1 through 3. On balance, what good are benchmarks? Are they just footballs to be kicked around by vendors? Are advertisers and publishers the only true beneficiaries? Do DBMS customers benefit from the efforts of TPC and like groups? How should customers use benchmarks?

---

[4]Jim Gray (Ed.), *The Benchmark Handbook for Database and Transaction Systems,* 2nd ed. (San Francisco: Morgan Kaufmann 1993).

Application Exercises

1. Neil at Flextime used his database with Excel to obtain the data that he needs. A more common scenario is to use Microsoft Access with Excel: Users process relational data with Access, import some of the data into Excel, and use Excel's tools for creating professional-looking charts and graphs. You will do exactly that in this exercise.

   Download the Access file **Ch05Ex01** from *www.pearsonhighered.com/ kroenke.* Open the database and select *Database Tools/Relationships.* As you can see, there are three tables: *Product, VendorProductInventory,* and *Vendor.* Open each table individually to familiarize yourself with the data.

   For this problem, we will define *InventoryCost* as the product of *Industry StandardCost* and *QuantityOnHand.* The query *InventoryCost* computes these values for every item in inventory for every vendor. Open that query and view the data to be certain you understand this computation. Open the other queries as well so that you understand the data they produce.

   a. Sum this data by vendor and display it in a pie chart like that shown in Figure AE-4. Proceed as follows:

   (1) Open Excel and create a new spreadsheet.
   (2) Click *Data* on the ribbon and select *Access* in the *Get External Data* ribbon category.
   (3) Navigate to the location in which you have stored the Access file **Ch05Ex01**.
   (4) Select the query that contains the data you need for this pie chart.
   (5) Import the data into a table.
   (6) Format the appropriate data as currency.
   (7) Select the range that contains the data, press the Function key, and proceed from there to create the pie chart. Name the data and pie chart worksheets appropriately.

   b. Follow a similar procedure to create the bar chart shown in Figure AE-5. Place the data and the chart in separate worksheets and name them appropriately.

2. Reread the Guide from earlier in the chapter. Suppose you are given the task of converting the salesperson's data into a database. Because his data is so poorly structured, it will be a challenge, as you will see.

Figure AE-4
Data Displayed in Pie-Chart Format

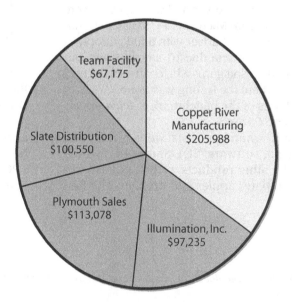

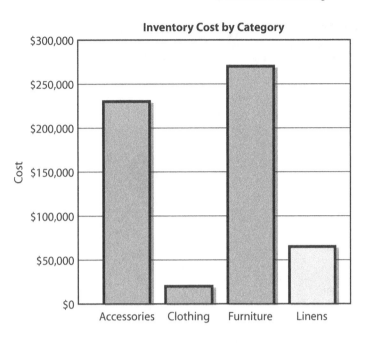

Figure AE-5
Data Displayed in Bar-Chart
Format

a. Download the Excel file named **Ch05Ex02** from *www.pearsonhighered.com/ kroenke*. This spreadsheet contains data that fits the salesperson's description in the Guide. Open the spreadsheet and view the data.

b. Download the Access file with the same name, **Ch05Ex02**. Open the database, select *Database Tools*, and click *Relationships*. Examine the four tables and their relationships.

c. Somehow, you have to transform the data in the spreadsheet into the table structure in the database. Because so little discipline was shown when creating the spreadsheet, this will be a labor-intensive task. To begin, import the spreadsheet data into a new table in the database; call that table *Sheet1* or some other name.

d. Copy the *Name* data in *Sheet1* onto the clipboard. Then, open the *Customer* table and paste the column of name data into that table.

e. Unfortunately, the task becomes messy at this point. You can copy the *Car Interests* column into *Make or Model of Auto*, but then you will need to straighten out the values by hand. Phone numbers will need to be copied one at a time.

f. Open the *Customer* form and manually add any remaining data from the spreadsheet into each customer record. Connect the customer to his or her auto interests.

g. The data in the finished database has much more structure than that in the spreadsheet. Explain why that is both an advantage and a disadvantage. Under what circumstances is the database more appropriate? Less appropriate?

3. In this exercise, you will create a two-table database, define relationships, create a form and a report, and use them to enter data and view results.

a. Download the Excel file **Ch05Ex03** from *www.pearsonhighered.com/ kroenke*. Open the spreadsheet and review the data in the *Employee* and *Computer* worksheets.

b. Create a new Access database with the name *Ch05Ex03_Solution*. Close the table that Access automatically creates and delete it.

c. Import the data from the Excel spreadsheet into your database. Import the *Employee* worksheet into a table named *Employee*. Be sure to check *First Row Contains Column Headings*. Select *Choose my own primary key* and use the ID field as that key.

d. Import the *Computer* worksheet into a table named *Computer*. Check *First Row Contains Column Headings*, but let Access create the primary key.

Figure AE-6
Employee Computer
Assignment Form

Employee   114

	Serial Number	Brand	Purchase Cost	Operating System
	100	Dell	$1,750	Vista
	800	HP	$750	Windows XP
*				

ID

First Name   Jane

Last Name   Ashley

Department   Mkt

Computer

Record: 1 of 2 — No Filter — Search

Record: 1 of 6 — No Filter — Search

e. Open the relationships window and add both *Employee* and *Computer* to the design space. Drag ID from *Employee* and drop it on *EmployeeID* in *Computer*. Check *Enforce Referential Integrity* and the two checkmarks below. Ensure you know what these actions mean.

f. Open the Form Wizard dialog box (under *Create, More Forms*) and add all of the columns for each of your tables to your form. Select *View your data by Customer*. Title your form *Employee* and your subform *Computer*.

g. Open the *Computer* subform and delete *EmployeeID* and *ComputerID*. These values are maintained by Access, and it is just a distraction to keep them. Your form should appear like the one shown in Figure AE-6.

h. Use your form to add two new computers to *Jane Ashley*. Both computers are Dells, and both use Vista; one costs $750, and the second costs $1,400.

i. Delete the Lenovo computer for Rex Scott.

j. Use the Report Wizard (under *Create*) to create a report having all data from both the *Employee* and *Computer* tables. Play with the report design until you find a design you like. Correct the label alignment if you need to.

Chapter 4 (original Chapter 6 of "Using MIS, 4/e")

Data Communication

From Chapter 6 of *Using MIS*, 4/e. David M. Kroenke. Copyright © 2012 by Pearson Education. Published by Prentice Hall.

Data Communication

FlexTime's building lease is about to expire and the owner wants to increase the rent by 30 percent. The building's facilities need to be repaired and upgraded, and the new lease calls for FlexTime to pay for those improvements. In response, Neil and Kelly have decided to buy their own building. They are walking through the door of the current building, discussing the difficult discussion they'd had with their banker.

"Neil, I don't want to put up the condo."

"Kelly, you were there. We heard him together: Our house valuation came in too low, and they want more collateral. It's either the condo or take another $150,000 out of the building infrastructure."

"If this economy doesn't improve, and if FlexTime can't support the new mortgage, we could lose it all. The business, our house, everything. The condo would be all we have left."

"OK, Kelly, let's look again at the costs."

Neil opens his laptop computer on his desk. They look at it together.

"The land, the basic building construction, the parking lots . . . I don't see how we get those costs down, but I'll talk to the contractor again. What about the locker rooms? Can we do anything to bring the locker room costs down?"

"Neil, I've been thinking about that. Maybe we go for a warehouse look. Of course we have to have showers and toilets and sinks and mirrors . . . and the lockers, but what if we go radical industrial? We could save on tile and fixtures."

"OK, Kelly, that's a start. What else?"

"Hey, Neil, what's this $175,000 for network infrastructure? What do we need that for?"

"Hooking up all the computers."

"$175,000 to hook up a computer? Come on, Neil, get real."

"Kelly, it's not just one computer, it's all of our computers. Plus all the new gear."

"Speaking of new gear!" Felix sticks his head into Neil's office, "Check out my new shoes. They talk to my wristband and, if I have a wireless network nearby, the wristband talks to the network and stores my workout data on my workout Web site. Cool! This gonna work in the new building?"

Felix heads down the hall.

"See what I mean, Kelly? Plus all the new machines have network adapters—either wired or wireless. And this is just the tip of the iceberg. Everybody wants to have their workout data collected and stored and processed. We're going to have to store more and more personal workout data. And it's got to get from the spinning machine, or the shoes, or the whatever, to the network somehow."

"Neil, I can understand spending money on wires; they're made of something and they have to be installed. But wireless? How come the air costs $175,000?"

"That's not fair, Kelly. The $175,000 includes wires installed in the walls, but actually, that's not a big expense. The major expenses are equipment items like switches and routers and other equipment that can give us the performance we need."

"Neil, this stuff is expensive. Cisco router??? Why do we need four of them? Or, hey, what is a VPN/firewall appliance? Appliance? Like a toaster? Pricey little number. Can we get by without it? There must be some fat in here we can remove."

Neil grimaces.

"Neil, why don't we just use iPhones? They talk to shoes, too."

"You mean have our clients use an iPhone app?"

"Yeah. I tried one last week, Neil, and it was great. I was out running and it worked just like my cell phone. I didn't have a wireless network anywhere near me. When I got back here I used the app to download the data to our computer. Why don't our clients do that?"

"Kelly, where is FlexTime in that transaction?"

"FlexTime? Nowhere. It was just me and shoes and the iPhone and the app and, ah Neil, I get the picture. Why would they need us?"

"Plus we have to do all we can to support whatever devices are coming down the road in the next 10 years."

"Neil, I'm in over my head on this. I don't even know the difference between a LAN and a WAN. But, I'll talk to our architect and try to get the locker room costs down. Meanwhile, can you take a look at this $175,000? Do we need all of it? Do we need all of it now? Can we shave even $20,000 off?" ■

Study Questions

Q1 What is a computer network?

Q2 What are the components of a LAN?

Q3 What are the alternatives for connecting to a WAN?

Q4 What are the fundamental concepts you should know about the Internet?

Q5 What processing occurs on a typical Web server?

Q6 How do organizations benefit from virtual private networks (VPNs) and firewalls?

Q7 2021?

If you go into business for yourself, there's an excellent chance you'll have a problem just like Neil's. How much do you really have to pay toward a network infrastructure? You'll need the knowledge of this chapter to understand the conversations you'll have to make that assessment. Of course, you can just rely on outside experts, but that probably doesn't work in the twenty-first century. Many of your competitors will be able to ask and understand those questions—and use the money their knowledge saves them for other facilities they need, like locker rooms and parking lots.

Or, what if you work in product management for a large company? Does your product "talk" to some network? If not, could it? Should it? Does it require a LAN or a WAN?

In this chapter, we will define essential data communications terms and explain basic concepts so that you won't find yourself in Kelly's position. We'll discuss LANs, WANs, and the fundamentals of the Internet. You'll also learn how Web servers function and be introduced to basic Web technologies. Finally, we'll discuss virtual private networks.

Q1 What Is a Computer Network?

A computer **network** is a collection of computers that communicate with one another over transmission lines or wirelessly. As shown in Figure 1, the three basic types of networks are local area networks, wide area networks, and internets.

A **local area network (LAN)** connects computers that reside in a single geographic location on the premises of the company that operates the LAN. The number of connected computers can range from two to several hundred. The distinguishing characteristic of a LAN is *a single location*. A **wide area network (WAN)** connects computers at different geographic locations. The computers in two separated company sites must be connected using a WAN. To illustrate, the computers for a College of Business located on a single campus can be connected via a LAN. The computers for a College of Business located on multiple campuses must be connected via a WAN.

The single- versus multiple-site distinction is important. With a LAN, an organization can place communications lines wherever it wants, because all lines reside on its premises. The same is not true for a WAN. A company with offices in Chicago and Atlanta cannot run a wire down the freeway to connect computers in the two cities. Instead, the company contracts with a communications vendor that is licensed by the government and that already has lines or has the authority to run new lines between the two cities.

An **internet** is a network of networks. Internets connect LANs, WANs, and other internets. The most famous internet is **"the Internet"** (with an uppercase letter *I*), the collection of networks that you use when you send email or access a Web site. In addition to the Internet, private networks of networks, called *internets*, also exist. A private internet that is used exclusively within an organization is sometimes called an **intranet**.

Many employees use computers for personal email, Facebook, Twitter, and other personal and social applications. Is such usage ethical? We consider that question in the Ethics Guide in this chapter.

Figure 1
Major Network Types

Type	Characteristic
Local area network (LAN)	Computers connected at a single physical site
Wide area network (WAN)	Computers connected between two or more separated sites
The Internet and internets	Networks of networks

The networks that comprise an internet use a large variety of communication methods and conventions, and data must flow seamlessly across them. To provide seamless flow, an elaborate scheme called a *layered protocol* is used. The details of protocols are beyond the scope of this text. Just understand that a **protocol** is a set of rules that programs on two communicating devices follow. There are many different protocols; some are used for LANs, some are used for WANs, some are used for internets and the Internet, and some are used for all of these. We will identify several common protocols in this chapter.

Social networking online is a new phenomenon created by the Internet. For information on social network theory and how it can benefit you, see the Guide later in this chapter.

Q2 What Are the Components of a LAN?

As stated, a LAN is a group of computers connected together on a single site. Usually the computers are located within a half mile or so of each other. The key distinction, however, is that all of the computers are located on property controlled by the organization that operates the LAN. This means that the organization can run cables wherever needed to connect the computers.

A Typical SOHO LAN

Figure 2 shows a LAN that is typical of those in a **small office or a home office (SOHO)**. Typically such LANs have fewer than a dozen or so computers and printers. Many businesses, of course, operate LANs that are much larger than this one. The principles are the same for a larger LAN, but the additional complexity is beyond the scope of this text.

The computers and printers in Figure 2 communicate via a mixture of wired and wireless connections. Computers 1 and 3 and printer 1 use wired connections; computers 2, 4, and 5 as well as printer 2 use wireless connections. The devices and protocols used differ for wired and wireless connectivity.

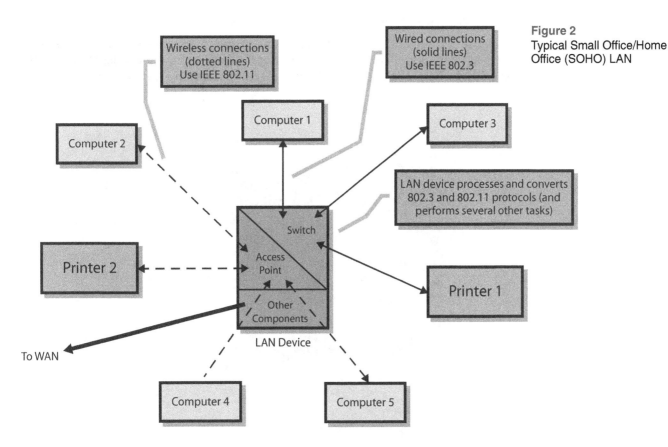

Figure 2
Typical Small Office/Home Office (SOHO) LAN

Wired Connectivity

Computers 1 and 3 and printer 1 are connected to a **switch**, which is a special-purpose computer that receives and transmits wired traffic on the LAN. In Figure 2, the switch is contained within the box labeled "LAN Device." When either of these two computers communicates with each other or with printer 1, it does so by sending the traffic to a switch, which redirects the traffic to the other computer or printer 1.

The **LAN device** is a small computer that contains the following networking components. It has a switch, as just described; it also has a device for wireless communication, as you are about to learn. In most cases, it has devices for connecting to a WAN and via the WAN to the Internet. It has numerous other elements, which are discussed in Q3. For SOHO applications, LAN devices are usually provided by the phone or cable vendor. They have many different names, depending on the brand. The example device in Figure 3 is called a gateway. It was manufactured by the 2Wire Corporation and was provided to the user by Qwest.

Each wired computer or printer on the LAN has a **network interface card (NIC)**, which is a device that connects the computer's or printer's circuitry to the network cables. The NIC works with programs in each device to implement the protocols necessary for communication. Most computers today ship from the factory with an **onboard NIC**, which is a NIC built into the computer's circuitry.

The computers, printers, and the switches on a wired LAN are connected using one of two wired media. Most LAN connections are made using **unshielded twisted pair (UTP) cable**. This cable contains sets of wires that are twisted together to improve signal quality. However, if the connection carries a lot of traffic, the UTP cable may be replaced by **optical fiber cables**. The signals on such cables are light rays, and they are reflected inside the glass core of the optical fiber cable.

LANs that are larger than the one in Figure 2 use more than one switch. Typically, in a building with several floors a switch is placed on each floor, and the computers on that floor are connected to the switch with UTP cable. The switches on each floor are connected to each other via the faster-speed optical fiber cable.

Wireless Connections

In Figure 2, three of the computers and one printer are connected to the LAN using wireless technology. The wireless computers and printer have a **wireless NIC (WNIC)** instead of a NIC. Today, nearly all personal computers ship from the factory with an

Figure 3
Gateway

Source: David M. Kroenke.

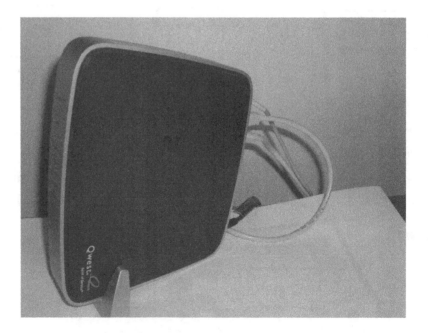

onboard WNIC. (By the way, in almost all cases a NIC or WNIC can be added to a computer that does not have one.)

As shown in Figure 2, the WNIC devices connect to an **access point**, which is the component of the LAN device that processes wireless traffic and communicates with the wired switch. Thus, with this design every device on the LAN, whether wired or wireless, can communicate with every other device. Wireless devices communicate to each other via the access point. If wireless devices need to connect to a wired device, they do so via the access point, then to the switch, and then to the wired devices. Similarly, wired devices communicate to each other via the switch. If the wired devices need to connect to wireless ones, they do so via the switch, then to the access point, and then to the wireless devices.

LAN Protocols

For two devices to communicate, they must use the same protocol. The Institute for Electrical and Electronics Engineers (IEEE, pronounced "I triple E") sponsors committees that create and publish protocols and other standards. The committee that addresses LAN standards is called the *IEEE 802 Committee.* Thus, IEEE LAN protocols always start with the numbers 802.

The **IEEE 802.3 protocol** is used for wired LAN connections. This protocol standard, also called **Ethernet**, specifies hardware characteristics, such as which wire carries which signals. It also describes how messages are to be packaged and processed for wired transmission over the LAN.

The NICs in most personal computers today support what is called **10/100/1000 Ethernet**. These products conform to the 802.3 specification and allow for transmission at a rate of 10, 100, or 1,000 Mbps (megabits per second). Switches detect the speed that a given device can handle and communicate with it at that speed. If you check computer listings at Dell, HP, Lenovo, and other manufacturers, you will see PCs advertised as having 10/100/1000 Ethernet.

By the way, the abbreviations used for communications speeds differ from those used for computer memory. For communications equipment, k stands for 1,000, not 1,024 as it does for memory. Similarly, M stands for 1,000,000, not 1,024 × 1,024; G stands for 1,000,000,000, not 1,024 × 1,024 × 1,024. Thus, 100 Mbps is 100,000,000 bits per second. Also, communications speeds are expressed in *bits*, whereas memory sizes are expressed in *bytes*.

Wireless LAN connections use the **IEEE 802.11 protocol**. Several versions of 802.11 exist, and as of 2010 the most popular one is IEEE 802.11g. The differences among these versions are beyond the scope of this discussion. Just note that the current standard, 802.11g, allows speeds of up to 54 Mbps.

Observe that the LAN in Figure 2 uses both the 802.3 and 802.11 protocols. The NICs operate according to the 802.3 protocol and connect directly to the switch, which also operates on the 802.3 standard. The WNICs operate according to the 802.11 protocol and connect to the wireless access point. The access point must process messages using both the 802.3 and 802.11 standards; it sends and receives wireless traffic using the 802.11 protocol and then communicates with the switch using the 802.3 protocol. Characteristics of LANs are summarized in the top two rows of Figure 4 on the next page.

Bluetooth is another common wireless protocol. It is designed for transmitting data over short distances, replacing cables. Some devices, such as wireless mice and keyboards, use Bluetooth to connect to the computer. Smartphones use Bluetooth to connect to automobile entertainment systems.

FlexTime has a LAN that connects computer workstations to each other and to the server. That network also makes Internet connections using a DSL modem. Fixed, desktop computers and some of the stationary workout equipment use wires and Ethernet. Laptops and some of the other workout equipment are wireless and use a version of IEEE 802.11. Some of the devices used by clients at FlexTime, like Kelly's talking shoes, connect to a network using Bluetooth.

Technology enables cost-effective communicating appliances . . . maybe next year they'll be tweeting one another. But, do you care? See the Guide later in the chapter for a discussion of the planning of exponential phenomena.

Type	Topology	Transmission Line	Transmission Speed	Equipment Used	Protocol Commonly Used	Remarks
Local area network	Local area network	UTP or optical fiber	10,100, or 1,000 Mbps	Switch NIC UTP or optical	IEEE 802.3 (Ethernet)	Switches connect devices, multiple switches on all but small LANs.
	Local area network with wireless	UTP or optical for non-wireless connections	Up to 54 Mbps	Wireless access point Wireless NIC	IEEE 802.11g	Access point transforms wired LAN (802.3) to wireless LAN (802.11).
Wide area network	DSL modem to ISP	DSL telephone	Personal: Upstream to 256 kbps, downstream to 6.544 Mbps	DSL modem DSL-capable telephone line	DSL	Can have computer and phone use simultaneously. Always connected.
	Cable modem to ISP	Cable TV lines to optical cable	Upstream to 256 kbps Downstream 300–600 kbps (10 Mbps in theory)	Cable modem Cable TV cable	Cable	Capacity is shared with other sites; performance varies depending on others' use.
	WAN wireless	Wireless connection to WAN	500 kbps to 1 Mbps	Wireless WAN modem	EVDO, HSDPA, WiMax	Sophisticated protocol enables several devices to use the same wireless frequency.

Figure 4
Summary of LAN and WAN
Networks

Q3 What Are the Alternatives for Connecting to a WAN?

A WAN connects computers located at physically separated sites. A company with offices in Detroit and Atlanta uses a WAN to connect the offices' computers together. Because the sites are physically separated, the company cannot string wire from one site to another. Rather, it must obtain connection capabilities from another company (or companies) licensed by the government to provide communications.

Although you may not have realized it, when you connect your personal computer, iPhone, iPad, or Kindle to the Internet, you are connecting to a WAN. You are connecting to computers owned and operated by an **Internet service provider (ISP)** that are not physically located at your site.

An ISP has three important functions. First, it provides you with a legitimate Internet address. Second, it serves as your gateway to the Internet. The ISP receives the communications from your computer and passes them on to the Internet, and it receives communications from the Internet and passes them on to you. Finally, ISPs pay for the Internet. They collect money from their customers and pay access fees and other charges on your behalf.

Figure 4 shows the three common WAN alternatives for connecting to the Internet. Notice that we are discussing how your computer connects to a WAN; we are not discussing the structure of the WAN itself. WAN architectures and their protocols are beyond the scope of this discussion. Search the Web for "leased lines" or "PSDN" if you want to learn more about WAN architectures.

SOHO LANs (like that in Figure 2) and individual home and office computers are commonly connected to an ISP in one of three ways: a special telephone line called a DSL line, a cable TV line, or a wireless-phone-like connection. All three of

122

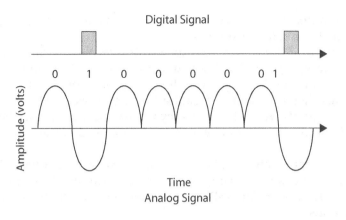

Figure 5
Analog Versus Digital Signals

these alternatives require that the *digital data* in the computer be converted to a wavy signal, or an **analog signal**. A device called a **modem**, or modulator/demodulator, performs this conversion. Figure 5 shows one way of converting the digital byte 01000001 to an analog signal.

(By the way, because LAN devices like the one shown in Figure 3 almost always contain a modem, they are sometimes called *modems*. As you have learned, however, they contain much more than just a modem, so we do not call them modems in this text.)

As shown in Figure 6, once the modem converts your computer's digital data to analog, that analog signal is then sent over the telephone line, TV cable, or air. If sent by telephone line, the first telephone switch that your signal reaches converts the signal into the form used by the international telephone system.

DSL Modems

A **DSL modem** is the first modem type. DSL stands for **digital subscriber line**. DSL modems operate on the same lines as voice telephones, but they operate so that their signals do not interfere with voice telephone service. Because DSL signals do not interfere with telephone signals, DSL data transmission and telephone conversations can occur simultaneously. A device at the telephone company separates the phone

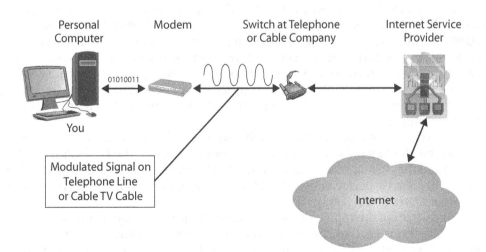

Figure 6
Personal Computer (PC)
Internet Access

123

signals from the computer signals and sends the latter signal to the ISP. DSL modems use their own protocols for data transmission.

There are gradations of DSL service and speed. Most home DSL lines can download data at speeds ranging from 256 kbps to 6.544 Mbps and can upload data at slower speeds—for example, 512 kbps. DSL lines that have different upload and download speeds are called **asymmetric digital subscriber lines (ADSL)**. Most homes and small businesses can use ADSL because they receive more data than they transmit (e.g., pictures in news stories), and hence they do not need to transmit as fast as they receive.

Some users and larger businesses, however, need DSL lines that have the same receiving and transmitting speeds. They also need performance-level guarantees. **Symmetrical digital subscriber lines (SDSL)** meet this need by offering the same fast speed in both directions.

Cable Modems

A cable modem is a second modem type. **Cable modems** provide high-speed data transmission using cable television lines. The cable company installs a fast, high-capacity optical fiber cable to a distribution center in each neighborhood that it serves. At the distribution center, the optical fiber cable connects to regular cable-television cables that run to subscribers' homes or businesses. Cable modems modulate in such a way that their signals do not interfere with TV signals.

Because up to 500 user sites can share these facilities, performance varies depending on how many other users are sending and receiving data. At the maximum, users can download data up to 50 Mbps and can upload data at 512 kbps. Typically, performance is much lower than this. In most cases, the speed of cable modems and DSL modems is about the same. Cable modems use their own protocols.

WAN Wireless Connection

A third way that you can connect your computer, iPhone, iPad, Kindle, or other communicating device is via a **WAN wireless** connection. Amazon.com's Kindle, for example, uses a Sprint wireless network to provide wireless data connections. The iPhone uses a LAN-based wireless network if one is available and a WAN wireless network if one is not. The LAN-based network is preferred because performance is considerably higher. As of 2010, WAN wireless provides average performance of 500 kbps, with peaks of up to 1.7 Mbps, as opposed to the typical 50 Mbps for LAN wireless.

A variety of WAN wireless protocols exist. Sprint and Verizon use a protocol called **EVDO**; AT&T, which supports the iPhone, and T-Mobile use one called **HSDPA**. Another protocol, **WiMax**, has been implemented by Clearwire and is available on Sprint's XOHM network (see the Case Study at the end of the chapter). The meaning of these acronyms and their particulars are unimportant to us; just realize that a marketing and technology battle is underway for WAN wireless. WiMax has the greatest potential for speed, but it is currently the least available. Figure 4 summarizes these alternatives.

When Kelly's shoes were communicating with her iPhone and the iPhone application was transferring data to a server, her shoes were using the Bluetooth wireless protocol and the iPhone was using a wireless WAN. Had she been inside the FlexTime building, to increase performance, the iPhone would have used the FlexTime wireless LAN rather than the wireless WAN.

Before we leave the topic of network connections, you should learn the meaning of two other terms used to classify network speed. **Narrowband** lines typically have transmission speeds less than 56 kbps. **Broadband** lines have speeds in excess of 256 kbps. Today, all popular communication technologies provide broadband capability, and so these terms are likely to fade from use.

Using MIS InClass *A Group Exercise*

Opening Pandora's Box

Superstock Royalty Free

Nearly free data communications and data storage have created unprecedented opportunities for businesses, as we have described numerous times. Inevitably, such technology will have a revolutionary impact in the home as well. The Guide from earlier in the chapter discusses why you should be wary of toasters and microwaves that talk to each other, but home entertainment is another matter.

Sonos is a good example. Sonos has leveraged emerging technologies, especially wireless technology, to develop easy-to-install, high-quality wireless audio systems. Customers hook up one of several different Sonos devices into their home LAN device using a wired Ethernet connection. That device then connects wirelessly to up to 32 other Sonos audio devices around the home. Each device can play its own music or other audio, some can play the same audio, or all can be forced to play the same audio.

Some Sonos devices provide wireless stereo to existing stereo systems; other devices include the wireless receiver and an amplifier, with the customer providing the speakers. Still other devices provide the wireless receiver, amplifier, and speakers in one unit.

Each Sonos device includes a computer running Linux. Those computers communicate wirelessly using a proprietary Sonos protocol. Because every device communicates with every other device, Sonos refers to its network of equipment as a *wireless mesh*. The benefit of this mesh to the consumer is flexibility and ease of installation. The devices find each other and determine their own data communications pathways (akin to, but different from, IP routing on the Internet).

Sonos works with any Internet radio source and with music services such as Pandora. With Pandora (and similar services), you establish a personal radio station by selecting a favorite song or musical work. Pandora then plays music based on your selection. You can vote thumbs up or thumbs down on

music that is played. Based on your ratings, Pandora selects similar music based on proprietary algorithms.

Form a group of students and answer the following questions:

1. Imagine that you have graduated, have the job of your dreams, and want to install a wireless stereo system in your new condo. Assume that you have a spare bedroom you use as an office that has a LAN device connected to the Internet. You have an existing stereo system in your living room, a pair of unused speakers, but no other stereo equipment. Assume that you want to play audio and music in your office, your living room, and your bedroom.
   a. Visit the Sonos Web site at *www.sonos.com* and select and price the equipment you will need.
   b. Go to the Web sites of Sonos' competitors at *www.logitechsqueezebox.com* and *http://soundbridge.roku.com* and select and price equipment you will need.
   c. Recommend one of the selections you identified in your answers to items a and b and justify your selection.
   d. Report your findings to the rest of the class.

2. Visit the Pandora Web site at *www.pandora.com*. Using the free trial membership, build a radio station for your group. Base your station on whatever song or music your group chooses.

3. The Sonos equipment has no on-off switch. Apparently, it is designed to be permanently on, like your LAN device. You can mute each station, but to turn a station off you must unplug it, an action few people take. Suppose you have tuned a Sonos device to a Pandora station, and you mute that device. Because the Sonos equipment is still on, it will continue downloading packets over the Internet to a device that no one is listening to.
   a. Describe the consequences of this situation on the Internet.
   b. You pay a flat fee for your Internet connection. In what ways does such a fee arrangement discourage efficiency?

4. Using your group's imagination and curiosity, describe the consequences of Internet-based audio on each of the following:
   a. Existing radio stations
   b. Vendors of traditional audio receivers
   c. Audio entertainment
   d. Cisco (a vendor of Internet routers)
   e. Your local ISP
   f. Any other companies or entities you believe will be impacted by wireless audio systems
   g. Report your conclusions to the rest of the class

5. Using history as a guide, we can image that audio leads the way for video.
   a. Explain how you could use a wireless video system in your new condo
   b. In the opinion of your group, is having multiple wireless video players in your condo more or less desirable than wireless audio? Explain.
   c. Answer a–f in item 4, but use wireless video rather than audio as the driving factor.
   d. Report your answers to the rest of the class.
6. Considering all of your answers to items 1–5:
   a. What industries are the winners and losers?
   b. What companies are the winners and losers?
   c. How does your answer to parts a and b guide your job search?
7. Use the knowledge you have gained in answering items 1–6 to prepare a 1-minute statement that you could make in a job interview about emerging opportunities in Internet-based audio and video. Assume that with this statement you wish to demonstrate your ability to think innovatively. Deliver your statement to the rest of the class.

Q4 What Are the Fundamental Concepts You Should Know About the Internet?

As discussed in Q1, the Internet is an *internet*, meaning that it is a network of networks. As you might guess, the technology that underlies the Internet is complicated and beyond the scope of this text. However, because of the popularity of the Internet, certain terms have become ubiquitous in twenty-first-century business society. In this question, we will define and explain terms that you need to know to be an informed business professional and consumer of Internet services.

An Internet Example

Figure 7 illustrates one use of the Internet. Suppose that you are sitting in snowbound Minneapolis and you want to communicate with a hotel in sunny, tropical, northern

Figure 7
Using the Internet for a Hotel Reservation

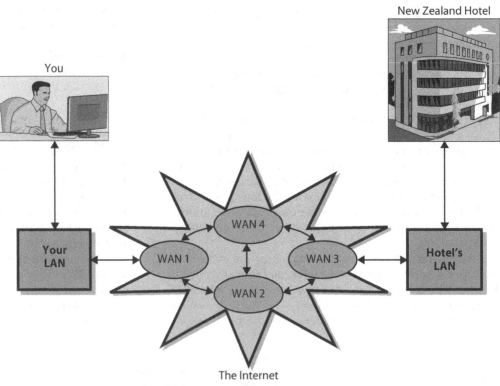

Layer	Name	Scope	Purpose	Example Protocol
5	Application	Program to program	Enable communication among programs	HTTP, HTTPS, SMTP, FTP
4	Transport	Internets	Reliable internet transport	TCP
3	Internet	Internets	Internet routing	IP
2	Data Link	Network	Flow among switches and access points	IEEE 802.3 IEEE 802.11
1	Physical	Two devices	Hardware specifications	IEEE 802.3 IEEE 802.11

Figure 8
TCP/IP Protocol Architecture

New Zealand. Maybe you are making a reservation using the hotel's Web site, or maybe you are sending an email to a reservations clerk inquiring about facilities or services.

To begin, note that this example is an internet because it is a network of networks. It consists of two LANs (yours and the hotel's) and four WANs. (In truth, the real Internet consists of tens of thousands of WANs and LANs, but to conserve paper we don't show all of them here.)

Your communication to the hotel involves nearly unimaginable complexity. Somehow, your computer communicates with a server in the New Zealand hotel, a computer that it has never "met" before and knows nothing about. Further, your transmission, which is too big to travel in one piece, is broken up into parts and each part passed along from WAN to WAN in such a way that it arrives intact. Then your original message is re-assembled, any parts that were lost or damaged (this happens) are resent, and the reconstructed message delivered to the server for processing. All of this is accomplished by computers and data communications devices that most likely have not interacted before.

What all these devices do know, however, is that they process the same set of protocols. Thus, we need to begin with Internet protocols.

The TCP/IP Protocol Architecture

The protocols used on the Internet are arranged according to a structure known as the **TCP/IP Protocol (TCP/IP) architecture**, which is a scheme of five protocol types arranged in layers. As shown in Figure 8, the top layer concerns protocols for applications like browsers and Web servers. The next two layers concern protocols about data communications across any internet (note the small *i*; this means any network of networks), including the Internet. The bottom two layers involve protocols that concern data transmission within a network. For example, the IEEE 802.3 and 802.11 LAN protocols operate at the bottom two layers.

As stated, a protocol is a set of rules and data structures for organizing communication. One or more protocols are defined at each layer. Data communications and software vendors write computer programs that implement the rules of a particular protocol. (For protocols at the bottom layer, the physical layer, they build hardware devices that implement the protocol.)

You are probably wondering, "Why should I know about this?" The reason is so that you will understand the terms you will hear and the products you will use, buy, or possibly invest in that relate to each other via this architecture.

Application-Layer Protocols

You will directly encounter at least three application-layer protocols in your professional life. (In fact, you have used two of them already). **Hypertext Transport Protocol (HTTP)** is the protocol used between browsers and Web servers. When you use a browser such as Internet Explorer, Safari, or Chrome, you are using a program that implements the HTTP protocol. At the other end, at the New Zealand Hotel for example, there is a server that also processes HTTP, as you will learn in Q5. Even though your browser and the server at the hotel have never "met" before, they can communicate with one another because they both follow the rules of HTTP. Your browser sends requests for service encoded in a predefined HTTP *request format*; the server receives that request, does something, and formats a response in a predefined HTTP *response format*.

There is secure version of HTTP called **HTTPS**. Whenever you see *https* in your browser's address bar, you have a secure transmission, and you can safely send sensitive data like credit card numbers. When you are on the Internet, if you do not see *https*, then you should assume that all of your communication is open and could be published on the front page of your campus newspaper tomorrow morning. Hence, when you are using HTTP, email, text messaging, chat, videoconferencing, or anything other than HTTPS, know that whatever you are typing or saying could be known by anyone else. Thus, in your classroom, when you send a text message to a fellow student, that message can be intercepted and read by anyone in your class, including your professor. The same is true of people at a coffee shop, an airport, or anywhere.

Two additional TCP/IP application-layer protocols are common. **SMTP**, or **Simple Mail Transfer Protocol**, is used for email transmissions (along with other protocols as well). **FTP**, or **File Transfer Protocol**, is used to move files over the Internet. One very common use for FTP is to maintain Web sites. When a Web site administrator wishes to post a new picture or story on a Web server, the administrator will often use FTP to move the picture or other item to the server. Like HTTP, FTP has a secure version as well, but do not assume you are using it.

With this knowledge, we can clear up one common misconception. You are using the Internet when you use any of these protocols. However, you are using the Web only when you use either HTTP or HTTPS. Thus, the **Web** is the Internet-based network of browsers and servers that process HTTP or HTTPS. When you send a file using FTP, you are using the Internet, but not the Web. It is incorrect to say you are using the Web to FTP files.

TCP and IP Protocols

You have some idea of the protocols used at the application (top) layer in Figure 8, and from the discussion in Q2 you have some idea of the LAN protocols used at the bottom two layers. But what is the purpose of the layers in between, the transport and internet layers? You know these two layers must be important because the architecture is named after their protocols.

These protocols manage traffic as it passes across an internet (including the Internet) from one network to another. The most important protocol in the transport layer is **TCP**, or the **Transmission Control Protocol**. As a transport protocol, TCP has many functions, most of which are beyond the scope of our discussion. One easily understood function, however, is that TCP programs break your traffic up into pieces and send each piece along its way. It then works with TCP programs on other devices in the internet to ensure that all of the pieces arrive at their destination. If one or more pieces are lost or damaged, TCP programs detect that condition and cause retransmission of that piece. Hence, the TCP layer is said to provide *reliable internet transport*.

The primary protocol of the Internet layer is called **IP (Internet Protocol)**, which is a protocol that specifies the routing of the pieces of your message through the networks that comprise any internet (including the Internet). In Figure 7, programs on devices at each of the networks (the two LANs and the four WANs) receive a portion of your message and route it to another computer in its network, or to another network altogether. A **packet** is a piece of a message that is handled by programs that implement IP. A **router** is a special-purpose computer that moves packet traffic according to the rules of the IP protocol.

Your message is broken into packets (for simplicity we're leaving a LOT out here) and each packet is sent out onto the Internet. The packet contains the address of where it is supposed to go. Routers along the way receive the packet, examine the destination IP address, and send it either to the desired destination, or to another router that is closer to the desired destination.

When your message starts on its way to the New Zealand hotel, no device knows what route the pieces will take. Until the last hop, a router just sends the packet to another router that it determines to be closer to the final destination. In fact, the packets that make up your message may take different pathways through the Internet (this is rare, but it does occur). Because of this routing scheme, the Internet is very robust. For example, in Figure 7, either WAN 2 or WAN 4 could fail and your packets will still get to the hotel.

To summarize, TCP provides reliable internet transport and IP provides internet routing.

IP Addressing

An **IP address** is a number that identifies a particular device. **Public IP addresses** identify a particular device on the public Internet. Because public IP addresses must be unique, worldwide, their assignment is controlled by a public agency known as **ICANN (Internet Corporation for Assigned Names and Numbers)**.

Private IP addresses identify a particular device on a private network, usually on a LAN. Their assignment is controlled within the LAN, usually by the LAN device shown in Figure 2. When you sign onto a LAN at a coffee shop, for example, the LAN device loans you a private IP address to use while you are connected to the LAN. When you leave the LAN, it reuses that address.

Use of Private IP Addresses

When your computer uses TCP/IP within a LAN, say to access a private Web server within the LAN, it uses a private IP address. However, and this is far more common, when you access a public site, say *www.LearningMIS.com* from within the LAN, your traffic uses your internal IP address until it gets to the LAN device. At that point, the LAN device substitutes your private IP address for its public IP address and sends your traffic out onto the Internet.

This private/public IP address scheme has two major benefits. First, public IP addresses are conserved. All of the computers on the LAN use only one public IP address. Second, by using private IP addresses, you need not register a public IP address for your computer with ICANN-approved agencies. Furthermore, if you had a public IP address for your computer, every time you moved it, say from home to school, the Internet would have to update its addressing mechanisms to route traffic to your new location. Such updating would be a massive burden (and a mess)!

Functions of the LAN Device

Before we continue with IP addressing, note all of the functions of the LAN device. A lot is happening in that little box shown in Figure 2:

- Switch processing IEEE 802.3 wired LAN traffic
- Access-point processing IEEE 802.11 wireless LAN traffic
- Translation between IEEE 802.3 and IEEE 802.11
- Modem converting between Analog and Digital
- Server that assigns private IP addresses assigning private IP addresses
- Private/public IP address translation converting between private and public IP addresses
- Internet router routing packets
- (And more that is beyond the scope of this discussion . . .)

Public IP Addresses and Domain Names

IP addresses have two formats. The most common form, called **IPv4**, has a four-decimal dotted notation like 165.193.123.253; the second, called **IPv6**, has a longer

Figure 9
Go Daddy Screenshot

Source: www.godaddy.com.

format and will not concern us here. In your browser, if you enter *http://165.193.123.253*, your browser will connect with the device on the public Internet that has been assigned to this address. Try it to find out who has this address.

Nobody wants to type IP addresses like *http://165.193.123.253* to find a particular site. Instead, we want to enter names like *www.pandora.com* or *www.woot.com* or *www.MyMISTutor.com*. To facilitate that desire, ICANN administers a system for assigning names to IP addresses. First, a **domain name** is a worldwide-unique name that is affiliated with a public IP address. When an organization or individual wants to register a domain name, it goes to a company that applies to an ICANN-approved agency to do so. Go Daddy (*www.GoDaddy.com*) is an example of such a company (Figure 9).

Go Daddy, or a similar agency, will first determine if the desired name is unique, worldwide. If so, then it will apply to register that name to the applicant. Once the registration is completed, the applicant can affiliate a public IP address with the domain name. From that point onward, traffic for the new domain name will be routed to the affiliated IP address.

Note two important points: First, several (or many) domain names can point to the same IP address. Right now, *www.MyMISProf.com* and *www.MyMISTutor.com* both point to the same public IP address. Second, the affiliation of domain names with IP addresses is dynamic. The owner of the domain name can change the affiliated IP addresses at its discretion.

Before we leave the Internet, you need to know one more term. A **URL (Uniform Resource Locator)** is an address on the Internet. Commonly, it consists of a protocol (like http:// or ftp://) followed by a domain name or public IP address. A URL is actually quite a bit more complicated than this description, but that detailed knowledge won't get you a good date, so we'll hurry along. The preferred pronunciation of URL is to say the letters U, R, L.

Q5 What Processing Occurs on a Typical Web Server?

At this point, you know basic networking terms and have a high-level view of how internets and the Internet work. To complete this chapter's high-level survey of data communications, you need to know a bit about the processing that occurs on a Web server. For this discussion, we will use the example of a Web storefront, which is a server on the Web from which you can buy products. Web storefronts are one type of

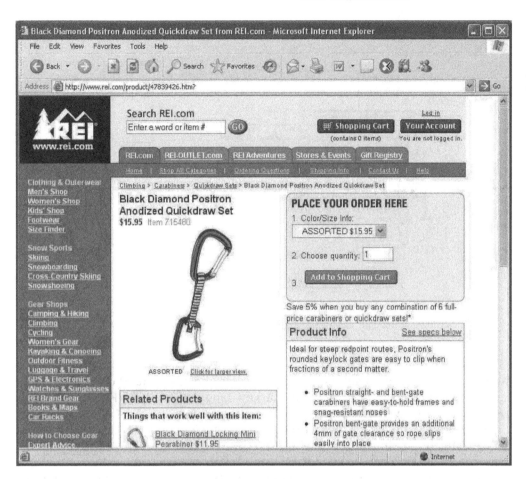

Figure 10
Sample of Commerce Server
Pages; Product Offer Pages

Source: Used with permission of REI and Black
Diamond.

e-commerce. Here, just consider the Web storefront as an example Web server.

Suppose you want to buy climbing equipment from REI, a co-op that sells outdoor clothing and equipment. To do so, you go to www.rei.com and navigate to the product(s) that you want to buy (see Figure 10). When you find something you want, you add it to your shopping cart and keep shopping. At some point, you check out by supplying credit card data.

In Q4, we discussed how your traffic crosses over the Internet to arrive at the REI server. The next question is: What happens at that server when it arrives? Or, from another perspective, if you want to set up a Web storefront for your company, what facilities do you need?

Three-Tier Architecture

Almost all e-commerce applications use the **three-tier architecture**, which is an arrangement of user computers and servers into three categories, or tiers, as shown in Figure 11. The **user tier** consists of computers, phones, and other devices that have browsers that request and process Web pages. The **server tier** consists of computers that run Web servers and process application programs. The **database tier** consists of computers that run a DBMS that processes SQL requests to retrieve and store data. Figure 11 shows only one computer at the database tier. Some sites have multicomputer database tiers as well.

When you enter *http://www.rei.com* in your browser, the browser sends a request that travels over the Internet to a computer in the server tier at the REI site. That request is formatted and processed according to the rules of HTTP. (Notice, by the way, that if you just type *www.rei.com*, your browser will add the *http://* to signify that it is using HTTP.) In response to your request, a server-tier computer sends back a

Three-Tier Architecture

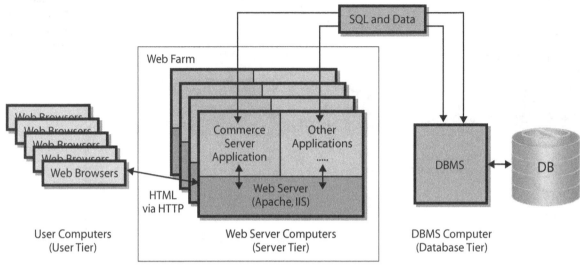

Figure 11
Three-Tier Architecture

Web page, which is a document that is coded in one of the standard page markup languages. The most popular page markup language is the *Hypertext Markup Language (HTML)*, which is described later in this section.

Web servers are programs that run on a server-tier computer and that manage HTTP traffic by sending and receiving Web pages to and from clients. A **commerce server** is an application program that runs on a server-tier computer. A commerce server receives requests from users via the Web server, takes some action, and returns a response to the users via the Web server. Typical commerce server functions are to obtain product data from a database, manage the items in a shopping cart, and coordinate the checkout process. In Figure 11, the server-tier computers are running a Web server program, a commerce server application, and other applications having an unspecified purpose.

To ensure acceptable performance, commercial Web sites usually are supported by several or even many Web server computers in a facility called a **Web farm**. Work is distributed among the computers in a Web farm so as to minimize customer delays. The coordination among multiple Web server computers is a fantastic dance, but, alas, we do not have space to tell that story here. Just imagine the coordination that must occur as you add items to an online order when, to improve performance, different Web server computers receive and process each addition to your order.

Watch the Three Tiers in Action!

To see a three-tier example in action, go to your favorite Web storefront site, place something in a shopping cart, and consider Figure 11 as you do so. When you enter an address into your browser, the browser sends a request for the default page to a server computer at that address. A Web server, and possibly a commerce server, process your request and send back the default page.

As you click Web pages to find products you want, the commerce server accesses the database to retrieve data about those products. It creates pages according to your selections and sends the results back to your browser via the Web server. Again, different computers on the server tier may process your series of requests and must constantly communicate about your activities. You can follow this process in Figure 11.

Figure 12
Shopping-Cart Page

Source: Used with permission of REI.

In Figure 10 the user has navigated through climbing equipment at REI.com to find a particular item. To produce this page, the commerce server accessed a database to obtain the product picture, price, special terms (a 5 percent discount for buying six or more), product information, and related products.

The user placed six items in her basket, and you can see the response in Figure 12. Again, trace the action in Figure 11 and imagine what occurred to produce the second page. Notice that the discount was applied correctly.

When the customer checks out, the commerce server program will be called to process payment, schedule inventory processing, and arrange for shipping. Truly this is an amazing capability!

Hypertext Markup Language (HTML)

Hypertext Markup Language (HTML) is the most common language for defining the structure and layout of Web pages. An HTML **tag** is a notation used to define a data element for display or other purposes. The following HTML is a typical heading tag:

<h2> <Price of Item> </h2>

Notice that tags are enclosed in < > (called *angle brackets*) and that they occur in pairs. The start of this tag is indicated by <h2>, and the end of the tag is indicated by </h2>. The words between the tags are the value of the tag. This HTML tag means to place the words "Price of Item" on a Web page in the style of a level-two heading. The creator of the Web page will define the style (font size, color, and so forth) for h2 headings and the other tags to be used.

Ethics
Guide

Personal Work at Work?

Let's suppose you go on a vacation to New Zealand and you decide to email pictures of your amazing surfing skills to a friend who works at, say, some company in Ohio. Your email does not concern your friend's work or his company's business. It is not an emergency email, nor is it even a request for a ride to your house from the airport. Your email concerns your surfing skills! Even worse, your email is not just a few sentences that would consume a little file space. Rather, your email contains a dozen pictures, and, without noticing it, you sent very high-quality pictures that were 6.2 megabytes in size, each.

"Come on," you're saying, "give me a break! What's the matter with an email and some pictures? It's me surfing, it's not some weird pornographic material."

Maybe you're right; maybe it's not a big deal. But consider the resources you've consumed by sending that email: Your message, over 60 megabytes of it, traveled over the Internet to your friend's company's ISP. The packets of the email and picture were then transmitted to the company's router and from that router to its email server. Your message consumed processing cycles on the router and on the email server computer. A copy of your picture was then stored on that email server until your friend deleted it, perhaps weeks later. Additionally, your friend will use his computer and the company LAN to download the pictures to his

desktop computer, where they will be stored. In fact, the entire computing infrastructure, from the ISP to your friend's desk, is owned, operated, and paid for by your friend's employer. Finally, if your friend reads his email during his working hours, he will be consuming company resources—his time and attention, which the company has paid for while he is at work.

[Update: 2008] Since this guide was written, the situation has become even more complicated. Now, in addition to (or instead of) emailing pictures, you're likely to be updating your Facebook page with the photos, and your friend is likely using his computer to view those photos and to comment on your page and to update his. Now, the pictures are no longer stored on the company's servers, but they are still being transmitted over its data communications network.

[Update: 2010] Since the 2008 update was written, personal, intelligent devices like the iPhone, the iPad, and Windows 7 Series phones, not to mention BlackBerry phones, have become affordable and popular. Consequently, your friend can choose to read your Facebook page, tweets, and so on from his phone or iPad. If his device connects to his company's LAN, then he is still using the company's data communications network. However, if that phone makes a WAN wireless connection, then he is no longer using any of his company's data communications network. He is, however, using company time. ■

Discussion Questions

Questions 1–4 concern the original scenario, before the 2008 and 2010 updates.

1. Is it ethical for you to send the email and picture to your friend at work?

2. Does your answer to question 1 change depending on the size of the pictures? Does your answer change if you send 100 pictures? If you send 1,000 pictures? If your answer does change, where do you draw the line?

3. Once the pictures are stored on the company's email server, who owns the pictures? Who controls those pictures? Does the company have the right to inspect the contents of its employees' mailboxes? If so, what should managers do when they find your picture that has absolutely nothing to do with the company's business?

4. What do you think is the greater cost to your friend's company: the cost of the infrastructure to transmit and store the email or the cost of the time your friend takes at work to read and view your pictures? Does this consideration change any of your answers above?

5. How does the 2008 update change the ethics of the situation? Is it ethical for your friend to read and update Facebook using the company's computers?

6. How does the 2010 update change the ethics of the situation? Is it any of the company's business what your friend does with his iPhone or other device at work?

7. Describe a reasonable policy for computer/phone/communicating device use at work. Consider email, Facebook, and Twitter, as well as the 2008 and 2010 updates. Try to develop a policy that will be robust in the face of likely data communication changes in the future.

Chris Batson/ Alamy Images Royalty Free

Figure 13a
Sample HTML Code Snippet

```
<title>UMIS Example HTML</title>
<style type="text/css">
.style1 {
    font-size: xx-large;
    text-align: center;
    font-family: Arial, Helvetica, sans-serif;
}
.style2 {
    color: #FF00FF;
}
.style3 {
    font-size: medium;
    text-align: center;
    font-family: Arial, Helvetica, sans-serif;
}
.style5 {
    font-size: medium;
    text-align: left;
    font-family: Arial, Helvetica, sans-serif;
}
</style>
</head>

<body>

<p class="style1">
    <span class="style2"><strong>Using</strong></span>
    <strong>MIS</strong></p>
<p class="style1"> </p>
<p class="style3"><em>Fourth Edition</em></p>
<p class="style3"> </p>
<p class="style5">Example HTML Document</p>
<p class="style5"> </p>
<p class="style5"> </p>
<p class="style5">Click <a href="http://www.PearsonHigherEd.com/kroenke">here</a>
for the textbook&#39;s web site at Pearson Education.</p>

</body>
```

Web pages include **hyperlinks**, which are pointers to other Web pages. A hyperlink contains the URL of the Web page to find when the user clicks the hyperlink. The URL can reference a page on the server that generated the page containing the hyperlink or it can reference a page on another server.

Figure 13(a) shows a sample HTML document. The document has a heading that provides metadata about the page and a body that contains the content. The tag <h1> means to format the indicated text as a level-one heading; <h2> means a level-two heading. The tag <a> defines a hyperlink. This tag has an **attribute**, which is a variable used to provide properties about a tag. Not all tags have attributes, but many do. Each attribute has a standard name. The attribute for a hyperlink is **href**, and its value indicates which Web page is to be displayed when the user clicks the link. Here, the page *www.pearsonhighered.com/kroenke* is to be returned when the user clicks the hyperlink. Figure 13(b) shows this page as rendered by Internet Explorer.

Figure 13b
Document Created from HTML Code in Figure 13a

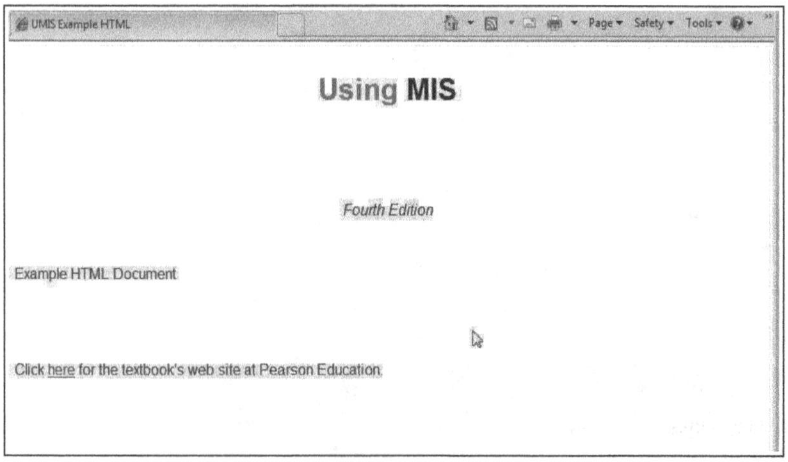

XML, Flash, Silverlight, and HTML 5

HTML has been the workhorse of the Web for more than 15 years. However, it has problems and limitations that have been overcome by newer technologies. **XML (eXtensible Markup Language)** is a markup language that fixes several HTML deficiencies and is commonly used for program-to-program interaction over the Web. **Flash** is an add-on to browsers that was developed by Adobe and is useful for providing animation, movies, and other advanced graphics inside a browser. **Silverlight** is a browser add-on that was developed by Microsoft for the same purposes as Flash. Silverlight has newer technology than Flash and greater functionality, but is less frequently used. Finally, HTML 5.0 is a new version of HTML that also supports animation, movies, and graphics.

Almost all experts agree that XML will continue to be most important for interprogram communication on the Web. Some people believe that HTML 5.0 will replace standard HTML, Flash, and Silverlight.

Q6 How Do Organizations Benefit from Virtual Private Networks (VPNs) and Firewalls?

Before we leave the topic of data communications, you need to learn about two more concepts that you are likely to encounter when you work in organizations: VPNs and firewalls.

Virtual Private Network

A **virtual private network (VPN)** uses the Internet to create the appearance of private point-to-point connections. In the IT world, the term *virtual* means something that appears to exist but in fact does not. Here, a VPN uses the public Internet to create the appearance of a private connection.

A Typical VPN

Figure 14 shows one way to create a VPN to connect a remote computer, perhaps an employee working at a hotel in Miami, to a LAN at a Chicago site. The remote user is the VPN client. That client first establishes a connection to the Internet. The connection can be obtained by accessing a local ISP, as shown in the figure, or, in some hotels, the hotel itself provides a direct Internet connection.

In either case, once the Internet connection is made, VPN software on the remote user's computer establishes a connection with the VPN server in Chicago. The VPN client and VPN server then have a point-to-point connection. That connection, called

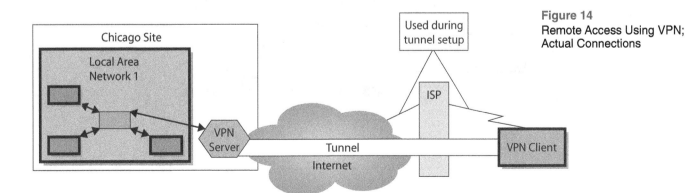

Figure 14
Remote Access Using VPN;
Actual Connections

Figure 15
Remote Access Using VPN;
Apparent Connection

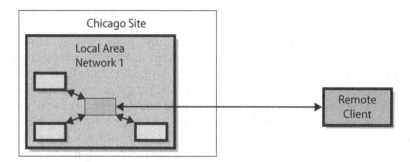

a **tunnel**, is a virtual, private pathway over a public or shared network from the VPN client to the VPN server. Figure 15 illustrates the connection as it appears to the remote user.

VPN communications are secure, even though they are transmitted over the public Internet. To ensure security, VPN client software *encrypts*, or codes, the original message so that its contents are protected from snooping. Then the VPN client appends the Internet address of the VPN server to the message and sends that package over the Internet to the VPN server. When the VPN server receives the message, it strips its address off the front of the message, *decrypts* the coded message, and sends the plain text message to the original address on the LAN. In this way, secure private messages are delivered over the public Internet.

VPNs offer the benefit of point-to-point leased lines, and they enable remote access, both by employees and by any others who have been registered with the VPN server. For example, if customers or vendors are registered with the VPN server, they can use the VPN from their own sites. Figure 16 shows three tunnels: one supports a point-to-point connection between the Atlanta and Chicago sites and the other two support remote connections.

Microsoft has fostered the popularity of VPNs by including VPN support in Windows. All versions of Microsoft Windows have the capability of working as VPN clients. Computers running Windows Server can operate as VPN servers.

FlexTime uses a VPN. Currently, its software can only be accessed via a LAN. But Kelly, Neil, and key employees need to be able to access that software from home

Figure 16
WAN Using VPN

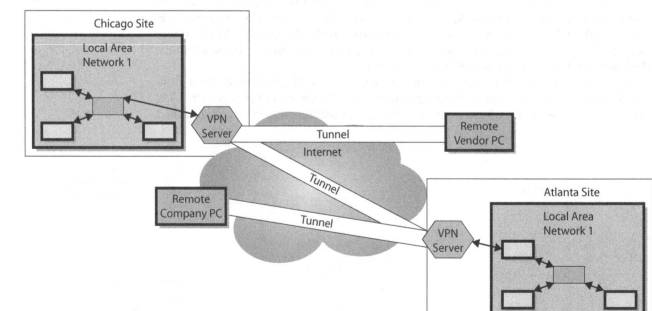

or from another remote location. Accordingly, FlexTime has set up a VPN. Remote users sign on to the VPN, and then they can work as if they were using a computer that is directly connected to the FlexTime LAN.

FlexTime could continue using the VPN in this way and not move to a thin-client application. However, it would still have the burden of installing and maintaining thick clients on user computers, and Neil wants to eliminate that burden. Furthermore, if it moved to a thin client, customers could access the FlexTime system using their browsers.

Firewalls

A **firewall** is a computing device that prevents unauthorized network access. A firewall can be a special-purpose computer, or it can be a program on a general-purpose computer or on a router.

Organizations normally use multiple firewalls. A **perimeter firewall** sits outside the organizational network; it is the first device that Internet traffic encounters. In addition to perimeter firewalls, some organizations employ **internal firewalls** inside their network. Figure 17 shows the use of a perimeter firewall that protects all of an organization's computers and a second internal firewall that protects a LAN.

A **packet-filtering firewall** examines each part of a message and determines whether to let that part pass. To make this decision, it examines the source address, the destination address(es), and other data.

Packet-filtering firewalls can prohibit outsiders from starting a session with any user behind the firewall. They can also disallow traffic from particular sites, such as known hacker addresses. They also can prohibit traffic from legitimate, but unwanted, addresses, such as competitors' computers. Firewalls can filter outbound traffic as well. They can keep employees from accessing specific sites, such as competitors' sites, sites with pornographic material, or popular news sites.

A firewall has an **access control list (ACL)**, which encodes the rules stating which addresses are to be allowed and which are to be prohibited. As a future manager, if you have particular sites with which you do not want your employees to communicate, you can ask your IS department to enforce that limit via the ACL in one or more routers. Most likely, your IS organization has a procedure for making such requests.

Packet-filtering firewalls are the simplest type of firewall. Other firewalls filter on a more sophisticated basis. If you take a data communications class, you will learn about them. For now, just understand that firewalls help to protect organizational computers from unauthorized network access.

No computer should connect to the Internet without firewall protection. Many ISPs provide firewalls for their customers. By nature, these firewalls are generic.

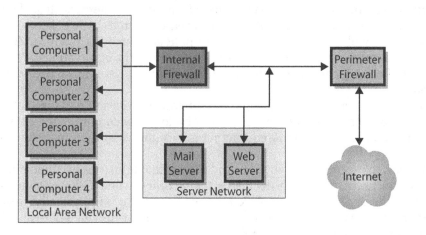

Figure 17
Use of Multiple Firewalls

Large organizations supplement such generic firewalls with their own. Most home routers include firewalls, and Windows XP, Vista, and Windows 7 have built-in firewalls as well. Third parties such as Norton and Symantec also license firewall products.

Q7 2021?

It can't last. Today's Internet access, that is. Right now you pay a fixed amount, say $35 to your ISP for Internet access. You can read just three emails a month, or you can download 1,000 movies a month; either way, you pay the same $35. But, that charging scheme just can't last; it's just too juicy a target. By 2021, ISPs will have figured out some way to charge based on the number of bits you transfer. So, enjoy it while you can.

State governments will find a way to get in on the Internet, too. Right now, in most states, businesses and individuals are legally required to pay taxes on goods they buy from out-of-state, over the Internet. But few do. States would like to require the sellers to collect the tax, but a 1992 U.S. Supreme Court ruling prohibits states from forcing a business to collect sales tax unless the business has a physical presence in that state. So, as long as you pick vendors that don't have facilities in your state, you can get away with paying no state sales tax for online purchases.

Like flat-rate Internet access, this just can't last. In fact, as of 2009, 22 states had enacted legislation to conform to a state-developed program called the Streamlined Sales Tax Project. This project requires vendors to collect taxes on behalf of the state in which the purchaser resides. In addition to the 22 core states, another 20 or so states have laws that provide some degree of compliance with this project. So, by 2021 it's a safe bet you'll be paying state taxes on Internet purchases.

On the technology front, by 2021 everything will be connected to everything, everywhere, and everything will be interconnected. Today, most companies have a phone system that is separate from their computer networks. Employees get email and instant messaging (IM) on their computers and telephone messages over the phone.

But such ubiquitous connectivity means more than better IM. **Remote access systems** provide computer-based activity or action at a distance. By enabling action at a distance, remote access systems save time and travel expense and make the skills and abilities of an expert available in places where he or she is not physically located.

Today, remote access systems include **telediagnosis**, which is used by health care professionals to provide expertise in rural or remote areas. **Telesurgery** uses telecommunications to link surgeons to robotic equipment at distant locations. In 2001, Dr. Jacques Marescaux, located in New York City, performed the first trans-Atlantic surgery when he successfully operated on a patient in Strasbourg, France.

Other uses for remote systems include **telelaw enforcement**, such as the RedFlex system that uses cameras and motion-sensing equipment to issue tickets for red-light and speeding violations. The RedFlex Group, headquartered in South Melbourne, Victoria, Australia, earns 87 percent of its revenue from traffic violations in the United States. It offers a turn-key traffic-citation information system that includes all five components.

Many remote systems are designed to provide services in dangerous locations, such as robots that clean nuclear reactors or biologically contaminated sites. Drones and other unoccupied military equipment are examples of remote systems used in war zones.

By 2021, tele-action will move beyond high-value industries like medicine. As the cost of teledistance technology decreases, tele-action will benefit lower-value services. Why does the world's best figure skating coach need to be physically present at a skater's practice? Why can't the world's best ski instructor provide high-value instruction to skiers on mountains all over the world?

Tele-action also reduces the value of local mediocrity. The claim "Well, I'm not the best, but at least I'm here" loses value in a tele-action world. In 1990, when former Secretary of Labor Robert Reich wrote *The Work of Nations*,[1] he could sensibly claim that those who provide routine face-to-face services are exempt from the dangers of off-shoring. That claim loses validity in the tele-action world.

However, the need for local support staff increases with tele-action. The remote hospital may not need its own mediocre heart surgeon, but it will need staff who can prepare the patient for surgery; it will need a local anesthesiologist, and it will need local nurses. This is also true of a remote figure skating coach. Someone needs to be on-scene.

Finally, tele-action increases the value of robotics. Someone needs to design, build, market, sell, and support the machines that are on the other end of the expert's action. If the value of the expert increases, so, too, does the value of the robot.

[1]Reich, Robert. *Work of Nations: Preparing Ourselves for 21st Century Capitalism.* Vintage Books: New York, 1992, p. 176.

Guide

Thinking Exponentially Is Not Possible, but . . .

Nathan Myhrvold, the chief scientist at Microsoft Corporation during the 1990s, once said that humans are incapable of thinking exponentially. Instead, when something changes exponentially, we think of the fastest linear change we can imagine and extrapolate from there, as illustrated in the figure on the next page. Myhrvold was writing about the exponential growth of magnetic storage. His point was that no one could then imagine how much growth there would be in magnetic storage and what we would do with it.

This limitation pertains equally well to the growth of computer network phenomena. We have witnessed exponential growth in a number of areas: the number of Internet connections, the number of Web pages, and the amount of data accessible on the Internet. And, all signs are that this exponential growth isn't over.

You might wonder how this will affect you. Well, suppose you are a product manager for home appliances. When most homes have a wireless network, it will be cheap and easy for appliances to talk to one another. When that day arrives, what happens to your existing product line? Will the competition's talking appliances take away your market share? However, talking appliances may not satisfy a real need. If a toaster and a coffee pot have nothing to say to each other, you'll be wasting money to create them.

Every business, every organization, needs to be thinking about the ubiquitous and cheap connectivity that is growing exponentially. What are the new opportunities? What are the new threats? How will our competition react? How should we position ourselves? How should we

respond? As you consider these questions, keep in mind that because humans cannot think exponentially, we're all just guessing.

So what can we do to better anticipate changes brought by exponential phenomena? For one, understand that technology does not drive people to do things they've never done before, no matter how much the technologists suggest it might. (Just because we *can do* something does not mean anyone will *want to do* that something.)

Social progress occurs in small, evolutionary, adaptive steps. Right now, for example, if you want to watch a movie with someone, you both need to be in the same room. It needn't be that way. Using data communications, several people can watch the same movie, at the same time, together, but not in the same location. They can have an open audio line to make comments to each other during the movie or even have a Web cam so they can see each other watching the same movie. That sounds like something people might want to do—it's an outgrowth of what people are already doing.

However, emerging network technology enables my dry cleaner to notify me the minute my clothes are ready. Do I want to know? How much do I care to know that my clothes are ready Monday at 1:45 rather than sometime after 4:00 on Tuesday? In truth, I don't care. Such technology does not solve a problem that I have.

So, even if technology enables a capability, that possibility doesn't mean that anyone wants that capability. People want to do what they're already doing, but more easily; they want to solve problems that they already have.

Another response to exponential growth is to hedge your bets. If you can't know the outcome of an exponential phenomenon, don't commit to one direction. Position yourself to move as soon as the direction is clear. Develop a few talking appliances, position your organization to develop more, but wait for a clear sign of market acceptance before going all out.

Finally, notice in the exponential curve that the larger the distance between Now and The Future, the larger the error. In fact, the error increases exponentially with the length of the prediction. So, if you hear that the market for talking kitchen appliances will reach $1 billion in 1 year, assign that statement a certain level of doubt. However, if you hear that it will reach $1 billion in 5 years, assign that statement an exponentially greater level of doubt. ■

Discussion Questions

1. In your own words, explain the meaning of the claim that no one can think exponentially. Do you agree with this claim?

2. Describe a phenomenon besides connectivity or magnetic memory that you believe is increasing exponentially. Explain why it is difficult to predict the consequences of this phenomenon in 3 years.

3. To what extent do you think technology is responsible for the growth in the number of news sources? On balance, do you think having many news sources of varying quality is better than having just a few high-quality ones?

4. List three products or services, such as group movie viewing, that could dramatically change because of increased connectivity. Do not include movie viewing.

5. Rate your answers to question 4 in terms of how closely they fit with problems that people have today.

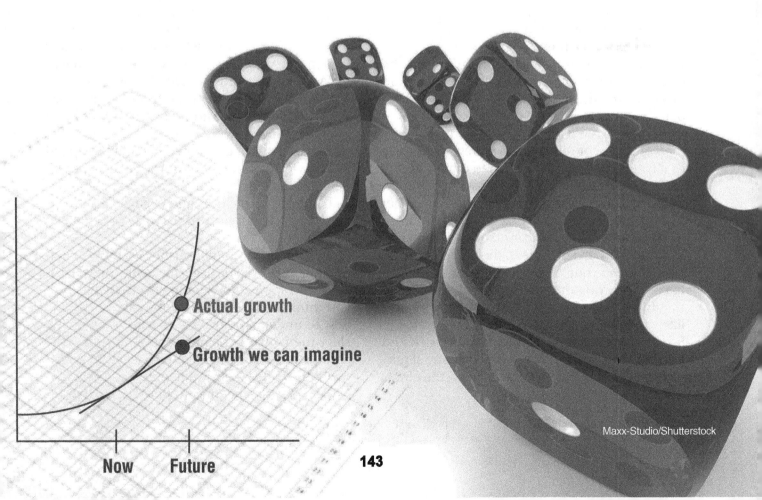

Actual growth

Growth we can imagine

Now   Future

Guide

Human Networks Matter More

In case you missed it, *Six Degrees of Separation* is a play by John Guare that was made into a movie starring Stockard Channing and Donald Sutherland. The title is related to the idea, originated by the Hungarian writer Frigyes Karinthy, that everyone on earth is connected to everyone else by five (Karinthy) or six (Guare) people.[2] For example, according to the theory, you are connected to Eminem by no more than five or six people, because you know someone who knows someone, who knows someone, and so on. By the same theory, you are also connected to a Siberian seal hunter. Today, in fact, with the Internet, the number may be closer to three people than to five or six, but, in any case, the theory points out the importance of human networks.

Suppose you want to meet your university's president. The president has a secretary who acts as a gatekeeper. If you walk up to that secretary and say, "I'd like a half an hour with President Jones," you're likely to be palmed off to some other university administrator. What else can you do?

If you are connected to everyone on the planet by no more than six degrees, then surely you are connected to your president in fewer steps. Perhaps you play on the tennis team, and you know that the president plays tennis. In that case, it is likely that the tennis coach knows the president. So, arrange a tennis match with your coach and the president. Voilà! You have your meeting. It may even be better to have the meeting on the tennis court than in the president's office.

The problem with the six-degree theory, as Stockard Channing said so eloquently, is that even though those six people do exist, we don't know who they are. Even worse, we often don't know who the person is with whom we want to connect. For example, there is someone, right now who knows someone who has a job for which you are perfectly suited. Unfortunately, you don't know the name of that person.

It doesn't stop when you get your job, either. When you have a problem at work, like the need to understand the basics of TCP/IP, there is someone who knows exactly how to help you. You, however, don't know who that is.

Accordingly, most successful professionals consistently build personal human networks. They use Facebook and LinkedIn to build and maintain their networks because they know that somewhere there is someone whom they need to know or will need to know. They also meet people at professional and social situations, collect and pass out cards, and engage in pleasant conversation (all part of a social protocol) to expand their networks.

You are undoubtedly using Facebook right now. You may even be using LinkedIn. But you can use these applications more effectively if you think about the power of weak ties. To understand weak ties, consider the network diagram above. Assume that each line represents a relationship between two people. Notice that the people in your

○ People in Accounting
● People in Your Department

---

[2]See "The Third Link" in Albert Laszlo Barabasi's book *Linked* (New York: Perseus Publishing, 2002) for background on this theory.
[3]See "The Third Link" in Albert Laszlo Barabasi's book *Linked* (New York: Perseus Publishing).

department tend to know each other, and the people in the accounting department also tend to know each other. That's typical.

Now suppose you are at the weekly employee after-hours party and you have an opportunity to introduce yourself either to Linda or Eileen. Setting aside personal considerations, thinking just about network building, which person should you meet?

If you introduce yourself to Linda, you shorten your pathway to her from two steps to one and your pathway to Shawna from three to two. You do not open up any new channels because you already have them to the people in your floor.

However, if you introduce yourself to Eileen, you open up an entirely new network of acquaintances. So, considering just network building, you use your time better by meeting Eileen and other people who are not part of your current circle. It opens up many more possibilities.

The connection from you to Eileen is called a weak tie in social network theory,[3] and such links are crucial in connecting you to everyone in six degrees. *In general, the people you know the least contribute the most to your network.* This phenomenon is true whether your network is face-to-face or virtual, like LinkedIn.

This concept is simple, but you'd be surprised by how few people pay attention to it. At most company events, everyone talks with the people they know, and, if the purpose of the function is to have fun, then that behavior makes sense. In truth, however, no business social function exists for having fun, regardless of what people say. Business functions exist for business reasons, and you can use them to create and expand networks. Given that time is always limited, you may as well use such functions efficiently. ■

Discussion Questions

1. Determine the shortest path from you to your university's president. How many links does it have?

2. Give an example of a network to which you belong that is like your department in the figure on the preceding page. Sketch a diagram of who knows whom for six or so members of that group.

3. Recall a recent social situation and identify two people, one of whom could have played the role of Linda (someone in your group whom you do not know) and one of whom could have played the role of Eileen (someone in a different group whom you do not know). How could you have introduced yourself to either person?

4. Does it seem too contrived and calculating to think about your social relationships in this way? Even if you do not approach relationships like this, are you surprised to think that others do? Under what circumstances does this kind of analysis seem appropriate, and when does it seem inappropriate?

5. Consider the phrase, "It's not what you know, it's whom you know that matters." Relate this phrase to the diagram. Under what circumstances is this likely to be true? When is it false?

6. Describe how you can apply the principle "The people you know the least contribute the most to your network" to your use of Facebook or LinkedIn during a search for a job.

Active Review

Use this Active Review to verify that you understand the ideas and concepts that answer the chapter's study questions.

Q1 What is a computer network?

Define *computer network.* Explain the differences among LANs, WANs, internets, and the Internet. Describe the purpose of a protocol.

Q2 What are the components of a LAN?

Explain the key distinction of a LAN. Describe the purpose of each component in Figure 2. Describe the placement of switches in a multistory building. Explain when optical fiber cables are used for a LAN. Define *IEEE 802.3* and *802.11* and explain how they differ.

Q3 What are the alternatives for connecting to a WAN?

Explain why your connection to an ISP is a WAN and not a LAN. Name three functions of an ISP. Describe the purpose of a modem. Explain three ways you can connect to the Internet. Describe the differences among DSL, cable, and WAN wireless alternatives.

Q4 What are the fundamental concepts you should know about the Internet?

Explain the statement, "The Internet is an internet." Define *TCP/IP* and name its layers. Explain, in general terms, the purpose of each layer. Explain the purpose of HTTP, HTTPS, SMTP, and FTP. Explain why TCP is said to provide *reliable internet transport.* Define *IP, packet,* and *router.* Explain why IP is said to provide internet routing. Describe the advantages of private and public IP addresses. List the purposes of the LAN device. Explain, in general terms, how you would obtain a domain name. Describe the relationship between domain names and public IP addresses. Define *URL.*

Q5 What processing occurs on a typical Web server?

Explain what a Web storefront is. Define *three-tier architecture* and name and describe each tier. Explain the function of a Web page, a Web server, and a commerce server. Explain the purpose of a Web farm. Explain the function of each tier in Figure 11 as the pages in Figures 10 and 12 are processed. Define *HTML* and explain its purpose. Define *href* and *attribute.* Explain the purpose of XML, Flash, Silverlight, and HTML 5.

Q6 How do organizations benefit from virtual private networks (VPNs) and firewalls?

Describe the problem that a VPN solves. Use Figure 15 to explain one way that a VPN is set up and used. Define *tunnel.* Describe how encryption is used in a VPN. Explain why a Windows user does not need to license or install other software to use a VPN. Define *firewall.* Explain the role for each firewall in Figure 16. Describe how a manager might ask to shut off access to or from a particular site.

Q7 2021?

Explain how ISP charges may change by 2021. Explain how payments for state taxes will change. Provide examples of how business communications today are not integrated. Define *remote access system* and give four examples. Explain how such systems create new opportunities for you.

 Key Terms and Concepts

10/100/1000 Ethernet	Attribute	Digital subscriber line (DSL)
Access control list (ACL)	Bluetooth	Domain name
Access point	Broadband	DSL modem
Analog signal	Cable modem	Ethernet
Asymmetric digital subscriber lines (ADSL)	Commerce server	EVDO
	Database tier	Firewall

Flash
FTP (File Transfer Protocol)
Href
HSDPA
HTML (Hypertext Markup Language)
HTTP (Hypertext Transport Protocol)
HTTPS
Hyperlinks
ICANN (Internet Corporation for Assigned Names and Numbers)
IEEE 802.3
IEEE 802.11
IEEE 802.16
Internal firewall
internet
Internet service provider (ISP)
Intranet
IP (Internet Protocol)
IP address
IPv4
IPv6
LAN device

Local area network (LAN)
Modem
Narrowband
Network
Network interface card (NIC)
Onboard NIC
Optical fiber cables
Packet
Packet-filtering firewall
Perimeter firewall
Private IP address
Problem of the last mile
Protocol
Public IP Address
Remote access system
Router
Server tier
Silverlight
SMTP (Simple Mail Transfer Protocol)
Small office/home office (SOHO)
Switch
Symmetrical digital subscriber lines (SDSL)
Tag

The Internet
TCP (Transmission Control Protocol)
TCP/IP Protocol (TCP/IP) architecture
Telediagnosis
Telelaw enforcement
Telesurgery
Three-tier architecture
Tunnel
URL (Uniform Resource Locator)
User tier
Unshielded twisted pair (UTP) cable
Virtual private network (VPN)
WAN wireless
Wide area network (WAN)
Web
Web farm
Web page
Web server
WiMax
Wireless NIC (WNIC)
XML (eXtensible Markup Language)

▬▬ Using Your Knowledge

1. Suppose you manage a group of seven employees in a small business. Each of your employees wants to be connected to the Internet. Consider two alternatives:

   Alternative A: Each employee has his or her own modem and connects individually to the Internet.

   Alternative B: The employees' computers are connected using a LAN, and the network uses a single modem to connect to the Internet.

   a. Sketch the equipment and lines required for each alternative.

   b. Explain the actions you need to take to create each alternative.

   c. Compare the alternatives using the criteria in Figure 16.

   d. Which of these two alternatives do you recommend?

2. Suppose that you have a consulting practice implementing LANs for fraternities and sororities on your campus.

   a. Consider a fraternity house. Explain how a LAN could be used to connect all of the computers in the house. Would you recommend an Ethernet LAN, an 802.11 LAN, or a combination? Justify your answer.

   b. This chapter did not provide enough information for you to determine how many switches the fraternity house might need. However, in general terms, describe how the fraternity could use a multiple-switch system.

   c. Considering the connection to the Internet, would you recommend that the fraternity house use a DSL modem, a cable modem, or WAN wireless? Although you can rule out at least one of these alternatives with the knowledge you already have, what additional information do you need in order to make a specific recommendation?

   d. Should you develop a standard package solution for each of your customers? What advantages accrue from a standard solution? What are the disadvantages?

3. Consider Neil's problem at FlexTime. He wants to carefully review the $175,000 network infrastructure proposal and eliminate any equipment or services that he can. At the same time, while the building is being remodeled the walls will be open, and this will be the best possible time to add cabling and any other equipment that FlexTime may eventually need.

   Assume that you have Neil's task. How would you proceed? We don't have enough information to analyze that proposal in detail. Instead, answer the following questions that concern how Neil might go about making this analysis.

   a. Describe FlexTime equipment that is likely to have a wired connection to a LAN.

b. Describe FlexTime equipment that is likely to have a wireless connection to a LAN.

c. Describe customer equipment that is likely to have a wireless connection to a FlexTime LAN.

d. Neil (and you) need to plan for the future. How are your answers to parts a–c likely to change in the next 5 years? In the next 10 years?

e. Describe a process for determining the total wireless demand for a room that contains 50 spinning bicycles.

f. Using the knowledge you have gained from this chapter, list all of the equipment and cabling that FlexTime will need for their new building. Just list equipment categories; you do not have sufficient information to specify particular brands or models of equipment.

g. Suppose Neil receives three different bids for the network infrastructure. Does he necessarily choose the lowest-cost one? Why or why not? What process should Neil use to analyze the three proposals?

Collaboration Exercise

Collaborate with students on the following exercise. In particular, consider using Google Docs, Windows Live SkyDrive, Microsoft SharePoint, or some other collaboration tool.

Consider the information technology skills and needs of your parents, relatives, family friends, and others in the Baby Boom generation. Although you may not know it, you possess many skills that generation wants but does not have. You know how to text chat, how to download music from iTunes, how to buy and sell items on eBay, how to use Craigslist, and how to use a PDA, an iPhone, and so forth. You probably can even run the navigation system in your parents' car.

1. Thinking about Baby Boomers whom you know, brainstorm with your team the skills that you possess that they do not. Consider all of the items just described and others that come to mind. If you have not read Using MIS InClass earlier in the chapter, do so now. Make a common team list of all those skills.

2. Interview, survey, or informally discuss the items on your list in part 1 with your parents and other Baby Boomers. As a team, determine the five most frustrating and important skills that these people do not possess.

3. The Baby Boomer market has both money and time, but not as much information technology capability as they need, and they do not like it.

   With your team, brainstorm products that you could sell to this market that would address the Baby Boomers' techno-ignorance. For example, you might create a video of necessary skills, or you might provide a consulting service setting up Microsoft Home Server computers. Consider other ideas and describe them as specifically as you can. You should consider at least five different product concepts.

4. Develop sales material that describes your services, the benefits they provide, and why your target market should buy those products. Try your sales pitch on friends and family.

5. How viable is your concept? Do you think you can make money with these products? If so, summarize an implementation plan. If not, explain why not.

Case Study

Keeping Up with Wireless

Data communications technology is one of the fastest-changing technologies, if not *the* fastest changing, in all of IT. Substantial portions of the knowledge you gain from this chapter will be obsolete within the first 5 years of your career. Unfortunately, we do not know which portions that will be.

Consider the example of WAN wireless technology. Three protocol standards are in competition: EVDO, HSDPA, and WiMax. Because WiMax has the greatest potential performance, we will consider it further in this case.

Craig McCaw built one of the world's first cellular networks in the early 1980s and brought cell phones to the masses. In the 1990s, he sold his company to AT&T for $11.5 billion. In 2003, McCaw started a new venture, Clearwire, by buying rights to technology based on WiMax to address what is called the "problem of the last mile." Will WiMax defeat the other WAN wireless technologies? We do not know. But, when someone with McCaw's knowledge, experience, and wealth starts a new venture based on that new technology, we should pay attention.

To begin, what is the **problem of the last mile**? The bottleneck on data communications into homes, and into smaller businesses, is the last mile. Fast optical fiber transmission lines lie in the street in front of your apartment or office; the problem is getting that capacity into the building and to your computer or TV. Digging up the street and backyard of every residence and small business to install optical fiber is not an affordable proposition. Even if that could be done, such infrastructure cannot be used by mobile devices. You cannot watch a downloaded movie on a commuter train using an optical fiber line.

The WiMax standard, **IEEE 802.16**, could be implemented by many companies, but only if those companies own wireless frequencies for data transmission. Hence the interest by people like McCaw and other cellular players such as Sprint. The WiMax standard includes two usage models: *fixed* and *mobile*. The former is akin to LAN wireless in existence today; mobile access allows users to move around, as they do with cell phones, staying connected.

On December 1, 2008, Clearwire merged with Sprint Nextel and received a $3.2 billion outside investment. In the process, Clearwire gained access to Sprint Nextel's spectrum holdings (authority to use certain frequencies for cellular signals). The merged company is called Clearwire and the products are marketed as Sprint Xohm.

Clearwire already provides fixed use in many cities. As of June 2010, mobile WiMax services were available only in selected cities, but roll out to many more cities is planned in the near future.

Questions

1. Read the "Thinking Exponentially" Guide from earlier in the chapter. Keeping the principles of that guide in mind, list five possible commercial applications for mobile WiMax. Consider applications that necessitate mobility.

2. Evaluate each of the possible applications in your answer to question 1. Select the three most promising applications and justify your selection.

3. Clearwire went public in March 2007 at an initial price of $27.25. As of April 2010, the price was $8.00. Go online and research the company to find out what happened to its share price. Explain why its share price has dropped.

4. AT&T and T-Mobile have endorsed HSDPA, but it does not have the same potential maximum transmission rates. Rather than jump on the WiMax bandwagon, those companies plan to deploy a different technology called Long Term Evolution (LTE). Search the Web for LTE versus WiMax comparisons and compare and contrast these two technologies.

5. Where will this end? On which of these technologies would you be willing to invest $100 million? Why?

Application Exercises

1. Numerous Web sites are available that will test your Internet data communications speed. You can find one good site at *www.speakeasy.net/speedtest/*. (If that site is no longer active, Google or Bing "What is my Internet speed?" to find another speed-testing site. Use it.)

   a. While connected to your university's network, go to Speakeasy and test your speed against servers in Seattle, New York City, and Atlanta. Compute your average upload and download speeds. Compare your speed to the speeds listed in Figure 4.

   b. Go home, or to a public wireless site, and run the Speakeasy test again. Compute your average upload and download speeds. Compare your speed to those listed in Figure 4. If you are performing this test at home, are you getting the performance you are paying for?

   c. Contact a friend or relative in another state. Ask him or her to run the Speakeasy test against those same three cities.

   d. Compare the results in parts a–c. What conclusion, if any, can you make from these tests?

2. Suppose you work for a company that installs computer networks. Assume that you have been given the task of creating spreadsheets to generate cost estimates.

   a. Create a spreadsheet to estimate hardware costs. Assume that the user of the spreadsheet will enter the number of pieces of equipment and the standard cost for each type of equipment. Assume that the networks can include the following components: NIC cards; WNIC cards; wireless access points; switches of two types, one faster, one slower, at two different prices; and routers. Also assume that the company will use both UTP and optical fiber cable and that prices for cable are stated as per foot. Use the network in Figure 2 as an example.

   b. Modify your spreadsheet to include labor costs. Assume there is a fixed cost for the installation of each type of equipment and a per foot cost for the installation of cable.

   c. Give an example of how you might use this spreadsheet for planning network installations. Explain how you could adapt this spreadsheet for project tracking and billing purposes.

Using IS for Competitive Advantage Opener

Using IS for Competitive Advantage

Fox Lake Country Club is a private golf and tennis club located in the suburbs of Hartford, Connecticut. Founded in 1982, the club includes two 18-hole golf courses, 14 tennis courts, a swimming pool, a restaurant, meeting rooms, and a pro shop that sells golf and tennis gear and clothing. The golf courses, designed by a leading golf professional, are beautiful and challenging. Indeed, all of the Fox Lake grounds are picturesque and meticulously maintained by the groundskeeping staff.

All of this beauty is not cheap; memberships cost $75,000, and the monthly fee is $425. The club's bylaws allow for up to 1,500 club memberships. Like most such organizations, member initiation fees are invested and the proceeds pay mortgages on the club's facilities as well as maintenance expenses on capital equipment. Monthly membership charges pay operational expenses, including salaries for Fox Lake's 35 full-time employees and hourly wages for about 100 seasonal workers. The restaurant and pro shop are intended to be profit-generating centers for the club.

Fox Lake employs golf and tennis professionals as subcontractors. These professionals staff the pro shop and activity centers for a few hours each week. They spend the bulk of their time giving private lessons to club members.

The recent recession hit Fox Lake hard. For the first time in 30 years, in December 2008 the club had open memberships. As of 2010, all the memberships have been sold, but the waiting list is months long, rather than years long, as it was before 2008. Further, both the pro shop and the restaurant lost money in 2009 and 2010.

In response to these financial challenges, the club's board of directors asked the club's general manager, Jeff Lloyd, to seek additional sources of revenue. Because of the beauty of its grounds, Fox Lake had been used as the site of several weddings, and Jeff developed a business plan to expand these occasional events into a wedding-hosting business. Fox Lake is gorgeous in the summer, of course, but even in the winter, when the grounds are covered with snow, the scene is lovely, and he reasoned that weddings and receptions could provide year-round revenue.

With the board's approval, Jeff hired Anne Foster to develop this new business. At the time, Foster was working as a successful independent wedding planner, and she wanted an opportunity to expand her business. It seemed to be a good match; Fox Lake provided her a beautiful venue and greater opportunity for more events, and her knowledge of the industry as well her contacts with vendors and potential clients jump-started Fox Lake into the wedding events business.

Alamy Images

Chapter 5 (original Chapter 7 of "Using MIS, 4/e")

Enterprise Systems

Enterprise Systems

"Mike, what are you telling me?"

Anne Foster struggles to keep her voice down as she talks with Mike Stone, the facilities manager.

"I'm saying that we've got to do the earthquake retrofit on the Oak Room."

"That's fine, Mike. Do it next winter. I'll work around it."

"Anne, that won't work. It's got to be done by November 1. The insurance company said so."

"Look, I'm a wedding planner—I plan weddings, in fact I've already got four of them for the first two weeks of October. The good news is that I only need the Oak Room for one."

"I'm sorry, Anne. I really am. I thought you knew."

"Knew? Would I plan a wedding that we can't do? What am I supposed to do, go back to the bride and say, 'Hey, change of plans, you'll have to do your wedding reception elsewhere!'"

"Sorry, but that's the way it is."

"Oh, no, Mike. You might be a good facilities manager; but you don't know anything about brides!" Anger and desperation fill her voice.

"Well, we can get 150 people into the Maple Suite, if we open the walls and set tables outside."

"Oh, great!!! Wonderful!!!! I've got two problems with that, Mike: One, what if the weather is bad? What if it's too cold to open the walls? But that's nothing compared to my second problem."

"Let's hear it."

"How old is your daughter, Mike?"

"Three."

"OK, I'll accept that you just don't get it. Our bride is having her special day. She and her betrothed sent out their save-the-date cards. In fact, they've even sent out their invitations. To 185 people, Mike! That's 185, not 150 if the weather is good."

"Anne, I scheduled this REQUIRED maintenance 6 months ago."

"Maybe so, Mike, but nobody told ME."

"OK, Anne. Imagine this: Let's say we put off this maintenance and, God forbid, we have an earthquake. You know what the lawyers would say if we knew we needed the work but didn't do it just for the revenue of another 35 people?"

"Lawyers!!!" Anne shouts, "You want to see lawyers???? Not only is the bride's father a partner in the biggest firm in Hartford, he is also a founding member of Fox Lake Country Club and a past president of the board."

"Then I'm sure he'll understand."

"Mike, you're an idiot."

"Let's go talk to Jeff . . . "

Study Questions

Q1 How do information systems vary by scope?

Q2 When are information silos a problem?

Q3 How do enterprise information systems eliminate silos?

Q4 How do CRM, ERP, and EAI support enterprise processes?

Q5 What are the elements of an ERP system?

Q6 How do the major ERP vendors compare?

Q7 What are the challenges when implementing new enterprise systems?

Q8 2021?

In this chapter, we will explore information systems within an organization. We will investigate the types and scope of information systems in organizations. We will also discuss *information silos* that occur with departmental information systems, explain why such silos can be problematic, and show how three types of enterprise systems can eliminate those problems. Enterprise resource planning (ERP) systems play a particularly important role in organizations today, and we will discuss their purpose and components and the major ERP vendors. Finally, we will wrap up the chapter by surveying the major challenges that occur when implementing enterprise systems and discussing future technology (2021) and enterprise systems in the cloud.

Q1 How Do Information Systems Vary by Scope?

Something is amiss at the Fox Lake Country Club. Months ago, the facilities department scheduled needed maintenance on the club's buildings. The wedding events group, unaware of this schedule, planned a wedding and reception that conflicts with the maintenance activity. Facilities claims that the maintenance cannot be delayed because of a directive from Fox Lake's insurance company. Eventually, Fox Lake will solve this problem. However, Fox Lake management will be in turmoil before a solution is found and implemented, and the solution will be so expensive that it exceeds the profits from wedding events for the second half of that year.

Fundamentally, this problem was caused by the existence of **information silos**, a condition that exists when data are isolated in separated information systems. (Isolated systems are referred to as *silos* because when drawn in diagrams they appear as long vertical columns . . . like silos.) Fox Lake's problem occurred because wedding events had one version of room-scheduling data and facilities had a second version of that same data. The two versions, each in their own silo, conflicted, but no one knew it.

In this chapter, we will discuss the problems of such silos and the role of enterprise information systems in eliminating them. To begin that discussion, consider the scope of the information systems summarized in Figure 1. In this figure, as you move from the top to the bottom, the scope of information systems widens to include more people and organizations.

Personal Information Systems

Personal information systems are used by a single individual. The contact manager in your iPhone or in your email account is an example of a personal information system. Because such systems have only one user, procedures are simple and probably not documented or formalized in any way.

You and the other members of your organization may duplicate data; many of you may have phone numbers and email addresses for the same people, but such data duplication is not normally important. When phone numbers change, for example, you all make that change in your own way, in your own time, without any problem.

It is easy to manage change to personal information systems. If you switch email from, say, MSN to Google, you'll have to move your contact list from one vendor to the other, and you'll have to inform your correspondents of your new address, but you control the timing of that change. Because you will be the sole user of the new system, if new procedures are required only you need to adapt. And, if there are problems, you can solve them yourself.

Scope	Fox Lake Example	Characteristics
Personal	Contact manager	Single user; procedures informal; problems isolated; data duplication among employees; easy to manage change
Workgroup	Scheduling of groundskeeping	10 to 100 of users; procedures understood within group; problem solutions within group; data duplication among departments; somewhat difficult to change
Enterprise	Charging of membership fees	100 to 1000s of users; procedures formalized; problem solutions affect enterprise; data duplication minimized; very difficult to change
Interenterprise	Ordering of restaurant supplies from suppliers	1000s of users; procedures formalized; problem solutions affect multiple organizations; controlled data duplication; difficult to change; interorganization IS required

Figure 1
Scope of Information Systems

Workgroup Information Systems

A **workgroup information system** is an information system that is shared by a group of people for a particular purpose. At Fox Lake, the groundskeepers (personnel who maintain the golf courses and club lawns and gardens) share a workgroup information system for scheduling employees and tasks.

Workgroup information systems that support a particular department are sometimes called **departmental information systems**. An example is the accounts payable system that is used by the accounts payable department. Other workgroup information systems support a particular business function and are called **functional information systems**. An example of a functional system is a Web storefront. Finally, the collaboration information systems are also workgroup information systems.

Workgroup information systems, whether departmental, functional, or collaboration, share the characteristics shown in Figure 1. Typical workgroup systems support 10 to 100 users. The procedures for using them must be understood by all members of the group. Often, procedures are formalized in documentation, and users frequently receive formal training in the use of those procedures.

When problems occur, they almost always can be solved within the group. If accounts payable duplicates the record for a particular supplier, the accounts payable group can make the fix. If the Web storefront has the wrong number of widgets in the inventory database, that count can be fixed within the storefront group.

(Notice, by the way, that the *consequences* of a problem are not isolated to the group. Because the workgroup exists to provide a service to the rest of the organization, its problems have consequences throughout the organization. The *fix* to the problem can be usually obtained within the group, however.)

Two or more workgroups within an organization can duplicate data, and such duplication can be very problematic to the organization, as we discuss in Q2. Finally, because workgroup information systems involve many users, changing them is more difficult than changing personal information systems. All the members of the workgroup need to be informed and trained on procedure changes when the system is altered.

157

Enterprise Information Systems

Enterprise information systems are information systems that span an organization and support activities in multiple departments. At Fox Lake, all customer charges are recorded against membership accounts; no cash or credit card transactions are allowed. The restaurant, the golf course, the pro shop, and the wedding events departments all use the same enterprise information system to record sales.

Enterprise information systems typically have hundreds to thousands of users. Procedures are formalized and extensively documented; users undergo formal procedure training. Sometimes enterprise systems include categories of procedures, and users are defined according to levels of expertise with the system as well as by level of security authorization.

The solutions to problems in an enterprise system usually involve more than one department. As you will learn in this chapter, a major advantage of enterprise systems is that data duplication is either eliminated altogether or, if it is allowed to exist, changes to duplicated data are carefully managed to maintain consistency.

Because enterprise systems span many departments and involve potentially thousands of users, they are very difficult to change. Changes must be carefully planned, cautiously implemented, and users given considerable training. Sometimes users are given incentives and other inducements to motivate them to change.

The Ethics Guide in this chapter demonstrates how one person's actions can affect an entire company.

We will discuss the most common examples of enterprise information systems in Q4 and the problems of implementing and changing these systems in Q7.

Interenterprise Information Systems

Interenterprise information systems are information systems that are shared by two or more independent organizations. At Fox Lake, the information system that the restaurant uses to order supplies and ingredients from its suppliers is an interorganizational system. Because such systems are used by employees of different organizations, procedures are formalized and user training is mandatory.

Such systems typically involve thousands of users, and solutions to problems require cooperation among different, usually independently owned, organizations. Problems are resolved by meeting, by contract, and sometimes by litigation.

Data are often duplicated between organizations, but such duplication is carefully managed. Because of the wide span, complexity, and multiple companies, such systems can be exceedingly difficult to change.

Q2 When Are Information Silos a Problem?

As stated, information silos exist when data are isolated in separated information systems. Information silos develop over time, as more and more personal and work-group information systems are implemented. As organizations grow, however, at some point the inevitable duplication of data in such systems will become a source of potentially serious problems.

How Do Information Silos Arise?

No organization plans to create information silos. They arise as a consequence of an organization's growth and increasing use of information systems.

Consider the example of Fox Lake in Figure 2. The wedding events department is new, and Anne, the manager, has been given incentives to grow the business. At the same time, both she and Fox Lake have a reputation to protect, so she wants to grow the business so that Fox Lake weddings and receptions have a superior reputation.

Golf operations has a very different set of goals. Golfing is the primary concern of club members, and the club must provide golfers with accurate tee times (starting

Figure 2
Fox Lake Country Club
Departmental Goals

Figure 2
Fox Lake Country Club
Departmental Goals

times) and with a pleasant golfing experience. The club contracts with professional golfers to teach golf lessons. The pros make most of their income from lessons, and in order to attract and keep quality pros the course needs to give them plenty of business. Other concerns of golf course operations are listed in Figure 2.

The goals of the facilities department are completely different from the other two groups. Facilities is concerned with maintenance for top-level appearance, protection of club assets, solving equipment problems, and so forth. Unlike wedding events or golf operations, facilities generates no revenue; it is all cost. So, the facilities manager is given incentives to carefully manage the facilities budget.

Before continuing, consider the different needs for information systems among these groups. Wedding events is concerned with growth in the number of one-time events. Golf operations is concerned with customer satisfaction and maintaining golf pro instruction. Facilities is concerned with accomplishing needed maintenance tasks on time and within budget and with solving problems quickly and efficiently.

Because of these different orientations, each group will develop information systems of a different character, as shown in Figure 3. Because these systems have

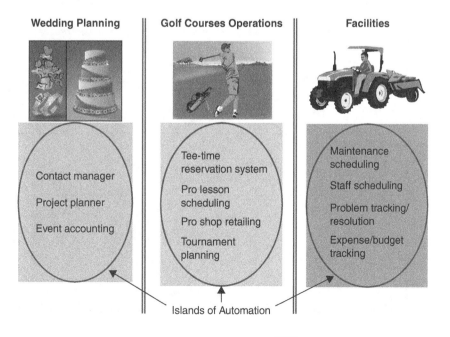

Figure 3
Fox Lake Country Club
Departmental Information
Systems

nearly nothing to do with each other, they can operate as isolated entities for a long time, without problem. In fact, **islands of automation** is another term for information silo; it just means groups of information systems that operate in isolation from one other.

Information silos (or, equivalently, islands of automation) are not a problem until they begin to share data about the same entities. Or, stated differently, until they duplicate data. At that point, they can become quite problematic, as Fox Lake learned when the wedding events department maintained its own copy of room reservation data that duplicated that same data in the facilities department.

What Are Common Departmental Applications?

Before we address the problems that information silos cause, realize that many, many departmental applications and information systems have been developed and are still in use today. Figure 4 lists common departmental applications. Like the departmental systems at Fox Lake, each of those systems was created to support a given department's information-processing needs. They work fine for those departments.

However, even a quick glance at this list indicates that these activities are likely to duplicate data. For example, many of these applications concern customers. Information systems for sales and marketing, operations, manufacturing, and customer service all process their own customer data. At least the first three of those process finished-goods inventory data. They all process order data. Human resources systems duplicate data about employees and personnel, their training, and their availability with other departments.

Even with this cursory review, you can see that such functional applications duplicate large amounts of data and are likely to cause problems.

Figure 4
Common Departmental
Information Systems

Department	Application
Sales and marketing	• Lead generation • Lead tracking • Customer management • Sales forecasting • Product and brand management
Operations	• Order entry • Order management • Finished-goods inventory management
Manufacturing	• Inventory (raw materials, goods-in-process) • Planning • Scheduling • Operations
Customer service	• Order tracking • Account tracking • Customer support and training
Human resources	• Recruiting • Compensation • Assessment • HR Planning
Accounting	• General ledger • Financial reporting • Cost accounting • Accounts receivable • Accounts payable • Cash management • Budgeting • Treasury management

What Problems Do Information Silos Cause?

We have seen one problem of information silos at Fox Lake. Because wedding events, facilities, and golf operations use the same physical structures, they duplicate data about those facilities in their isolated systems. By processing isolated data, their plans can conflict, as they did.

Consider, however, the more complex example in Figure 5. Every day, patients are discharged from hospitals. Think about the numerous departments that need to be notified when that occurs. Doctors issue the discharge order. In response, nurses need to prepare the patient, the pharmacy needs to prepare take-home medications, the kitchen needs to stop making meals for the discharged patient, housekeeping needs to clean the vacated room, and the family needs to be notified to ensure that someone is available to take the patient home. If each of these departments maintains its own island of automation, it will make decisions in isolation from the others. For example, the kitchen will prepare food for patients who have been discharged. Or, families will attempt to visit patients who have been moved to new locations. In short, patients, families, doctors, nurses, and staff will come to believe that "no one seems to know what is going on."

Figure 6 summarizes the problems of the information silos created by isolated information systems. First, data are duplicated, because each application has its own database. If accounting and sales/marketing applications are separated, customer data will be duplicated and may become inconsistent. Changes to customer data made in the sales/marketing application may take days or weeks to reach the accounting application's database. During that period, shipments may reach the customer without delay, but invoices will be sent to the wrong address.

Additionally, when applications are isolated, business processes are disjointed. Suppose a business has a rule that credit orders over $20,000 must be preapproved by the accounts receivable department. If the supporting applications are separated, it will be difficult for the two activities to reconcile their data, and the approval will be slow-to-grant and possibly erroneous.

In the second row of Figure 6, sales and marketing wants to approve a $20,000 order with Ajax. According to the sales and marketing database, Ajax has a current balance of $17,800, so sales requests a total credit amount of $37,800. The accounting database, however, shows Ajax with a balance of $12,300, because the accounts receivable application has credited Ajax for a return of $5,500. According to

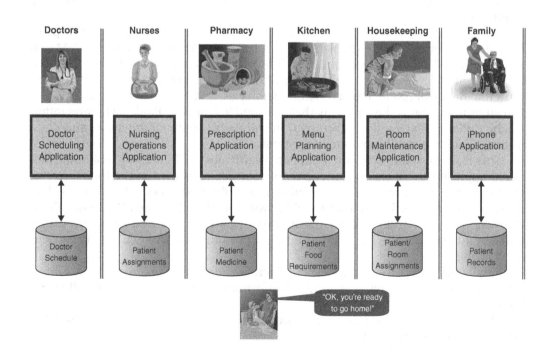

Figure 5

Examples of Islands of Automation at a Hospital

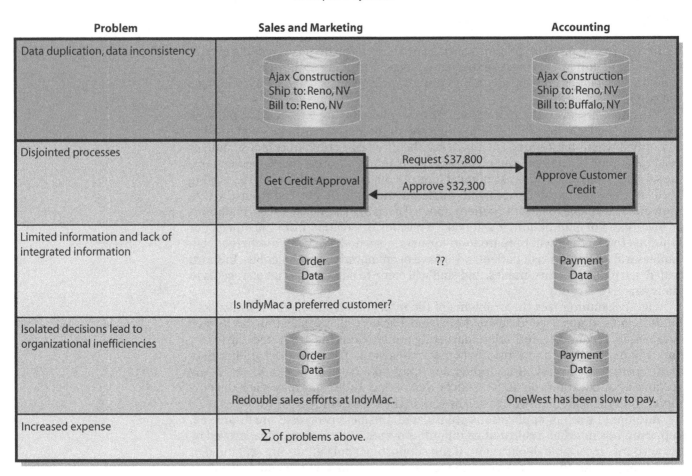

Problem	Sales and Marketing	Accounting
Data duplication, data inconsistency	Ajax Construction Ship to: Reno, NV Bill to: Reno, NV	Ajax Construction Ship to: Reno, NV Bill to: Buffalo, NY
Disjointed processes	Get Credit Approval — Request $37,800 → Approve Customer Credit ← Approve $32,300	
Limited information and lack of integrated information	Order Data ?? Is IndyMac a preferred customer?	Payment Data
Isolated decisions lead to organizational inefficiencies	Order Data Redouble sales efforts at IndyMac.	Payment Data OneWest has been slow to pay.
Increased expense	Σ of problems above.	

Figure 6
Problems Created by
Information Silos

accounting's records, only $32,300 is needed in order to approve the $20,000 order, so that is all they grant. Sales and marketing doesn't understand what to do with a credit approval of $32,300. Was only $14,500 of the order approved? And why that amount? Both departments want to approve the order. It will take numerous emails and phone calls, however, to sort this out. The interacting business processes are disjointed.

A consequence of such disjointed systems is the lack of integrated enterprise information. For example, suppose sales and marketing wants to know if IndyMac is still a preferred customer. Assume that determining a customer's status requires a comparison of order history and payment history data. However, with information silos, that data will reside in two different databases, and, in one of them, IndyMac is known by the name of the company that acquired it, OneWest Bank. Data integration will be difficult. Making the determination will require manual processes and days, when it should be readily answered in seconds.

This leads to the fourth consequence: inefficiency. When using isolated functional applications, decisions are made in isolation. As shown in the fourth row of Figure 6, sales and marketing decided to redouble its sales effort with IndyMac. However, accounting knows that IndyMac was foreclosed by the FDIC and sold to OneWest and that there are far better prospects for increased sales attention. Without integration, the left hand of the organization doesn't know what the right hand is doing.

Finally, information silos can result in increased costs for the organization. Duplicated data, disjointed systems, limited information, and inefficiencies all mean higher costs.

These problems are solved by enterprise information systems, and we consider them for the rest of this chapter.

Q3 How Do Enterprise Information Systems Eliminate Silos?

The fundamental problem of information silos is that data are duplicated in isolated systems. The most obvious fix is to eliminate that duplicated data by storing a single copy of data in a shared database and revising business processes (and applications) to use that database. Another remedy is to allow the duplication, but to manage it to avoid problems. We will discuss both techniques.

An Enterprise System at Fox Lake

Figure 7 shows how the first remedy is applied at Fox Lake. First, a database is created that contains reservations for club facilities. Each department then alters its business processes (and applications) to use the shared database. In this simple example, the only change needed is to develop procedures to check availability before scheduling activities and to record any intended use for shared resources in the database. One or more database applications may need to be developed to enable availability checking.

However, with this solution, each department must be mindful that it is processing a shared resource. For example, prior to the shared database, the facilities department would block out weeks of time on its calendar for building maintenance, much more time than it actually needed. It would then work in maintenance activities during that block in accordance with its own tasks and priorities. If facilities continues this practice, it will needlessly block out wedding events and reduce potential club revenue. With the shared database, facilities needs to schedule specific activities against specific buildings for the minimum necessary blocks of time.

Before we go on, this simple example illustrates a phenomenon that creates difficult management challenges. When the enterprise system is implemented, all the departments that use it must change their business processes. People do not like to change; in fact, unless the benefit of the change is easily recognized, people resist change. However, in some cases, new enterprise systems require departments to change without any obvious benefit *to that department*. In the Fox Lake example, when moving to the system in Figure 7, facilities will need to change its processes for the benefit of wedding events (and for Fox Lake as an enterprise), but for no benefit to itself. Facilities personnel may perceive the new system as a lot of trouble for nothing.

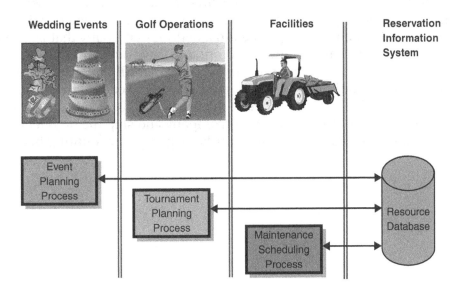

Figure 7
Fox Lake Country Club
Enterprise Reservation System

Ethics Guide

Dialing for Dollars

Suppose you are a salesperson, and your company's CRM forecasts that your quarterly sales will be substantially under quota. You call your best customers to increase sales, but no one is willing to buy more.

Your boss says that it has been a bad quarter for all of the salespeople. It's so bad, in fact, that the vice president of sales has authorized a 20-percent discount on new orders. The only stipulation is that customers must take delivery prior to the end of the quarter so that accounting can book the order. "Start dialing for dollars," she says, "and get what you can. Be creative."

Using your CRM, you identify your top customers and present the discount offer to them. The first customer balks at increasing her inventory, "I just don't think we can sell that much."

"Well," you respond, "how about if we agree to take back any inventory you don't sell next quarter?" (By doing this, you increase your current sales and commission, and you also help your company make its quarterly sales projections. The additional product is likely to come back next quarter, but you think, "Hey, that's then and this is now.")

"OK," she says, "but I want you to stipulate the return option on the purchase order."

You know that you cannot write that on the purchase order because accounting won't book all of the order if you do. So you tell her that you'll send her an email with that stipulation. She increases her order, and accounting books the full amount.

With another customer, you try a second strategy. Instead of offering the discount, you offer the product at full price, but agree to pay a 20-percent credit in the next quarter. That way you can book the full price now. You pitch this offer as follows: "Our marketing department analyzed past sales using our fancy new computer system, and we know that increasing advertising will cause additional sales. So, if you order more product now, next quarter we'll give you 20 percent of the order back to pay for advertising."

In truth, you doubt the customer will spend the money on advertising. Instead, they'll just take the credit and sit on a bigger inventory. That will kill your sales to them next quarter, but you'll solve that problem then.

Even with these additional orders, you're still under quota. In desperation, you decide to sell product to a fictitious company that is "owned" by your brother-in-law. You set up a new account, and when accounting calls your brother-in-law for a credit check he cooperates with your scheme. You then sell $40,000 of product to the fictitious company and ship the product to your brother-in-law's garage. Accounting books the revenue in the quarter, and you have finally made quota. A week into the next quarter, your brother-in-law returns the merchandise.

Meanwhile, unknown to you, your company's ERP system is scheduling production. The program that creates the production schedule reads the sales from your activities (and those of the other salespeople) and finds a sharp increase in product demand. Accordingly, it generates a schedule that calls for substantial production increases and schedules workers for the production runs. The production system, in turn, schedules the material requirements with the inventory application, which increases raw materials purchases to meet the increased production schedule. ■

Discussion Questions

1. Is it ethical for you to write the email agreeing to take the product back? If that email comes to light later, what do you think your boss will say?

2. Is it ethical for you to offer the "advertising" discount? What effect does that discount have on your company's balance sheet?

3. Is it ethical for you to ship to the fictitious company? Is it legal?

4. Describe the impact of your activities on next quarter's inventories.

5. Setting aside the ethical issues, would you say the enterprise system is more a help or a hindrance in this example?

The system in Figure 7 is an enterprise information system in that different departments share data. However, notice that the business processes do not overlap departments; they are still isolated. This is not the case in most organizations. Usually, enterprise business processes span departments. When they do so, the development of enterprise systems is considerably more difficult but potentially more beneficial. Consider the hospital example previously introduced.

An Enterprise System for Patient Discharge

Figure 8 shows some of the hospital departments and processes involved in discharging a patient from a hospital. A doctor initiates the process by issuing a discharge patient order. That order is delivered to the appropriate nursing staff member, who initiates activities at the pharmacy, the patient's family, and housekeeping. Some of those activities initiate activities back at the nursing staff. In this figure, the enterprise information system is represented by a dotted gold line.

Prior to the enterprise system, the hospital had developed procedures for using a paper-based system and informal messaging via the telephone. Each department kept its own records. When the new enterprise information system was implemented, not only was the data integrated into a database, but new computer-based forms and reports were created. To use the new system, the staff needed to transition from the paper-based system to the computer-based one. They also needed to stop making phone calls and let the new information system make notifications across departments. These measures involved substantial change, and most organizations experience considerable anguish when undergoing such transitions.

Business Process Reengineering

Enterprise systems like the one in Figure 8 were not feasible until network, data communication, and database technologies reached a sufficient level of capability and maturity in the late 1980s and early 1990s. At that point, many organizations began to develop enterprise systems.

As they did so, organizations realized that their existing business processes needed to change. In part, they needed to change to utilize the shared databases and to utilize new computer-based forms and reports. However, an even more important reason for changing business processes was that integrated data and enterprise

Figure 8
Example Enterprise
Process and Information
System

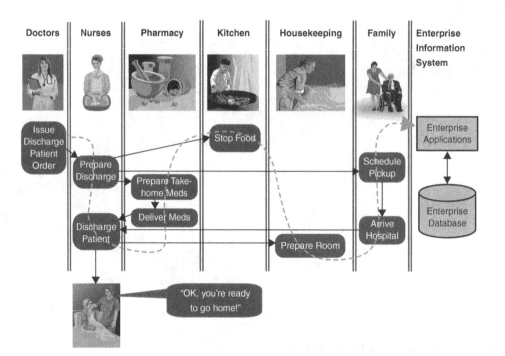

systems offered the potential of substantial operational efficiencies. It became possible to do things that had been impossible before. Using Porter's language, enterprise systems enabled the creation of stronger, faster, more effective linkages among value chains.

For example, when the hospital used a paper-based system, the kitchen would prepare meals for everyone who was a patient at the hospital as of midnight the night before. It was not possible to obtain data about discharges until the next midnight. Consequently, considerable food was wasted at substantial cost.

With the enterprise system, the kitchen can be notified about patient discharges as they occur throughout the day, resulting in substantial reductions in wasted food. But when should the kitchen be notified? Immediately? And what if the discharge is cancelled before completion? Notify the kitchen of the cancelled discharge? Many possibilities and alternatives exist. So, to design its new enterprise system, the hospital needed to determine how best to change its processes to take advantage of the new capability. Such projects came to be known as **business process reengineering**, which is the activity of altering and designing business processes to take advantage of new information systems.

Unfortunately, business process reengineering is difficult, slow, and exceedingly expensive. Systems analysts need to interview key personnel throughout the organization to determine how best to use the new technology. Because of the complexity involved, such projects require high-level and expensive skills and considerable time. Many early projects stalled when the enormity of the project became apparent. This left some organizations with partially implemented systems, which had disastrous consequences. Personnel didn't know if they were using the new system, the old system, or some hacked-up version of both.

The stage was set for the emergence of enterprise application vendors, which we discuss next.

Q4 How Do CRM, ERP, and EAI Support Enterprise Processes?

When the need for business process reengineering emerged, most organizations were still developing their applications in-house. At the time, organizations perceived their needs as being "too unique" to be satisfied by off-the-shelf or altered applications. However, as applications became more and more complex, in-house development costs became infeasible. Systems built in-house are expensive not only because of their high initial development costs, but also because of the continuing need to adapt those systems to changing requirements.

In the early 1990s, as the costs of business process reengineering were coupled to the costs of in-house development, organizations began to look more favorably on the idea of licensing pre-existing applications. "Maybe we're not so unique, after all."

Some of the vendors who took advantage of this change in attitude were People-Soft, which licensed payroll and limited-capability human resources systems; Siebel, which licensed a sales lead tracking and management system, and SAP, which licensed something new, a system called *enterprise resource management*.

These three companies, and ultimately dozens of others like them, offered not just software and database designs. They also offered standardized business processes. These **inherent processes**, which are predesigned procedures for using the software products, saved organizations from the expense, delays, and risks of business process reengineering. Instead, organizations could license the software and obtain, as part of the deal, prebuilt procedures, which the vendors assured them were based on "industry best practices."

Some parts of that deal were too good to be true because, as you'll learn in Q7, inherent processes are almost never a perfect fit. But, the offer was too much for many

Despite the clear benefits of inherent processes and ERP, there can be an unintended consequence. See the Guide later in the chapter and consider that risk.

organizations to resist. Over time, three categories of enterprise applications emerged: customer relationship management,, enterprise resource planning, and enterprise application integration. Consider each.

Customer Relationship Management (CRM)

A **customer relationship management (CRM) system** is a suite of applications, a database, and a set of inherent processes for managing all the interactions with the customer, from lead generation to customer service. Every contact and transaction with the customer is recorded in the CRM database. Vendors of CRM systems claim that using their products makes the organization *customer-centric*. Though that term reeks of sales hyperbole, it does indicate the nature and intent of CRM packages.

Figure 9 shows four phases of the **customer life cycle**: marketing, customer acquisition, relationship management, and loss/churn. Marketing sends messages to the target market to attract customer prospects. When prospects order, they become customers who need to be supported. Additionally, relationship management processes increase the value of existing customers by selling them more product. Inevitably, over time the organization loses customers. When this occurs, win-back processes categorize customers according to value and attempt to win back high-value customers.

Figure 10 illustrates the major components of a CRM application. Notice that components exist for each stage of the customer life cycle. As shown, all applications process a common customer database. This design eliminates duplicated customer data and removes the possibility of inconsistent data. It also means that each department knows what has been happening with the customer at other departments. Customer support, for example, will know not to provide $1,000 worth of support labor to a customer that has generated $300 worth of business over time. However, they'll know to bend over backwards for the customers that have generated hundreds of thousands of dollars of business. The result to the customer is that he or she feels like they are dealing with one entity and not many.

Figure 9
The Customer Life Cycle

Source: *The Customer Life Cycle.* Used with permission from Professor Douglas Maclachian, University of Washington Business School, University of Washington, Seattle, Washington.

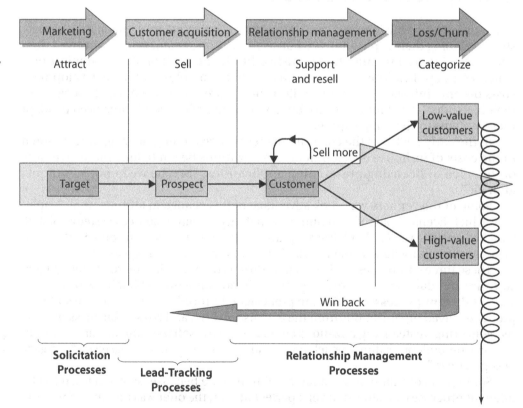

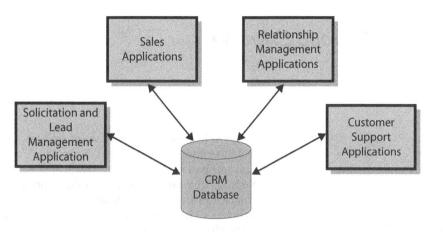

Figure 10
CRM Applications

CRM systems vary in the degree of functionality they provide. One of the primary tasks when selecting a CRM package is to determine the features you need and to find a package that meets that set of needs. You might be involved in just such a project during your career.

Enterprise Resource Planning (ERP)

Enterprise resource planning (ERP) is a suite of applications called **modules**, a database, and a set of inherent processes for consolidating business operations into a single, consistent, computing platform. An **ERP system** is an information system based on ERP technology. As shown in Figure 11, ERP systems include the functions of CRM systems, but also incorporate accounting, manufacturing, inventory, and human resources applications.

The primary purpose of an ERP system is integration; an ERP system allows the left hand of the organization to know what the right hand is doing. This integration allows real-time updates globally, whenever and wherever a transaction takes place. Critical business decisions can then be made on a timely basis using the latest data.

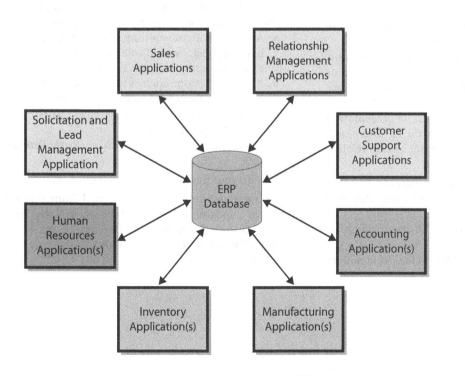

Figure 11
ERP Applications

169

Using MIS InClass   *A Group Exercise*

Choosing a CRM Product

Newscom

Choosing a CRM product is complicated. Dozens of CRM products exist, and it's difficult to determine their different features and functions, let alone how easy they are to learn and use, how difficult they are to implement, and so forth. Choosing a CRM product requires knowledge of the organization's requirements, and oftentimes those requirements aren't fully known, or, if they are known, they are changing as the organization grows.

This exercise is designed to give you a sense of the challenges involved when choosing a CRM product. Form a team of students, fire up your browsers, and answer the following questions:

1. Act! and Goldmine are two lower-end CRM products. They began as sales lead tracking tools for individuals and small offices but have evolved since then.
   a. To learn about those products, visit *www.act.com* and *www.frontrange.com/goldmine.aspx.*
   b. It is difficult compare the products based on the information just on those sites. To learn more, Google or Bing the phrase "Act vs. Goldmine." Read several comparisons.
   c. Summarize your findings in a 2-minute presentation to the rest of the class. Include in your summary each product's intended market, costs, and relative strengths and weaknesses.

2. Salesforce.com and Sugar are CRM products that are intended for use by larger organizations than Act! and Goldmine are.
   a. To learn about those products, visit *www.salesforce.com* and *www.sugarcrm.com.*
   b. These two products seem to differ in their orientation.

To learn how others view these differences, Google or Bing the phrase "Salesforce vs. Sugar CRM." Read several comparisons.
   c. Summarize your findings in a 2-minute presentation to the rest of the class. Include in your summary each product's intended market, costs, and relative strengths and weaknesses.

3. Of course, the major software vendors have CRM offerings as well. Using a combination of acquisition and internal development, Microsoft created the Dynamics CRM product. Oracle, meanwhile, through acquisition of Siebel Systems in 2005 and other acquisitions, has developed a suite of CRM applications.
   a. To learn about those products, visit *http://crm.dynamics.com/en-us/Default.aspx* and *www.oracle.com/us/solutions/crm/index.htm.*
   b. List and briefly describe Oracle's product suite. List and briefly describe Microsoft's CRM offering. To learn more, Google or Bing "Microsoft CRM vs. Oracle CRM."
   c. Summarize your findings in a 2-minute presentation to the rest of the class. Include in your summary each product's intended market, costs, and relative strengths and weaknesses.

4. Given your answers to items 1–3 (and those of other teams if you have been presenting to each other), consider the desirability of CRM product offerings for a variety of businesses. Specifically, suppose you have been asked to recommend two of the CRM products for further research. For each of following businesses, recommend two such products and justify your recommendation:
   a. An independent wedding planner who is working in her own business as a sole proprietor (as Anne Foster was before she joined Fox Lake).
   b. An online vendor, such as *www.sephora.com.*
   c. A musical venue, such as *http://santafeopera.org.*
   d. A vendor of consulting services, such as *www.crmsoftwaresolutions.ca.*
   e. A vacation cruise ship line, such as *www.hollandamerica.com.*

   Present your findings to the rest of the class.

5. Summarize what you have learned from this exercise about choosing a CRM product. Formulate your summary as an answer to a job interviewer's question about the difficulties that organizations face when choosing software products.

To understand the utility of this integration, consider the pre-ERP systems shown in Figure 12. It includes five different databases, one each for vendors, raw materials, finished goods, manufacturing plan, and CRM. Consider the problems that appear with such separated data when the sales department closes a large order, say, for 1,000 bicycles.

First, should the company take the order? Can it meet the schedule requirements for such a large order? Suppose one of the primary parts vendors recently lost capacity due to an earthquake, and the manufacturer cannot obtain parts for the order in time. If so, the order schedule ought not to be approved. However, with such separated systems this situation is unknown.

Even if parts can be obtained, until the order is entered into the finished goods database, purchasing is unaware of the need to buy new parts. The same comment applies to manufacturing. Until the new order is entered into the manufacturing plan, the production department doesn't know that it needs to increase manufacturing. And, as with parts, does the company have sufficient machine and floor capacity to fill the order on a timely basis? Does it have sufficient personnel with the correct skill sets? Should it be hiring? Can production meet the order schedule? No one knows before the order is approved.

Figure 12 does not show accounting. We can assume, however, that the company has a separate accounting system that is similarly isolated. Eventually, records of business activity find their way to the accounting department and will be posted into the general ledger. With such a pre-ERP system, financial statements are always outdated, available several weeks after the close of the quarter or other accounting period.

Figure 12
Pre-ERP Information
Systems

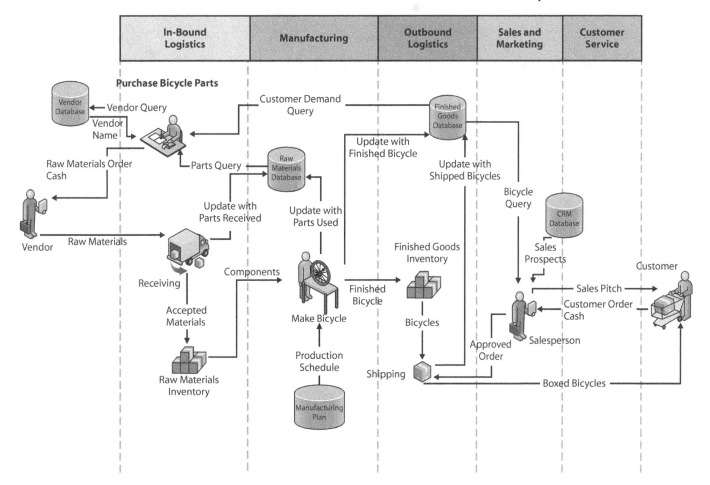

Contrast this situation with the ERP system in Figure 13. Here, all activity is processed by ERP application programs and consolidated data are stored in a centralized ERP database. When sales is confronted with the opportunity to sell 1,000 bicycles, the information that it needs to confirm that the order, schedule, and terms are possible can be obtained from the ERP system immediately. Once the order is accepted, all departments, including purchasing, manufacturing, human resources, and accounting, are notified. Further, transactions are posted to the ERP database as they occur; the result is that financial statements are available quickly, in most cases correct financial statements can be produced in real time. With such integration, ERP systems can display the current status of critical business factors to managers and executives, as shown in the sales dashboard in Figure 14.

Of course, the devil is in the details. It's one thing to draw a rectangle on a chart, label it "ERP Application Programs," and assume that data integration takes all the problems away. It is far more difficult to write those application programs and to design the database to store that integrated data. Even more problematic, what procedures should employees and others use to process those application programs? Specifically, for example, what actions should salespeople take before they approve a large order? Here are some of the questions that need to be answered or resolved:

- How does the sales department determine that an order is considered large? By dollars? By volume?
- Who approves customer credit (and how)?
- Who approves production capacity (and how)?

Figure 13
ERP Information Systems

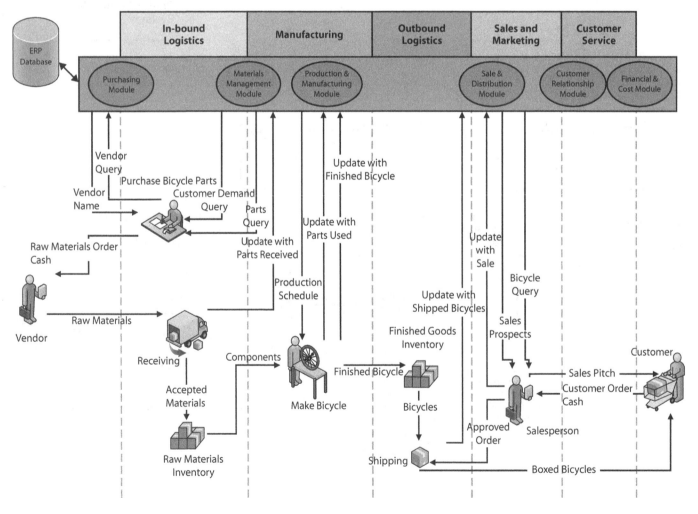

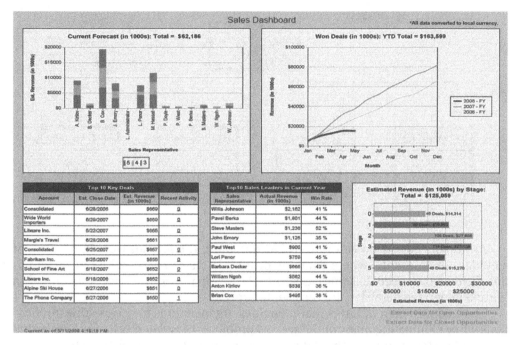

Figure 14
Sales Dashboard

Source: Microsoft Corporation.

- Who approves schedule and terms (and how)?
- What actions need to be taken if the customer modifies the order?
- How does management obtain oversight on sales activity?

As you can imagine, many other questions must be answered as well. Because of its importance to organizations today, we will discuss ERP in further detail in questions Q5 and Q6. Before we do so, however, consider the third type of enterprise system: EAI.

Enterprise Application Integration (EAI)

ERP systems are not for every organization. For example, some nonmanufacturing companies find the manufacturing orientation of ERP inappropriate. Even for manufacturing companies, some find the process of converting from their current system to an ERP system too daunting. Others are quite satisfied with their manufacturing application systems and do not wish to change them.

Companies for which ERP is inappropriate still have the problems associated with information silos, however, and some choose to use **enterprise application integration (EAI)** to solve those problems. EAI is a suite of software applications that integrates existing systems by providing layers of software that connect applications together. EAI does the following:

- It connects system "islands" via a new layer of software/system.
- It enables existing applications to communicate and share data.
- It provides integrated information.
- It leverages existing systems—leaving functional applications as is, but providing an integration layer over the top.
- It enables a gradual move to ERP.

The layers of EAI software shown in Figure 15 enable existing applications to communicate with each other and to share data. For example, EAI software can be configured to automatically make the data conversion required to make data conversions among different systems. When the CRM applications send data to the manufacturing application system, for example, the CRM system sends its data to an EAI software program. That EAI program makes the conversion and then sends the converted data to the ERP system. The reverse action is taken to send data back from the ERP to the CRM.

Figure 15
Design and Implementation
for the Five Components

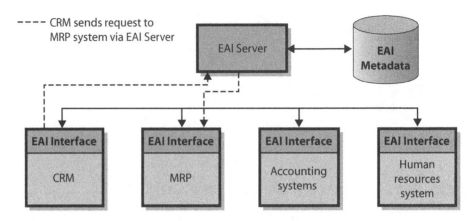

Although there is no centralized EAI database, the EAI software keeps files of metadata that describe where data are located. Users can access the EAI system to find the data they need. In some cases, the EAI system provides services that provide a "virtual integrated database" for the user to process.

The major benefit of EAI is that it enables organizations to use existing applications while eliminating many of the serious problems of isolated systems. Converting to an EAI system is not nearly as disruptive as converting to an ERP system, and it provides many of the benefits of ERP. Some organizations develop EAI applications as a stepping-stone to complete ERP systems.

Q5 What Are the Elements of an ERP System?

Because of its importance to organizations today, we will consider ERP in more depth than CRM or EAI. To begin, the term *ERP* has been applied to a wide array of application solutions, in some cases erroneously. Some vendors attempted to catch the buzz for ERP by misapplying the term to applications that provided only one or two integrated functional applications.

The organization ERPsoftware360 publishes a wealth of information about ERP vendors, products, solutions, and applications. According to its Web site (*www.erpsoftware360.com/erp-101.htm*), for a product to be considered a true ERP product it must include applications that integrate:

- Supply chain (procurement, sales order processing, inventory management, supplier management, and related activities)
- Manufacturing (scheduling, capacity planning, quality control, bill of materials, and related activities)
- CRM (sales prospecting, customer management, marketing, customer support, call center support)
- Human resources (payroll, time and attendance, HR management, commission calculations, benefits administration, and related activities)
- Accounting (general ledger, accounts receivable, accounts payable, cash management, fixed asset accounting)

An ERP solution consists of application programs, databases, business process procedures, and training and consulting. We consider each, in turn.

ERP Application Programs

ERP vendors design application programs to be configurable so that development teams can alter them to meet an organization's requirements without changing program code. Accordingly, during the ERP development process, the development team sets configuration parameters that specify how ERP application programs will operate. For example, an hourly payroll application is configured to specify the number of hours in the standard workweek, hourly wages for different job categories, wage adjustments for overtime and holiday work, and so forth.

Of course, there are limits to how much configuration can be done. If a new ERP customer has requirements that cannot be met via program configuration, then it either needs to adapt its business to what the software can do or write (or pay another vendor to write) application code to meet its requirement. Such custom programming is expensive, both initially and in long-term maintenance costs. Thus, choosing an ERP solution that has applications that function close to the organization's requirements is critical to its successful implementation.

ERP Databases

An ERP solution includes a database design as well as initial configuration data. It does not, of course, contain the company's operational data. During development, the team must enter the initial values for that data as part of the development effort.

If your only experience with databases is creating a few tables in Microsoft Access, then you probably underestimate the value and importance of ERP database designs. SAP, the leading vendor of ERP solutions, provides ERP databases that contain over 15,000 tables. The design includes the metadata for those tables, as well as their relationships to each other, and rules and constraints about how the data in some tables must relate to data in other tables. The ERP solution also contains tables filled with initial configuration data.

Reflect on the difficulty of creating and validating data models, and you will have some idea of the amount of intellectual capital invested in a database design of 15,000 tables. Also, consider the magnitude of the task of filling such a database with users' data!

Large organizational databases contain two types of program code. The first, called a **trigger**, is a computer program stored within the database that runs to keep the database consistent when certain conditions arise. The second, called a **stored procedure**, is a computer program stored in the database that is used to enforce business rules. An example of such a rule would be never to sell certain items at a discount. Triggers and stored procedures are also part of the ERP solution. Much of this program code needs to be configured during the ERP implementation as well.

Business Process Procedures

The third component of an ERP solution is a set of inherent procedures that implement standard business processes. ERP vendors develop hundreds, or even thousands, of procedures that enable the ERP customer organization to accomplish its work using the applications provided by the vendor. Figure 16 shows a part of the SAP ordering business process; this process implements a portion of the inbound logistics activities. Some ERP vendors call the inherent processes that are defined in the ERP solution **process blueprints**.

Without delving into the details, you should be able to understand the flow of work outlined in this process. Every function (rounded rectangles in Figure 16) consists of a set of procedures for accomplishing that function. Typically, these procedures require an ERP user to use application menus, screens, and reports to accomplish the activity.

As with application programs, ERP users must either adapt to the predefined, inherent processes and procedures or design new ones. In the latter case, the design of new procedures may necessitate changes to application programs and to database structures as well. Perhaps you can begin to understand why organizations attempt to conform to vendor standards.

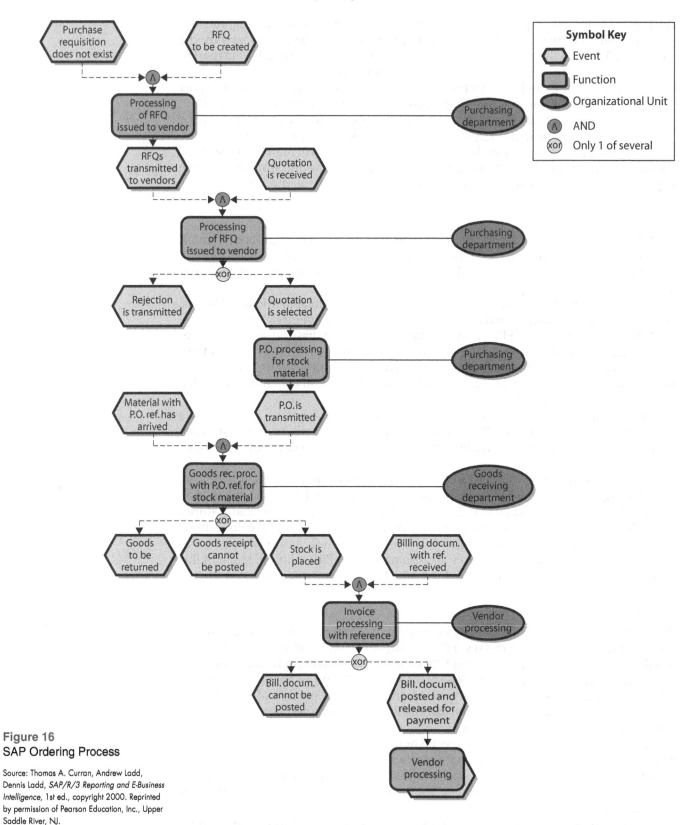

Figure 16
SAP Ordering Process

Source: Thomas A. Curran, Andrew Ladd, Dennis Ladd, *SAP/R/3 Reporting and E-Business Intelligence*, 1st ed., copyright 2000. Reprinted by permission of Pearson Education, Inc., Upper Saddle River, NJ.

Training and Consulting

Because of the complexity and difficulty of implementing and using ERP solutions, ERP vendors have developed training curricula and classes. SAP operates universities, in which customers and potential customers receive training both before and after the ERP implementation. In addition, ERP vendors typically conduct classes on site. To reduce expenses, the vendors sometimes train the organization's employees, called Super Users, to become in-house trainers in training sessions called **train the trainer**.

ERP training falls into two broad categories. The first category is training about how to implement the ERP solution. This training includes topics such as obtaining top-level management support, preparing the organization for change, and dealing with the inevitable resistance that develops when people are asked to perform work in new ways. The second category is training on how to use the ERP application software; this training includes specific steps for using the ERP applications to accomplish the activities in processes like those in Figure 16.

ERP vendors also provide on-site consulting for implementing and using the ERP system. Additionally, an industry of third-party ERP consultants has developed to support new ERP customers and implementations. These consultants provide knowledge gained through numerous ERP implementations. Such knowledge is valued because most organizations only go through an ERP conversion once. Ironically, having done so, they now know how to do it. Consequently, some employees, seasoned by an ERP conversion with their employer, leave that company to become ERP consultants

Industry-Specific Solutions

As you can tell, considerable work needs to be done to customize an ERP application to a particular customer. To reduce that work, ERP vendors provide starter kits for specific industries called **industry-specific solutions**. These solutions contain program and database configuration files as well as process blueprints that apply to ERP implementations in specific industries. Over time, SAP, which first provided such solutions, and other ERP vendors created dozens of such starter kits for manufacturing, sales and distribution, health care, and other major industries.

Q6 How Do the Major ERP Vendors Compare?

Although more than 100 different companies advertise ERP products, not all of those products meet the minimal ERP criteria in Q5. Even of those that do, the bulk of the market is held by the five vendors shown in Figure 17.

ERP Vendor Market Ranking

Figure 17 shows market rank rather than market share because it is difficult to obtain comparable revenue numbers. Infor is owned by private equity investors and does not publish financial data. Microsoft's ERP revenue is combined with its CRM revenue, and its true ERP revenue is unknown. Similarly, Oracle and SAP combine ERP revenue with revenue from other products.

The rankings were obtained as follows. Epicor, a publicly traded company, reported 2009 revenue of $410 million. Microsoft Dynamics revenue is reported to be in the range of $1.3 billion, but that revenue includes general ledger accounting systems sales. Still, even though Dynamic's ERP-only revenue is uncertain, it is most likely greater than Epicor's $410 million. Industry estimates for Infor's revenue are in the range of $2 billion. Oracle's ERP revenue is known to be more than $2 billion, but, judging by the number of installations and the size of the company's customers, Oracle's ERP revenue is considerably less than SAP's.

In 2005, AMR Research reported that SAP had 42 percent of the market, Oracle 20 percent, Microsoft 4 percent, Infor 2 percent, and Epicor 1 percent.[1] However, Infor has substantially increased its market position since 2005 and has surpassed Microsoft's revenue.

---

[1]Marianne Bradford, *Modern ERP* (Far Rockaway, NY: H&M Book's, 2008), p. 11.

Company	ERP Market Rank	Remarks	Future
Epicore	5	Strong-industry specific solutions, especially retail.	Epicore 9 designed for flexibility (SOA). Highly configurable ERP. Lower cost.
Microsoft Dynamics	4	Four products acquired: AX, Nav, GP, and Solomon. AX & Nav more comprehensive. Solomon on the way out? Large VAR channel.	Products not well integrated with Office. Not integrated at all with Microsoft development languages. Product direction uncertain. Watch for Microsoft ERP announcement on the cloud (Azure).
Infor	3	Privately held corporation that has acquired an ERP product named Baan, along with more than 20 others.	Span larger small companies to smaller large companies. Offers many solutions.
Oracle	2	Combination of in-house and acquired (PeopleSoft, Siebel) products.	Intensely competitive company with strong technology base. Large customer base. Flexible SOA architecture. Expensive. Oracle CEO Ellison owns 70% of NetSuite.
SAP	1	Led ERP success. Largest vendor, most comprehensive solution. Largest customers.	Technology older. Expensive and seriously challenged by less expensive alternatives. Huge customer base. Future growth uncertain.

Figure 17
Characteristics of Top ERP Vendors

ERP Products

Figure 18 shows how the ERP products from each of these companies relate to the size of their customers. Both Epicor and Microsoft Dynamics address the needs of small and midsized organizations. Infor has a product for almost everyone, as you'll see. Oracle and SAP serve the largest organizations. Specific product details are as follows.

Figure 18
Top ERP Vendors and Customer Size

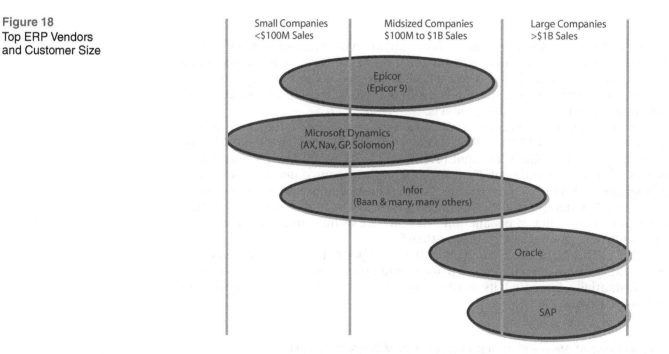

178

Epicor

Epicor is known primarily for its retail-oriented ERP software, although it is broadening its penetration in other industry segments. Its lead ERP product, called Epicor 9, is based on a modern software development design pattern called *service-oriented architecture (SOA)*, which we discuss in Q8. For now, understand that SOA enables cost-effective application flexibility and allows organizations to connect their application programs with Epicor 9 in highly customizable ways. Epicor's products are lower in cost than those from other companies.

Microsoft Dynamics

Microsoft offers five ERP products, all obtained via acquisition: AX (pronounced "A and X," not "axe"), Nav, GP, Solomon, and Dynamics CRM. AX and Nav have the most capability; GP is smaller and easier to use. The future of Solomon is cloudy; supposedly Microsoft outsources the maintenance of the code to provide continuing support to existing customers. To add to the confusion, although Dynamics CRM is primarily a CRM product, vendors extend it by combining it with the accounting features in Dynamics GP to create a *de facto* ERP application.

The future direction of Microsoft's products is uncertain. Most likely AX will continue going forward as a true ERP product for larger organizations. Dynamics CRM will serve both as a CRM product as well as a platform for more generalized relationship management. Dynamics GP, which is the easiest of the products to install, will continue as a general ledger program and possibly be combined with the CRM product to create a true, albeit custom, ERP solution.

Microsoft relies heavily on its network of independent software vendors to create customer solutions using the Dynamics platform. These vendors adapt off-the-shelf Dynamics products to customize them for particular situations. Further developments in the Dynamics product line are likely. Search *www.microsoft.com* for the keyword "dynamics" to learn more.

Infor

Infor was purchased in 2002 by private equity investors, primarily Golden Gate Partners. The company then went on an acquisition binge to consolidate many product offerings under one sales and marketing organization. It purchased Baan, a well-known and successful ERP company, along with more than 20 other companies. Today, Infor sells many ERP products for many different industries.

As you might imagine, Infor's products vary in purpose, scope, and quality. They span the mid-range, serving higher-end small companies and lower-end large companies. The Infor story is still being written; it is little known, considering its revenue size and product portfolio.

Oracle

Oracle is an intensely competitive company with a deep base of technology and high-quality technical staff. Oracle developed some of its ERP products in-house and has complemented those products through the acquisition of PeopleSoft (high-quality HR products) and Siebel (high-quality CRM products).

Oracle's ERP products are designed according to SOA principles and hence are adaptable and customizable. Beginning with its first DBMS product release, Oracle has never been known to create easy-to-use products. It is known, however, for producing fully featured products with superior performance. They are also expensive.

Oracle CEO Larry Ellison owns 70 percent of NetSuite, a company that offers a cloud-based solution for integrated financial reporting for large, international organizations. It would not be unexpected for Oracle to acquire that company as the part of a future ERP product in the cloud.

SAP

SAP is the gold standard of ERP products. It led the direction of the ERP industry in the 1990s and first decade of the twenty-first century. SAP sells to the largest companies and offers the most expensive of the ERP products.

Ironically, SAP's past success creates a problem today. SAP uses classic, thick-client, client-server architecture. Because of its installed base, SAP cannot make a rapid move to thin-client, cloud-based solutions. Instead, it must focus resources and attention on the needs of its current customers (and the attendant, large revenue stream from their maintenance contracts).

In 2003, SAP announced NetWeaver, which is a software architecture that serves as the backbone to integrate existing SAP applications. NetWeaver is believed to be the way in which SAP will gradually move its products and installed based to a more flexible and modern product architecture. As of 2010, however, NetWeaver has not achieved prominence in the SAP installed base.

Q7 What Are the Challenges When Implementing New Enterprise Systems?

Implementing new enterprise systems, whether CRM, ERP, or EAI, is challenging, difficult, expensive, and risky. It is not unusual for enterprise system projects to be well over budget and a year or more late. The expense and risks arise from four primary factors (see Figure 19).

Collaborative Management

Unlike departmental systems in which a single department manager is in charge, enterprise systems have no clear boss. Examine the discharge process in Figure 8; there is no manager of discharge. The discharge process is a collaborative effort among many departments (and customers).

With no single manager, who resolves the disputes that inevitably arise? All of these departments ultimately report to the CEO, so there is a single boss over all of them, but employees can't go to the CEO with a problem about, say, coordinating discharge activities between nursing and housekeeping. The CEO would throw them out of his or her office. Instead, the organization needs to develop some sort of collaborative management for resolving process issues.

Usually this means that the enterprise develops committees and steering groups for providing enterprise process management. Although this can be an effective solution, and in fact may be the *only* solution, the work of such groups is both slow and expensive.

Requirements Gaps

As stated in Q3, few organizations today create their own enterprise systems from scratch. Instead, they license an enterprise product that provides specific functions

Figure 19
Four Primary Factors

- Collaborative management
- Requirements gaps
- Transition problems
- Employee resistance

and features and that includes inherent procedures. But, such licensed products are never a perfect fit. Almost always there are gaps between the organization's requirements and the application's capabilities.

The first challenge is identifying the gaps. To specify a gap, an organization must know both what it needs and what the new product does. However, it can be very difficult for an organization to determine what it needs; that difficulty is one reason organizations choose to license rather than to build. Further, the features and functions of complex products like CRM or ERP are not easy to identify. Thus, gap identification is a major task when implementing enterprise systems.

The second challenge is deciding what to do with gaps, once they are identified. Either the organization needs to change the way it does things to adapt to the new application, or the application must be altered to match what the organization does. Either choice is problematic. Employees will resist change, but paying for alterations is expensive and the organization is committing to maintaining those alterations as the application is changed over time. Here, organizations fill gaps by choosing their lesser regret.

Transition Problems

Transitioning to a new enterprise system is also difficult. The organization must somehow change from using isolated departmental systems to using the new enterprise system, while continuing to run the business. It's like having heart surgery while running a 100-yard dash.

Such transitions require careful planning and substantial training. Inevitably, problems will develop. Knowing this will occur, senior management needs to communicate the need for the change to the employees and then stand behind the new system as the kinks are worked out. It is an incredibly stressful time for all involved.

Employee Resistance

People resist change. Change requires effort and it engenders fear. Considerable research and literature exists about the reasons for change resistance and how organizations can deal with it. Here we will summarize the major principles.

First, senior-level management needs to communicate the need for the change to the organization, and reiterate this, as necessary, throughout the transition process. Second, employees fear change because it threatens **self-efficacy**, which is a person's belief that he or she can be successful at his or her job. To enhance confidence, employees need to be trained and coached on the successful use of the new system. Word-of-mouth is a very powerful factor, and in some cases key users are trained ahead of time to create positive buzz about the new system. Video demonstrations of employees successfully using the new system are also effective.

Some companies may change too often. See the Guide later in the chapter for a discussion on how management fads can grow tiresome for employees.

Third, employees may need to be given extra inducement to change to the new system. As one experienced change consultant said, "Nothing succeeds like praise or cash, especially cash." Straight-out pay for change is bribery; but contests with cash prizes among employees or groups can be very effective at inducing change.

Implementing new enterprise systems can solve many problems and bring great efficiency and cost savings to an organization, but it is not for the faint of heart.

Q8 2021?

The problem with functional systems is that they exist in isolation. Organizations have seen great benefits by moving to integrated applications such as CRM and ERP. However, moving to those applications has been fraught with difficulty, as just described.

To ease the creation of integrated systems, information systems developers studied best-of-practice techniques and from these developed a design philosophy known as *service-oriented architecture (SOA)*. SOA was originally used to design interacting computer programs. More recently, systems designers have applied SOA principles to business process activities, whether those activities are manual, partly automated, or fully automated.

SOA offers great flexibility, ease of use, and adaptability, and we can expect that it will see even greater use by 2021. In fact, by that time, it is likely that all new systems and business processes will be developed using SOA principles. So, what are those principles?

To begin, **service-oriented architecture (SOA)** is a design philosophy in which every activity is modeled as an encapsulated service and exchanges among those services are governed by standards. This definition has three key terms: *service, encapsulation,* and *standards.* Consider each.

First, a **service** is a repeatable task that a business needs to perform. At Fox Lake, the following are examples of services:

- Reserve a tee time (start time) on a golf course
- Reserve facilities for a wedding
- Bill a member's account
- Cancel a wedding event

To understand the importance of services, consider the process in Figure 20, in which the activities in the circles are people or job titles, not services, and the result is a mess. To begin, the customer requests that a good or service be charged to his or her member account. Each of the employees or departments in this diagram responds in a different way. Golf pro Norman makes no check at all, whereas golf pro Nicholas checks the account status on a computer. The golf pro shop and restaurant catering make still other checks.

Consider some of the problems of this process. First, because the circles are people or departments and not services, the means by which they check account status is individualistic. What would a third golf pro do? If the pro shop changes sales application software, will that software check the account status in yet a different way? When Fox Lake added the wedding events department, what kind of account status checking did it do? What would a circle labeled "Anne" mean?

Figure 20
Non-SOA Account Status
Checking

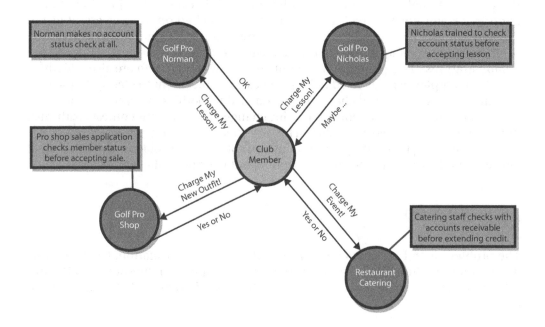

As a result of this individualistic account checking, results vary. One of Norman's customers can run up bad debt because Norman does not check accounts. Nicholas does something, checking account status, somewhere, but we don't know how or what the results will be. Restaurant catering checks with accounts receivable, and the pro shop has an application that performs some other type of checking.

Now, imagine that each of these people or departments is supported by an information system. The logic for checking member accounts when extending credit will be spread over many different computer programs. If Fox Lake decides to change its credit policies, many different computer programs will need to be changed. Such change will be difficult and expensive.

To convert this process to an SOA process, the first task is to replace people and departments with defined, standardized services (repeatable business tasks). Figure 21 shows the same business activity, but modeled as services like *Sell Golf Lesson* and *Accept Catering Reservation*. Of course, those services are provided by someone, but the processes are standardized and employees are trained to use them.

The next step is to consolidate the checking of an account into a single service. Figure 21 shows a standard service called *Check Account Status* within the accounts receivable department. Using SOA principles, this service, like all SOA services, is designed to be independent. No other service is aware of how *Check Account Status* works, and none need be. Instead, services need only to agree on the structure of the data they exchange. In Figure 21, the customer-facing services pass a *Charge Request* to *Check Account Status*, and they receive *Approval* or *Rejection* back. The full design stipulates the particular data items and the format of those items included in the *Approval* or *Rejection* notices.

None of the services that send a *Charge Request* to *Check Account Status* need to know how the checking will be done. The *Check Account Status* process could involve flipping a coin, throwing darts, checking outstanding balances, or performing some

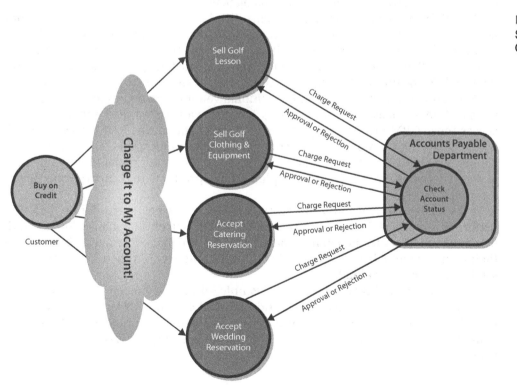

Figure 21
SOA Account Status
Checking

sophisticated data mining on the member's payment history. None of the services that call *Check Account Status* know or need to know how the decision is made to authorize or reject the charge request.

When the logic for some service is isolated in this way, the logic is said to be **encapsulated** in the service. **Encapsulation** places the logic in one place, which is exceedingly desirable. For one, all other services know to go to that one place for that service. Even more important, if the managers of the accounts receivable department decide to change the criteria for approvals or rejections, no other process or activity is affected. As long as the structure and meaning of *Charge Request* and *Approval* or *Rejection* data do not change, all activities are isolated from changes in *Check Account Status* (or any other SOA-designed service).

Because of encapsulation, service implementations are easily adapted to new requirements, technologies, or methodologies. In fact, it does not matter who performs the services or where they are performed. *Check Account Status* could be done by Fox Lake on a single computer. Later, it could be performed by a different company, say a service bureau, on different computers, in another part of the world. As long as the interfaces among the services do not change, *Check Account Status* is free to change its implementation.

The third key term in the SOA definition is *standards*. Data, and more generically messages, are exchanged among services using standardized formats and techniques, which are referred to as **SOA standards**. In the past, the programmers of the *Sell Clothing and Equipment* application program would meet with the programmers of the *Check Account Status* application program and design a unique, proprietary means for exchanging data. Such a design is expensive and time consuming. Consequently, the computer industry developed standard ways for formatting messages for describing services and standard protocols for managing the exchanges among services. SOA standards eliminated the need for proprietary designs and expanded the scope and importance of SOA design principles.

We will not consider the particulars of SOA standards in this text. If you wish to learn more, Google or Bing the terms "SOA standards," "XML," "WSDL," and "REST." For now, just understand that by 2021 most organizations and software vendors will design their processes and applications using SOA.

Which brings us to enterprise systems. CRM and ERP systems vendors cannot ignore new innovations such as powerful thin-client technology using HTML 5, portable devices like the iSomethings, and new technology movements like enterprise 2.0 and social CRM. Somehow vendors must adapt to these new requirements while continuing to support their existing customers.

SOA provides them a solution. If traditional vendors can repackage their applications as SOA services, then new devices, say, for example, an iPad application, can access those CRM or ERP components using SOA standards. In this way, SOA will open up existing CRM and ERP functionality to new applications. Thus, established companies like SAP and Oracle can maintain control of traditional ERP functionality, and smaller vendors will create complementary products that incorporate newer technologies.

SOA design provides another advantage. SOA services, once defined, can be performed anywhere, including the cloud. By 2021, it is likely that many CRM and ERP functions will be performed in the cloud, and it may be that companies will assemble their own, individualized versions of CRM, ERP, and even EAI by repackaging SOA services hosted in the cloud.

Workday, started by the founder of PeopleSoft, offers hosted HR applications. Ellison's NetSuite offers accounting and financial systems for large, international organizations in the cloud. SAP's NetWeaver also provides a hosted ERP solution. Some companies will assemble their own, unique enterprise systems from these components.

Even if traditional vendors of enterprise systems can maintain an exclusive hold on their customers, you can expect that, by 2021, enterprise products will be redesigned to use SOA principles. They will run as thin-client applications on any computing device and will access data and programs using virtualized servers in the cloud. Competition, customer demands for lower costs, and organizational needs to adapt will force traditional vendors to make these changes or lose their customers. Such dramatic change in such a critical business endeavor will create many new opportunities for young business professionals like you and your classmates.

Guide

The Flavor-of-the-Month Club

"Oh, come on. I've been here 30 years and I've heard it all. All these management programs. . . . Years ago, we had Zero Defects. Then it was Total Quality Management, and after that, Six Sigma. We've had all the pet theories from every consultant in the Western Hemisphere. No, wait, we had consultants from Asia, too.

"Do you know what flavor we're having now? We're redesigning ourselves to be 'customer-centric.' We are going to integrate our functional systems into a CRM system to transform the entire company to be 'customer-centric.'

"You know how these programs go? First, we have a pronouncement at a 'kick-off meeting' where the CEO tells us what the new flavor is going to be and why it's so important. Then a swarm of consultants and 'change management' experts tell us how they're going to 'empower' us. Then HR adds some new item to our annual review, such as, 'Measures taken to achieve customer-centric company.'

"So, we all figure out some lame thing to do so that we have something to put in that category of our annual review. Then we forget about it because we know the next new flavor of the month will be along soon. Or worse, if they actually force us to use the new system, we comply, but viciously. You know, go out of our way to show that the new system can't work, that it really screws things up.

"You think I sound bitter, but I've seen this so many times before. The consultants and rising stars in our company get together and dream up one of these programs. Then they present it to the senior managers. That's when they make their first mistake: They think that if they can sell it to management, then it must be a good idea. They treat senior management like the customer. They should have to sell the idea to those of us who actually sell, support, or make things. Senior management is just the banker; the managers should let us decide if it's a good idea.

"If someone really wanted to empower me, she would listen rather than talk. Those of us who do the work have hundreds of ideas of how to do it better. Now it's customer-centric? As if we haven't been trying to do that for years!

"Anyway, after the CEO issues the pronouncements about the new system, he gets busy with other things and forgets about it for a while. Six months might go by, and then we're either told we're not doing enough to become customer-centric (or whatever the flavor is) or the company announces another new flavor.

"In manufacturing they talk about push versus pull. You know, with push style, you make things and push them onto the sales force and the customers. With pull style, you let the customers' demand pull the product out of manufacturing. You build when you have holes in inventory. Well, they should adapt those ideas to what they call 'change management.' I mean, does anybody need to manage real change? Did somebody have a 'Use the iPhone program'? Did some CEO announce, 'This year, we're all going to use the iPhone'? Did the HR department put a line into our annual evaluation form that asked how many times we'd used an iPhone? No, no, no, and no. Customers pulled the iPhone through. We wanted it, so we bought and used iPhones. Same with Kindles, iPads, Twitter, and Facebook.

"That's pull. You get a group of workers to form a network, and you get things going among the people who do the work. Then you build on that to obtain true organizational change. Why don't they figure it out?

"Anyway, I've got to run. We've got the kick-off meeting of our new initiative—something called business process management. Now they're going to empower me to manage my own activities, I suppose. Like, after 30 years, I don't know how to do that. Oh, well, I plan to retire soon.

"Oh, wait. Here, take my T-shirt from the knowledge management program 2 years ago. I never wore it. It says, 'Empowering You Through Knowledge Management.' That one didn't last long." ■

Discussion Questions

1. Clearly, this person is cynical about new programs and new ideas. What do you think might be the cause of her antagonism? What seems to be her principal concern?

2. What does she mean by "vicious" compliance? Give an example of an experience you've had that exemplifies such compliance.

3. Consider her point that the proponents of new programs treat senior managers as the customer. What does she mean? To a consultant, is senior management the customer? What do you think she's trying to say?

4. What does she mean when she says, "If someone wants to empower me, she would listen rather than talk"? How does listening to someone empower that person?

5. Her examples of "pull change" all involve the use of new products. To what extent do you think pull works for new management programs?

6. How do you think management could introduce new programs in a way that would cause them to be pulled through the organization? Consider the suggestion she makes, as well as your own ideas.

7. If you managed an employee who had an attitude like this, what could you do to make her more positive about organizational change and new programs and initiatives?

Gregory Gerber/Shutterstock

Guide

ERP and the Standard, Standard Blueprint

Designing business processes is difficult, time consuming, and very expensive. Highly trained experts conduct seemingly countless interviews with users and domain experts to determine business requirements. Then, even more experts join those people, and together this team invests thousands of labor hours to design, develop, and implement effective business processes that meet those requirements. All of this is a very high-risk activity, prone to failure. And it all must be done before IS development can even begin.

ERP vendors such as SAP have invested millions of labor hours into the business blueprints that underlie their ERP solutions. Those blueprints consist of hundreds or thousands of different business processes. Examples are processes for hiring employees, processes for acquiring fixed assets, processes for acquiring consumable goods, and processes for custom "one-off" (a unique product with a unique design) manufacturing, to name just a few.

Additionally, ERP vendors have implemented their business processes in hundreds of organizations. In so doing, they have been forced to customize their standard blueprint for use in particular industries. For example, SAP has a distribution-business blueprint that is customized for the auto parts industry, for the electronics industry, and for the aircraft industry. Hundreds of other customized solutions exist as well.

Even better, the ERP vendors have developed software solutions that fit their business-process blueprints. In theory, no software development is required at all if the organization can adapt to the standard blueprint of the ERP vendor.

As described in this chapter, when an organization implements an ERP solution, it first identifies any differences that exist between its business processes and the standard blueprint. Then, the organization must remove that difference, which can be done in one of two ways: It changes business processes to fit the standard blueprint. Or, the ERP vendor or a consultant modifies the standard blueprint (and software solution that matches that blueprint) to fit the unique requirements.

In practice, such variations from the standard blueprint are rare. They are difficult and expensive to implement, and they require the using organization to maintain the variations from the standard as new versions of the ERP software are developed. Consequently, most organizations choose to *modify their processes* to meet the blueprint, rather than the other way around. Although such process changes are also difficult to implement, once the organization has converted to the standard blueprint, they need no longer support a "variation."

So, from a standpoint of cost, effort, risk, and avoidance of future problems, there is a huge incentive for organizations to adapt to the standard ERP blueprint.

Initially, SAP was the only true ERP vendor, but other companies have developed and acquired ERP solutions as well. Because of competitive pressure across the software industry, all of these products are beginning to have the same sets of features and functions. ERP solutions are becoming a commodity.

All of this is fine, as far as it goes, but it introduces a nagging question: If, over time, every organization tends to implement the standard ERP blueprint, and if, over time, every software company develops essentially the same ERP features and functions, then won't every business, worldwide, come to look just like every other business, worldwide? How will organizations gain a competitive advantage if they all use the same business processes?

If every auto parts distributor uses the same business processes, based on the same software, are they not all clones of one another? How will one distinguish itself? How will innovation occur? Even if one parts distributor does successfully innovate a business process that gives it a competitive advantage, will the ERP vendors be conduits to transfer that innovation to competitors? Does the use of "commoditized" standard blueprints mean that no company can sustain a competitive advantage? ■

Discussion Questions

1. Explain in your own words why an organization might choose to change its processes to fit the standard blueprint. What advantages accrue by doing so?

2. Explain how competitive pressure among software vendors will cause the ERP solutions to become commodities. What does this mean to the ERP software industry?

3. If two businesses use exactly the same processes and exactly the same software, can they be different in any way at all? Explain why or why not.

4. Explain the following statement: An ERP software vendor can be a conduit to transfer innovation. What are the consequences to the innovating company? To the software company? To the industry? To the economy?

5. In theory, such standardization might be possible, but worldwide, there are so many different business models, cultures, people, values, and competitive pressures, can any two businesses ever be exactly alike?

iStockphoto.com

Active Review

Use this Active Review to verify that you understand the ideas and concepts that answer the chapter's study questions.

Q1 How do information systems vary by scope?

Explain how information systems vary by scope. Name the scope, give an example using a club like Fox Lake, but use a different example than the one in Figure 1. Describe characteristics of information systems of each type.

Q2 When are information silos a problem?

Define *information silo,* and explain how such silos come into existence. When do such silos become a problem? Name and describe five common functional applications. Describe data that are likely duplicated among those five applications. Summarize the problems caused by information silos.

Q3 How do enterprise information systems eliminate silos?

Explain how the information silo at Fox Lake led to the conflict between wedding events and facilities at Fox Lake. Describe how the system in Figure 7 solves this problem. Describe a situation in which an enterprise system creates a burden for one department without any benefit to that department. Explain a key difference between the enterprise system at Fox Lake and the one at the hospital in Figure 8. Describe a key benefit to kitchen operations of the enterprise system to the hospital. Define *business process reengineering,* and explain why it is difficult and expensive.

Q4 How do CRM, ERP, and EAI support enterprise processes?

Explain two major reasons why developing enterprise information systems in-house is expensive. Explain the advantages of inherent processes. Define and differentiate among *CRM, ERP,* and *EAI.* Explain how the nature of CRM and ERP is more similar than that of EAI.

Q5 What are the elements of an ERP system?

Describe the minimum capability of a true ERP product. Explain the nature of each of the following ERP solution components: programs, data, procedures, and training and consulting. For each, summarize the work that customers must perform.

Q6 How do the major ERP vendors compare?

List the top five ERP vendors in decreasing order of market share. Using Figure 18 as a guide, summarize the differences among the top five vendors. Explain, using Figure 19 as a guide, how the use and application of the ERP products from these five vendors compares.

Q7 What are the challenges when implementing new enterprise systems?

Name and describe four sources of challenges when implementing enterprise systems. Describe why enterprise systems management must be collaborative. Explain two major tasks required to identify requirements gaps. Summarize the challenges of transitioning to an enterprise system. Explain why employees resist change, and describe three ways of responding to that resistance.

Q8 2021?

Define *SOA,* and explain its origin. Explain the meaning of the three key components of this definition. Give examples of services not in this text. Summarize the advantages of encapsulation. In your own words, summarize the challenges that enterprise software vendors face. Explain how SOA could enable traditional vendors to maintain control of their products while opening the doors to complementary products from smaller vendors. Summarize how SOA facilitates CRM, ERP, and EAI in the cloud. Summarize the factors that will force enterprise vendors to change.

Key Terms and Concepts

Business process reengineering
Customer life cycle
Customer relationship management
 (CRM) system
Departmental information
 system
Encapsulation (encapsulated)
Enterprise application
 integration (EAI)
Enterprise information system
Enterprise resource planning
 (ERP)

ERP system
Functional information system
Industry-specific solutions
Information silo
Inherent processes
Interenterprise information
 system
Island of automation
Modules
Personal information system
Process blueprints
Self-efficacy

Service
Service-oriented
 architecture (SOA)
SOA standards
Stored procedures
Train the trainer
Trigger
Workgroup information
 system

Using Your Knowledge

1. Using the example of your university, give examples of information systems for each of the four levels of scope shown in Figure 1. Describe three workgroup information systems that are likely to duplicate data. Explain how the characteristics of information systems in Figure 1 relate to your examples.

2. In your answer to question 1, explain how the three workgroup information systems create information silos. Describe the kinds of problems that these silos are likely to cause. Use Figure 6 as a guide.

3. Using your answer to question 2, describe an enterprise information system that will eliminate the silos. Explain whether your information system is more like the one in Figure 7 or more like the one in Figure 8. Would the implementation of your system require business process reengineering? Explain why or why not.

4. Using the patient discharge process in Figure 8, explain how the hospital benefits from an ERP solution. Describe why integration of patient records has advantages over separated databases. Explain the value of an industry-specific ERP solution to the hospital.

5. Consider the problem at Fox Lake at the start of this chapter. Explain why this problem was caused by a lack of integration. In what ways would ERP help Fox Lake? If Fox Lake decided to implement ERP, which vendors are likely to have suitable products? Do you think you would recommend an ERP system to Fox Lake? Why or why not?

6. Google or Bing each of the five vendors in Figure 17. In what ways have their product offerings changed since this text was written? Do these vendors have new products? Have they made important acquisitions? Have they been acquired? Have any new companies made important inroads into their market share? Update Figure 17 with any important late-breaking news.

7. Reread the explanation of SOA in Q8. In your own words, explain how an SOA-designed ERP system enables ERP customers to better integrate existing and new company applications into the vendor's ERP package. Explain how SOA creates an opportunity for smaller companies to develop and sell ERP-related applications.

Collaboration Exercise

Collaborate with students on the following exercise. In particular, consider using Google Docs, Windows Live SkyDrive, Microsoft SharePoint, or some other collaboration tool.

The county planning office issues building permits, septic system permits, and county road access permits for all building projects in a county in an eastern state. The planning office issues permits to homeowners and builders for the construction of new homes and buildings and for any remodeling projects that involve electrical, gas, plumbing, and other utilities, as well as the conversion of unoccupied spaces, such as garages, into living or working space. The office also issues permits for new or upgraded septic systems and permits to provide driveway entrances to county roads.

Figure 22 shows the permit process that the county used for many years. Contractors and homeowners found this process to be slow and very frustrating. For one, they did not like its sequential nature. Only after a permit had been approved or rejected by the engineering review process would they find out that a

Figure 22
Building Permit Process,
Old Version

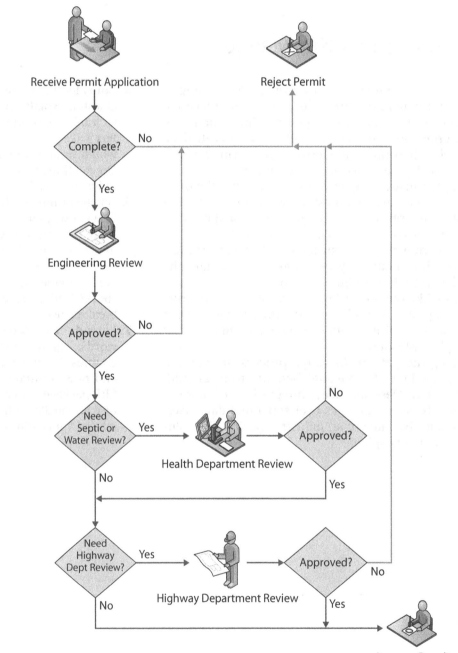

health or highway review was also needed. Because each of these reviews could take 3 or 4 weeks, applicants requesting permits wanted the review processes to be concurrent rather than serial. Also, both the permit applicants and county personnel were frustrated because they never knew where a particular application was in the permit process. A contractor would call to ask how much longer, and it might take an hour or longer just to find which desk the permits were on.

Accordingly, the county changed the permit process to that shown in Figure 23. In this second process, the permit office made three copies of the permit and distributed one to each department. The departments reviewed the permits in parallel; a clerk would analyze the results and, if there were no rejections, approve the permit.

Unfortunately, this process had a number of problems, too. For one, some of the permit applications were lengthy; some included as many as 40 to 50 pages of large architectural drawings. The labor and copy expense to the county was considerable.

Second, in some cases departments reviewed documents unnecessarily. If, for example, the highway department rejected an application, then neither the engineering nor health departments needed to continue their reviews. At first, the county responded to this problem by having the clerk who analyzed results cancel the reviews of other departments when he or she received a rejection. However, that policy was exceedingly unpopular with the permit applicants, because once an application was rejected and the problem corrected the permit had to go back through the other departments. The permit would go to the end of the line and work its way back into the departments from which it had been pulled. Sometimes this resulted in a delay of 5 or 6 weeks.

Canceling reviews was unpopular with the departments as well, because permit-review work had to be repeated. An application might have been nearly

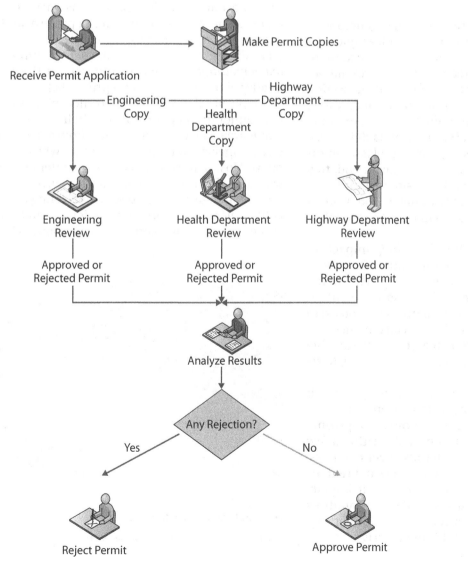

Figure 23
Building Permit Process,
Revised Version

completed when it was cancelled due to a rejection in another department. When the application came through again, the partial work results from the earlier review were lost.

1. Explain why the processes in Figures 22 and 23 are classified as enterprise processes rather than as departmental processes. Why are these processes not interorganizational processes?
2. Using Figure 8 as an example, redraw Figure 22 using an enterprise information system that processes a shared database. Explain the advantages of this system over the paper-based system in Figure 22.
3. Using Figure 8 as an example, redraw Figure 23 using an enterprise information system that processes a shared database. Explain the advantages of this system over the paper-based system in Figure 23.
4. Assuming that the county has just changed from the system in Figure 22 to the one in Figure 23, which of your answers in questions 2 and 3 do you think is better? Justify your answer.
5. Assume your team is in charge of the implementation of the system you recommend in your answer to question 4. Describe how each of the four challenges discussed in Q5 pertain to this implementation. Explain how your team will deal with those challenges.
6. Read the Guide on the flavor of the month earlier in the chapter, if you have not already done so. Assume that person is a key player in the implementation of the new system. How will your team deal with her?

 ## Case Study

Process Cast in Stone

Bill Gates and Microsoft were exceedingly generous in the allocation of stock options to Microsoft employees, especially during Microsoft's first 20 years. Because of that generosity, Microsoft created 4 billionaires and an estimated 12,000 millionaires as Microsoft succeeded and the value of employee stock options soared. Not all of those millionaires stayed in the Seattle/Redmond/Bellevue, Washington, area, but thousands did. These thousands of millionaires were joined by a lesser number who made their millions at Amazon.com and, to a lesser extent, at RealNetworks, Visio (acquired by Microsoft), and Aldus (acquired by Adobe). Today, some Google employees who work at Google's Seattle office are joining these ranks.

The influx of this wealth had a strong impact on Seattle and the surrounding communities. One result has been the creation of a thriving industry in high-end, very expensive homes. These Microsoft and other millionaires are college educated; many were exposed to fine arts at the university. They have created homes that are not just large and situated on exceedingly valuable property, but that also are appointed with the highest-quality components.

Today, if you drive through a small area just south of central Seattle, you will find a half dozen vendors of premium granite, marble, limestone, soapstone, quartzite, and other types of stone slabs within a few blocks of each other. These materials cover counters, bathrooms, and other surfaces in the new and remodeled homes of this millionaire class. The stone is quarried in Brazil, India, Italy, Turkey, and other countries and either cut at its origin or sent to Italy for cutting. Huge cut slabs, 6 feet by 10 feet, arrive at the stone vendors in south Seattle, who stock them in their warehouses. The stone slabs vary not only in material, but also in color, veining pattern, and overall beauty. Choosing these slabs is like selecting fine art (see Figure 24). (Visit *www.pentalonline.com* or *www.metamarble.com* to understand the premium quality of these vendors and products.)

Typically, the client (homeowner) hires an architect who either draws plans for the kitchen, bath, or other stone area as part of the overall house design or who hires a specialized kitchen architect who draws those plans. Most of these clients also hire interior decorators who help them select colors, fabrics, furniture, art, and other home furnishings. Because selecting a stone slab is like selecting a work of art, clients usually visit the stone vendors' warehouses personally. They walk

Figure 24
High-end countertops from Pental

Source: Used with permission of Pental Granite and Marble.

through the warehouses, often accompanied by their interior designer, and maybe also their kitchen architect, carrying little boxes into which stone vendor employees place chips of slabs in which the client expresses interest.

Usually, the team selects several stone slabs for consideration, and those are set aside for that client. The name of the client or the decorator is written in indelible ink on the side of the stone to reserve it. When the client or design team makes a final selection, the name is crossed out on the stone slabs they do not purchase. The purchased slabs are set aside for shipping.

During the construction process, the contractor will have selected a stone fabricator, who will cut the stone slab to fit the client's counters. The fabricator will also treat the stone's edges, possibly repolish the stone, and cut holes for sinks and faucets. Fabricators move the slabs from the stone vendor to their workshops, prepare the slab, and eventually install it in the client's home.

Questions

1. Identify the key actors in this scenario. Name their employer (if appropriate), and describe the role that they play. Include as a key player the operations personnel who move stones in the warehouse as well as who load stones on the fabricators' trucks.

2. Using the below figure as an example, diagram the stone-selection process. Classify this process as a personal, a workgroup, an enterprise, or an inter-enterprise process.

3. The current system is not a paper-based system; it is a stone-based system. Explain why this is so.

4. Create an enterprise system that uses a shared database. Change the diagram you created in your answer to question 2 to include this database. (Assume every slab of stone and every location in the warehouse have a unique identifier.) Does the shared database system solve the problems of the stone-based system? Why or why not?

5. Do you think the customers, designers, and fabricators would prefer the stone-based system or the database system? Explain.

6. Suppose you manage the stone vendor company. If you implement the system in your answer to question 4, what problems can you expect? If you do not implement that system, what problems can you expect? What course of action would you take and why?

7. Explain how a knowledge of enterprise systems can help you become a stone slab client rather than a stone chipper.

Phase	Decisions and Procedures
Starting	What is the team's authority? What is the purpose of the team? Who is on the team? What is expected from team members? What are team members' roles and authorities?
Planning	What tasks need to be accomplished? How are the tasks related to one another? Who is responsible for each task? When will tasks be completed?
Doing	Executing project tasks Task status reporting Managing exceptions
Wrapping-up	Are we done? Documenting team results Documenting team learnings for future teams Closing down the project

Decisions and Procedures
for Project Phases

Application Exercises

1. Assume that you have been hired to develop an Access database for a portion of the Fox Lake Country Club Enterprise Reservation System shown in Figure 7. You have been given the following design for implementation:

   FACILITY   (FacilityID, FacilityName, Description, StandardRentalFee)
      RESERVATION (ReservationNumber, *FacilityID*, Date, StartTime, EndTime)

   Where FacilityID and ReservationNumber are AutoNumber primary keys. RESERVATION.FacilityID is a foreign key to FACILITY. Assume the appropriate data types for the other columns.

   a. Create these tables in Access.
   b. Create the appropriate relationship in Access.
   c. Import the data from the file **Ch07Ex1.txt** into the FACILITY table.
   d. Create a reservation form for creating and viewing specific reservations.
   e. Create a parameterized query for finding a reservation by value of ReservationNumber.
   f. Create a report that shows all the reservations for all facilities.
   g. Create a parameterized report that shows all of the reservations for a particular date.

2. Suppose your manager asks you to create a spreadsheet to compute a production schedule. Your schedule should stipulate a production quantity for seven products that is based on sales projections made by three regional managers at your company's three sales regions.

   a. Create a separate worksheet for each sales region. Use the data in the Word file **Ch07Ex02**, which you can download from the text's Web site. This file contains each manager's monthly sales projections for the past year, actual sales results for those same months, and projections for sales for each month in the coming quarter.
   b. Create a separate worksheet for each manager's data. Import the data from Word into Excel.
   c. On each of the worksheets, use the data from the prior four quarters to compute the discrepancy between the actual sales and the sale projections. This discrepancy can be computed in several ways: You could calculate an overall average, or you could calculate an average per quarter or per month. You could also weight recent discrepancies more heavily than earlier ones. Choose a method that you think is most appropriate. Explain why you chose the method you did.
   d. Modify your worksheets to use the discrepancy factors to compute an adjusted forecast for the coming quarter. Thus, each of your spreadsheets will show the raw forecast and the adjusted forecast for each month in the coming quarter.
   e. Create a fourth worksheet that totals sales projections for all of the regions. Show both the unadjusted forecast and the adjusted forecast for each region and for the company overall. Show month and quarter totals.
   f. Create a bar graph showing total monthly production. Display the unadjusted and adjusted forecasts using different colored bars.

Figure AE-7
Bill of Materials Example

3. Figure AE-7 is a sample bill of materials, a form that shows the components and parts used to construct a product. In this example, the product is a child's wagon. Such bills of materials are an essential part of manufacturing functional applications as well as ERP applications.

This particular example is a form produced using Microsoft Access. Producing such a form is a bit tricky, so this exercise will guide you through the steps required. You can then apply what you learn to produce a similar report. You can also use Access to experiment on extensions of this form.

a. Create a table named *PART* with columns *Part Number, Level, Description, QuantityRequired,* and *PartOf. Description* and *Level* should be text, *PartNumber* should be AutoNumber, and *Quantity Required* and *PartOf* should be numeric, long integer. Add the *PART* data shown in Figure AE-7 to your table.

b. Create a query that has all columns of *PART*. Restrict the view to rows having a value of 1 for *Level*. Name your query *Level1*.

c. Create two more queries that are restricted to rows having values of 2 or 3 for *Level*. Name your queries *Level2* and *Level3*, respectively.

d. Create a form that contains *PartNumber, Level,* and *Description* from *Level1*. You can use a wizard for this if you want. Name the form *Bill of Materials*.

e. Using the subform tool in the Toolbox, create a subform in your form in part d. Set the data on this form to be all of the columns of *Level2*. After you have created the subform, ensure that the Link Child Fields property is set to *PartOf* and that the Link Master Fields property is set to *PartNumber*. Close the *Bill of Materials* form.

f. Open the subform created in part e and create a subform on it. Set the data on this subform to be all of the columns of *Level3*. After you have created the subform, ensure that the Link Child Fields property is set to *PartOf* and that the Link Master Fields property is set to *PartNumber*. Close the *Bill of Materials* form.

g. Open the *Bill of Materials* form. It should appear as in Figure AE-7. Open and close the form and add new data. Using this form, add sample BOM data for a product of your own choosing.

h. Following the process similar to that just described, create a *Bill of Materials Report* that lists the data for all of your products.

i. (**Optional, challenging extension**) Each part in the BOM in Figure AE-7 can be used in at most one assembly (there is space to show just one *PartOf* value). You can change your design to allow a part to be used in more than one assembly as follows: First, remove *PartOf* from PART. Next, create a second table that has two columns: *AssemblyPartNumber* and *ComponentPart Number*. The first contains a part number of an assembly and the second a part number of a component. Every component of a part will have a row in this table. Extend the views described previously to use this second table and to produce a display similar to Figure AE-7.

Chapter 6 (original Chapter 8 of "Using MIS, 4/e")

E-Commerce, Web 2.0, and Social Networking Systems

From Chapter 8 of *Using MIS*, 4/e. David M. Kroenke. Copyright © 2012 by Pearson Education. Published by Prentice Hall.

E-Commerce, Web 2.0, and Social Networking Systems

"I would *totally recommend Fox Lake Country Club for your wedding reception if you want to be told to disinvite your close friends and family. I dreamed my whole life about having my wedding reception there, and I was so excited . . . little did I know that they were TOTAL liars who planned ballroom renovations DURING my wedding reception—told me to cut 35 people from my guest list!! What is the point of having your dream wedding if the people you love aren't there to enjoy it with you!!?? They are just greedy business people who want to get your money no matter what!!! Whatever you do, don't ever work with Fox Lake Country Club!!!!!"*

—Posting on Fox Lake's Facebook Page

"She said WHAT?" asked Jeff Lloyd, general manager of Fox Lake Country Club.

"She said that we're a bunch of greedy business people who want to get your money, no matter what,'" Anne responded.

"On our Facebook page????" Jeff is incredulous.

"Yup."

"Well, delete it then. That shouldn't be too hard." Jeff turns to look out the window at the golfers headed to the first tee.

"Jeff, we can do that, but I think we should be careful here," Anne offers this opinion cautiously as she pushes back.

"No, of course, let's leave it out there. Let's tell the whole world that you and I are greedy business people out to take advantage of our customers. What did she say, 'Don't ever work with Fox Lake?' Yeah, let's leave that there, too . . . maybe put a link to it on our Web site. That'll help at the next board meeting." Sarcasm drips from his voice.

"Well, Jeff, here's the deal. You don't want to enrage the connected . . . they have power. Remember what happened to Nestlé?"

"No, what? Are they greedy business people, too?"

"They got some bad PR on their site and just deleted it. Bingo, it came back, but a thousandfold. Worse, someone at Nestlé got high handed and posted a criticism of the commenters; it was pouring gas on a raging fire."

"Anne, you're tedious. Tell me what we CAN do!"

"Be open. The key is open, honest communication. We fix the problem—get the maintenance done ahead of schedule or delay, I don't care. Then, we tell our upset and nervous bride that we fixed it . . . maybe ask her, gently, to write that on our page. Possibly we follow up with our side of the story, briefly and not defensively."

"Too passive for me. Let's sue her for defamation." Jeff's sarcasm turns to anger.

"No, Jeff. No. That's not the way. You have any idea of the comments we'd get?"

"A lot."

"Besides, we have another problem." Anne represses a smile as she thinks.

"What's that, Anne?"

"Her father. He's a partner in the club's law firm. You gonna hire him to sue his own daughter? Over her wedding plans?" Anne tries hard not to chuckle.

Jeff stares at the golfers out the window, "Weddings. Why did I think weddings were a good idea? What's the matter with golf? It's a good business . . . you water the grass, put out the flags, move the tees around. . . ."

Study Questions

Q1 How do organizations use e-commerce?

Q2 How do organizations use Web 2.0?

Q3 How do social networking information systems increase social capital?

Q4 What are business applications for Facebook, Twitter, and User-Generated Content (UGC)?

Q5 How does social CRM empower customers?

Q6 How can organizations manage the risks of social networking applications?

Q7 2021?

This chapter addresses **interorganizational information systems**, which we define as information systems used between or among organizations that are independently owned and managed. In this discussion, we include customers as organizations, even if they are only a sole individual. Figure 1 shows four types of interorganizational system in use today. These types are presented in the order in which they developed.

With **pre-Internet systems**, organizations communicated via postal mail, telephone, and fax. As you would expect, by today's standards the pace was incredibly slow. Vendors, through their use of advertising and public relations, were in control of the customer relationship. They decided when and how frequently they would contact the customer. Except for limited customer support, communication was one-way, from the vendor to the customer. Because such systems are fading from use, we will not consider them further in this text.

E-commerce is the buying and selling of goods and services over public and private computer networks. E-commerce became feasible with the creation and widespread use of HTTP, HTML, and server applications such as Web storefronts that enabled browser-based transactions. As you'll learn in Q2, e-commerce brought vendors closer to their customers, and in the process changed market characteristics and dynamics.

As browsers with extensions like Flash became more powerful, they enabled thin-client applications to perform sophisticated operations without the user having to download or install a program. The collection of many of these capabilities, along with new business models, has come to be known as Web 2.0. You'll learn about Web 2.0 in Q3.

We begin our discussion of social networking by investigating the theory and application of social capital in Q4. Then, Q5 extends that discussion to consider the business applications of Facebook, Twitter, and User-Generated Content. We next investigate social CRM in Q5. Social CRM is an implementation of Enterprise 2.0, and we'll consider it as well in Q5. Then, we'll wrap up the discussion of social networking systems by describing, in Q6, some of the ways organizations can manage the risks of these new applications.

Finally, in Q7, we'll forecast how all of these new technologies and movements are likely to impact interorganizational information systems during the early

Figure 1
Types of Interorganizational Systems

Type	Supporting Technologies	Characteristics
Pre-Internet	Postal mail, telephone, fax	Slow. Vendors in control of relationship. Primitive interorganizational IS.
E-commerce	HTTP, HTML, Web storefronts	Faster. Vendors and customers closer. New market dynamics.
Web 2.0	Thin clients, Flash	Even faster. Advertising revenue models; flexibility. Rise of User Generated Content (UGC).
Enterprise 2.0	Facebook, Twitter, social CRM; service-oriented architecture (SOA)	Emergent relationships; customer selects relationship characteristics; vendors lose control of relationship. Dynamic interorganizational IS.

---

[1]Andrew McAfee, "Enterprise 2.0: The Dawn of Emergent Collaboration," *MIT Sloan Management Review*, Spring 2006. Available at: *http://sloanreview.mit.edu/the-magazine/files/saleablepdfs/47306.pdf* (accessed May, 2010).

years of your career.

Q1 How Do Organizations Use E-Commerce?

As stated, e-commerce is the buying and selling of goods and services over public and private computer networks. Notice that this definition restricts e-commerce to buying and selling transactions. Checking the weather at *www.yahoo.com* is not e-commerce, but buying a weather-service subscription that is paid for and delivered over the Internet is.

Figure 2 lists categories of e-commerce companies. The U.S. Census Bureau, which publishes statistics on e-commerce activity, defines **merchant companies** as those that take title to the goods they sell. They buy goods and resell them. It defines **nonmerchant companies** as those that arrange for the purchase and sale of goods without ever owning or taking title to those goods. With regard to services, merchant companies sell services that they provide; nonmerchant companies sell services provided by others. Of course, a company can be both a merchant and nonmerchant company.

E-Commerce Merchant Companies

The three main types of merchant companies are those that sell directly to consumers, those that sell to companies, and those that sell to government. Each uses slightly different information systems in the course of doing business. **B2C, or business-to-consumer**, e-commerce concerns sales between a supplier and a retail customer (the consumer). Traditional B2C information systems rely on a **Web storefront** that customers use to enter and manage their orders. Amazon.com, REI.com, and LLBean.com are examples of companies that use B2C information systems.

The term **B2B, or business-to-business**, e-commerce refers to sales between companies. As Figure 3 shows, raw materials suppliers use B2B systems to sell to manufacturers, manufacturers use B2B systems to sell to distributors, and distributors uses B2B systems to sell to retailers.

B2G, or business-to-government, e-commerce refers to sales between companies and governmental organizations. In Figure 3, the manufacturer that uses an e-commerce site to sell computer hardware to the U.S. Department of State is engaging in B2G commerce. Suppliers, distributors, and retailers sell to the government as well.

B2C applications first captured the attention of mail-order and related businesses. However, companies in all sectors of the economy soon realized the enormous potential of B2B and B2G. The number of companies engaged in B2B and B2G commerce now far exceeds those engaged in B2C commerce. Furthermore, today's B2B and B2G applications implement just a small portion of their potential capabilities. Their full utilization is some years away, as you'll learn in Q7.

Interorganizational information systems often require meetings to reach a joint agreement on the process for sharing data. You may be asked to attend such meetings, and, if so, you need to know the proper etiquette for such meetings, as described in the Guide later in the chapter.

Merchant companies	Nonmerchant companies
– Business-to-consumer (B2C) – Business-to-business (B2B) – Business-to-government (B2G)	– Auctions – Clearinghouses – Exchanges

Figure 2
E-Commerce Categories

Figure 3
Example of Use of B2B, B2G, and B2C

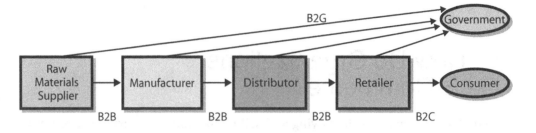

Nonmerchant E-Commerce

The most common nonmerchant e-commerce companies are auctions and clearing-houses. E-commerce **auctions** match buyers and sellers by using an e-commerce version of a standard auction. This e-commerce application enables the auction company to offer goods for sale and to support a competitive-bidding process. The best-known auction company is eBay, but many other auction companies exist; many serve particular industries.

Clearinghouses provide goods and services at a stated price and arrange for the delivery of the goods, but they never take title. One division of Amazon.com, for example, operates as a nonmerchant clearinghouse, allowing individuals and used bookstores to sell used books on the Amazon.com Web site. As a clearinghouse, Amazon.com matches the seller and the buyer and then takes payment from the buyer and transfers the payment to the seller, minus a commission.

Another type of clearinghouse is an **electronic exchange** that matches buyers and sellers; the business process is similar to that of a stock exchange. Sellers offer goods at a given price through the electronic exchange, and buyers make offers to purchase over the same exchange. Price matches result in transactions from which the exchange takes a commission. Priceline.com is an example of an exchange used by consumers.

How Does E-Commerce Improve Market Efficiency?

E-commerce improves market efficiency in a number of different ways. For one, e-commerce leads to **disintermediation**, which is the elimination of middle layers of distributors and suppliers. You can buy a 3D TV from a typical "bricks-and-mortar" electronics store, or you can use e-commerce to buy it from the manufacturer. If you take the latter route, you eliminate the distributor, the retailer, and possibly more companies. The product is shipped directly from the manufacturer's finished goods inventory to you. You eliminate the distributor's and retailer's inventory-carrying costs, and you eliminate shipping overhead and handling activity. Because the distributor and associated inventories have become unnecessary waste, disintermediation increases market efficiency.

E-commerce also improves the flow of price information. As a consumer, you can go to any number of Web sites that offer product price comparisons. You can search for the 3D TV you want and sort the results by price and vendor reputation. You can find vendors that avoid your state sales tax or that omit or reduce shipping charges. The improved distribution of information about price and terms enables you to pay the lowest possible cost and serves ultimately to remove inefficient vendors. The market as a whole becomes more efficient.

From the seller's side, e-commerce produces information about price elasticity that has not been available before. **Price elasticity** measures the amount that demand rises or falls with changes in price. Using an auction, a company can learn not just what the top price for an item is, but also the second, third, and other prices from the losing bids. In this way, the company can determine the shape of the price elasticity curve.

Similarly, e-commerce companies can learn price elasticity directly from experiments on customers. For example, in one experiment, Amazon.com created three groups of similar books. It raised the price of one group 10 percent, lowered the price of the second group 10 percent, and left the price of the third group unchanged. Customers provided feedback to these changes by deciding whether to buy books at the offered prices. Amazon.com measured the total revenue (quantity times price) of each group and took the action (raise, lower, or maintain prices) on all books that maximized revenue. Amazon.com repeated the process until it reached the point at which the best action was to maintain current prices.

Managing prices by direct interaction with the customer yields better information than managing prices by watching competitors' pricing. By experimenting, companies learn how customers have internalized competitors' pricing, advertising, and messaging. It might be that customers do not know about a competitor's lower prices, in which case there is no need for a price reduction. Or, it may be that the competitor is using a price that, if lowered, would increase demand sufficiently to increase total revenue. Figure 4 summarizes the ways e-commerce generates market efficiencies.

What Economic Factors Disfavor E-Commerce?

Although there are tremendous advantages and opportunities for many organizations to engage in e-commerce, the economics of some industries may disfavor e-commerce activity. Companies need to consider the following economic factors:

- Channel conflict
- Price conflict
- Logistics expense
- Customer-service expense

Consider the example of the manufacturer selling directly to the government agency shown in Figure 3. Before engaging in such e-commerce, the manufacturer must consider the unfavorable economic factors just listed. First, what **channel conflict** will develop? Suppose the manufacturer is a computer maker that is selling directly, B2G, to the State Department. When the manufacturer begins to sell goods B2G that State Department employees used to purchase from a retailer down the street, that retailer will resent the competition and might drop the manufacturer. If the value of the lost sales is greater than the value of the B2G sales, e-commerce is not a good solution, at least not on that basis.

When a business engages in e-commerce, it may also cause **price conflict** with its traditional channels. Because of disintermediation, the manufacturer may be able to offer a lower price and still make a profit. However, as soon as the manufacturer offers the lower price, existing channels will object. Even if the manufacturer and the retailer are not competing for the same customers, the retailer still will not want a lower price to be readily known via the Web.

Also, the existing distribution and retailing partners do provide value; they are not just a cost. Without them, the manufacturer will have the increased *logistics expense* of entering and processing orders in small quantities. If the expense of processing a 1-unit order is the same as that for processing a 12-unit order (which it might be), the average logistics expense per item will be much higher for goods sold via e-commerce.

> **Market Efficiencies**
>
> – Disintermediation
> – Increased information on price and terms
> – Knowledge of price elasticity
> • Losing-bidder auction prices
> • Price experimentation
> • More accurate information obtained
>   directly from customer

Figure 4
E-Commerce Market
Efficiencies

Similarly, *customer-service* expenses are likely to increase for manufacturers that use e-commerce to sell directly to consumers. The manufacturer will be required to provide service to less sophisticated users and on a one-by-one basis. For example, instead of explaining to a single sales professional that the recent shipment of 100 Gizmo 3.0s requires a new bracket, the manufacturer will need to explain that 100 times to less knowledgeable, frustrated customers. Such service requires more training and more expense.

All four economic factors are important for organizations to consider when they contemplate e-commerce sales.

Q2 How Do Organizations Use Web 2.0?

E-commerce sites duplicate the experience of shopping in a grocery store or other retail shop. The customer moves around the store, places items in a shopping cart, and then checks out. Shopping carts and other e-commerce techniques have been a boon to business, especially B2C commerce, but they do not take full advantage of the Web's potential.

Amazon.com was one of the first to recognize other possibilities when it added the "Customers Who Bought This Book Also Bought" feature to its Web site. With that feature, e-commerce broke new ground. No grocery store could or would have a sign that announced, "Customers who bought this tomato soup, also bought. . . ." That idea was the first step toward what has come to be known as Web 2.0.

What Is Web 2.0?

Although the specific meaning of **Web 2.0** is hard to pin down, it generally refers to a loose grouping of capabilities, technologies, business models, and philosophies. Figure 5 compares Web 2.0 to traditional processing. (For some reason, the term *Web 1.0* is not used.)

Software as a (Free) Service

Google, Amazon.com, and eBay exemplify Web 2.0. These companies do not sell software licenses, because software is not their product. Instead, they provide **software as a service (SAAS)**. You can search Google, run Google Docs, use Google Earth, process Gmail, and access Google Maps—all from a thin-client browser, with the bulk of the processing occurring in the cloud, somewhere on the Internet. Like all

Figure 5
Comparison of Web 2.0 with Traditional Processing

Web 2.0 Processing	Traditional Processing
Major winners: Google, Amazon.com, eBay	Major winners: Microsoft, Oracle, SAP
Software as a (Free) Service	Software as product
Frequent releases of thin-client applications	Infrequent, controlled releases
Business model relies on advertising or other revenue-from-use	Business model relies on sale of software licenses
Viral marketing	Extensive advertising
Product value increases with use and users	Product value fixed
Organic interfaces, mashups encouraged	Controlled, fixed interface
Participation	Publishing
Some rights reserved	All rights reserved

Web 2.0 programs, Google releases new versions of its programs frequently. Instead of software license fees, the Web 2.0 business model relies on advertising or other revenue that results as users employ the software as a service.

Web 2.0 applications are thin clients. As such, they do not require an installation on the users' computers. Web servers download Web 2.0 programs as code within HTML, as Flash, or as Silverlight code. Because this is so, they are readily (and frequently) updated. New features are added with little notice or fanfare. Web 2.0 users are accustomed to, and even expect, frequent updates to their license-free software.

Figure 6 shows new features that Google is considering adding to Google Maps (as of May 2010, that is). Notice the warning that they "may change, break, or disappear at any time." By providing frequent updates this way, Google maintains it reputation as an innovative company while obtaining testing and usability feedback on new features.

Software as a service clashes with the software model used by traditional software vendors, such as Microsoft, Oracle, and SAP. Software is their product. They release new versions and new products infrequently. For example, 3 years separated the release of Microsoft Office 2007 from 2010. Releases are made in a very controlled fashion, and extensive testing and true beta programs precede every release.

Traditional software vendors depend on software license fees. If a large number of Office users switched to free word processing and spreadsheet applications, the hit on Microsoft's revenue would be catastrophic. Because of the importance of software licensing revenue, substantial marketing efforts are made to convert users to new releases.

In the Web 2.0 world, no such marketing is done; new features are released and vendors wait for users to spread the news to one another, one friend sending a message to many friends; most of whom send that message, in turn, to their friends; and so forth, in a process called **viral marketing**. Google has never announced any software in a formal marketing campaign. Users carry the message to one another. In fact, if a product requires advertising to be successful, then it is not a Web 2.0 product.

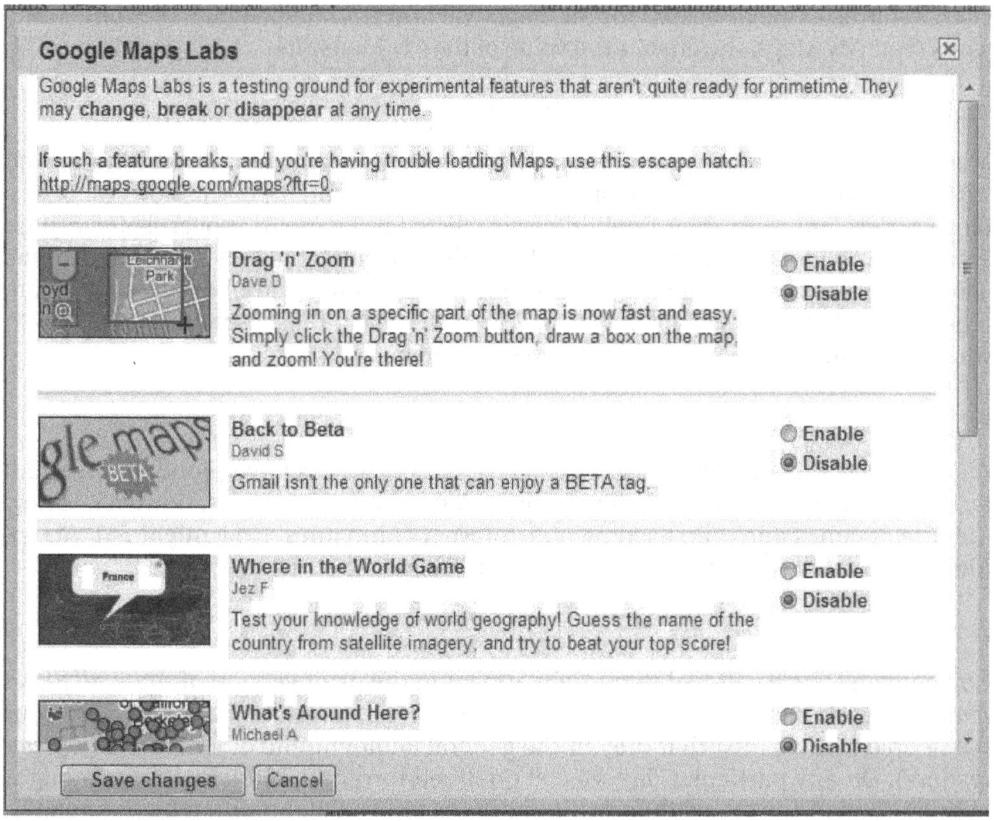

Figure 6
Potential New Features in Google Maps

By the way, traditional software companies do use the term *software as a service*. However, they use it only to mean that they will provide their software products via the cloud rather than having customers install that software on their computers. Software licenses for their products still carry a sometimes hefty license fee. So, we need to say that in the Web 2.0 world software is provided as a *free* service.

Use Increases Value

Another characteristic of Web 2.0 is that the value of the site increases with users and use. Amazon.com gains more value as more users write more reviews. Amazon.com becomes *the* place to go for information about books or other products. Similarly, the more people who buy or sell on eBay, the more eBay gains value as a site.

Organic User Interfaces and Mashups

The traditional software model carefully controls the users' experience. All Office programs share a common user interface; the ribbon (toolbar) in Word is similar to the ribbon in PowerPoint and in Excel. In contrast, Web 2.0 interfaces are organic. Users find their way around eBay and PayPal, and if the user interface changes from day to day, well, that is just the nature of Web 2.0. Further, Web 2.0 encourages **mashups**, which occur when the output from two or more Web sites is combined into a single user experience.

Google's **My Maps** is an excellent mashup example. Google publishes Google Maps and provides tools for users to make custom modifications to those maps. Thus, users mash the Google Map product with their own knowledge. One user demonstrated the growth of gang activity to the local police by mapping new graffiti sites on Google Maps. Other users share their experiences or photos of hiking trips or other travel.

In Web 2.0 fashion, Google provides users a means for sharing their mashed-up map over the Internet and then indexes that map for Google search. If you publish a mashup of a Google map with your knowledge of a hiking trip on Mt. Pugh, anyone who performs a Google search for Mt. Pugh will find your map. Again, the more users who create My Maps, the greater the value of the My Maps site.

Participation and Ownership Differences

Mashups lead to another key difference. Traditional sites are about publishing; Web 2.0 is about participation. Users provide reviews, map content, discussion responses, blog entries, and so forth. A final difference, listed in Figure 5, concerns *ownership*. Traditional vendors and Web sites lock down all the legal rights they can. For example, Oracle publishes content and demands that others obtain written permission before reusing it. Web 2.0 locks down only some rights. Google publishes maps and says, "Do what you want with them. We'll help you share them."

How Can Businesses Benefit from Web 2.0?

Amazon.com, Google, eBay, and other Web 2.0 companies have pioneered Web 2.0 technology and techniques to their benefit. A good question today, however, is how these techniques might be used by non-Internet companies. How might 3M, Alaska Airlines, Procter & Gamble, or the bicycle shop down the street use Web 2.0?

Advertising

Consider an Oracle CRM ad that might appear in the print version of the *Wall Street Journal*. Oracle has no control over who reads that ad, nor does it know much about the people who do (just that they fit the general demographic of *Wall Street Journal* readers). On any particular day, 10,000 qualified buyers for Oracle products might happen to read the ad, or then again, perhaps only 1,000 qualified buyers read it.

Neither Oracle nor the *Wall Street Journal* knows the number, but Oracle pays the same amount for the ad, regardless of the number of readers or who they are.

In the Web 2.0 world, advertising is specific to user interests. Someone who searches online for "customer relationship management" is likely an IT person (or a student) who has a strong interest in Oracle and its competing products. Oracle would like to advertise to that person.

Google pioneered Web 2.0 advertising. With its **AdWords** software, vendors pay a certain amount for particular search words. For example, FlexTime might agree to pay $2 for the word *workout*. When someone Googles that term, Google will display a link to FlexTime's Web site. If the user clicks that link (and *only* if the user clicks that link), Google charges FlexTime's account $2. FlexTime pays nothing if the user does not click. If it chooses, FlexTime, which is based in Indianapolis, can agree to pay only when users in the Indianapolis area click the ad.

The amount that a company pays per word can be changed from day to day, and even hour to hour. If FlexTime is about to start a new spinning class, it will be willing to pay more for the word *spinning* just before the class starts than it will afterward. The value of a click on *spinning* is low when the start of the next spinning class is a month away.

AdSense is another advertising alternative. Google searches an organization's Web site and inserts ads that match content on that site. When users click those ads, Google pays the organization a fee. Other Web 2.0 vendors offer services similar to AdWords and AdSense.

With Web 2.0, the cost of reaching a particular, qualified person is much smaller than in the traditional advertising model. As a consequence, many companies are switching to the new lower-cost medium, and newspapers and magazines are struggling with a sharp reduction in advertising revenue.

Mashups

How can two non-Internet companies mash the content of their products? Suppose you're watching a hit movie and you would like to buy the jewelry, dress, or watch worn by the leading actress. Suppose that Nordstrom sells all those items. With Web 2.0 technology, the movie's producer and Nordstrom can mash their content together so that you, watching the movie on computer at home, can click the item you like and be directed to Nordstrom e-commerce site that will sell it to you. Or, perhaps Nordstrom is disintermediated out of the transaction, and you are taken to the e-commerce site of the watch's manufacturer.

Q3 How Do Social Networking Information Systems Increase Social Capital?

You don't need this text to learn how to use Facebook or Twitter. You already know how to do that. But when you use such sites, there is more going on than you realize. If you are using such sites solely for entertainment or self-expression, then deeper understanding isn't too important. But, if, like many professionals, you use such sites for both self-expression and for professional purposes, then understanding how such sites contribute to your social capital and how such capital influences and benefits organizations is important.

What Is Social Capital?

Business literature defines three types of capital. Karl Marx defined **capital** as the investment of resources for future profit. This traditional definition refers to investments into resources such as factories, machines, manufacturing equipment, and the like. **Human capital** is the investment in human knowledge and skills for

How honest are people with social networking? Reflect on ethical issues for social networking in the Ethics Guide in this chapter.

future profit. By taking this class, you are investing in your own human capital. You are investing your money and time to obtain knowledge that you hope will differentiate you from other workers and ultimately give you a wage premium in the workforce.

According to Nan Lin, **social capital** is the investment in social relations with the expectation of returns in the marketplace.[2] When you attend a business function for the purpose of meeting people and reinforcing relationships, you are investing in your social capital. Similarly, when you join LinkedIn or contribute to Facebook, you are (or can be) investing in your social capital.

According to Lin, social capital adds value in four ways:

* Information
* Influence
* Social credentials
* Personal reinforcement

Relationships in social networks can provide *information* about opportunities, alternatives, problems, and other factors important to business professionals. They also provide an opportunity to *influence* decision makers in one's employer or in other organizations who are critical to your success. Such influence cuts across formal organizational structures, such as reporting relationships. Third, being linked to a network of highly regarded contacts is a form of *social credential.* You can bask in the glory of those with whom you are related. Others will be more inclined to work with you if they believe critical personnel are standing with you and may provide resources to support you. Finally, being linked into social networks reinforces a professional's image and position in an organization or industry. It reinforces the way you define yourself to the world (and to yourself).

Social networks differ in value. The social network you maintain with your high school friends probably has less value than the network you have with your business associates, but not necessarily so. According to Henk Flap,[3] the **value of social capital** is determined by the number of relationships in a social network, by the strength of those relationships, and by the resources controlled by those related. If your high school friends happened to have been Bill Gates and Paul Allen, and if you maintain strong relations with them via your high school network, then the value of that social network far exceeds any you'll have at work. For most of us, however, it is the network of our current professional contacts that provides the most social capital.

So, when you use social networking professionally, consider those three factors. You gain social capital by adding more friends and by strengthening the relationships you have with existing friends. Further, you gain more social capital by adding friends and strengthening relationships with people who control resources that are important to you. Such calculations may seem cold, impersonal, and possibly even phony. When applied to the recreational use of social networking, they may be. But when you use social networking for professional purposes, keep them in mind.

How Do Social Networks Add Value to Businesses?

Organizations have social capital just as humans do. Historically, organizations created social capital via salespeople, via customer support, and via public relations. Endorsements by high-profile people are a traditional way of increasing social capital, but there are tigers in those woods.

---

[2]Nan Lin, *Social Capital: The Theory of Social Structure and Action* (Cambridge, UK: Cambridge University Press, 2002), Location 310 of the Kindle Edition.

[3]Henk D. Flap, "Social Capital in the Reproduction of Inequality," *Comparative Sociology of Family, Health, and Education,* Vol. 20, pages 6179–6202 (1991). Cited in Nan Lin, *Social Capital: The Theory of Social Structure and Action* (Cambridge, UK: Cambridge University Press, 2002), Kindle location 345.

Using MIS InClass *A Group Exercise*

Computing Your Social Capital

Superstock Royalty Free

Social capital is not an abstract concept that applies only to organizations; it applies to you as well. You and your classmates are accumulating social capital now. What is the value of that capital? To see, form a group and complete the following items:

1. Define *capital, human capital,* and *social capital.* Explain how these terms differ.

2. How does the expression "It's not what you know, but who you know that matters" pertain to the terms you defined in item 1?

3. Do you, personally, agree with the statement in item 2? Form your own opinion before discussing it with your group.

4. As a group, discuss the relative value of human and social capital. In what ways is social capital more valuable than human capital? Form a group consensus view on the validity of the statement in item 2.

5. Visit the Facebook, LinkedIn, Twitter, or other social networking presence site of each group member.
   a. Using the definition of social capital value in this chapter, assess the value of each group member's social networking presence.
   b. Recommend at least one way to add value to each group member's social capital at each site.

6. Suppose you each decide to feature your Facebook or other social networking page on your professional résumé.
   a. How would you change your presence that you evaluated in item 5 in order to make it more appropriate for that purpose?
   b. Describe three or four types of professionals that you could add to your social network that would facilitate your job search.

7. Imagine that you are the CEO of a company that has just one product to sell: You!
   a. Review the Enterprise 2.0 SLATES principles in Figure 16 and assess how each could pertain to the selling of your "product" (i.e., obtaining a quality job that you want). You can find the McAfee article at *http://sloanreview.mit.edu/the-magazine/files/saleable-pdfs/47306.pdf.*
   b. Explain how you could use your social networking presence to facilitate social CRM selling of your product.
   c. Devise a creative and interesting way to use this exercise as part of your social CRM offering.

8. Present your answers to items 4 and 7 to the rest of the class.

Today, progressive organizations maintain a presence on Facebook, LinkedIn, Twitter, and possibly other sites. They include links to their social networking presence on their Web sites and make it easy for customers and interested parties to leave comments. In most cases, such connections are positive, but they can backfire, as you saw at Fox Lake in the opening of this chapter.

To understand how social networks add value to businesses, consider each of the elements of social capital: number of relationships, strength of relationships, and resources controlled by "friends."

Using Social Networking to Increase the Number of Relationships

The term **social networking (SN)** refers to any activity that an entity (individual, project, or organization) takes with entities with which it is related. As shown in Figure 7, in a traditional business relationship clients (you) have some experience with a business, such

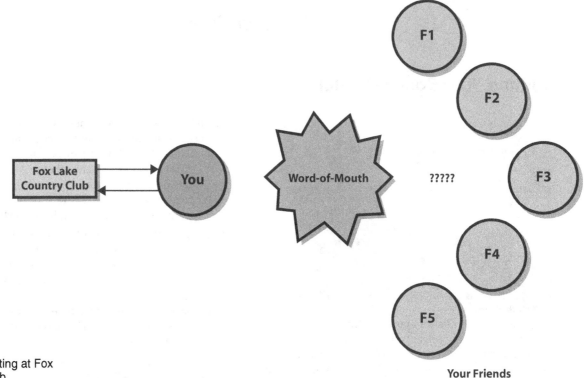

Figure 7
Traditional Marketing at Fox
Lake Country Club

as the restaurant at Fox Lake. Traditionally, you may express your opinions about that experience by word-of-mouth to your social network (here denoted by friends F1, F2, etc.). However, such communication is unreliable and brief: You are more likely to say something to your friends if the experience was particularly good or bad; but, even then, you are likely only to say something to those friends whom you encounter while the experience is still recent. And once you have said something, that's it; your words don't live on for days or weeks.

A **social networking information system** is an information system that facilitates interactions on a social network. Social networking information systems have numerous characteristics, one of which is that they make the transmission of your opinions more reliable and longer lasting. For example, suppose the Fox Lake restaurant establishes a presence on a social network, maybe it has a page on Facebook. The nature of the presence is unimportant here.

When you mention the Fox Lake restaurant on your social network, something about that business will be broadcast to your friends, as shown in Figure 8. That messaging is automatic; "I just had the Sunday night lobster dinner at Fox Lake, Yummm!" will be reliably broadcast to all of your friends and, unlike word-of-mouth, that message will last for hours, even days. That, in itself, is a powerful marketing program.

However, social networking provides even greater possibilities. As shown in Figure 9, you have friends (OK, you have more than five friends, but space is limited), and your friends have friends, and those friends have friends. If something about your message, induces F5 (for example) to broadcast about Fox Lake to her friends, and if that message induces F7 to broadcast about Fox Lake to his friends, and so forth, the messaging will be viral. The something that induces people to share your message is called a **viral hook**.

As shown in Figure 9, some of the social capital you contribute to Fox Lake is the relationships you have with your friends, and the relationships they have with their friends. But those relationships are indirect. Viral marketing will be even more powerful if your message induces your friends (and their friends, etc.) to form a direct relationship with Fox Lake's social networking presence, as shown in Figure 10.

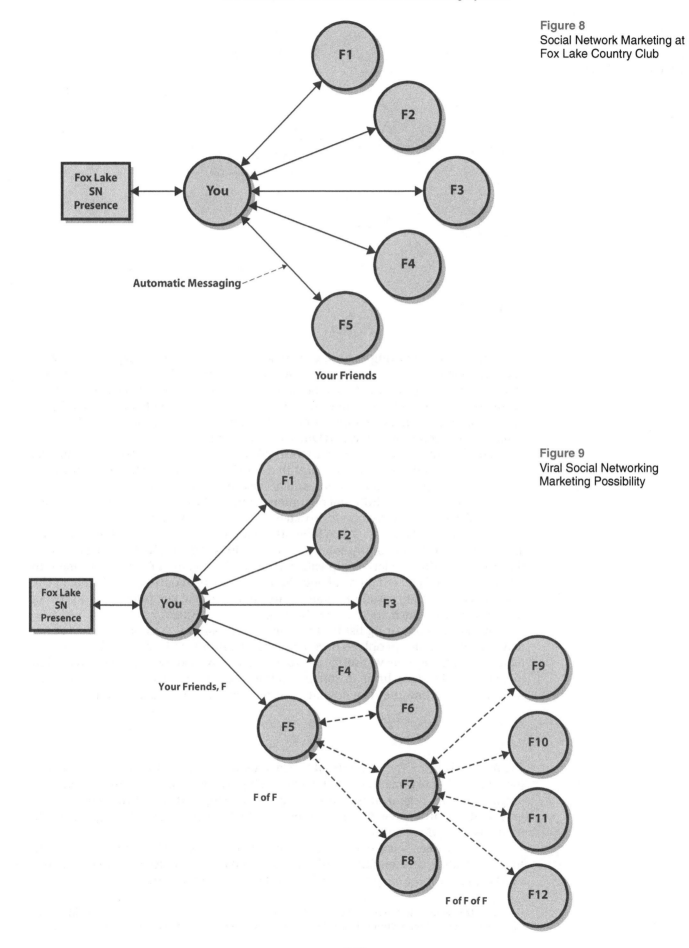

Figure 8
Social Network Marketing at
Fox Lake Country Club

Figure 9
Viral Social Networking
Marketing Possibility

Figure 10
Viral Message Causes Your
Friends (and Theirs) to
Connect with Fox Lake

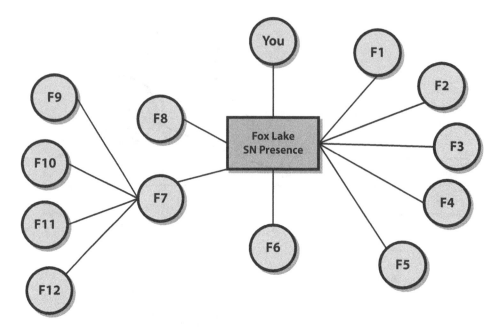

Consider the following example. Microsoft Office 2010 has the capability to store documents in the cloud on a virtual server called Windows Live SkyDrive. It's a handy way to store backup copies of documents, but, even more useful, you can share those documents with friends. You enter their email addresses to enable them to read your documents. However, if you want your friends to be able to add, modify, or delete documents, your friends must have an Office Live account.

Here's how this situation creates a viral hook: Last month, I posted some documents on my Windows Live SkyDrive account that I wanted another professor to review. I entered his university email account, and he was able to read those documents. However, he wanted to add additional documents, and to do so he needed an Office Live account. The easiest way for him to do that was to create a new Hotmail account.

Thus, Microsoft used its Office franchise to induce me to create a viral hook, bait, as it were, to cause one of my colleagues to obtain an Office Live/Hotmail account, thus forming a direct relationship with Microsoft. The beauty of this arrangement to Microsoft is that I created the viral hook for them; they paid nothing for the hook. The only direct cost to Microsoft of obtaining this new Hotmail customer was the cost of the storage I use, which, as you know by now, is essentially zero.[4]

Fox Lake has a waiting list for new memberships, so it is unlikely to use social networking to induce people to become members. However, brides need not be club members to have their weddings at Fox Lake, so Fox Lake would be interested in inducing one Fox Lake bride to convince a friend to have her wedding at Fox Lake as well. You'll learn how they can do that using groups and applications in Q4.

Using Social Networks to Increase the Strength of Relationships

To an organization, the **strength of a relationship** is the likelihood that the entity (person or other organization) in the relationship will do something that benefits the organization. An organization has a strong relationship with you if you buy its products, write positive reviews about it, post pictures of you using the organization's products or services, and so on.

As stated earlier, social networks provide four forms of value: influence, information, social credentials, and reinforcement. If an organization can induce those in its relationships to provide more of any of those factors, it has strengthened that relationship.

---

[4]This was true when I wrote it in May of 2010, but is no longer as you can now change directories without a Windows Live account. This is just another example of how quickly technology changes.

214

In his autobiography, Benjamin Franklin[5] provided a key insight. He said that if you want to strengthen your relationship with someone in power, ask them to do you a favor. Before he invented the public library, he would ask powerful strangers to lend him their expensive books. In that same sense, organizations have learned that they can strengthen their relationships with you by asking you to do them a favor. In Q4, we will discuss information systems that encourage the creation of User-Generated Content as a way of getting you to do them a favor. When you provide that favor, it strengthens your relationship with the organization.

Traditional capital depreciates. Machines wear out, factories get old, technology and computers become obsolete, and so forth. Does social capital also depreciate? Do relationships wear out from use? So far, the answer seems to be both yes and no.

Clearly, there are only so many favors you can ask of someone in power. And, there are only so many times a company can ask you to review a product, post pictures, or provide connections to your friends. At some point, the relationship deteriorates due to overuse. So, yes, social capital does depreciate.

However, frequent interactions strengthen relationships and hence increase social capital. The more you interact with a company, the stronger your commitment and allegiance. But continued frequent interactions occur only when both parties see value in continuing the relationship. Thus, at some point, the organization must do something to make it worth your while to continue to do them a favor.

So, social capital does depreciate, but such depreciation can be ameliorated by adding something of value to the interaction. And, continuing a successful relationship over time substantially increases relationship strength.

Connecting to Those with More Assets

The third measure of the value of social capital is the size of the assets controlled by those in the relationships. An organization's social capital is thus partly a function of the social capital of those to whom it relates. The most visible measure is the number of relationships. Someone with 1,000 loyal Twitter followers is usually more valuable than someone with 10. But the calculation is more subtle than that; if those 1,000 followers are college students, and if the organization's product is adult diapers, the value of the relationship to the followers is low. A relationship with 10 Twitter followers who are in retirement homes would be more valuable.

There is no formula for computing social capital, but the three factors would seem to be more multiplicative than additive. Or, stated in other terms, the value of social capital is more in the form of

$$SocialCapital = NumberRelationships \times RelationshipStrength \times EntityResources$$

Than it is:

$$SocialCapital = NumberRelationships + RelationshipStrength + EntityResources$$

Again, do not take these equations literally; take them in the sense of the interaction of the three factors.

The multiplicative nature of social capital means that a huge network of relationships to people who have few resources may be lower than that of a smaller network with people with substantial resources. Furthermore, those resources must be

---

[5]Founding father of the United States. Author of *Poor Richard's Almanac*. Successful businessman; owner of a chain of print shops. Discoverer of groundbreaking principles in the theory of electricity. Inventor of bifocals, the potbelly stove, the lightning rod, and much more. Founder of the public library and the postal service. Darling of the French court and salons, and now, contributor to social network theory!

Ethics Guide

Hiding the Truth?

No one is going to publish their ugliest picture on their Facebook page, but how far should you go to create a positive impression? If your hips and legs are not your best features, is it unethical to stand behind your sexy car in your photo? If you've been to one event with someone very popular in your crowd, is it unethical to publish photos that imply you meet as an everyday occurrence? Surely there is no obligation to publish pictures of yourself at boring events with unpopular people just to balance the scale for those photos in which you appear unrealistically attractive and overly popular.

As long as all of this occurs on a Facebook or MySpace account that you use for personal relationships, well, what goes around comes around. But consider social networking in the business arena.

a. Suppose that a river rafting company starts a group on a social networking site for promoting rafting trips. Graham, a 15-year-old high school student who wants to be more grown-up than he is, posts a picture of a handsome 22-year-old male as a picture of himself. He also writes witty and clever comments on the site photos and claims to play the guitar and be an accomplished masseuse. Are his actions unethical? Suppose someone decided to go on the rafting trip, in part because of Graham's postings, and was disappointed with the truth about Graham. Would the rafting company have any responsibility to refund that person's fees?

b. Suppose you own and manage the rafting company. Is it unethical for you to encourage your employees to write positive reviews about your company? Does your assessment change if you ask your employees to use an email address other than the one they have at work?

c. Again, suppose you own and manage the rafting company and that you pay your employees a bonus for every client they bring to a rafting trip. Without specifying any particular technique, you encourage your employees to be creative in how they obtain clients. One employee invites his MySpace friends to a party at which he shows photos of prior rafting trips. On the way to the party, one of the friends has an automobile accident and dies. His spouse sues your company. Should your company be held accountable? Does it matter if you knew about the presentation? Would it matter if you had not encouraged your employees to be creative?

d. Suppose your rafting company has a Web site for customer reviews. In spite of your best efforts at camp cleanliness, on one trip (out of dozens) your staff accidentally served contaminated food and everyone became ill with food-poisoning. One of those clients from that trip writes a poor review because of that experience. Is it ethical for you to delete that review from your site?

e. Assume you have a professor who has written a popular textbook. You are upset with the grade you received in his class, so you write a scandalously poor review of that professor's book on Amazon.com. Are your actions ethical?

f. Instead of owner, suppose you were at one time employed by this rafting company and you were, undeservedly you think, terminated. To get even, you use Facebook to spread rumors to your friends (many of whom are river guides) about the safety of the company's trips. Are your actions unethical? Are they illegal? Do you see any ethical distinctions between this situation and that in item d?

g. Again, suppose that you were at one time employed by the rafting company and were undeservedly terminated. You notice that the company's owner does not have a Facebook account, so you create one for her. You've known her for many years and have dozens of photos of her, some of which were taken at parties and are unflattering and revealing. You post those photos along with critical comments that she made about clients or employees. Most of the comments were made when she was tired or frustrated, and they are hurtful, but because of her wit, also humorous. You send friend invitations to people whom she knows, many of whom are the target of her biting and critical remarks. Are your actions unethical? ▓

Discussion Questions

1. Read the situations in items a through g and answer the questions contained in each.

2. Based on your answers in question 1, formulate ethical principles for creating or using social networks for business purposes.

3. Based on your answers in question 1, formulate ethical principles for creating or using User-Generated Content for business purposes.

4. Summarize the risks that a business assumes when it chooses to sponsor User-Generated Content.

5. Summarize the risks that a business assumes when it uses social networks for business purposes.

relevant to the organization. Students with pocket change are relevant to Pizza Hut; they are irrelevant to a BMW dealership.

This discussion brings us to the brink of social networking practice. Most organizations today (2010) ignore the value of entity assets and simply try to connect to more people with stronger relationships. This area is ripe for innovation. Data aggregators like ChoicePoint and Acxiom maintain detailed data about people, worldwide. It would seem that such data could be used by information systems to calculate the potential value of a relationship to a particular individual. This possibility would enable organizations to better understand the value of their social networks as well as guide their behavior with regard to particular individuals.

Stay tuned; many possibilities exist, and some ideas, maybe yours, will be very successful.

Q4 What Are Business Applications for Facebook, Twitter, and User-Generated Content (UGC)?

Innovative organizations have developed and continue to develop Facebook, Twitter, and User-Generated Content systems for increasing their social capital. In this question, we will consider each.

Facebook

The easiest way for an organization to use Facebook is to create a page and manage that page for business purposes using the same techniques that you use to manage your personal Facebook page. Organizations can build the number of relationships by inducing Facebook members to "Like" them, as discussed in Q3. Here, we will consider how organizations use groups and applications.

Using Facebook Groups

A **social networking group** is an association of SN members related to a particular topic, event, activity, or other collective interest. In addition to members, SN groups have resources such as photos, videos, documents, discussion threads, a wall, and features. In some cases, groups have one or more events.

Three types of groups are possible:

- **Public.** Anyone can find the group by searching, and anyone can join it.
- **Invitation.** Anyone can find the group by searching, but he or she must be invited to join.
- **Private.** The group cannot be found by searching, and members must be invited to join.

Businesses can use groups to strengthen relationships among customers and to create the possibility of a viral hook. For example, Fox Lake could create an invitation group for each wedding to use as its wedding Web site. The bride then invites everyone on the guest list to join the group. Prior to the wedding, the bride and groom could place photos and videos of their relationship and engagement on the group site. The happy couple could also provide links to gift registries, directions to Fox Lake, weather forecasts, and any other information of interest to the wedding attendees. They could also start a discussion list.

If Fox Lake can convince wedding parties to use its groups, it can form relationships with the wedding invitees, as shown for the two weddings in Figure 11.

Additionally, at some point Fox Lake may ask the bride if it can create a public version of the wedding as part of its club news site. Club members who see wedding pictures of members' families will be more likely to consider Fox Lake for themselves or their friends.

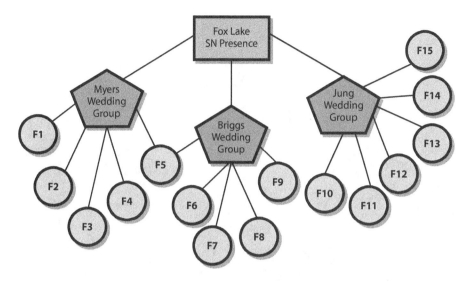

Figure 11
Strengthening Relationships
with Wedding Groups

Notice that social networking groups can be used for more than marketing. To help plan weddings, Anne might create a private group for just the wedding party. That group could have information about the rehearsal, rehearsal dinner, logistics, and so forth. Brides might be more willing to share the email addresses of these people with Fox Lake than they would be willing to share email addresses of all invitees. Of course, once the wedding is over, Fox Lake has the email addresses of the wedding party, and we're back to . . . marketing!

Using Facebook Applications

A **social networking application** is a computer program that interacts with and processes information in a social network. For example, consider Survey Hurricane, a Facebook application created by Infinistorm (*www.infinistorm.com*). Users who install that application on their page can survey their friends on topics of interest. The *New York Times* quiz is another application, as are applications for buying and selling items, comparing movies, and so on.

Social networking applications run on servers provided by the application's creator. When someone accesses the application on the SN vendor's site (e.g., Facebook or MySpace), the request for that service is passed to the application provider's server. That application can call back to the SN vendor to create friend requests, find existing friends, generate email, make requests, poke friends, or take other actions. In the process, it can collect data about you and your friends for individualized marketing or for data mining.

Organizations can use social networking applications to increase their competitive advantage as well as to increase the value of their social networks. For example, Fox Lake could create an application called "Plan Your Fox Lake Wedding" and make the application part of its product offering. If the application has features that greatly simplify and facilitate wedding planning and includes ideas, dos and don'ts, recommended vendors, and other resources of interest to wedding planners, it would be one more reason for brides to choose Fox Lake. Figure 12 shows this application supporting three different weddings. Note that Person 5 is an attendant in two weddings. By creating this application, Fox Lake will obtain the name, email address, and possibly the postal address of all the attendants. Using this data, Fox Lake can begin to build stronger relationships with each person.

Applications give the application vendor more control over the users' experience than groups do. An application can be developed to require passwords and user accounts. Fox Lake would need to implement user accounts to be able to ensure that only members of the wedding party can access the planning application. That application would probably also have rules and restrictions about who could add, edit, or delete content.

Figure 12
Strengthening Relationships
with a Wedding Application

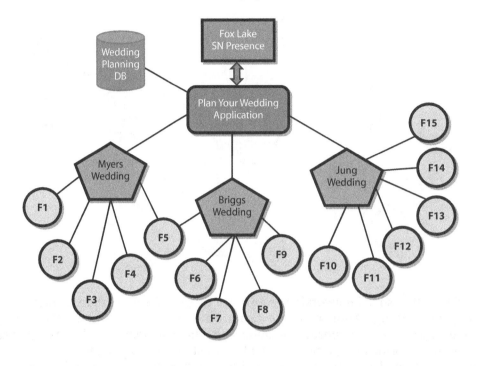

The key to success is, of course, to make the application compelling. Facebook publishes considerable documentation and advice to its developers, including four principles for designing meaningful applications. Consider each:

- **Social.** *Meaningful applications use information in the social graph.* A **social graph** is a network of relationships; Figure 12 shows a portion of the social graph among three different wedding parties. A survey application uses information from the social graph because it uses the links to your friends to ask the survey questions. If "Plan Your Wedding" asks friends to label photos of the groom in amusing situations, it is using the social graph in a compelling way. Both you and your friends will find it far more meaningful than an application that just shows wedding pictures.
- **Useful.** *Meaningful applications address real needs, from entertainment to practical tasks.* In a business setting, no one cares what you had for breakfast or where you put your toothbrush this morning. They might, however, be interested in what cities you'll be visiting on your next business trip. Similarly, "Plan Your Wedding" could have features that enable the wedding party to plan ride sharing.
- **Expressive.** *Meaningful applications share a personal perspective on the world.* People participate in SN activities because they want to share something about themselves. An SN application that publishes generic photos, or even personal photos in a generic way, does not allow the user to express his or her individuality. Fox Lake would add expressivity to "Plan Your Wedding" if it allowed members of the wedding party to describe how they first met the bride or groom, what they thought when they heard about the wedding, or any other expressive perspective. Such personal reflections induce clients to author more comments and their friends to read them more frequently.
- **Engaging.** *Meaningful applications compel users to come back again, and again, and again.* Engaging applications are dynamic; they give participants a reason to come back. A dynamic application slowly reveals more of its content, changes its content, or alters the actions that participants can take. This principle is less appropriate to weddings, because they are a one-time event. Fox Lake, however, might have a golfing application that includes a feature like "Shot of the Day," "Duffer of the Day," or something similar.

Social Networking Applications Versus Web Sites

Social networking applications share many features and functions with Web sites. Fox Lake can develop a Web site with photos, even particular wedding photos. It can also develop a site that has a "Shot of the Day" feature. So why develop an SN application rather than a Web site?

The answer lies with the degree to which the application requires a social graph. Does the application use or benefit from social network communication? Is there a need for social collaboration? For feedback and iteration? If not, the organization could develop a Web application that would be just as effective, possibly cheaper, and would not run the risks described in Q6.

Twitter

Twitter has taken the business world by storm. If you think of Twitter as a place for teenage girls to describe the lipstick they're wearing today, think again. Hundreds of businesses are now using Twitter for legitimate business purposes.

First, in the unlikely case you haven't heard of Twitter, it is a Web 2.0 application that allows users to publish 140-character descriptions of . . . well, anything. Users can follow other Twitter users, and users can, in turn, be followed. Twitter is an example of a category of applications called *microblogs*. A **microblog** is a Web site on which users can publish their opinions, just like a Web blog, but the opinions are restricted to small amounts of text, such as Twitter's 140 characters.

You might think that 140 characters is too limiting. However, Twitter has demonstrated the design adage that "structure is liberating." Thousands more people microblog than blog because microblogging is less intimidating. You don't have space to write a well-constructed paragraph; in fact, the character limitation forces you to abbreviate words and grammar. It isn't necessary to spell correctly or to know that sentences need a subject and a verb, either. Microbloggers just have to be (barely) comprehensible to their audience. It is easy to fit a headline and a link to a Web site that provides more information.

Microblog competitors to Twitter are emerging, and it is possible that by the time you read this Twitter will be old news. If so, as you read, replace Twitter with the name of whatever microblog application is currently the rage.

We Are All Publishers Now

Microblogs like Twitter make everyone a publisher. Anyone can join, for free, and immediately publish his or her ideas, worldwide. If you happen to be the world's expert on making pine-bark tea and you have developed innovative techniques for harvesting pine bark, you have a free, worldwide platform for publishing those techniques.

Before we continue, think about that statement. As recently as 10 years ago, worldwide publishing was expensive and restricted to the very few. The *New York Times*, the *Wall Street Journal*, and a few other newspapers and large television networks were the only worldwide publishing venues in the United States. Publishing was a one-way street. They published, and we consumed.

Microblogging enables two-way publishing, worldwide. You publish your ideas on pine-bark harvesting, and others can publish you back. Notice that, unlike email, you are both *publishing*, not just communicating to each other. Your interchange, your conversation, is available for others to read, worldwide.

By the way, microblogging would be far less important if it lacked search features. Unfortunately for you, only four other people, worldwide, care about pine-bark harvesting. Were it not for the ability to search microblogs, they and you would never find one another. So, microblogging is important not just because it turns us all into publishers—by itself, that would not be very useful. Equally important is that microblogging enables users with similar interests to find each other.

Be careful what you publish! Social networking at work may be problematic. The Guide later in the chapter explores social networking opinions of employees at Pearson Education (the publisher of this text).

221

How Can Businesses Benefit from Microblogging?

As of October, 2010, businesses are actively experimenting with microblogging. Three obvious applications have emerged so far:

- Public relations
- Relationship sales
- Market research

We'll examine each of these, in turn, but stay tuned! Newer innovative applications are in the works.

PUBLIC RELATIONS   Microblogging enables any employee or business owner to communicate with the world. No longer is it necessary to meet with editors and writers at newspapers and magazines and attempt to influence them to publish something positive about your product or other news. Instead, write it yourself and click "Update." The only requirements are having something to say that your customers want to read and using keywords on which your customers are likely to search.

Possible examples are a product manager who's excited about a new use for his product. He can publish the idea and a summary of instructions. If the concept is longer than 140 words, he can include a link to a blog or Web site that has the rest of the description. Or, a customer service representative can publish warnings about possible misuse of a product or provide instructions for a new way of performing product maintenance, again with a link to a Web site, if necessary.

Pete Carroll, former coach of the University of Southern California football team, introduced microblogging by college football coaches. Coaches can increase fan awareness by blogging with insider details, how the practice went, comments about the recent game, and so on. Coaches no longer have to depend on sportswriters and sportscasters for team public relations. In addition, microblogging means that coaches can control the content that is published.

By the way, these new public relations capabilities are stressing existing institutions. The NCAA has many rules and regulations about how and when coaches can contact potential recruits. How does a coach's microblogging fit into this scheme? The NCAA and others are scrambling to figure it out.

RELATIONSHIP SALES   Social networking in general and microblogging in particular are all about relationships—forming new relationships and strengthening existing ones. Such relationships can serve as an ideal channel for sales. For example, suppose you are the owner of a plant nursery and you've just received a shipment of 100 hard-to-get plants. If you've formed Twitter relationships with your customers, you can Tweet the arrival of the plants and include a link to a Web site with pictures of how gorgeous these plants can be.

However, experience has shown that pure sales pitches are ineffective when microblogging. People stop following sources that only publish ads and sales pitches. Instead, people look for Tweeters who offer something they value, such as advice, links to resources, and interesting and thought-provoking opinions. So you, as the plant nursery owner, should offer advice and assistance, such as reminders that it's time to prune the roses or fertilize the azaleas.

From time to time, you can publish an ad, but, even then, it should be published in a way like that you would use with a friend. Hard come-ons won't work; instead, make the pitch in terms of "I thought you might want to know about the arrival of the. . . ." just as you would pass advice on to a friend. You can find many other sales ideas in books, such as *Twitter Revolution: How Social Media and Mobile Marketing Is Changing the Way We Do Business and Market Online*.[6]

---

[6]Warren Whitlock and Deborah Micek, *Twitter Revolution: How Social Media and Mobile Marketing Is Changing the Way We Do Business and Market Online* (Las Vegas, NV: Xeno Press, 2008).

MARKET RESEARCH   Market research is the third promising business use of microblogging. Want to know what people think of your product? Search Twitter to find out. Office 2010 is an interesting example. Office 2010 was prereleased to a limited set of expert users as a beta version in the fall of 2008 and to a larger group of experienced users as a release candidate in the spring of 2009. Users of both these releases used Twitter to comment about their experience as well as to ask for help or provide assistance to each other. Meanwhile, Microsoft product managers were searching the Twitter traffic to learn the buzz about the new product. They used knowledge of what users especially liked to craft the launch of the actual product in 2010. Product developers and technical writers also learned about features that were hard to understand and use.

User-Generated Content

Users have been generating content on the Internet since its beginning. However, with Web 2.0 many companies have found (and are finding) innovative ways of using User-Generated Content (UGC) for business functions. This section surveys common types of UGC and discusses their business applications.

Figure 13 lists the common types of UGC. You are undoubtedly familiar with most, if not all, of these. Product ratings and surveys have been used for years. Product opinions are also common. Recent research indicates that ratings and opinions of fellow customers are far more trusted than any advertising. In March 2007, Jupiter Research found that social network users were three times more likely to trust their peers' opinions over advertising when making purchase decisions.[7]

Some companies find it advantageous to facilitate customers' storytelling about the use of the company's products. According to Bazaarvoice (*www.bazaarvoice.com*), "Giving visitors a place to share their stories will increase brand involvement, interaction, intimacy and influence. Far beyond just increasing time on site, personal stories engage visitors and writers alike, all increasing overall loyalty to your site—and your brand."[8]

Still other companies sponsor discussion groups for customers to offer advice and assistance to one another. In addition to customer support, those sites provide the company with useful information for product marketing and development. Wikis and blogs are another form of UGC in which customers and partners can offer advice and assistance regarding products.

Video is increasingly used to tell stories, offer product demonstrations, and apply products to specific needs and problems. The amount of UGC video is staggering. According to YouTube, 10 hours of UGC video are uploaded to its site *every minute.* That video is equivalent to 57,000 feature-length movies every week.[9]

- Ratings and surveys
- Opinions
- Customer stories
- Discussion groups
- Wikis
- Blogs
- Video

Figure 13
Types of User-Generated Content

---

[7]Jupiter Research, "Social Networking Sites: Defining Advertising Opportunities in a Competitive Landscape," March 2007.

[8]Quote from *www.bazaarvoice.com/stories.html* (accessed August 2008).

[9]N'Gai Croal, "The Internet Is the New Sweatshop," *Newsweek,* July 7–14, 2008, *www.newsweek.com/id/143740* (accessed July 2008).

Figure 14
UGC Applications

Application	Example
Sale (ratings, reviews, recommendations, stories)	www.amazon.com
Marketing (crowdsourcing)	www.ryzwear.com
Product support (problem solving, Q&A, advice, applications)	www.msdn.com
Product development (research and development)	www.spore.com www.ryzwear.com
UGC as bait for advertising	www.youtube.com www.funnyordie.com
UGC as part of product	www.finewoodworking.com www.woodenboat.com

UGC Applications

Figure 14 lists the most common applications for UGC. In sales, the presence of ratings, reviews, and recommendations increases conversion rates—in some cases doubling the rate of purchase. Interestingly, conversion rates are higher for products with less-than-perfect reviews than for products with no reviews at all.[10] Furthermore, return rates fall dramatically as the number of product reviews increases.[11]

Crowdsourcing is the process by which users provide services to or on behalf of the vendor. On some sites, users provide customer support and advice to one another. Even more dramatic, some crowdsourcers participate in the creation of product specifications, designs, and complete products. As shown in Figure 15, the shoe company RYZ (*www.ryzwear.com*) sponsors shoe design contests to help it understand which shoes to create and how to market those designs.

Crowdsourcing combines social networking, viral marketing, and open-source design, saving considerable cost while cultivating customers. With crowdsourcing, the

Figure 15
Design by Crowdsourcing

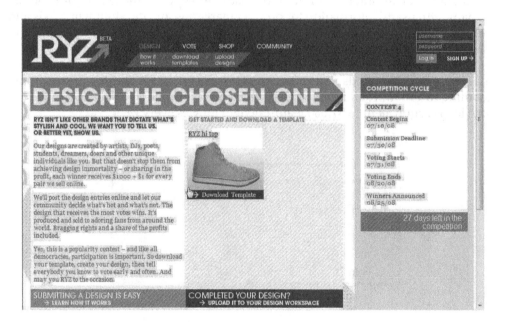

[10]Bazaarvoice, "Industry Statistics, July 2008," *www.bazaarvoice.com/industryStats.html* (accessed August 2008).
[11]Matt Hawkings, "PETCO.com Significantly Reduces Return Rates," *Marketing Data Analyst*, June 27, 2006, *www.bazaarvoice.com/cs_rr_returns_petco.html* (accessed August 2008).

crowd performs classic in-house market research and development and does so in such a way that customers are being set up to buy.

As another UGC example, Microsoft supports its software, database, and other developers on its MSDN Web site (*www.msdn.com*; MSDN stands for "Microsoft Developer Network"). Developers post answers to questions, articles, best practices, blogs, code samples, and other resources for developing Microsoft applications.

YouTube is famous for hosting UGC videos provided as bait for advertising. Finally, some sites include UGC as part of the product. The magazines *Fine Woodworking* and *Wooden Boat* both include UGC video as part of their product offerings.

The use of UGC has been increasing with the growth of e-commerce and Web 2.0. Undoubtedly, many successful applications have yet to be invented. UGC for business will be an exciting field during the early years of your career.

Q5 How Does Social CRM Empower Customers?

Prior to the Internet, organizations controlled their relationships with customers. In fact, the primary purpose of traditional CRM was to manage customer touches. Traditional CRM ensured that the organization spoke to customers with one voice and that it controlled the messages, offers, and even the support that customers received based on the value of a particular customer. In 1990, if you wanted to know something about an IBM product you'd contact its local sales office; that office would classify you as a prospect and use that classification to control the literature, documentation, and your access to IBM personnel.

Today, the vendor–customer relationship is far more complex and is not controlled by the vendor. Businesses offer many different customer touch points, and customers craft their own relationship with the business by their use of those touch points. **Social CRM** is the creation and use of the Enterprise 2.0 collaborative relationship between businesses and customers. Because social CRM is a manifestation of Enterprise 2.0, we begin with it.

What Are the Characteristics of Enterprise 2.0?

Enterprise 2.0 is the application of Web 2.0 technologies, collaboration systems, social networking, and related technologies to facilitate the cooperative work of people in organizations. You can think of Enterprise 2.0 as the migration and use of Web 2.0 tools and techniques within organizations. Enterprise 2.0 provides a set of capabilities that workers use to collaborate and that allows content to emerge, rather than be preplanned.

McAfee defined six characteristics of Enterprise 2.0 that he refers to with the acronym **SLATES** (see Figure 16). Workers want to be able to *search* for content inside the organization just like they do on the Web. Most workers find that searching is more effective than navigating content structures such as lists and tables of content. Workers want to access organizational content by *link*, just as they do on the Web. They also want to *author* organizational content using blogs, wikis, discussion groups, published presentations, and so on.

Enterprise 2.0 content is *tagged*, just like content on the Web, and tags are organized into structures, as is done on the Web at sites like Delicious (*www.delicious.com*). These structures organize tags as a taxonomy does, but, unlike taxonomies, they are not preplanned; they emerge. A **folksonomy** is content structure that has emerged from the processing of many user tags. Additionally, Enterprise 2.0 workers want applications to enable them to rate tagged content and to use the tags to predict content that will be of interest to them (as with Pandora), a process McAfee refers to as *extensions*. Finally, Enterprise 2.0 workers want relevant content pushed to them; they want to be *signaled* when something of interest to them happens in organizational content.

225

Figure 16
McAffee's SLATES Enterprise
2.0 Model

Enterprise 2.0 Component	Remarks
Search	People have more success searching than they do in finding from structured content
Links	Links to enterprise resources (like on the Web)
Authoring	Create enterprise content via blogs, wikis, discussion groups, presentations ...
Tags	Flexible tagging (like del.icio.us) results in folksonomies of enterprise content
Extensions	Using usage patterns to offer enterprise content via tag processing (like Pandora)
Signals	Pushing enterprise content to users based on subscriptions and alerts

Social CRM Is Enterprise 2.0 CRM

As stated, social CRM is customer relationship management done in the style of Enterprise 2.0. The relationships between organizations and customers emerge as both parties create and process content. In addition to the traditional forms of promotion, employees in the organization create wikis, blogs, discussion lists, frequently asked questions, sites for user reviews and commentary, and other dynamic content. Customers search this content, contribute reviews and commentary, ask more questions, create user groups, and so forth. With social CRM, each customer crafts his or her own relationship with the company.

Social CRM flies in the face of the principles of traditional CRM. Because relationships emerge from joint activity, customers have as much control as companies. This characteristic is an anathema to traditional sales managers who want control over what the customer is reading, seeing, and hearing about the company and its products. The general manager at Fox Lake is incensed because a negative review was published on his organization's Facebook page. He wants to delete it but finds he has insufficient social power to do so.

Further, traditional CRM is centered on lifetime value; customers that are likely to generate the most business get the most attention and have the most impact on the organization. However, with social CRM the customer who spends 10 cents but who is an effective reviewer, commentator, or blogger can have more influence than the quiet customer who purchases $10 million a year. Such imbalance is incomprehensible to traditional sales managers.

This brings us to the leading edge of the use of Web 2.0, social networking, and Enterprise 2.0 in business. What happens next is yet to be told; you will have exciting opportunities to work with these technologies early in your career! But remember to tell the world you learned it here first: *www.facebook.com/david.kroenke*!

Q6 How Can Organizations Manage the Risks of Social Networking Applications?

Before we get too carried away with the potential for emergent relationships via social CRM, Enterprise 2.0, and Web 2.0, note that not all business information systems benefit from flexibility and organic growth. Any information system that deals with assets, whether financial or material, requires some level of control. You probably do not want to mash up your credit card transactions to emerge via UGC, nor do you want them mashed up on a map that is shared with the world. As CFO, you probably do not want your accounts payable or general ledger system to have an emergent user interface; in fact, the Sarbanes-Oxley Act prohibits that possibility.

Problem Sources

Before a business plunges headlong into any commercial application of social networking, it should be aware of the risks that these tools entail. Some of the major risks are:

- Junk and crackpots
- Inappropriate content
- Unfavorable reviews
- Mutinous movements
- Dependency on the SN vendor

When a business participates in a social network or opens its site to UGC, it opens itself to misguided people who post junk unrelated to the site's purpose. Crackpots may also use the network or UGC site as a way of expressing passionately held views about unrelated topics, such as UFOs, government cover-ups, weird conspiracy theories, and so forth. Because of the possibility of such content, employees of the hosting business must regularly monitor the site and remove objectionable material immediately. Companies like Bazaarvoice offer services not only to collect and manage ratings and reviews, but also to monitor the site for irrelevant content.

Unfavorable reviews are another risk. Research indicates that customers are sophisticated enough to know that few, if any, products are perfect. Most customers want to know the disadvantages of a product before purchasing it so they can determine if those disadvantages are important for their application. However, if every review is bad, if the product is rated 1 star out of 5, then the company is using Web 2.0 technology to publish its problems. In this case, corrective action must be taken.

Mutinous movements are an extension of bad reviews. The campaign Web site *www.my.barackobama.com* had a strong social networking component, and when then-Senator Obama changed his position on immunity for telecoms engaged in national security work 22,000 members of his site joined a spontaneous group to object. Hundreds of members posted very critical comments of Obama, on his own site! This was an unexpected backlash to a campaign that had enjoyed unprecedented success raising money from small donors via social networking.

Although it is possible for organizations to develop their own social networking capability, many organizations use social networking vendors such as Facebook and MySpace. Those organizations are vulnerable to the success and policies of Facebook, MySpace, and others. These SN vendors are new companies with unproven business models; they may not survive. Also, using a social networking vendor for a business purpose makes the business vulnerable to the reliability and performance the SN vendor provides.

The license agreements of SN vendors are strongly biased in favor of the vendor. In some cases, the vendor owns the content that is developed; in other cases, the vendor can remove social networking applications at its discretion. In July 2008, for example, under pressure from Hasbro, the owner of Scrabble, Facebook required the creators of "Scrabulous" to redesign its game into "Wordscraper."[12]

The vulnerability is real, but the choices are limited. As stated, companies can create their own social networking capability, but doing so is expensive and requires

---

[12]Caroline McCarthy, "Why Facebook Left 'Scrabulous' Alone," *CNET News*, August 1, 2008, *http://news.cnet.com/8301-13577_3-10003821-36.html?part=rss&subj=news&tag=2547-1_3-0-5* (accessed August 2008).

highly skilled employees. And, having developed its own capability, no company will have the popularity and mindshare of Facebook or MySpace.

Responding to Social Networking Problems

The first task in managing social networking risk is to know the sources of potential problems and to monitor sites for problematic content. Once such content is found, however, organizations must have a plan for creating the organization's response. Three possibilities are:

* Leave it
* Respond to it
* Delete it

If the problematic content represents reasonable criticism of the organization's products or services, the best response may be to leave it where it is. Such criticism indicates that the site is not just a shill for the organization, but contains legitimate user content. Such criticism also serves as a free source of product reviews, which can be useful for product development. To be useful, the development team needs to know about the criticism, so systems to ensure that it is found and communicated to the development team are important.

A second response is to respond to the problematic content. This response is, however, dangerous. If the response could be construed, in any way, as patronizing or insulting to the content contributor, the response can enrage the user community and generate a strong backlash. Also, if the response appears defensive, it can become a strong public relations negative. In most cases, responses are best reserved for when the problematic content has caused the organization to do something positive as a result. For example, suppose a user publishes that he or she was required to hold for customer support for 45 minutes. If the organization has done something to reduce wait times, then an effective response to the criticism is to recognize it as valid and state, nondefensively, what had been done to reduce wait times.

Deleting content should be reserved for contributions that are inappropriate because they are contributed by crackpots, because they have nothing to do with the site, or because they contain obscene or otherwise inappropriate content. However, deleting legitimate negative comments can result in a strong user backlash. As Anne mentions in the Fox Lake case that opens this chapter, Nestlé created a PR nightmare on its Facebook account with its response to criticism it received about its use of palm oil. Someone altered the Nestlé logo, and in response Nestlé decided to delete all Facebook contributions that used that altered logo, and did so in an arrogant, heavy-handed way. The result was a negative firestorm on Twitter.[13]

A sound principle in business is to never ask a question to which you do not want the answer. We can extend that principle to social networking; never set up a site that will generate content for which you have no effective response!

Q7 2021?

So much change is in the air: Web 2.0, social networking, Enterprise 2.0. Is there an enterprise 3.0 around the corner? We don't know. However, new devices like the iSomethings and their copycats, along with dynamic and agile information systems based on cloud computing and virtualization, guarantee that monumental changes will occur in interorganizational systems between now and 2021.

---

[13]Bernhard Warner, "Nestlé's 'No Logo' Policy Triggers Facebook Revolt," *Social Media Influence*, March 19, 2010, *http://socialmediainfluence.com/2010/03/19/nestles-no-logo-policy-triggers-facebook-revolt/* (accessed August 2010).

In Brazil, Unilever placed GPS devices in 50 packages of its Omo detergent.[14] The GPS devices were activated when customers removed the package from the shelf. The devices then reported the customer's home location back to Unilever. Unilever employees then contacted the customers at home and gave them pocket video cameras. The point? Promotion. But what's next?

Advance the clock 10 years. You're now the product marketing manager for an important new product series for your company . . . the latest in a line of, say, intelligent home appliances. How are you going to promote your products? GPS, with a team following them home? That's probably a gross understatement for promotion in 2021.

Think about your role as a manager in enterprise 2021. Your team has 10 people, half of whom report to you and half of whom work for other managers; two work for a different company. Your company uses SharePoint 2021, which has many features that enable employees to publish their ideas in blogs, wikis, movies, and whatever other means have become available. Your employees have computers assigned to them at work; computers that they almost never use. Instead, they use their $29 slate computers that are always connected via wireless WAN to an ISP that they pay for themselves. Of course, your employees have their own Facebook, Twitter, Foursquare and other social networking sites to which they regularly contribute.

How do you manage this team? If "management" means to plan, organize, and control, how can you accomplish any of these functions in this emergent network of employees? For example, classic marketing principles dictate that you take your product line to market with a single, consistent message. Back in the days when you could approve everything printed via public relations and advertising, you could manage to obtain that single consistent messaging.

In this new world, how do you keep each of your employees from publishing commentary that is way off-message? How do you keep them from publishing personal opinions that conflict with your communication goals? You might be able to control their access to SharePoint, but how do you control their access to your company's Facebook page? You cannot. They're not even using your company's computer or network.

Suppose you try to clamp down on individual messaging. Next thing you know, your private email messages to your employees are published on the Web. Your competitor's sales force seizes on this evidence of dissension in your group to claim to prospects that your company doesn't know the benefits of its new product line.

In the context of CRM, emergence means that the vendor loses control of the customer relationship. Customers use all the touch points they can find with the vendor to craft their own relationships. Emergence in the context of management means loss of control of employees. Employees craft their own relationships with their employers, whatever that might mean by 2021. Certainly it means a loss of control, one that is readily made public, to the world.

What are the new management principles for the Enterprise 2.0 world? We don't know. In Enterprise 2.0 style, they will probably emerge, so pay attention. You will manage in very interesting and dynamic times.

---

[14]Laurel Wentz, "Is Your Detergent Stalking You?" *Advertising Age,* July 29, 2010, *http://adage.com/globalnews/article?article_id=145183* (accessed August, 2010).

Guide

Blending the Personal and the Professional

Many businesses are beginning to use social networking sites such as Facebook and MySpace for professional purposes. It began with coworkers sharing their accounts with each other socially, just as they did in college. The first interactions concerned activities such as photos of the company softball team or photos at a cocktail party at a recent sales meeting. However, every business social function is a *business* function, so even sharing photos and pages with the work softball team began to blur the personal–professional boundary.

The employees of Pearson, the publisher of this text, are no exception. When I began work on this chapter, I started a Facebook group called "Experiencing MIS." I then queried Facebook for Pearson employees I guessed might have Facebook accounts and invited them to be "friends." Most accepted, and I asked them to join the Experiencing MIS group.

The first day I checked my account, I found an entry from Anne, one of my new friends, who stated that she had been out too late the prior night. That day she happened to be working on the sales plan for this text, and I realized that I didn't want to know her current condition. So, in the group, I asked whether the blending of the personal and the professional is a good thing, and the following conversation resulted:

Anne: I think that for a lot of reasons it is a good thing . . . within reason. I think that people seeing a personal side of you can humanize you. For example, my "I was out too late last night" post didn't mean that I was not into work early and ready to go (which I was, just with a larger

coffee than usual), just that I like to have a good time outside of my work life. Also, with all the time we spend at work, our social lives are intertwined with our work lives.

Also, 9–5 work hours are becoming more and more obsolete. I may be updating my Facebook page at noon on a Friday, but you will surely find me working at least part of my day on Saturday and Sunday.

Bob: I definitely see Anne's point of view. There is the temptation to believe that we are all family. I am too old to believe that, but corporate advancement is always going to be predicated to some degree on your willingness to surrender the personal for the professional and/or allow blur. Technology may give you the illusion that you can safely have it both ways.

I am skeptical of business applications for Facebook. My guess is most folks find them lame in the way that business blogs and Xmas cards from your insurance agent are.

Lisa: I actually think there is a place for Facebook in business . . . For example, think about how it's connected a team like ours—where everyone is located all over the country—to have a place where we actually get to know each other a little better. It's corny, perhaps, but reading people's status updates on my iPhone gives me a better sense of who they are in "real life," not just on the job. I'd get that if we all sat in the same office every day; given that we don't, it's a pretty decent substitute.

I totally agree with Anne's notion that, in many ways, the personal and the professional already do blur . . . but I think that's more to do with who we are and what we do, than any specific notion of "corporations." Our work is portable and always on—and judged by results, not hours logged (I think!). In a work universe like that, the lines sort of slowly and inevitably blur . . . PS: Anne, I was out too late too. :)

Clearly, I am the curmudgeon here. But, just as I was reflecting on these comments, I received a private email from another person who chose not to be identified:

Other person: A few weeks ago, Pearson started getting really into Facebook. I went from not really using it to getting tons of "friend requests" from coworkers. Then, I got a request from somebody in an executive position at Pearson. I was worried at first—I had heard so many stories of people who had lost their jobs due to social networking, blogging, or other information they posted on the Internet. When I received this request, I must have gone over my profile 10 times to ensure there was nothing that could any way be misconstrued as offensive or illegal. I think many people at the company already know a lot about me, but I . . . I think you would have to be more careful if you're in the introductory months of a new job. ▪

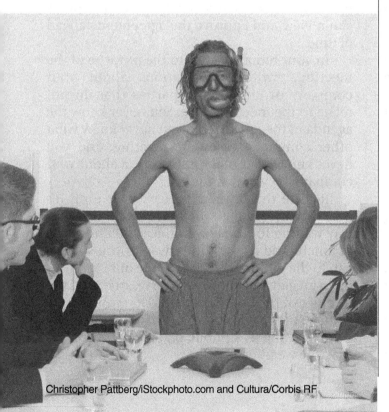

Discussion Questions

1. Do you think Anne's post that she was "Out too late last night" was inappropriate, given that she knew that her professional colleagues were reading her page? Explain your answer.

2. Anne and Lisa contend that Facebook allows employees to get to know each other better in "real life" and not just on the job. Both of these women are very successful business professionals, and they believe such knowledge is important. Do you? Why or why not?

3. Bob is skeptical that Facebook has potential business applications. He thinks social networking sites will become as lame and as uninteresting as business blogs and corporate holiday cards. Do you agree? Why or why not?

4. In the olden days before social networking, instant messaging, email, and "free" long-distance phone calls, social networking was restricted to the people in your department, or maybe those who worked on your floor. You knew the people to whom you revealed personal data, and they were close to you in the organizational hierarchy. You would have had almost no contact with your manager's manager's manager, and what contact you did have would have been in the context of a formal meeting. How do you think management is affected when personal data is readily shared far up and down the organizational hierarchy?

5. Do you think it was appropriate for the senior manager to invite distant subordinates in the organization to be friends? Why did this action put the junior employees in a tight spot? What advantages accrue to the senior manager of having very junior friends? What advantages accrue to the junior professional of having a senior friend?

6. All of the people in this dialog update Facebook using iPhones that they purchased with their own money. Because they are not using a corporate asset, managers at Pearson would be unable to stop these employees from using Facebook, if they wanted to. How does this fact change the power structure within an organization? Consider, for example, what would happen if senior management announced an unpopular change in employee benefits or some other program.

7. As the lawyers say, "You cannot un-ring the bell." Once you've revealed something about yourself, you cannot take it back. Knowing that, what criteria will you use to decide what you will post on a social networking site that is read by your professional colleagues? How do those criteria differ from the criteria you use at school?

Guide

Interorganizational Information Exchange

Interorganizational information systems—information systems that connect two or more organizations—require collaborative agreements among independent companies and organizations. Such agreements can be successful only if all parties have a clear idea of the goals, benefits, costs, and risks of working together. The creation of collaborative agreements requires many joint meetings in which the parties make their goals and objectives clear and decide how best to share information and other resources.

During your career, you may be asked to participate is such meetings. You should understand a few basic guidelines before participating.

First, when you meet with employees of another company, realize that you must apply stronger limits on your conversation than when you meet with employees in your own firm. For all you know, the company you are meeting with may become your strongest competitor. In general, you should assume that whatever you say to an employee of another company could be general knowledge in your industry the next day.

Of course, the goal of such meetings is to develop a collaborative relationship, and you cannot accomplish that goal without saying something. The best strategy, however, is to reveal exactly what you must reveal and no more.

Before you meet with another company, you and your team should have a clear and common understanding of the purpose of the meeting. Your team needs to agree beforehand on the topics that are to be addressed and those that are to be avoided. Relationships often develop in stages: Two companies meet, establish one level of understanding, meet again with another level of understanding, and so forth, feeling one another out on the way to some type of relationship.

You may be asked to sign a nondisclosure agreement. Such agreements are contracts that stipulate the responsibilities of each party in protecting the other's proprietary information. Such agreements vary in length; some are a page long and some are 30 pages long. You need to understand the policy of your organization with regard to such agreements before the meeting starts. Sometimes, companies exchange their standard nondisclosure agreements before the meeting so that the respective legal departments can review and approve the agreements ahead of time.

In your remarks, stick to the purpose of the meeting. Avoid conversations about your company or about third parties that do not relate to the meeting topic. You never know the agenda of the other party; you never know what other companies they are meeting; and you never know what other information about your company they may want.

Realize that a meeting isn't over until it's over. The meeting is still underway in the hallway waiting for the elevator. It's still underway at lunch. And it's still underway as you share a cab to the airport. By the way, the only two topics in an elevator should be the weather and the number of the floor you want. Don't embarrass yourself or the employees of the other company by discussing in a public place anything other than the weather.

All of these suggestions may seem paranoid, but even paranoid companies have competitors. There is simply no reason, other than carelessness or stupidity, to discuss topics with another company that do not relate to the matter at hand. Your company will assume enough risk just setting up the interorganizational system. Don't add to that risk by making gratuitous comments about your or any other company. ■

Discussion Questions

1. Suppose you are asked to attend a meeting with your suppliers to discuss the sharing of your sales data. You have no idea as to the specific purpose of the meeting, why you were invited, or what will be expected of you. What should you do?

2. Suppose you flew 1,500 miles for a meeting and at the start of the meeting the other company asks you to sign a nondisclosure statement. You knew nothing about the need to sign such an agreement. What do you do?

3. Some companies have an open, democratic style with lots of collaboration and open discussion. Others are closed and authoritarian, and employees wait to be told what to do. Describe what will happen when employees from two such companies meet. What can be done to improve the situation?

4. Suppose during lunch an employee of another company asks you, "What are you all doing about social networking monitoring?" Assume that this topic has little to do with the purpose of your meeting. You think about it and decide that it doesn't seem too risky to respond, so you say, "Not much." What information have you conveyed by this statement? What is a better way to respond to the question?

5. Suppose you are in a joint meeting and you are asked, "So who else are you working with on this problem?" Describe guidelines you could use in deciding how to answer this question.

6. Explain the statement, "A meeting isn't over until it's over." How might this statement pertain to other meetings—say, a job interview?

7. Reread this guide in the context of a virtual meeting, say a Webinar. Webinars can be recorded, and you never know for sure who is in the meeting. How do the principles expressed in this guide change in the context of a Webinar?

Active Review

Use this Active Review to verify that you understand the ideas and concepts that answer this chapter's study questions.

Q1 How do organizations use e-commerce?

Name four types of interorganizational systems, and explain the characteristics of each. Define *e-commerce.* Define *B2C, B2B,* and *B2G.* Distinguish among auctions, clearinghouses, and exchanges. How does e-commerce improve market efficiency? Define and explain *disintermediation,* and give an example other than one in this text. Explain how e-commerce improves the flow of price information. Define *price elasticity,* and explain how e-commerce companies can estimate it. Name four factors that disfavor e-commerce. Explain the impact of each factor.

Q2 How do organizations use Web 2.0?

How did Amazon.com usher in Web 2.0? Explain the term *software as a (free) service* and how it differs from traditional software licensing. Describe the difference in business models between Web 2.0 and traditional software companies. Explain the statement, "If a product requires advertising, then it is not Web 2.0." Explain how use increases value in Web 2.0. Define *mashup.* In what way are Web 2.0 interfaces organic? How does rights management differ between Web 2.0 and traditional software? Summarize the ways that businesses can benefit from Web 2.0.

Q3 How do social networking information systems increase social capital?

Define *capital, human capital,* and *social capital.* Name and explain four ways that social capital adds value. Name and explain three factors that determine the value of social capital. Explain how companies traditionally increased their social capital. Define *viral hook,* and give an example other than one in this text. Describe how organizations can use information systems to increase the strength of relationships. Explain the dynamics of social networking depreciation. Explain the statement "the three factors of social capital are more multiplicative than additive." Discuss the potential role for data aggregators for increasing the value of social capital.

Q4 What are business applications for Facebook, Twitter, and User-Generated Content (UGC)?

Define *social networking group,* and give an example from your own experience. Name and define three types of Facebook groups. Explain how Fox Lake might use Facebook groups. Define *social networking application.* Explain the role of services in an SN application. Name and explain four characteristics of a meaningful application and give an example of each, other than ones in this book. Define *microblog.* Explain why Twitter's 140-character limit is liberating. Describe how microblogging makes everyone a publisher. Explain the role and importance of being able to search microblogs. Identify and describe three applications for microblogging in business. Give an example of each of the types of UGC in Figure 13, other than ones in this textbook.

Q5 How does social CRM empower customers?

Characterize the differences between traditional and social CRM. Define *Enterprise 2.0,* and explain the meaning of the SLATES acronym. Define *social CRM.* Explain the statement, "Social CRM is CRM done in the style of Enterprise 2.0." How does social CRM conflict with the traditional view of CRM?

Q6 How can organizations manage the risks of social networking applications?

Summarize the risks of social networking. Show how those risks apply to Fox Lake's use of groups.

Q7 2021?

Summarize the systems and technology described in this chapter that will cause significant change by 2021. Using an example other than the one in this book, give an example of how these systems and technologies will challenge traditional management functions. What does the term *emergence* mean in relation to management? Using the knowledge of this chapter, and the hints in this question, create three questions that you could ask in a job interview that would indicate your awareness of changes in management that will be needed in the next 10 years.

Key Terms and Concepts

AdSense
AdWords
Auctions
Business-to-business (B2B)
Business-to-consumer (B2C)
Business-to-government (B2G)
Capital
Channel conflict
Clearinghouses
Crowdsourcing
Disintermediation
E-commerce
Electronic exchange
Enterprise 2.0
Folksonomy

Human capital
Interorganizational
  information system
Mashup
Merchant companies
Microblog
My Maps
Nonmerchant companies
Pre-Internet system
Price conflict
Price elasticity
SLATES
Social capital
Social graph
Social CRM

Social networking (SN)
Social networking
  application
Social networking group
Social networking
  information system
Software as a service (SAAS)
Strength of a relationship
Twitter
Value of social capital
Viral hook
Viral marketing
Web 2.0
Web storefront

Using Your Knowledge

1. Recall the process that you used when you applied for admission to your university. Classify that process in terms of the four interorganizational system types in Figure 1. Do you have a system of a type other than the one you used would be better? Why or why not?

2. Shop for a Sonos S5 audio system (or any other Sonos audio product). You can buy this product from Sonos itself, or you can buy it from online vendors of electronic equipment. Compare prices and terms. Describe how Sonos has channel conflict. Explain how it appears to deal with that conflict.

3. Google or Bing "Chloe" and search for sites that deal with Chloe fashion products. Identify companies that have purchased the Chloe AdWord. Follow three or four such links. Identify as many Web 2.0 features in the sites that you encounter as you can. Explain what you think the business rationale is for each site.

4. Visit *www.lie-nielsen.com* or *www.sephora.com*. On the site you chose, find links to social networking

sites. In what ways are those sites sharing their social capital with you? In what ways are they attempting to cause you to share your social capital with them? Describe the business value of social networking to the business you chose.

5. According to Paul Greenberg, Amazon.com is the master of the 2-minute relationship and Boeing is the master of the 10-year relationship.[15] Visit *www.boeing.com* and *www.amazon.com*. From Greenberg's statement and from the appearance of these Web sites, it appears that Boeing is committed to traditional CRM and Amazon.com to social CRM. Give evidence from each site that this might be true. Explain why the products and business environment of both companies cause this difference. Is there any justification for traditional CRM at Amazon.com? Why or why not? Is there any justification for social CRM at Boeing? Why or why not? Based on these companies, is it possible that a company might endorse Enterprise 2.0 but not endorse social CRM? Explain.

Collaboration Exercise

Collaborate with students on the following exercise. In particular, consider using Google Docs, Windows Live SkyDrive, Microsoft SharePoint, or some other collaboration tool.

Suppose your team has been hired by Anne Foster to investigate the use of Web 2.0, social networking, and social CRM for wedding events at Fox Lake. Work with your group to answer the following questions:

1. Describe how Fox Lake could use AdWords and AdSense to advertise its wedding events business.

Which, if either, of these would you recommend for Fox Lake? Why?

2. Explain how to assess the social capital of a wedding party. Is it possible to compare the social capital of two different wedding parties? If so, how? If not, why not? In what ways is knowledge of the relative social value of two wedding parties useful to Fox Lake? Are such considerations tawdry? Why or why not?

3. Describe techniques that Fox Lake could use to encourage wedding parties to contribute their social

---

[15]Paul Greenberg, *CRM at the Speed of Light,* 4th ed. (New York: McGraw-Hill, 2010), p. 105.

capital to Fox Lake. On the surface, Fox Lake appears to be the primary beneficiary of such a contribution. What can Fox Lake do to increase the value of such contributions to wedding parties?

4. Describe ways that Fox Lake can make it easy for wedding parties to contribute their social capital to Fox Lake via Facebook and via Twitter.

5. Traditional CRM, in which resources are allocated to customers on the basis of their lifetime value, makes no sense for weddings, unless Fox Lake wants to market to those most likely to divorce. Anne understands this and decides that social CRM makes more sense. Suppose she wants to create a variety of touch points for those who are in the market for wedding sites. Using the SLATES model, specify how Fox Lake could create a social CRM site with the following elements:

   a. Search
   b. Links
   c. Author
   d. Tags
   e. Extensions
   f. Signals

Summarize your recommendations for Anne in a one-page memo.

6. Prepare a 2-minute summary of what you have learned from this exercise that your group's members could use in a job interview. Give your presentation to the rest of the class.

Case Study

Tourism Holdings Limited (THL)

Tourism Holdings Limited (THL) is a publicly listed New Zealand corporation that owns multiple brands and businesses in the tourism industry. THL's principal holdings include:

- New Zealand tourist attractions, including Waitomo Black Water Rafting and Waitomo Glowworm Caves
- Kiwi Experience and Feejee Experience, hop-on, hop-off tourist bus services
- Four brands of holiday rental vehicles
- Ci Munro, a van-customization manufacturing facility

In 2009, THL earned $5 million in profit before interest and taxes on $170 million in revenue. It operates in New Zealand, Australia, and Fiji and has sales offices in Germany and the United Kingdom as well.

THL originated as The Helicopter Line, which provided scenic helicopter flights over New Zealand. Over the years, THL sold the helicopter business and has since owned and operated numerous tourism organizations and brands. THL continues to frequently buy and sell tourism businesses. For the current list of businesses, visit *www.thlonline.com/THLBusinesses*.

According to Grant Webster, THL's CEO, "THL is a house of brands and not a branded house." Thus, in the holiday rental business, THL owns and operates four different van rental brands: Maui, Britz, Backpacker, and ExploreMore. These brands are differentiated on price; Maui is the most expensive line, whereas ExploreMore appeals to the most budget-conscious traveler. Britz is the next step down in price from Maui, and Backpacker falls between Britz and ExploreMore.

Tourism Market

In 2008, an estimated 866 million international visitors toured the world. That number is expected to grow to more than 1.6 billion by 2020, according to *Tourism Business Magazine.* In 2008, travel and tourism was the world's largest business sector, accounting for 230 million jobs and over 10 percent of the world's GDP.

In spite of these long-term growth prospects, international tourism has contracted recently, following the financial crisis of fall 2008. As of June 2009, an annual total of 1.15 million international travelers visited New Zealand, a decrease of 5 percent from the year before, and 5.5 million international travelers visited Australia, a decline of 2 percent.

According to Webster, "While we believe the long-term prospects of tourism in our traditional markets of New Zealand, Australia, and Fiji will remain strong, THL's substantial growth opportunities will be achieved by expanding to other countries, possibly the United States, or Europe."

Investment in Information Systems

THL considers information systems and technology as a core component of its business value and has invested in a variety of innovative information systems and Web 2.0 technologies. Webster speaks knowledgeably about information technologies, including SharePoint, Microsoft Office SharePoint Services (MOSS), Microsoft Report Server, OLAP, and data mining.

Because of its acquisition of multiple brands and companies, THL accumulated a disparate set of information systems, based on a variety of different technologies. These disparate technologies created excessive software maintenance activity and costs. To reduce costs and simplify IS management, THL converted its customer-facing Web sites to use Microsoft SharePoint and MOSS. "Having a single development platform reduced our maintenance expenses and enabled us to focus management attention, development, and personnel training on a single set of technologies," according to Steve Pickering, manager of Interactive Information Systems.

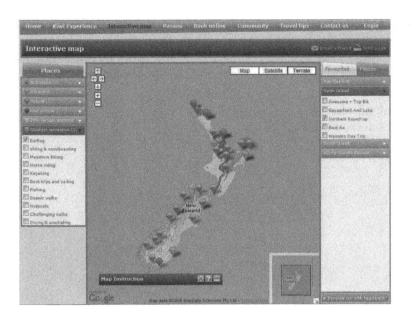

Figure 17
Interactive Map of
New Zealand at
www.KiwiExperience.com

Source: Used with permission of
Tourism Holdings Limited.

THL uses SharePoint not for collaboration, but rather as a development and hosting platform for sophisticated, highly interactive Web sites. You can find an example of such sophisticated capability at *www.kiwiexperience.com.* Click "Design Your Own Trip . . ." and the Web site will display a map of New Zealand as well as a menu of instructions. You can then select different locations, experiences, and sites from a menu, and the Web site will recommend particular tours, as shown in the right-hand pane in Figure 17. Visit the site to get a sense of the interactivity and sophistication of processing.

Web 2.0 technologies enable the tourism industry to disintermediate sales channels. According to the New Zealand Ministry of Tourism, in 2006 the Internet was used by 49 percent of international travelers to research travel options. That percentage has increased dramatically, and it is likely well over 50 percent today.

As with all disintermediation, when THL sells directly to the consumer it saves substantial distribution costs. To facilitate direct sales, THL actively uses Google AdWords and Google Analytics, a Google-supplied information system that enables AdWords customers to better understand how their sites are processed. THL is also experimenting with online chat, both voice and video. "A camper rental can cost $5,000 to $10,000 or more, and we believe our customers want a trusted relationship with a salesperson in order to commit," according to Webster. "We think that video online chat might give us that relationship with our customers."

Sources: Tourism Business Magazine, November 2009, p. 20; *www.tourismbusinessmag.co.nz* (accessed July 2010); New Zealand Ministry of Tourism, *www.tourismresearch.govt.nz* (accessed July 2010); Tourism of Australia, *www.tourism.australia.com* (accessed July 2010).

Questions

1. This case implies that the frequent acquisition and disposition of tourism brands poses problems for information systems. Summarize what you think those problems might be. Consider all five components of an information system. To what extent does standardizing on a single development platform solve those problems? Which of the five components does such standardization help the most?

2. Using the image below as a guide, summarize the ways in which IS gives THL a competitive advantage. Discuss each of the elements in the figure.

Product Implementations
1. Create a new product or service
2. Enhance products or services
3. Differentiate products or services

Process Implementations
4. Lock in customers and buyers
5. Lock in suppliers
6. Raise barriers to market entry
7. Establish alliances
8. Reduce costs

Principles of
Competitive
Advantage

3. Visit *www.kiwiexperience.com* and click "Design Your Own Trip." Select a variety of locations in the Adrenalin, Nature, and Kiwi Culture menus. Select several locations in each category and then select a pass that fits your destinations.

   a. Evaluate this user interface. Describe its strengths and weaknesses.

   b. Evaluate the Map Instructions. Do you find these instructions to be adequate? Explain why or why not.

   c. Summarize the ways in which this site uses social networking.

   d. Explain why this site is an example of a mashup.

4. Consider the Kiwi Experience site in the context of social CRM.

   a. Identify the customer touch points.

   b. Which of the elements of the SLATES model does this site contain?

   c. Consider the SLATES model elements that this site does not contain. Which ones do you think might be appropriate?

   d. Explain one way to implement each of the elements you identified in part c.

   e. Describe how your recommended social CRM capabilities would help to generate a trusted relationship.

Application Exercises

1. Microsoft created Windows Live SkyDrive and the Office Web applications as part of the Office 2010 launch. Somewhere in the middle of that launch, the Microsoft Fuse team realized that it would be a simple matter to put Facebook trappings (in tech parlance, Facebook Chrome) on top of a SkyDrive, call it Docs, and enable Windows Live SkyDrive to take advantage of Facebook's momentum. The question is, does Docs deliver value or hype?

   a. Go to *www.skydrive.com* and create a presentation having a few slides using the Microsoft PowerPoint Web App. For the purpose of this exercise, it doesn't matter what is in your presentation; choose a presentation for another class if you want. Save that presentation and share it with several friends or team members.

   b. Ask one or two of your friends to make several changes to the presentation.

   c. Repeat part a, but this time go to Docs at *http://docs.com* and join. Add a Profile tab for Docs to your Facebook account. Share the PowerPoint presentation as in part a.

   d. Ask one or two of your friends to make several changes to the presentation.

   e. Reflect on your experience using Windows Live SkyDrive and Docs. Does Docs add value, or is it just hype? Explain.

2. Assume that you have been given the task of compiling evaluations that your company's purchasing agents make of their e-commerce vendors. Each month, every purchasing agent evaluates all of the vendors that he or she has ordered from in the past month on three factors: price, quality, and responsiveness. Assume the ratings are from 1 to 5, with 5 being the best. Because your company has hundreds of vendors and dozens of purchasing agents, you decide to use Access to compile the results.

   a. Create a database with three tables: VENDOR (*VendorNumber, Name, Contact*), PURCHASER (*EmpNumber, Name, Email*), and RATING (*EmpNumber, VendorNumber, Month, Year, Price Rating, QualityRating, ResponsivenessRating*). Assume that *VendorNumber* and *EmpNumber* are the keys of VENDOR and PURCHASER, respectively. Decide what you think is the appropriate key for RATING.

   b. Create appropriate relationships.

   c. Go to this text's Web site and import the data in the Excel file **Ch08Ex02**. Note that data for Vendor, Purchaser, and Rating are stored in three separate worksheets.

   d. Create a query that shows the names of all vendors and their average scores.

   e. Create a query that shows the names of all employees and their average scores. *Hint:* In this and in part f, you will need to use the *Group By* function in your query.

   f. Create a parameterized query that you can use to obtain the minimum, maximum, and average ratings on each criterion for a particular vendor. Assume you will enter *VendorName* as the parameter.

   g. Using the information created by your queries, what conclusions can you make about vendors or purchasers?

Chapter 7 (original Chapter 9 of "Using MIS, 4/e")

Business Intelligence Systems

From Chapter 9 of *Using MIS*, 4/e. David M. Kroenke. Copyright © 2012 by Pearson Education. Published by Prentice Hall.
All rights reserved.

Business Intelligence Systems

"I'm not sure." Jeff rocks back in his chair, looks out the window, and watches two sweaty tennis players come in from their match.

"Come on, Jeff, the data's there. Just let me have it." Anne is pleading about her need for information.

"Let me be sure I get this. You want to go into our membership database and extract the names of all the members who have daughters between 20 and 30 years of age?"

"Right."

"Why not older than 30?" Jeff asks out of curiosity.

"Because they'll be less influenced by their families. But, OK, let's say 35. And I want their email addresses, too." Anne's not letting up the pressure.

"You gonna send out a blanket email? 'Hey, you've got a daughter, how about a wedding right here at Fox Lake?'"

"No, I'm going to write something quite a bit more sophisticated than that."

"What if their daughter is already married?"

"Well, that's a problem. I've got two ways to go. I can either write the promotion in a general way . . . you know, 'Fox Lake is a wonderful wedding site, blah, blah, and if your daughter or any of her friends are recently engaged, consider Fox . . .' Something like that."

"That's not too bad. I'm warming up to this idea."

"Or, I could be a lot more direct. We buy the marital data. My brother-in-law was telling me it's amazing the data you can buy about people's personal lives."

"Oh, no. We're not spying on our membership."

"He says this isn't spying. All the data is from public records. They just put all this public data together and sell it."

"Two problems: One, members are going to feel like they're being spied on. And two, that data's got to be pricey."

"Ah, now we're just talking price!"

"No, I said two problems: price and I don't like the appearance of spying."

"Look, Jeff, how will they know? I'm not gonna say, 'Hey, our records indicate you've got a pregnant, unmarried daughter, better hurry in to set up the wedding.'"

"Like, you've got 60,000 miles on your car, time for an oil change?"

"Yeah, no, I mean, no, I'm not going to say that."

"What are you going to say?"

"I don't say anything about them. It's about us! It looks like the promo went out to everyone, but, in truth, it just goes to families that we learn have unmarried, 20-something daughters. If we do it that way, I can spend a lot more on each promo piece. Maybe send out a package by courier. That'd be classy . . . with a flower for the Mom. Or . . ."

"Hey, kid, stop dreaming and get back to this meeting. If I agree, can we do this? Does anyone know how to get qualified names from the database?"

"I talked to Mike. He's got this groundskeeper guy who's a techno-whiz. Anyway, that guy knows how to query our database. In fact, he already looked at the data; we've got nearly 450 families with daughters of the right age."

"And sons? What about sons?"

"Yeah, I know. Just because the daughter's family pays . . . Maybe. But, for now, let's start with daughters."

"I have a bad feeling about this."

"Jeff, you told me to increase the wedding revenue. We're sitting on all this data. I want to make it pay. Let's do it!"

"OK. Find out what data we can buy and how much it costs. Make sure it's all public data. And, all the expenses, including any data purchases, come out of your budget. Got it?"

"I have it. I'll get going. Thanks, Jeff!"

Study Questions

Q1 Why do organizations need business intelligence?

Q2 What business intelligence systems are available?

Q3 What are typical reporting applications?

Q4 What are typical data-mining applications?

Q5 What is the purpose of data warehouses and data marts?

Q6 What are typical knowledge management applications?

Q7 How are business intelligence applications delivered?

Q8 2021?

Information systems generate enormous amounts of data. Most of these data are used for operational purposes, such as tracking orders, inventories, payables, and so forth. These operational data have a potential windfall: They contain patterns, relationships, clusters, and other information that can facilitate management, especially planning and forecasting. Business intelligence systems produce such information from operational data.

In addition to information in data, an even more important source of information is employees themselves. Employees come to the organization with expertise, and as they gain experience in the organization they add to that expertise. Vast amounts of collective knowledge exist in every organization's employees. How can that knowledge be shared? Knowledge management applications address this need, and we will conclude this chapter with a description of the purpose, features, and functions of these applications.

This chapter surveys the most common business intelligence and knowledge management applications, discusses the need and purpose for data warehouses, and explains how business intelligence applications are delivered to users as business intelligence systems. Along the way, you'll learn tools and techniques that Fox Lake can use to identify the guides that contribute the most (and least) to its competitive strategy. We'll wrap up by discussing some of the potential benefits and risks of mining credit card data.

Q1 Why Do Organizations Need Business Intelligence?

Because data communications and data storage are essentially free, enormous amounts of data are created and stored every day. A study done at the University of California at Berkeley[1] found that a total of 2 exabytes of data were created in 2002. That number has grown exponentially. In 2008, Michael Wesch stated that 70 exabytes of data would be generated in 2009; that is, 12,000 gigabytes per person of data, worldwide. Further, according to Wesch, less than .01 percent of that data will be printed on paper, and 88 percent of it will be new and original.[2]

The terms **petabyte** and **exabyte** are defined in Figure 1. As shown there, 70 exabyte is equivalent to 14 times the total number of words ever spoken by humans. That is indeed a lot of data, and it represents only the amount generated in 2008!

Somewhere in all that data is **business intelligence (BI)**—information containing patterns, relationships, and trends. But that information needs to be found and produced. For example, somewhere in the more than 300 million individual demographic records that Acxiom Corporation collects[3] is evidence that someone is going to default on a loan. That information is in the data. The question is: How can Acxiom get it out?

---

[1] "How Much Information, 2003," *http://sims.berkeley.edu/research/projects/how-much-info-2003* (accessed July 2009).

[2] *http://umanitoba.ca/ist/production/streaming/podcast_wesch.html* (accessed July 2009).

[3] *www.acxiom.com/about_us/Pages/AboutAcxiom.aspxm* (accessed July 2009).

Kilobyte (KB)	*1,000 bytes OR 10³ bytes* 2 Kilobytes: A typewritten page 100 Kilobytes: A low-resolution photograph
Megabyte (MB)	*1,000,000 bytes OR 10⁶ bytes* 2 Megabytes: A high-resolution photograph 5 Megabytes: The complete works of Shakespeare 10 Megabytes: A minute of high-fidelity sound 100 Megabytes: One meter of shelved books 500 Megabytes: A CD-ROM
Gigabyte (GB)	*1,000,000,000 bytes OR 10⁹ bytes* 1 Gigabyte: A pickup truck filled with books 20 Gigabytes: A good collection of the works of Beethoven 100 Gigabytes: A library floor of academic journals
Terabyte (TB)	*1,000,000,000,000 bytes OR 10¹² bytes* 1 Terabyte: 50,000 trees made into paper and printed 2 Terabytes: An academic research library 10 Terabytes: The print collections of the U.S. Library of Congress 400 Terabytes: National Climactic Data Center (NOAA) database
Petabyte (PB)	*1,000,000,000,000,000 bytes OR 10¹⁵ bytes* 2 Petabytes: All U.S. academic research libraries 200 Petabytes: All printed material
Exabyte (EB)	*1,000,000,000,000,000,000 bytes OR 10¹⁸ bytes* 2 Exabytes: Total volume of information generated in 1999 5 Exabytes: All words ever spoken by human beings

Figure 1
How Big Is an Exabyte?

Source: Used with permission of Peter Lyman and Hal R. Varian, University of California at Berkeley.

Businesses use business intelligence systems to process this immense ocean of data; to produce patterns, relationships, and other forms of information; and to deliver that information on a timely basis to users who need it.

Q2 What Business Intelligence Systems Are Available?

A **business intelligence (BI) system** is an information system that employs business intelligence tools to produce and deliver information. The characteristics of a particular BI system depend on the tool in use, so we will begin by categorizing such tools.

Business Intelligence Tools

A **business intelligence (BI) tool** is one or more computer programs that implement a particular BI technique. We can categorize BI tools in three ways: as reporting tools, as data mining tools, and as knowledge management tools.

Reporting tools are programs that read data from a variety of sources, process that data, format it into structured reports, and deliver those reports to the users who need them. The processing of the data is simple: Data are sorted and grouped, and simple totals and averages are calculated, as you will see. Reporting tools are used primarily for *assessment*. They are used to address questions like: What has happened in the past? What is the current situation? How does the current situation compare to the past?

Data mining tools process data using statistical techniques, many of which are sophisticated and mathematically complex. We will explore data mining later in this chapter. For now, it is enough to say that *data mining* involves searching for patterns and relationships among data. In most cases, data mining tools are used to make *predictions*. For example, we can use one form of analysis to compute the probability that a customer will default on a loan or the probability that a customer is likely to respond positively to a promotion. Another data-mining technique predicts products that tend to be purchased together. In one famous example, a data mining analysis determined that customers who buy diapers are likely to buy beer.[4] The information prompted store managers to locate beer and diapers near each other in store displays.

Although reporting tools *tend to be* used to assess and data mining tools *tend to be* used to predict, that distinction is not always true. A better way to distinguish between these two BI tools is that reporting tools use simple operations such as sorting, grouping, and summing, and data mining tools use sophisticated statistical techniques.

Knowledge management tools are used to store employee knowledge and to make that knowledge available to employees, customers, vendors, auditors, and others who need it. Knowledge management tools differ from reporting and data mining tools because the source of their data is human knowledge, rather than recorded facts and figures. Nonetheless, they are important BI tools.

Tools Versus Applications Versus Systems

It will be easier for you to understand this chapter if you distinguish among three terms. As stated, a *BI tool* is one or more computer programs. BI tools implement the logic of a particular procedure or process. A **business intelligence (BI) application** is the use of a tool on a particular type of data for a particular purpose. A business intelligence (BI) system is an information system having all five components that delivers the results of a BI application to users who need those results.

Consider an example. Later in this chapter, you will learn about a BI tool called *decision-tree analysis*. That BI tool can be used in a BI application to assess the risk of default on an existing loan. A BI system delivers the results of the decision-tree analysis on a particular loan to a banking officer, who then decides whether to buy or sell that loan and for what price.

Given this introduction, we will now illustrate applications of each type of BI tool.

Q3 What Are Typical Reporting Applications?

A **reporting application** is a BI application that inputs data from one or more sources and applies a reporting tool to that data to produce information. The resulting information is subsequently delivered to users by a **reporting system**, which is a BI system that delivers reports to authorized users at appropriate times. This section describes operations commonly used by reporting tools and then illustrates two important reporting applications: RFM analysis and OLAP.

---

[4]Michael J. A. Berry and Gordon Linoff, *Data Mining Techniques for Marketing, Sales, and Customer Support* (New York: John Wiley, 1997).

CustomerName	CustomerEmail	DateOfSale	Amount
Ashley, Jane	JA@somewhere.com	5/5/2010	$110.00
Corning,Sandra	KD@somewhereelse.com	7/7/2010	$375.00
Ching, Kam Hoong	KHC@somewhere.com	5/17/2010	$55.00
Rikki, Nicole	GC@righthere.com	6/19/2008	$155.00
Corning,Sandra	SC@somewhereelse.com	2/4/2009	$195.00
Scott, Rex	RS@somewhere.com	7/15/2010	$56.00
Corovic,Jose	JC@somewhere.com	11/12/2010	$55.00
McGovern, Adrian	BL@righthere.com	11/12/2008	$47.00
Wei, Guang	GW@ourcompany.com	11/28/2009	$385.00
Dixon,Eleonor	ED@somewhere.com	5/17/2010	$108.00
Lee,Brandon	BL@somewhereelse.com	5/5/2008	$74.00
Duong,Linda	LD@righthere.com	5/17/2009	$485.00
Dixon, James T	JTD@somewhere.com	4/3/2009	$285.00
La Pierre,Anna	SG@righthere.com	9/22/2010	$120.00
La Pierre,Anna	WS@somewhere.com	3/14/2009	$47.50
La Pierre,Anna	TR@righthere.com	9/22/2009	$580.00
Ryan, Mark	MR@somewhereelse.com	11/3/2009	$42.00
Rikki, Nicole	MR@righthere.com	3/14/2010	$175.00
Scott, Bryan	BS@somewhere.com	3/17/2009	$145.00
Warrem, Jason	JW@ourcompany.com	5/12/2010	$160.00
La Pierre,Anna	ALP@somewhereelse.com	3/15/2009	$52.00
Angel, Kathy	KA@righthere.com	9/15/2010	$195.00
La Pierre,Anna	JQ@somewhere.com	4/12/2010	$44.00
Casimiro, Amanda	AC@somewhere.com	12/7/2009	$52.00
McGovern, Adrian	AM@ourcompany.com	3/17/2009	$52.00
Menstell,Lori Lee	LLM@ourcompany.com	10/18/2010	$72.00
La Pierre,Anna	DJ@righthere.com	12/7/2009	$175.00
Nurul,Nicole	NN@somewhere.com	10/12/2010	$84.00
Menstell,Lori Lee	VB@ourcompany.com	9/24/2010	$120.00

Figure 2
Raw Sales Data

Basic Reporting Operations

Reporting tools produce information from data using five basic operations:

- Sorting
- Grouping
- Calculating
- Filtering
- Formatting

Consider the sales data shown in Figure 2. This list of raw data contains little or no information; it is just data. We can create information from this data by *sorting* by customer name, as shown in Figure 3. In this format, we can see that some customers have ordered more than once, and we can readily find their orders.

This is a step forward, but we can produce even more information by *grouping* the orders, as shown in Figure 4. Notice that the reporting tool not only grouped the orders but also *computed* the number of orders for each customer and the total purchase amount per customer.

Suppose we are interested in repeat customers. If so, we can *filter* the groups of orders to select only those customers that have two or more orders. The results of these operations are shown in Figure 5. The report in this figure not only has filtered the results, but it also has *formatted* them for easier understanding. Compare Figure 5 to 2. If your goal is to identify your best customers, the report in Figure 5 is far more useful and will save you considerable work.

The five operations just discussed may seem too simple to produce important results, but that is not the case. Reporting tools can produce incredibly interesting and insightful information. We will consider the use of two such tools next.

Figure 3
Sales Data Sorted by
Customer Name

CustomerName	CustomerEmail	DateOfSale	Amount
Adams, James	JA3@somewhere.com	1/15/2010	$145.00
Angel, Kathy	KA@righthere.com	9/15/2010	$195.00
Ashley, Jane	JA@somewhere.com	5/5/2010	$110.00
Austin, James	JA7@somewhere.com	1/15/2009	$55.00
Bernard, Steven	SB@ourcompany.com	9/17/2010	$78.00
Casimiro, Amanda	AC@somewhere.com	12/7/2009	$52.00
Ching, Kam Hoong	KHC@somewhere.com	5/17/2010	$55.00
Corning,Sandra	KD@somewhereelse.com	7/7/2010	$375.00
Corning,Sandra	SC@somewhereelse.com	2/4/2009	$195.00
Corovic,Jose	JC@somewhere.com	11/12/2010	$55.00
Daniel, James	JD@somewhere.com	1/18/2010	$52.00
Dixon, James T	JTD@somewhere.com	4/3/2009	$285.00
Dixon,Eleonor	ED@somewhere.com	5/17/2010	$108.00
Drew, Richard	RD@righthere.com	10/3/2009	$42.00
Duong,Linda	LD@righthere.com	5/17/2009	$485.00
Garrett, James	JG@ourcompany.com	3/14/2010	$38.00
Jordan, Matthew	MJ@righthere.com	3/14/2009	$645.00
La Pierre,Anna	DJ@righthere.com	12/7/2009	$175.00
La Pierre,Anna	SG@righthere.com	9/22/2010	$120.00
La Pierre,Anna	TR@righthere.com	9/22/2009	$580.00
La Pierre,Anna	ALP@somewhereelse.com	3/15/2009	$52.00
La Pierre,Anna	JQ@somewhere.com	4/12/2010	$44.00
La Pierre,Anna	WS@somewhere.com	3/14/2009	$47.50
Lee,Brandon	BL@somewhereelse.com	5/5/2008	$74.00
Lunden,Haley	HL@somewhere.com	11/17/2007	$52.00
McGovern, Adrian	BL@righthere.com	11/12/2008	$47.00
McGovern, Adrian	AM@ourcompany.com	3/17/2009	$52.00
Menstell,Lori Lee	LLM@ourcompany.com	10/18/2010	$72.00
Menstell,Lori Lee	VB@ourcompany.com	9/24/2010	$120.00

Figure 4
Sales Data, Sorted by
Customer Name and Grouped
by Orders and Purchase
Amount

CustomerName	NumOrders	TotalPurcha
Adams, James	1	$145.00
Angel, Kathy	1	$195.00
Ashley, Jane	1	$110.00
Austin, James	1	$55.00
Bernard, Steven	1	$78.00
Casimiro, Amanda	1	$52.00
Ching, Kam Hoong	1	$55.00
Corning,Sandra	2	$570.00
Corovic,Jose	1	$55.00
Daniel, James	1	$52.00
Dixon, James T	1	$285.00
Dixon,Eleonor	1	$108.00
Drew, Richard	1	$42.00
Duong,Linda	1	$485.00
Garrett, James	1	$38.00
Jordan, Matthew	1	$645.00
La Pierre,Anna	6	$1,018.50
Lee,Brandon	1	$74.00
Lunden,Haley	1	$52.00
McGovern, Adrian	2	$99.00
Menstell,Lori Lee	2	$192.00
Nurul,Nicole	1	$84.00
Pham,Mary	1	$38.00
Redmond, Louise	1	$140.00
Rikki, Nicole	2	$330.00
Ryan, Mark	1	$42.00
Scott, Bryan	1	$145.00
Scott, Rex	1	$56.00
UTran,Diem Thi	1	$275.00
Warrem, Jason	1	$160.00

Repeat Customers

Figure 5
Sales Data Filtered to Show
Repeat Customers

NumOrders	CustomerName	TotalPurchases
6	La Pierre,Anna	$1,018.50
2	Corning,Sandra	$570.00
2	Rikki, Nicole	$330.00
2	Menstell,Lori Lee	$192.00
2	McGovern, Adrian	$99.00

RFM Analysis

RFM analysis, a technique readily implemented using reporting tools, is used to analyze and rank customers according to their purchasing patterns.[5] RFM considers how *recently* (R) a customer has ordered, how *frequently* (F) a customer ordered, and how much *money* (M) the customer has spent.

To produce an RFM score, the RFM reporting tool first sorts customer purchase records by the date of their most recent (R) purchase. In a common form of this analysis, the tool then divides the customers into five groups and gives customers in each group a score of 1 to 5. The 20 percent of the customers having the most recent orders are given an R score of 1, the 20 percent of the customers having the next most recent orders are given an R score of 2, and so forth, down to the last 20 percent, who are given an R score of 5.

The tool then re-sorts the customers on the basis of how frequently they order. The 20 percent of the customers who order most frequently are given an F score of 1, the next 20 percent of most frequently ordering customers are given a score of 2, and so forth, down to the least frequently ordering customers, who are given an F score of 5.

Finally, the tool sorts the customers again according to the amount spent on their orders. The 20 percent who have ordered the most expensive items are given an M score of 1, the next 20 percent are given an M score of 2, and so forth, down to the 20 percent who spend the least, who are given an M score of 5.

Figure 6 shows sample RFM results. The first customer, Ajax, has ordered recently and orders frequently. Ajax's M score of 3 indicates, however, that it does not order the most expensive goods. From these scores, the sales team can conclude that Ajax is a good, regular customer, and that they should attempt to up-sell more-expensive goods to Ajax.

Customer	RFM Score		
Ajax	1	1	3
Bloominghams	5	1	1
Caruthers	5	4	5
Davidson	3	3	3

Figure 6
Example of RFM Score Data

---

[5]Arthur Middleton Hughes, "Boosting Response with RFM," *Marketing Tools*, May 1996. See also *http://dbmarketing.com*.

The second customer in Figure 6 could represent a problem. Bloominghams has not ordered in some time, but when it did order in the past it ordered frequently, and its orders were of the highest monetary value. This data suggests that Bloominghams might have taken its business to another vendor. Someone from the sales team should contact this customer immediately.

No one on the sales team should even think about the third customer, Caruthers. This company has not ordered for some time; it did not order frequently; and, when it did order, it bought the least-expensive items, and not many of them. Let Caruthers go to the competition; the loss will be minimal.

The last customer, Davidson, is right in the middle. Davidson is an OK customer, but probably no one in sales should spend much time with it. Perhaps sales can set up an automated contact system or use the Davidson account as a training exercise for an eager departmental assistant or intern.

Online Analytical Processing

Online analytical processing (OLAP), a second type of reporting tool, is more generic than RFM. OLAP provides the ability to sum, count, average, and perform other simple arithmetic operations on groups of data. The remarkable characteristic of OLAP reports is that they are dynamic. The viewer of the report can change the report's format, hence the term *online*.

An OLAP report has measures and dimensions. A **measure** is the data item of interest. It is the item that is to be summed or averaged or otherwise processed in the OLAP report. Total sales, average sales, and average cost are examples of measures. A **dimension** is a characteristic of a measure. Purchase date, customer type, customer location, and sales region are all examples of dimensions.

Figure 7 shows a typical OLAP report. Here, the measure is *Net Store Sales*, and the dimensions are *Product Family* and *Store Type*. This report shows how net store sales vary by product family and store type. Stores of type *Supermarket* sold a net of $36,189 worth of nonconsumable goods, for example.

A presentation like that in Figure 7 is often called an **OLAP cube**, or sometimes simply a *cube*. The reason for this term is that some software products show these displays using three axes, like a cube in geometry. The origin of the term is unimportant here, however. Just know that an *OLAP cube* and an *OLAP report* are the same thing.

The OLAP report in Figure 7 was generated by Microsoft SQL Server Analysis Services and is displayed in an Excel pivot table. The data were taken from a sample instructional database, called Food Mart, that is provided with SQL Server.

It is possible to display OLAP cubes in many ways besides with Excel. Some third-party vendors provide more extensive graphical displays. For more information about such products, check for OLAP vendors and products at the Data Housing Review at *http://dwreview.com/OLAP/index.html.*

Figure 7
OLAP Product Family and Store Type

	A	B	C	D	E	F	G
1							
2							
3	Store Sales Net	Store Type ▼					
4	Product Family ▼	Deluxe Supermarket	Gourmet Supermarket	Mid-Size Grocery	Small Grocery	Supermarket	Grand Total
5	Drink	$8,119.05	$2,392.83	$1,409.50	$685.89	$16,751.71	$29,358.98
6	Food	$70,276.11	$20,026.18	$10,392.19	$6,109.72	$138,960.67	$245,764.87
7	Non-Consumable	$18,884.24	$5,064.79	$2,813.73	$1,534.90	$36,189.40	$64,487.05
8	Grand Total	$97,279.40	$27,483.80	$14,615.42	$8,330.51	$191,901.77	$339,610.90

	A	B	C	D	E	F	G	H	I
1									
2									
3	Store Sales Net			Store Type ▼					
4	Product Family ▼	Store ▼	Store State	Deluxe Superma	Gourmet Supermar	Mid-Size Groce	Small Grocery	Supermarket	Grand Total
5	Drink	USA	CA		$2,392.83		$227.38	$5,920.76	$8,540.97
6			OR	$4,438.49				$2,862.45	$7,300.94
7			WA	$3,680.56		$1,409.50	$458.51	$7,968.50	$13,517.07
8		USA Total		$8,119.05	$2,392.83	$1,409.50	$685.89	$16,751.71	$29,358.98
9	Drink Total			$8,119.05	$2,392.83	$1,409.50	$685.89	$16,751.71	$29,358.98
10	Food	USA	CA		$20,026.18		$1,960.53	$47,226.11	$69,212.82
11			OR	$37,778.35				$23,818.87	$61,597.22
12			WA	$32,497.76		$10,392.19	$4,149.19	$67,915.69	$114,954.83
13		USA Total		$70,276.11	$20,026.18	$10,392.19	$6,109.72	$138,960.67	$245,764.87
14	Food Total			$70,276.11	$20,026.18	$10,392.19	$6,109.72	$138,960.67	$245,764.87
15	Non-Consumable	USA	CA		$5,064.79		$474.35	$12,344.49	$17,883.63
16			OR	$10,177.89				$6,428.53	$16,606.41
17			WA	$8,706.36		$2,813.73	$1,060.54	$17,416.38	$29,997.01
18		USA Total		$18,884.24	$5,064.79	$2,813.73	$1,534.90	$36,189.40	$64,487.05
19	Non-Consumable Total			$18,884.24	$5,064.79	$2,813.73	$1,534.90	$36,189.40	$64,487.05
20	Grand Total			$97,279.40	$27,483.80	$14,615.42	$8,330.51	$191,901.77	$339,610.90

Figure 8
OLAP Product Family and
Store Location by Store Type

As stated earlier, the distinguishing characteristic of an OLAP report is that the user can alter the format of the report. Figure 8 shows such an alteration. Here, the user added another dimension, *Store Country* and *Store State*, to the horizontal display. Product-family sales are now broken out by store location. Observe that the sample data only includes stores in the United States, and only in the western states of California, Oregon, and Washington.

With an OLAP report, it is possible to **drill down** into the data. This term means to further divide the data into more detail. In Figure 9, for example, the user has drilled down into the stores located in California; the OLAP report now shows sales data for the four cities in California that have stores.

Notice another difference between Figures 8 and 9. The user has not only drilled down, she has also changed the order of the dimensions. Figure 8 shows *Product Family* and then store location within *Product Family*. Figure 9 shows store location and then *Product Family* within store location.

Both displays are valid and useful, depending on the user's perspective. A product manager might like to see product families first and then store location data. A sales manager might like to see store locations first and then product data. OLAP reports provide both perspectives, and the user can switch between them while viewing the report.

Unfortunately, all of this flexibility comes at a cost. If the database is large, doing the necessary calculating, grouping, and sorting for such dynamic displays will require substantial computing power. Although standard commercial DBMS products do have the features and functions required to create OLAP reports, they are not designed for such work. They are designed, instead, to provide rapid response to transaction-processing applications, such as order entry or manufacturing planning.

Accordingly, special-purpose products called **OLAP servers** have been developed to perform OLAP analysis. As shown in Figure 10, an OLAP server reads data from an operational database, performs preliminary calculations, and stores the results of those calculations in an OLAP database. Several different schemes are used for this storage, but the particulars of those schemes are beyond this discussion. (Search the Web for the terms "MOLAP," "ROLAP," and "HOLAP" if you want to learn more.) Normally, for performance and security reasons the OLAP server and the DBMS run on separate servers.

For a discussion of security issues relating to reporting tools and reporting systems, see the Guide later in the chapter.

Using MIS InClass   *A Group Exercise*

Do You Have a Club Card?

Shutterstock and Superstock Royalty Free

A **data aggregator** is a company that obtains data from public and private sources and stores, combines, and publishes it in sophisticated ways. When you use your grocery store club card, the data from your grocery shopping trip are sold to a data aggregator. Credit card data, credit data, public tax records, insurance records, product warranty card data, voter registration data, and hundreds of other types of data are sold to aggregators.

Not all of the data are identified in the same way, not all of it has the same primary key). But, using a combination of phone number, address, email address, name, and other partially identifying data, such companies can integrate that disparate data into an integrated, coherent whole. They then query, report, and mine the integrated data to form detailed descriptions about companies, communities, zip codes, households, and individuals.

Laws limit the types of data that federal and other governmental agencies can acquire and store. There are also some legal safeguards on data maintained by credit bureaus and medical facilities. However, no such laws limit data storage by most companies (nor are there laws that prohibit governmental agencies from buying results from data aggregators).

Acxiom Corporation, a data aggregator with $1.2 billion in sales in 2009, has been described as the "biggest company you never heard of." Visit *www.acxiom.com* and complete the following tasks:

1. Navigate the Acxiom Web site and make a list of 10 different products that Acxiom provides.

2. Describe Acxiom's top customers.

3. Examine your answers to parts 1 and 2 and describe, in general terms, the kinds of data that Acxiom must collect to be able to provide these products to its customers.

4. In what ways might companies like Acxiom need to limit their marketing so as to avoid a privacy outcry from the public?

5. According to the Web site, what is Acxiom's privacy policy? Are you reassured by its policy? Why or why not?

6. Should there be laws governing companies like Acxiom? Why or why not?

7. Prepare a 3-minute presentation of your answers to items 3, 4, 5, and 6. Give your presentation to the rest of the class.

Q4 What Are Typical Data-Mining Applications?

Data mining is the application of statistical techniques to find patterns and relationships among data for classification and prediction. As shown in Figure 11, data mining resulted from a convergence of disciplines. Data-mining techniques emerged from statistics and mathematics and from artificial intelligence and machine-learning fields in computer science. As a result, data mining terminology is an odd blend of terms from these different disciplines. Sometimes people use the term *knowledge discovery in databases (KDD)* as a synonym for data mining.

Store Sales Net				Store Type					
Store Country	Store Sta	Store City	Product Family	Deluxe Super	Gourmet Supermar	Mid-Size Groce	Small Grocery	Supermarket	Grand Total
USA	CA	Beverly Hills	Drink		$2,392.83				$2,392.83
			Food		$20,026.18				$20,026.18
			Non-Consumable		$5,064.79				$5,064.79
		Beverly Hills Total			$27,483.80				$27,483.80
		Los Angeles	Drink					$2,870.33	$2,870.33
			Food					$23,598.28	$23,598.28
			Non-Consumable					$6,305.14	$6,305.14
		Los Angeles Total						$32,773.74	$32,773.74
		San Diego	Drink					$3,050.43	$3,050.43
			Food					$23,627.83	$23,627.83
			Non-Consumable					$6,039.34	$6,039.34
		San Diego Total						$32,717.61	$32,717.61
		San Francisco	Drink				$227.38		$227.38
			Food				$1,960.53		$1,960.53
			Non-Consumable				$474.35		$474.35
		San Francisco Total					$2,662.26		$2,662.26
	CA Total				$27,483.80		$2,662.26	$65,491.35	$95,637.41
	OR		Drink	$4,438.49				$2,862.45	$7,300.94
			Food	$37,778.35				$23,818.87	$61,597.22
			Non-Consumable	$10,177.89				$6,428.53	$16,606.41
	OR Total			$52,394.72				$33,109.85	$85,504.57
	WA		Drink	$3,680.56		$1,409.50	$458.51	$7,968.50	$13,517.07
			Food	$32,497.76		$10,392.19	$4,149.19	$67,915.69	$114,954.83
			Non-Consumable	$8,706.36		$2,813.73	$1,060.54	$17,416.38	$29,997.01
	WA Total			$44,884.68		$14,615.42	$5,668.24	$93,300.57	$158,468.91
USA Total				$97,279.40	$27,483.80	$14,615.42	$8,330.51	$191,901.77	$339,610.90
Grand Total				$97,279.40	$27,483.80	$14,615.42	$8,330.51	$191,901.77	$339,610.90

Figure 9

OLAP Product Family and Store Location by Store Type, Drilled Down to Show Stores in California

253

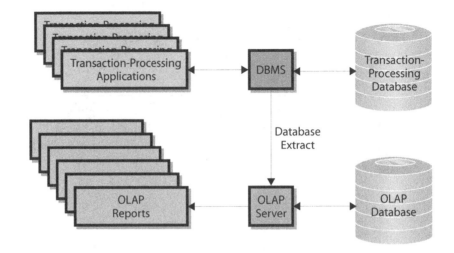

Figure 10
Role of OLAP Server
and OLAP Database

Data-mining techniques take advantage of developments in data management for processing the enormous databases that have emerged in the last 10 years. Of course, these data would not have been generated were it not for fast and cheap computers, and without such computers the new techniques would be impossible to compute.

Most data-mining techniques are sophisticated, and many are difficult to use well. Such techniques are valuable to organizations, however, and some business professionals, especially those in finance and marketing, have become expert in their use. In fact, today there are many interesting and rewarding careers for business professionals who are knowledgeable about data-mining techniques.

Data-mining techniques fall into two broad categories: unsupervised and supervised. We explain both types in the following sections.

Unsupervised Data Mining

With **unsupervised data mining**, analysts do not create a model or hypothesis before running the analysis. Instead, they apply the data-mining technique to the data and observe the results. With this method, analysts create hypotheses *after the analysis*, in order to explain the patterns found.

One common unsupervised technique is **cluster analysis**. With it, statistical techniques identify groups of entities that have similar characteristics. A common use for cluster analysis is to find groups of similar customers from customer order and demographic data.

Figure 11
Convergence Disciplines
for Data Mining

For example, suppose a cluster analysis finds two very different customer groups: One group has an average age of 33, owns two iPhones, has an expensive home entertainment system, drives a Lexus SUV, and tends to buy expensive children's play equipment. The second group has an average age of 64, owns Arizona vacation property, plays golf, and buys expensive wines. Suppose the analysis also finds that both groups buy designer children's clothing.

These findings are obtained solely by data analysis. There is no prior model about the patterns and relationships that exist. It is up to the analyst to form hypotheses, after the fact, to explain why two such different groups are both buying designer children's clothes.

Supervised Data Mining

With **supervised data mining**, data miners develop a model *prior to the analysis* and apply statistical techniques to data to estimate parameters of the model. For example, suppose marketing experts in a communications company believe that cell phone usage on weekends is determined by the age of the customer and the number of months the customer has had the cell phone account. A data mining analyst would then run an analysis that estimates the impact of customer and account age.

One such analysis, which measures the impact of a set of variables on another variable, is called a **regression analysis**. A sample result for the cell phone example is:

$$\text{CellphoneWeekendMinutes} = 12 + (17.5 \times \text{CustomerAge}) + (23.7 \times \text{NumberMonthsOfAccount})$$

Using this equation, analysts can predict the number of minutes of weekend cell phone use by summing 12, plus 17.5 times the customer's age, plus 23.7 times the number of months of the account.

As you will learn in your statistics classes, considerable skill is required to interpret the quality of such a model. The regression tool will create an equation, such as the one shown. Whether that equation is a good predictor of future cell phone usage depends on statistical factors, such as *t* values, confidence intervals, and related statistical techniques.

Neural networks are another popular supervised data-mining technique used to predict values and make classifications such as "good prospect" or "poor prospect" customers. The term *neural networks* is deceiving because it connotes a biological process similar to that in animal brains. In fact, although the original *idea* of neural nets may have come from the anatomy and physiology of neurons, a neural network is nothing more than a complicated set of possibly nonlinear equations. Explaining the techniques used for neural networks is beyond the scope of this text. If you want to learn more, search *http://kdnuggets.com* for the term *neural network*.

In the next sections, we will describe and illustrate two typical data mining tools—market-basket analysis and decision trees—and show applications of those techniques. From this discussion, you can gain a sense of the nature of data mining. These examples should give you, a future manager, a sense of the possibilities of data-mining techniques. You will need additional coursework in statistics, data management, marketing, and finance, however, before you will be able to perform such analyses yourself.

Data mining and other business intelligence systems are useful, but they are not without problems, as discussed in the Guide later in the chapter.

Market-Basket Analysis

Suppose you run a dive shop, and one day you realize that one of your salespeople is much better at up-selling to your customers. Any of your sales associates can fill a customer's order, but this one salesperson is especially good at selling customers items *in addition* to those for which they ask. One day, you ask him how he does it.

"It's simple," he says. "I just ask myself what is the next product they would want to buy. If someone buys a dive computer, I don't try to sell her fins. If she's buying a dive computer, she's already a diver and she already has fins. But, these dive computer displays are hard to read. A better mask makes it easier to read the display and get the full benefit from the dive computer."

A **market-basket analysis** is a data-mining technique for determining sales patterns. A market-basket analysis shows the products that customers tend to buy together. In marketing transactions, the fact that customers who buy product X also buy product Y creates a **cross-selling** opportunity; that is, "If they're buying X, sell them Y" or "If they're buying Y, sell them X."

Figure 12 shows hypothetical sales data from 400 sales transactions at a dive shop. The first row of numbers under each column is the total number of times an item was sold. For example, the 270 in the first row of Mask means that 270 of the 400 transactions included masks. The 90 under Dive Computer means that 90 of the 400 transactions included dive computers.

We can use the numbers in the first row to estimate the probability that a customer will purchase an item. Because 270 of the 400 transactions were masks, we can estimate the probability that a customer will buy a mask to be 270/400, or .675.

In market-basket terminology, **support** is the probability that two items will be purchased together. To estimate that probability, we examine sales transactions and count the number of times that two items occurred in the same transaction. For the data in Figure 12, fins and masks appeared together 250 times, and thus the support for fins and a mask is 250/400, or .625. Similarly, the support for fins and weights is 20/400, or .05.

These data are interesting by themselves, but we can refine the analysis by taking another step and considering additional probabilities. For example, what proportion

Figure 12
Market-Basket Example

	Mask	Tank	Fins	Weights	Dive Computer
Mask	270	10	250	10	90
Tank	10	200	40	130	30
Fins	250	40	280	20	20
Weights	10	130	20	130	10
Dive Computer	90	30	20	10	120
	Support				
Num Trans	400				
Mask	0.675	0.025	0.625	0.025	0.225
Tank	0.025	0.5	0.1	0.325	0.075
Fins	0.625	0.1	0.7	0.05	0.05
Weights	0.025	0.325	0.05	0.325	0.025
Dive Computer	0.225	0.075	0.05	0.025	0.3
	Confidence				
Mask	1	0.05	0.892857143	0.076923077	0.75
Tank	0.037037037	1	0.142857143	1	0.25
Fins	0.925925926	0.2	1	0.153846154	0.166666667
Weights	0.037037037	0.65	0.071428571	1	0.083333333
Dive Computer	0.333333333	0.15	0.071428571	0.076923077	1
	Lift (Improvement)				
Mask		0.074074074	1.322751323	0.113960114	1.111111111
Tank	0.074074074		0.285714286	2	0.5
Fins	1.322751323	0.285714286		0.21978022	0.238095238
Weights	0.113960114	2	0.21978022		0.256410256
Dive Computer	1.111111111	0.5	0.238095238	0.256410256	

of the customers who bought a mask also bought fins? Masks were purchased 270 times, and of those individuals who bought masks, 250 also bought fins. Thus, given that a customer bought a mask, we can estimate the probability that he or she will buy fins to be 250/270, or .926. In market-basket terminology such a conditional probability estimate is called the **confidence**.

Reflect on the meaning of this confidence value. The likelihood of someone walking in the door and buying fins is 250/400, or .625. But the likelihood of someone buying fins, given that he or she bought a mask, is .926. Thus, if someone buys a mask, the likelihood that he or she will also buy fins increases substantially, from .625 to .926. Thus, all sales personnel should be trained to try to sell fins to anyone buying a mask.

Now consider dive computers and fins. Of the 400 transactions, fins were sold 250 times, so the probability that someone walks into the store and buys fins is .625. But of the 90 purchases of dive computers, only 20 appeared with fins. So the likelihood of someone buying fins, given he or she bought a dive computer, is 20/90, or .1566. Thus, when someone buys a dive computer, the likelihood that she will also buy fins falls from .625 to .1566.

The ratio of confidence to the base probability of buying an item is called **lift**. Lift shows how much the base probability increases or decreases when other products are purchased. The lift of fins and a mask is the confidence of fins given a mask, divided by the base probability of fins. In Figure 13, the lift of fins and a mask is .926/.625, or 1.32. Thus, the likelihood that people buy fins when they buy a mask increases by 32 percent. Surprisingly, it turns out that the lift of fins and a mask is the same as the lift of a mask and fins. Both are 1.32.

We need to be careful here, though, because this analysis only shows shopping carts with two items. We cannot say from this data what the likelihood is that customers, given that they bought a mask, will buy both weights and fins. To assess that probability, we need to analyze shopping carts with three items. This statement illustrates, once again, that we need to know what problem we're solving before we start to build the information system to mine the data. The problem definition will help us decide if we need to analyze three-item, four-item, or some other sized shopping cart.

Many organizations are benefiting from market-basket analysis today. You can expect that this technique will become a standard CRM analysis during your career.

Decision Trees

A **decision tree** is a hierarchical arrangement of criteria that predict a classification or a value. Here we will consider decision trees that predict classifications. Decision-tree analyses are an unsupervised data-mining technique: The analyst sets up the computer program and provides the data to analyze, and the decision-tree program produces the tree.

A Decision Tree for Student Performance

The basic idea of a decision tree is to select attributes that are most useful for classifying entities on some criterion. Suppose, for example, that we want to classify students according to the grades they earn in the MIS class. To create a decision tree, we first gather data about grades and attributes of students in past classes.

We then input that data into the decision-tree program. The program analyzes all of the attributes and selects an attribute that creates the most disparate groups. The logic is that the more different the groups, the better the classification will be. For example, if every student who lived off campus earned a grade higher than 3.0, and every student who lived on campus earned a grade lower than 3.0, then the program would use the variable *live-off-campus* or *live-on-campus* to classify students. In this unrealistic example, the program would be a perfect classifier, because each group is pure, with no misclassifications.

Figure 13
Grades of Students from Past
MIS Class (Hypothetical Data)

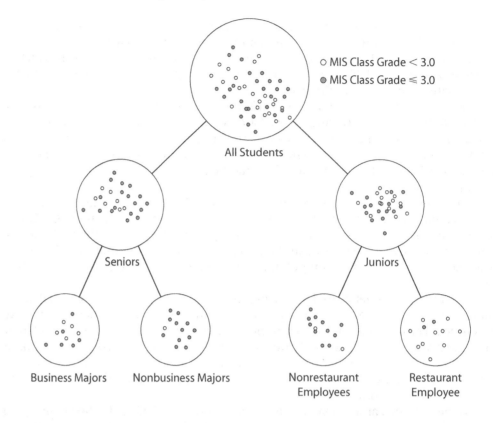

More realistically, consider Figure 13, which shows a hypothetical decision tree analysis of MIS class grades. Again, assume we are classifying students depending on whether their grade was greater than 3.0 or less than or equal to 3.0.

The decision-tree tool that created this tree examined student characteristics such as students' class (junior or senior), their major, their employment, their age, their club affiliations, and other student characteristics. It then used values of those characteristics to create groups that were as different as possible on the classification grade above or below 3.0.

For the results shown here, the decision-tree program determined that the best first criterion is whether the students are juniors or seniors. In this case, the classification was imperfect, as shown by the fact that neither of the senior nor the junior groups consisted only of students with GPAs above or below 3.0. Still, it did create groups that were less mixed than in the *All Students* group.

Next, the program examined other criteria to further subdivide *Seniors* and *Juniors* so as to create even more pure groups. The program divided the senior group into subgroups: those who are business majors and those who are not. The program's analysis of the junior data, however, determined that the difference between majors is not significant. Instead, the best classifier (the one that generated the most different groups) is whether the junior worked in a restaurant.

Examining this data, we see that junior restaurant employees do well in the class, but junior nonrestaurant employees and senior nonbusiness majors do poorly. Performance in the other senior group is mixed. (Remember, these data are hypothetical.)

A decision tree like the one in Figure 13 can be transformed into a set of decision rules having the format, **If ... then ....** Decision rules for this example are:

- If student is a junior and works in a restaurant, then predict grade > 3.0.
- If student is a senior and is a nonbusiness major, then predict grade ≤ 3.0.
- If student is a junior and does not work in a restaurant, then predict grade ≤ 3.0.
- If student is a senior and is a business major, then make no prediction.

258

As stated, decision-tree algorithms create groups that are as pure as possible, or, stated otherwise, as different from each other as possible. The algorithms use several metrics for measuring difference among groups. Further explanation of those techniques is beyond the scope of this text. For now, just understand that maximum difference among groups is used as the criterion for constructing the decision tree.

Let's now apply the decision-tree technique to a business situation.

Many problems arise with classification schemes, especially those that classify people. The Ethics Guide later in this chapter examines some of these problems.

A Decision Tree for Loan Evaluation

A common business application of decision trees is to classify loans by likelihood of default. Organizations analyze data from past loans to produce a decision tree that can be converted to loan-decision rules. A financial institution could use such a tree to assess the default risk on a new loan. Sometimes, too, financial institutions sell a group of loans (called a *loan portfolio*) to one another. An institution considering the purchase of a loan portfolio can use the results of a decision-tree program to evaluate the risk of a given portfolio.

Figure 14 shows an example provided by Insightful Corporation, a vendor of business intelligence tools. This example was generated using its Insightful Miner product. This tool examined data from 3,485 loans. Of those loans, 72 percent had no default and 28 percent did default. To perform the analysis, the decision-tree tool examined six different loan characteristics.

In this example, the decision-tree program determined that the percentage of the loan that is past due (*PercPastDue*) is the best first criterion. Reading Figure 14, you can see that of the 2,574 loans with a *PercPastDue* value of 0.5 or less (amount past due is less than half the loan amount), 94 percent were not in default. Reading down several lines in this tree, 911 loans had a value of *PercPastDue* greater than 0.5; of those loans, 89 percent were in default.

These two major categories are then further subdivided into three classifications: *CreditScore* is a creditworthiness score obtained from a credit agency; *MonthsPastDue* is the number of months since a payment; and *CurrentLTV* is the current ratio of outstanding balance of the loan to the value of the loan's collateral.

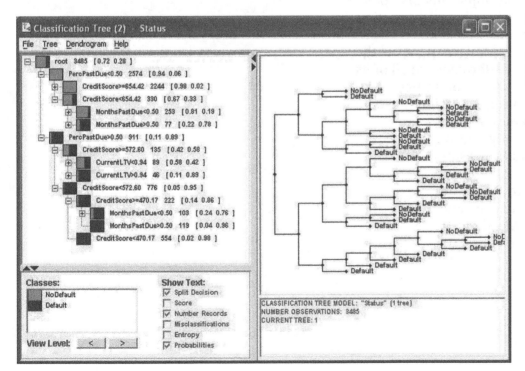

Figure 14
Credit Store Decision Tree

Ethics Guide

The Ethics of Classification

Classification is a useful human skill. Imagine walking into your favorite clothing store and seeing all of the clothes piled together on a center table. T-shirts and pants and socks intermingle, with the sizes mixed up. Retail stores organized like this would not survive, nor would distributors or manufacturers who managed their inventories this way. Sorting and classifying are necessary, important, and essential activities. But those activities can also be dangerous.

Serious ethical issues arise when we classify people. What makes someone a good or bad "prospect"? If we're talking about classifying customers in order to prioritize our sales calls, then the ethical issue may not be too serious. What about classifying applicants for college? As long as there are more applicants than positions, some sort of classification and selection process must be done. But what kind?

Suppose a university collects data on the demographics and the performance of all of its students. The admissions committee then processes these data using a decision tree data mining program. Assume the analysis is conducted properly and the tool uses statistically valid measures to obtain statistically valid results. Thus, the following resulting tree accurately represents and explains variances found in the data; no human judgment (or prejudice) was involved. ■

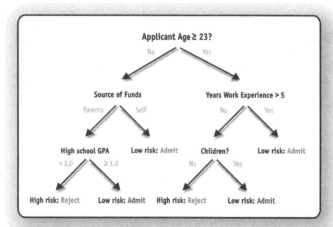

Discussion Questions

1. Explain what conditions in the data could have caused this particular structure to emerge. For example, what conditions may have existed for self-funding students under the age of 23 to be classified as low risk? Explain how you think the three other branches in this tree may have come about.

2. Consider this tree from the standpoint of:

    a. A 23-year-old woman whose job experience is 3 years as a successful Wall Street financial analyst.

    b. A 28-year-old gay male with 4 years' job experience who has no children and pays his own college education.

    c. The university fund-raising committee that wants to raise money from parent donations.

    d. A student who was seriously ill while attending a top-notch high school but managed to graduate with a GPA of 2.9 by working independently on her classes from her hospital room.

3. Suppose you work in admissions and your university's public relations department asks you to meet with the local press for an article they are preparing regarding your admittance policy. How do you prepare for the press meeting?

4. Would your answer to question 3 change if you work at a private rather than public institution? Would it change if you work at a small liberal arts college rather than a large engineering-oriented university?

5. What conclusions do you make regarding the use of decision trees for categorizing student applicants?

6. What conclusions do you make regarding the use of decision trees for categorizing prospects in general?

Andrew Johnson/ iStockphoto.com

With a decision tree like this, the financial institution can develop decision rules for accepting or rejecting the offer to purchase loans from another financial institution. For example:

- If percent past due is less than 50 percent, then accept the loan.
- If percent past due is greater than 50 percent *and*
  - If *CreditScore* is greater than 572.6 *and*
  - If *CurrentLTV* is less than .94, then accept the loan.
- Otherwise, reject the loan.

Of course, the financial institution will need to combine these risk data with an economic analysis of the value of each loan to determine which loans to take.

Decision trees are easy to understand and, even better, easy to implement using decision rules. They also can work with many types of variables, and they deal well with partial data. Organizations can use decision trees by themselves or combine them with other techniques. In some cases, organizations use decision trees to select variables that are then used by other types of data mining tools. For example, decision trees can be used to identify good predictor variables for neural networks.

Q5 What Is the Purpose of Data Warehouses and Data Marts?

Whereas basic reports and simple OLAP analyses can be made directly from operational data, more sophisticated reports and nearly all data mining applications cannot. One problem is that missing values and inconsistencies in the data can adversely affect results. Also, some analyses necessitate merging operational data with data purchased from outside sources. Yet another problem is data format. Operational data is designed to support fast transaction processing and might need to be reformatted to be useful for BI applications.

To address these problems, many organizations choose to extract operational data into facilities called **data warehouses** and **data marts**, both of which prepare, store, and manage data specifically for data mining and other analyses. (We will explain the differences between data warehouses and data marts in a few pages.)

Figure 15 shows the components in a data warehouse. Programs read production and other data and extract, clean, and prepare that data for BI processing. The prepared data are stored in a data-warehouse database using a data-warehouse

Figure 15

Components of a Data Warehouse

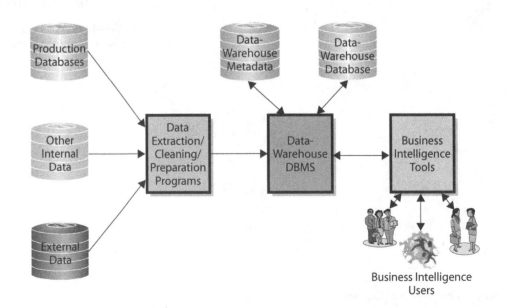

Business Intelligence Users

• Name, address, phone	• Magazine subscriptions
• Age	• Hobbies
• Gender	• Catalog orders
• Ethnicity	• Marital status, life stage
• Religion	• Height, weight, hair and
• Income	eye color
• Education	• Spouse name, birth date
• Voter registration	• Children's names and
• Home ownership	birth dates
• Vehicles	

Figure 16
Consumer Data Available for
Purchase from Data Vendors

DBMS, which can be different from the organization's operational DBMS. For example, an organization might use Oracle for its operational processing, but use SQL Server for its data warehouse. Other organizations use SQL Server for operational processing, but use DBMSs from statistical package vendors such as SAS or SPSS in the data warehouse.

Data warehouses include data that are purchased from outside sources such as Acxiom Corporation. A typical example is customer credit data. Figure 16 lists some of the consumer data that can be purchased from commercial vendors today. An amazing (and from a privacy standpoint, frightening) amount of data is available.

Metadata concerning the data—its source, its format, its assumptions and constraints, and other facts about the data—is kept in a data-warehouse metadata database. The data-warehouse DBMS extracts and provides data to BI tools such as data mining programs.

Problems with Operational Data

Unfortunately, most operational and purchased data have problems that inhibit their usefulness for business intelligence. Figure 17 lists the major problem categories. First, although data that are critical for successful operations must be complete and accurate, data that are only marginally necessary need not be. For example, some systems gather demographic data in the ordering process. But, because such data are not needed to fill, ship, and bill orders, their quality suffers.

Problematic data are termed **dirty data**. Examples are a value of *B* for customer gender and of *213* for customer age. Other examples are a value of *999–999–9999* for a U.S. phone number, a part color of *gren*, and an email address of *WhyMe@Guess WhoIAM.org*. All of these values can be problematic for data mining purposes.

Purchased data often contain *missing* elements. Most data vendors state the percentage of missing values for each attribute in the data they sell. An organization buys such data because for some uses, some data are better than no data at all. This is especially true for data items whose values are difficult to obtain, such as *Number of Adults in Household, Household Income, Dwelling Type*, and *Education of Primary Income Earner*. For data mining applications, though, a few missing or erroneous data points can be worse than no data at all because they bias the analysis.

Inconsistent data, the third problem in Figure 17, is particularly common for data that have been gathered over time. When an area code changes, for example, the phone

• Dirty data	• Wrong granularity
• Missing values	– Too fine
• Inconsistent data	– Not fine enough
• Data not integrated	• Too much data
	– Too many attributes
	– Too many data points

Figure 17
Problems of Using Transaction
Data for Analysis and Data
Mining

number for a given customer before the change will not match the customer's number after the change. Likewise, part codes can change, as can sales territories. Before such data can be used, they must be recoded for consistency over the period of the study.

Some data inconsistencies occur from the nature of the business activity. Consider a Web-based order-entry system used by customers worldwide. When the Web server records the time of order, which time zone does it use? The server's system clock time is irrelevant to an analysis of customer behavior. Coordinated Universal Time (formerly called Greenwich Mean Time) is also meaningless. Somehow, Web server time must be adjusted to the time zone of the customer.

Another problem is *nonintegrated data*. Suppose, for example, that an organization wants to perform an RFM analysis but wants to consider customer payment behavior as well. The organization wants to add a fourth factor (which we will call *P*) and scale it from 1 to 5 on the basis of how quickly a customer pays. Unfortunately, however, the organization records such payment data in an Oracle financial management database that is separate from the Microsoft CRM database that has the order data. Before the organization can perform the analysis, the data must somehow be integrated.

Data can also have the wrong **granularity**—it can be too fine or too coarse. For the former, suppose we want to analyze the placement of graphics and controls on an order-entry Web page. It is possible to capture the customers' clicking behavior in what is termed **clickstream data**. Those data, however, include everything the customer does at the Web site. In the middle of the order stream are data for clicks on the news, email, instant chat, and a weather check. Although all of that data may be useful for a study of consumer computer behavior, it will be overwhelming if all we want to know is how customers respond to an ad located differently on the screen. To proceed, the data analysts must throw away millions and millions of clicks.

Data can also be too coarse. For example, a file of order totals cannot be used for a market-basket analysis. For market-basket analysis, we need to know which items were purchased with which others. This does not mean the order-total data are useless. They can be adequate for an RFM analysis, for example; they just will not do for a market-basket analysis.

In general, it is better to have too fine a granularity than too coarse. If the granularity is too fine, the data can be made coarser by summing and combining. Only analysts' labor and computer processing are required. If the granularity is too coarse, however, there is no way to separate the data into constituent parts.

The final problem listed in Figure 17 is to have *too much data*. As shown in the figure, we can have either too many attributes or too many data points. We can have too many columns or too many rows.

Consider the first problem: too many attributes. Suppose we want to know the factors that influence how customers respond to a promotion. If we combine internal customer data with purchased customer data, we will have more than a hundred different attributes to consider. How do we select among them? Because of a phenomenon called the **curse of dimensionality**, the more attributes there are, the easier it is to build a model that fits the sample data but that is worthless as a predictor. There are other good reasons for reducing the number of attributes, and one of the major activities in data mining concerns efficient and effective ways of selecting attributes.

The second way to have too much data is to have too many data points—too many rows of data. Suppose we want to analyze clickstream data on CNN.com. How many clicks does that site receive per month? Millions upon millions! In order to meaningfully analyze such data we need to reduce the amount of data. There is a good solution to this problem: statistical sampling. Organizations should not be reluctant to sample data in such situations.

Data Warehouses Versus Data Marts

So, how is a data warehouse different from a data mart? In a way, you can think of a *data warehouse* as a distributor in a supply chain. The data warehouse takes data from the data manufacturers (operational systems and purchased data), cleans and

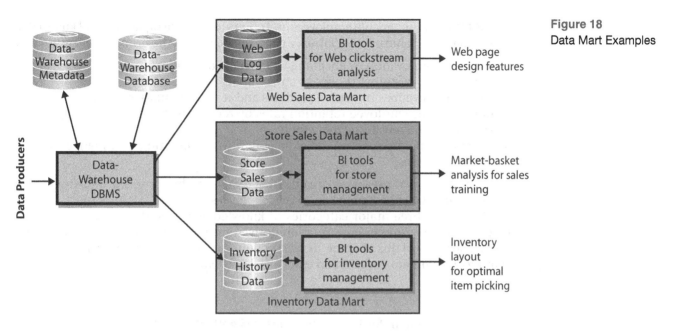

Figure 18
Data Mart Examples

processes the data, and locates the data on the shelves, so to speak, of the data warehouse. The people who work with a data warehouse are experts at data management, data cleaning, data transformation, and the like. However, they are not usually experts in a given business function.

A *data mart* is a data collection, smaller than the data warehouse, that addresses a particular component or functional area of the business. If the data warehouse is the distributor in a supply chain, then a data mart is like a retail store in a supply chain. Users in the data mart obtain data that pertain to a particular business function from the data warehouse. Such users do not have the data management expertise that data warehouse employees have, but they are knowledgeable analysts for a given business function.

Figure 18 illustrates these relationships. The data warehouse takes data from the data producers and distributes the data to three data marts. One data mart is used to analyze clickstream data for the purpose of designing Web pages. A second analyzes store sales data and determines which products tend to be purchased together. This information is used to train salespeople on the best way to up-sell to customers.

The third data mart is used to analyze customer order data for the purpose of reducing labor for item picking from the warehouse. A company like Amazon.com, for example, goes to great lengths to organize its warehouses to reduce picking expenses.

As you can imagine, it is expensive to create, staff, and operate data warehouses and data marts. Only large organizations with deep pockets can afford to operate a system like that shown in Figure 18. Smaller organizations operate subsets of this system; they may have just a simple data mart for analyzing promotion data, for example.

Q6 What Are Typical Knowledge Management Applications?

Knowledge management (KM) is the process of creating value from intellectual capital and sharing that knowledge with employees, managers, suppliers, customers, and others who need it. Whereas reporting and data mining are used to create new information from data, knowledge management systems concern the sharing of knowledge that is known to exist, either in libraries of documents or in the heads of employees.

KM applications enable employees and others to leverage organizational knowledge to work smarter. Santosus and Surmacz cite the following as the primary benefits of KM:

1. KM fosters innovation by encouraging the free flow of ideas.
2. KM improves customer service by streamlining response time.
3. KM boosts revenues by getting products and services to market faster.
4. KM enhances employee retention rates by recognizing the value of employees' knowledge and rewarding them for it.
5. KM streamlines operations and reduces costs by eliminating redundant or unnecessary processes.[6]

In addition, KM preserves organizational memory by capturing and storing the lessons learned and best practices of key employees.

There are three major categories of knowledge assets: data, documents, and employees. We addressed information derived from data in the reporting and data mining sections of this chapter. In this section, we will consider KM as it pertains to sharing of document content and employee knowledge.

Sharing Document Content

The focus on content for KM applications is slightly different. Whereas collaboration systems are concerned with document creation and change management, KM applications are concerned with maximizing content use. In this section, we focus on two key technologies for sharing content: indexing and RSS.

Indexing

Indexing is the single most important content function in KM applications. KM users need an easily accessible and robust means of determining whether content they need exists, and, if so, a link to obtain that content. Users need a keyword search that provides quick response and high document relevancy. The higher the relevancy, the more productive users will be.

The largest collection of documents ever assembled exists on the Internet, and the world's best-known indexing engine is operated by Google. When you "Google" a term, you are tapping into the world's largest content-indexing system. Google's limitation is that it can index only publicly accessible documents.

When organizations protect their content by placing it behind firewalls, Google's indexing software cannot find it. If you want to access documents published in, say, *Forbes*, you will have to use an indexing service that has an indexing agreement with *Forbes*. Similarly, organizations must develop their own indexing systems, or license indexing systems from others, in order to make their own protected content available to their employees and other authorized users.

Real Simple Syndication (RSS)

Real Simple Syndication (RSS) is a standard for subscribing to content sources. (Actually, as of 2009 there are *seven* different RSS standards; not all of them mean *real simple syndication*, but we will ignore that issue here. Perform an online search on *RSS standards* to learn more.)

You can think of RSS as an email system for content. With a program called an **RSS reader**, you can subscribe to magazines, blogs, Web sites, and other content sources. The RSS reader will periodically check the sources to which you subscribe to determine whether any content has changed. If so, the RSS reader will place a summary of the change and link to the new content in what is essentially an RSS inbox. You can

---

[6]Megan Santosus and John Surmacz, "The ABCs of Knowledge Management," *CIO Magazine*, May 23, 2001, *http://cio.com/research/knowledge/edit/kmabcs.html* (accessed July 2005).

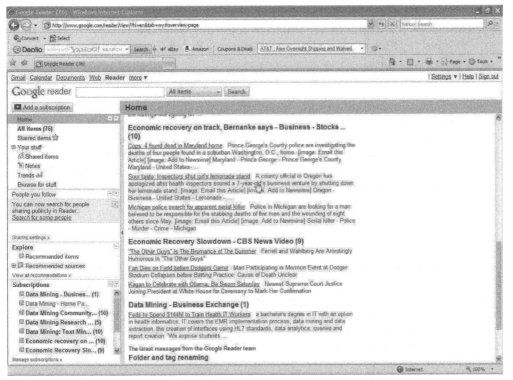

Figure 19
Interface of a Typical RSS
Reader

process your RSS inbox just like your email inbox. You read content changes, delete them in your RSS inbox, and, depending on your reader's features, forward notices of changes to others via email.

Figure 19 shows the interface of a typical RSS reader. The left-hand pane shows the RSS sources to which this user is subscribed. Entries are grouped into categories such as business, technology, and sports. In order to subscribe, the data source must provide what is termed an **RSS feed**. This simply means that the site posts changes according to one of the RSS standards.

Today, the employees in many organizations share their knowledge via personal blogs. Figure 20 shows the blog posts of one of the key employees on the Microsoft SharePoint team. Blogs like this include RSS feeds so that you can subscribe to them using an RSS reader. You can also configure SharePoint and other content-management systems to provide an RSS feed on lists or document libraries. Users who subscribe to those feeds will be notified whenever content changes.

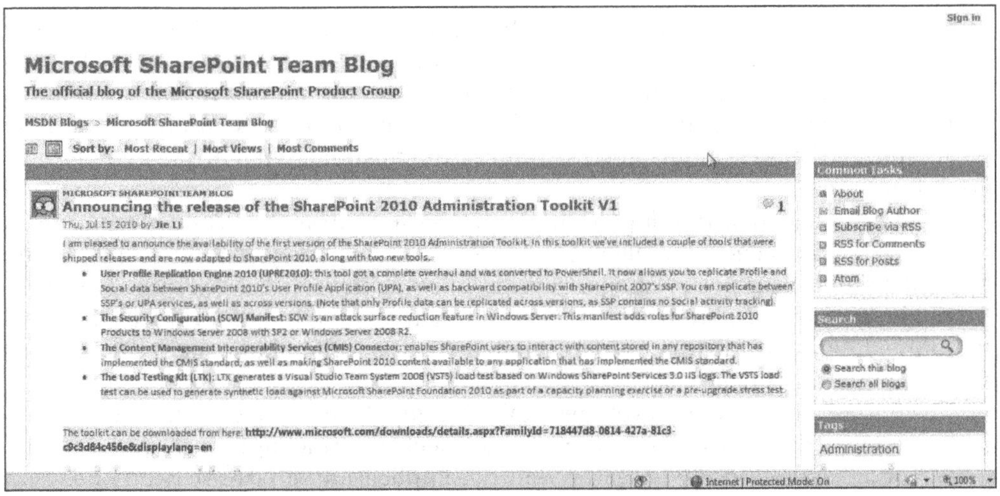

Figure 20
Blog Posts of SharePoint
Team Member

Source: Microsoft Office SharePoint Product
Group.

Content-sharing systems are flexible and organic. They are closer to Web 2.0 applications than are applications such as reporting and data mining. In fact, some people would say that content-sharing systems *are* Web 2.0 applications.

Expert Systems

Expert systems attempt to capture human expertise and put it into a format that can be used by nonexperts. Expert systems are rule-based systems that use If . . . then rules similar to those created by decision-tree analysis. However, decision trees' If . . . then rules are created by mining data. The If . . . then rules in expert systems are created by interviewing experts in a given business domain and codifying the rules stated by those experts. Also, decision trees typically have fewer than a dozen rules, whereas expert systems can have hundreds or thousands of rules.

Problems of Expert Systems

Many expert systems were created in the late 1980s and early 1990s, and a few of them have been successful. They suffer from three major disadvantages, however. First, they are difficult and expensive to develop. They require many labor hours from both experts in the domain under study and designers of expert systems. This expense is compounded by the high opportunity cost of tying up domain experts. Such experts are normally some of the most sought-after employees in the organization.

Second, expert systems are difficult to maintain. Because of the nature of rule-based systems, the introduction of a new rule in the middle of hundreds of others can have unexpected consequences. A small change can cause very different outcomes. Unfortunately, such side effects cannot be predicted or eliminated. They are the nature of complex rule-based systems.

Finally, expert systems have been unable to live up to the high expectations set by their name. Initially, proponents of expert systems hoped to be able to duplicate the performance of highly trained experts, such as doctors. It turned out, however, that no expert system has the same diagnostic ability as knowledgeable, skilled, and experienced doctors. Even when expert systems were developed that came close in ability, changes in medical technology required constant changing of the expert system, and the problems caused by unexpected consequences made such changes very expensive.

Today, however, there are successful, less-ambitious expert systems. Typically these systems address more restricted problems than duplicating a doctor's diagnostic ability. We consider one next.

Expert Systems for Pharmacies

The Medical Informatics group at Washington University School of Medicine in St. Louis, Missouri, develops innovative and effective information systems to support decision making in medicine. The group has developed several expert systems that are used as a safety net to screen the decisions of doctors and other medical professionals. These systems help to achieve the hospital's goal of state-of-the-art, error-free care.

Medical researchers developed early expert systems to support, and in some cases to replace, medical decision making. MYCIN was an expert system developed in the early 1970s for the purpose of diagnosing certain infectious diseases. Physicians never routinely used MYCIN, but researchers used its expert system framework as the basis for many other medical systems. For one reason or another, however, none of those systems has seen extensive use.

In contrast, the systems developed at Washington University are routinely used, in real time, every day. One of the systems, DoseChecker, verifies appropriate dosages on prescriptions issued in the hospital. Another application, PharmADE, ensures that

Pharmacy Clinical Decision Support
Version 2.0

Developed by The Division of Medical Informatics at Washington University School of Medicine for the Department of Pharmacy at Barnes Jewish Hospital.

Figure 21

Alert from Pharmacy Clinical Decision Support System

Source: The Division of Medicine at Washington University School of Medicine for the Department of Pharmacy at Barnes Jewish Hospital Informatics. *www.wustl.edu*. Used with permission of Medical Informatics at Washington University School of Medicine and BJC Healthcare.

Data as of: Mar 10 2000 4:40 AM　　　　**Alert #: 13104**　　　　**Satellite: CHNE**

Patient Name	Registration	Age	Sex	Weight(kg)	Height(in)	IBW(kg)	Location
SAMPLE,PATIENT	9999999	22	F	114	0	0	528

Creatinine Clearance Lab Results (last 3):

Collection Date	Serum Creatinine	Creatinine Clearance
Mar 9 2000 9:55 PM	7.1	14

DoseChecker Recommendations and Thoughts:

Order	Start Date	Drug Name	Route	Dose	Frequency
295	Mar 10 2000 12:00 AM	MEPERIDINE INJ 25MG	IV	25 MG	Q4H
Recommended Dose/Frequency:				**0.0 MG**	**PER DAY**
Comments:	0 <= CrCl < 20. Mependine should not be used for more than 48 hours or at doses > 600 mg per day in patients with renal or CNS disease. Serious consideration should be given to using an alternative analgesic in this patient population.				

patients are not prescribed drugs that have harmful interactions. The pharmacy order-entry system invokes these applications as a prescription is entered. If either system detects a problem with the prescription, it generates an alert like the one shown in Figure 21.

A pharmacist screens an alert before sending it to the doctor. If the pharmacist disagrees with the alert, it is discarded. If the pharmacist agrees there is a problem with either the dosage or a harmful drug interaction, she sends the alert to the doctor. The doctor can then alter the prescription or override the alert. If the doctor does not respond, the system will escalate the alert to higher levels until the potential problem is resolved.

Neither DoseChecker nor PharmADE attempts to replace the decision making of medical professionals. Rather, they operate behind the scenes, as a reliable assistant helping to provide error-free care.

Apparently, the systems work. According to the Informatics Web site, "Over a 6-month period at a 1,400 bed teaching hospital, the system [DoseChecker] screened 57,404 orders and detected 3,638 potential dosing errors." Furthermore, since the hospital implemented the system, the number of alerts has fallen by 50 percent, indicating that the prescribing process has been improved because of the feedback provided by the alerts.[7]

---

[7]The Division of Medical Informatics at Washington University School of Medicine for the Department of Pharmacy at Barnes Jewish Hospital. *http://informatics.wustl.edu* (accessed January 2005). Used with permission of Medical Informatics at Washington University School of Medicine and BJC Healthcare.

Q7 How Are Business Intelligence Applications Delivered?

By now you should have a good understanding of the potential power and utility of business intelligence applications. However, to make a practical difference the results of the BI analyses need to be delivered to people who can use them. For that, some sort of BI server is needed. Figure 22 summarizes the components of a generic business intelligence system. A *data source* is processed by a *BI tool* to produce *application results*. A **business intelligence (BI) application server** delivers those results in a variety of formats to *devices* for consumption by *BI users*.

What Are the Management Functions of a BI Server?

BI servers provide two major functions: management and delivery. The management function maintains metadata about the authorized allocation of BI results to users. The BI server tracks what results are available, what users are authorized to view those results, and the schedule upon which the results are provided to the authorized users. It adjusts allocations as available results change and users come and go.

BI servers vary in complexity and functionality, and their management function varies as well. Some BI servers are simply Web sites from which users can download, or **pull**, BI application results. For example, a BI Web server might post the results of an RFM analysis for salespeople to query to obtain RFM scores for their customers. The management function for such a site would simply be to track authorized users and restrict access to the site to them.

Another option is for the BI server to operate as a portal server, or as part of one. **Portal servers** are like Web servers except that they have a customizable user interface. You have probably used a portal, though you may not have realized it. If you establish an account with iGoogle, for example, you will be given the opportunity to customize the interface to your particular interests. You might, for example, choose to see the weather in certain cities, the values of particular stocks and markets, the results of particular sports events, and so forth. Whenever you sign on to iGoogle, it will present your customized interface. Figure 23 shows a sample portal.

Figure 22
Components of a Generic
Business Intelligence System

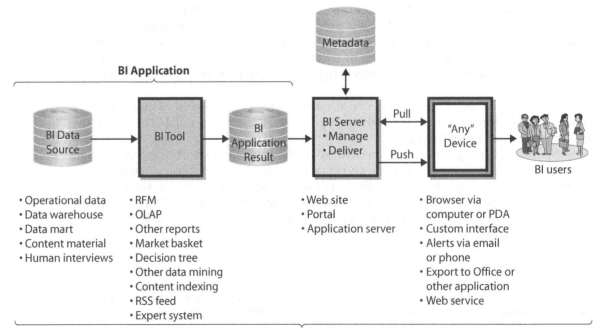

- Operational data
- Data warehouse
- Data mart
- Content material
- Human interviews

- RFM
- OLAP
- Other reports
- Market basket
- Decision tree
- Other data mining
- Content indexing
- RSS feed
- Expert system

- Web site
- Portal
- Application server

- Browser via
  computer or PDA
- Custom interface
- Alerts via email
  or phone
- Export to Office or
  other application
- Web service

BI System

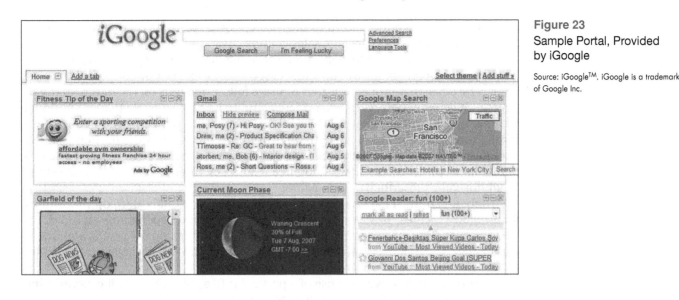

Figure 23
Sample Portal, Provided
by iGoogle

Source: iGoogle™. iGoogle is a trademark
of Google Inc.

Some organizations establish similar portal servers for use by employees within the company. Such portals might provide common data such as local weather, but they would also have links to company news, and, for our purposes, to BI application results such as reports on daily sales, operations, new employees, and so forth. Results of data mining applications could be presented as well.

To implement such a portal, the organization provides authorized user accounts on the portal server and allows users to place reports, data mining results, or other BI application results on their customized pages. Of course, selections are limited to results that the user is authorized to see. For example, a bank might publish a loan evaluation application based on a decision-tree analysis. Authorized bankers can place that evaluation application on their portal interface and invoke it when necessary. Management functions for BI portals are to track the available BI results, the users and their authorities, and, like all portal servers, the customizations in each user's interface.

A BI application server extends the functionality provided by portals to support user subscriptions to particular BI application results. For example, a user can subscribe to a daily sales report, requesting that it be delivered each morning. Or, the user might request that RFM analyses be delivered whenever a new result is posted on the server. Users can also subscribe to **alerts**, which are messages delivered via email or phone whenever a particular event occurs. A sales manager might want to be alerted, for example, whenever sales in his region exceed $1 million during the week. The BI application server **pushes** the subscribed results to the user.

A **report server** is a special case of a BI application server that serves only reports. BI application servers track results, users, authorizations, page customizations, subscriptions, alerts, and data for any other functionality provided.

As shown in Figure 22, all management data needed by any of the BI servers is stored in metadata. The amount and complexity of such data depends, of course, on the functionality of the BI server.

What Are the Delivery Functions of a BI Server?

BI servers use metadata to determine what results to send to which users and, possibly, on which schedule. Today, the expectation is that BI results can be delivered to "any" device. In practice, *any* is interpreted to mean computers, PDAs, phones, other applications such as Microsoft Office, and as an SOA service.

As stated, alerts are simply messages transmitted via email or phone that notify a user that a particular condition has occurred. The condition might be expected, such as the arrival of a new report on the BI server. Or, it might be unexpected, such as an

exception alert that notifies the user of an exceptional event, such as a dramatic fall in a stock price or exceptionally high sales volume.

A BI system, like all information systems, has hardware, software, data, procedures, and people. So far, we have discussed all of the components except procedures. The particular procedures that BI users follow depends on the nature of the BI system. In general, however, such systems tend to be more flexible than operational systems, such as order entry, CRM, or ERP. BI users tend to be engaged in nonstructured, nonroutine work. In such an environment, procedures are limited to basic operational instructions, such as how to obtain a user account, how to subscribe to a particular BI product, and how to obtain a result. The interpretation of the BI results is not normally prescribed by procedure.

There are, however, a few exceptions. The sales force might develop procedures for using RFM scores. "Always do this for a [2, 1, 1]," or "Never spend time on a [5, 5, 5]" are examples. Similarly, users might have instructions for using the results of market-basket analyses. "If the user orders a widget, attempt to up-sell a widget bracket" is an example.

In most cases, however, the use of a particular BI application result is nonroutine and is determined by the users' unique requirements.

Q8 2021?

Business intelligence systems truly add value. As described in the Guide later in the chapter, not every system is a success, but simple ones like RFM and OLAP often are, and even complicated and expensive data mining applications can generate tremendous return if they are applied to appropriate problems and are well-designed and implemented.

For example, suppose you never buy expensive jewelry on your credit card. If you travel to South America and attempt to buy a $5,000 diamond bracelet using that credit card, watch what happens! Especially if you make the attempt on a credit card other than the one for which you paid for the travel. A data mining application integrated into the credit card agency's purchase-approval process will detect the unusual pattern, on the spot, and require you to personally verify the purchase on the telephone or in some other way before it will accept the charge. Such applications are exceedingly accurate because they are well designed and implemented by some of the world's best data miners.

How will this change by 2021? We know that data storage is free, that CPU processors are becoming nearly so, that the world is generating and storing exponentially more information about customers, and that data-mining techniques are only going to get better. I think it likely that by 2021 some companies will know more about your purchasing psyche than you, your mother, or your analyst.

In fact, credit card companies already know a lot. According to MSN, if you use your card to purchase "secondhand clothing, retread tires, bail bond services, massages, casino gambling, or betting,"[8] you alert the credit card company of potential financial problems and, as a result, it may cancel your card or reduce your credit limit.

This practice raised enough concern that in May 2009 the U.S. Congress passed a credit card reform law that requires the Federal Trade Commission (FTC) to investigate data mining by credit card companies. In November 2009, the U.S. Judiciary passed the Personal Data Privacy and Security Act, which gives consumers more privacy rights in terms of information collected and distributed by commercial data brokers.

---

[8]MSN.com, "Can Lifestyle Hurt Your Credit?" *http://articles.moneycentral.msn.com/Banking/FinancialPrivacy/can-your-lifestyle-hurt-your-credit.aspx* (accessed August 2009).

However, despite the passage of the law, companies are still looking for new ways to gain access to information on consumers. The San Francisco–based data mining firm Rapleaf, for example, monitors social networks such as Facebook, Twitter, and MySpace and then makes a prediction based on who your friends are whether you are a worthy credit risk. Joel Jewitt, vice president of Rapleaf says, "Who you hang around with has empirical implications with how you behave."[9]

But, should there be limits? Suppose you stop shopping at Whole Foods (a high-value grocery store chain) and switch to Safeway (a lower-cost grocery store chain). If you pay both with a credit card, the evidence of this switch is obvious in your account record. The credit card company could notify Whole Foods that it lost you as a customer. And, in fact, credit card companies could sell such facts as well as similar data mining results to the vendors who accept its cards. They could notify Exxon where you buy gas, notify local restaurants where you dine out, and notify airlines when and where you fly with competing airlines. What else might data mining reveal from your credit card purchases? If you take a vacation every year, and you haven't yet taken one, you may be ripe for a personal contact from a travel agency. However, if you just came back from your annual vacation, why bother?

Absent laws to the contrary, by 2021 your credit card data will be fully integrated with personal and family data maintained by the data aggregators (like Acxiom and ChoicePoint). Sophisticated data mining programs will use cluster analyses, decision tree analyses, regression analyses, and other techniques to accurately predict when you are likely to get married, have a baby (or another baby), buy an auto, buy a house, sell a house, pay college expenses, retire, or die.

Much of this information will be useful for something. But what? You and your classmates will have a chance to develop innovative applications for it during your careers. It should be fascinating!

---

[9]Lucas Conley, "How Rapleaf Is Data Mining Your Friend Lists to Predict Your Credit Risk," *Fast Company*, November 16, 2009, *www.fastcompany.com/blog/lucas-conley/advertising-branding-and-marketing/company-we-keep.*

Guide
Semantic Security

Security is a very difficult problem—and risks grow larger every year. Not only do we have cheaper, faster computers (remember Moore's Law). We also have more data, more systems for reporting and querying that data, and easier, faster, and broader communication. All of these combine to increase the chances that we inadvertently divulge private or proprietary information.

Physical security is hard enough: How do we know that the person (or program) who signs on as Megan Cho really is Megan Cho? We use passwords, but files of passwords can be stolen. Setting that issue aside, we need to know that Megan Cho's permissions are set appropriately. Suppose Megan works in the HR department, so she has access to personal and private data of other employees. We need to design the reporting system so that Megan can access all of the data she needs to do her job, and no more.

Also, the delivery system must be secure. An application server is an obvious and juicy target for any would-be intruder. Someone can break in and change access permissions. Or, a hacker could pose as someone else to obtain reports. Application servers help the authorized user, resulting in faster access to more information. But, without proper security reporting servers also ease the intrusion task for unauthorized users.

All of these issues relate to physical security. Another dimension to security is equally serious and far more problematic: **semantic security**. Semantic security concerns the unintended release of protected information through the release of a combination of reports or documents that are independently not protected.

Take an example from class. Suppose I assign a group project, and I post a list of groups and the names of students assigned to each group. Later, after the assignments have been completed and graded, I post a list of grades on the Web site. Because of university privacy policy, I cannot post the grades by student name or identifier; so instead, I post the grades for each group. If you want to get the grades for each student, all you have to do is combine the list from Lecture 5 with the list from Lecture 10. You might say that the release of grades in this example does no real harm—after all, it is a list of grades from one assignment.

But go back to Megan Cho in HR. Suppose Megan evaluates the employee compensation program. The COO believes salary offers have been inconsistent over time and that they vary too widely by department. Accordingly, the COO authorizes Megan to receive a report that lists *SalaryOfferAmount* and *OfferDate* and a second report that lists *Department* and *AverageSalary*.

Those reports are relevant to her task and seem innocuous enough. But Megan realizes that she could use the information they contain to determine individual salaries—information she does not have and is not authorized to receive. She proceeds as follows.

Like all employees, Megan has access to the employee directory on the Web portal. Using the directory, she can obtain a list of employees in each department, and using the facilities of her ever-so-helpful report-authoring system she combines that list with the department and average-salary report. Now she has a list of the names of employees in a group and the average salary for that group.

Megan's employer likes to welcome new employees to the company. Accordingly, each week the company publishes an article about new employees who have been hired. The article makes pleasant comments about each person and encourages employees to meet and greet them.

Megan, however, has other ideas. Because the report is published on the Web portal, she can obtain an electronic copy of it. It's an Acrobat report, and using Acrobat's handy Search feature, she soon has a list of employees and the week they were hired.

She now examines the report she received for her study, the one that has *SalaryOfferAmount* and the offer date, and she does some interpretation. During the week of July 21, three offers were extended: one for $35,000, one for $53,000, and one for $110,000. She also notices from the "New Employees" report that a director of marketing programs, a product test engineer, and a receptionist were hired that same week. It's unlikely that they paid the receptionist $110,000; that sounds more like the director of marketing programs. So, she now "knows" (infers) that person's salary.

Next, going back to the department report and using the employee directory, she sees that the marketing director is in the marketing programs department. There are just three people in that department, and their average salary is $105,000. Doing the arithmetic, she now knows that the average salary for the other two people is $102,500. If she can find the hire week for one of those other two people, she can find out both the second and third person's salaries.

You get the idea. Megan was given just two reports to do her job. Yet she combined the information in those reports with publicly available information and is able to deduce salaries, for at least some employees. These salaries are much more than she is supposed to know. This is a semantic security problem. ▪

Discussion Questions

1. In your own words, explain the difference between access security and semantic security.

2. Why do reporting systems increase the risk of semantic security problems?

3. What can an organization do to protect itself against accidental losses due to semantic security problems?

4. What legal responsibility does an organization have to protect against semantic security problems?

5. Suppose semantic security problems are inevitable. Do you see an opportunity for new products from insurance companies? If so, describe such an insurance product. If not, explain why not.

SALARY INFORMATION

Guide

Data Mining in the Real World

"I'm not really a contrarian about data mining. I believe in it. After all, it's my career. But data mining in the real world is a lot different from the way it's described in textbooks.

"There are many reasons it's different. One is that the data are always dirty, with missing values, values way out of the range of possibility, and time values that make no sense. Here's an example: Somebody sets the server system clock incorrectly and runs the server for a while with the wrong time. When they notice the mistake, they set the clock to the correct time. But all of the transactions that were running during that interval have an ending time before the starting time. When we run the data analysis, and compute elapsed time, the results are negative for those transactions.

"Missing values are a similar problem. Consider the records of just 10 purchases. Suppose that two of the records are missing the customer number and one is missing the year part of transaction date. So you throw out three records, which is 30 percent of the data. You then notice that two more records have dirty data, and so you throw them out, too. Now you've lost half your data.

"Another problem is that you know the least when you start the study. So you work for a few months and learn that if you had another variable; say the customer's Zip code, or age, or something else, you could do a much better analysis. But those other data just aren't available. Or, maybe they are available, but to get the data you have to reprocess millions of transactions, and you don't have the time or budget to do that.

"Overfitting is another problem, a huge one. I can build a model to fit any set of data you have. Give me 100 data points and in a few minutes, I can give you 100 different equations that will predict those 100 data points. With neural networks, you can create a model of any level of complexity you want, except that none of those equations will predict new cases with any accuracy at all. When using neural nets, you have to be very careful not to overfit the data.

"Then, too, data mining is about probabilities, not certainty. Bad luck happens. Say I build a model that predicts the probability that a customer will make a purchase. Using the model on new-customer data, I find three customers who have a .7 probability of buying something. That's a good number, well over a 50–50 chance, but it's still possible that none of them will buy. In fact, the probability that none of them will buy is $.3 \times .3 \times .3$, or .027, which is 2.7 percent.

"Now suppose I give the names of the three customers to a salesperson who calls on them, and sure enough, we have a stream of bad luck and none of them buys. This bad result doesn't mean the model is wrong. But what does the salesperson think? He thinks the model is worthless and can do better on his own. He tells his manager who tells her associate, who tells the Northeast Region, and sure enough, the model has a bad reputation all across the company.

"Another problem is seasonality. Say all your training data are from the summer. Will your model be valid for the winter? Maybe, but maybe not. You might even know that it won't be valid for predicting winter sales, but if you don't have winter data, what do you do?

"When you start a data mining project, you never know how it will turn out. I worked on one project for 6 months, and when we finished, I didn't think our model was any good. We had too many problems with data: wrong, dirty, and missing. There was no way we could know ahead of time that it would happen, but it did.

"When the time came to present the results to senior management, what could we do? How could we say we took 6 months of our time and substantial computer resources to create a bad model? We had a model, but I just didn't think it would make accurate predictions. I was a junior member of the team, and it wasn't for me to decide. I kept my mouth shut, but I never felt good about it. Fortunately, the project was cancelled later for other reasons.

"However, I'm only talking about my bad experiences. Some of my projects have been excellent. On many, we found interesting and important patterns and information, and a few times I've created very accurate predictive models. It's not easy, though, and you have to be very careful. Also, lucky!" ■

Discussion Questions

1. Summarize the concerns expressed by this contrarian.

2. Do you think the concerns raised here are sufficient to avoid data mining projects altogether?

3. If you were a junior member of a data mining team and you thought that the model that had been developed was ineffective, maybe even wrong, what would you do? If your boss disagrees with your beliefs, would you go higher in the organization? What are the risks of doing so? What else might you do?

Allen Dellinger/ iStockphoto.com and kkymek/Shutterstock

Active Review

Use this Active Review to verify that you understand the ideas and concepts that answer the chapter's study questions.

Q1 Why do organizations need business intelligence?

Identify the economic factors that have caused so much data to be created. Define *petabyte* and *exabyte*. Explain the opportunities that all of this data presents to business.

Q2 What business intelligence systems are available?

Define *business intelligence system* and *business intelligence tool*. Name and describe the use of three categories of BI tools. Define *business intelligence application* and use an example to explain the differences among BI tools, applications, and systems.

Q3 What are typical reporting applications?

Name and describe five basic reporting operations. Explain why the report in Figure 5 is more useful than the list in Figure 2. Define *RFM analysis* and explain the actions that should be taken with customers who have the following scores: [1, 1, 1,], [5, 1, 1,], [1, 1, 3], and [1, 4, 1]. Explain OLAP and describe its unique characteristics. Explain the roles for measure and dimension in an OLAP cube. Illustrate an OLAP cube with a single measure and five dimensions, two dimensions on one axis and three on another. Show how drill down applies to your example.

Q4 What are typical data-mining applications?

Define *data mining*, and explain how its use typically differs from reporting applications. Explain why data mining tools are difficult to use well. Describe the differences between unsupervised and supervised data mining. Use an example to illustrate cluster analysis and regression analysis. Define *neural networks*, and explain why the term is a misnomer. Define *support*, *confidence*, and *lift*, and illustrate these terms using the data in Figure 12. Describe a good application for market-basket analysis results. Describe the purpose of decision trees and explain how the data in Figure 14 is used to evaluate loans for possible purchase.

Q5 What is the purpose of data warehouses and data marts?

Describe the need and functions of data warehouses and data marts. Name and describe the role of data warehouse components. List and explain the problems that can exist in data used for data mining and sophisticated reporting. Use the example of a supply chain to describe the differences between a data warehouse and data mart.

Q6 What are typical knowledge management applications?

Define *knowledge management*, and describe its primary benefits. Explain how KM document sharing differs from content management. Explain the importance of indexing, and describe when Google indexing is useful and when it is not. Explain the statement, "RSS is like email for content." Define *RSS reader* and *RSS feed*, and explain how they interact. Define *expert system*, and explain why expert systems have a checkered reputation. Describe the purpose of the expert systems in use at the Washington University School of Medicine.

Q7 How are business intelligence applications delivered?

Name the components of a business intelligence system, and briefly describe the nature or purpose of each. Explain the management functions of a BI server, and describe three types of servers defined in this chapter. Explain the difference between push and pull systems. Describe the devices that receive BI results. Summarize the nature of procedures used in BI systems.

Q8 2021?

Summarize the function of the credit card approval application. Explain how you think that application uses data. Describe the factors that favor greater sophistication in business intelligence systems. Explain how credit card companies use purchase patterns to reduce credit limits and revoke cards and how such practices could be discriminatory. Summarize other uses for credit card data. Explain how even more information could be generated if credit card data is combined with personal and family data stored by data aggregators.

▬ Key Terms and Concepts

Alerts
Business intelligence (BI)
Business intelligence
   (BI) application
Business intelligence (BI)
   application server
Business intelligence (BI)
   system
Business intelligence (BI) tool
Clickstream data
Cluster analysis
Confidence
Cross-selling
Curse of dimensionality
Data aggregator
Data marts
Data mining
Data mining tools
Data warehouses

Decision tree
Dimension
Dirty data
Drill down
Exabyte
Exception alert
Expert systems
Granularity
If . . . then . . .
Indexing
Knowledge management (KM)
Knowledge management
   tools
Lift
Market-basket analysis
Measure
Neural networks
OLAP cube
OLAP servers

Online analytical processing
   (OLAP)
Petabyte
Portal servers
Pull (results)
Push (results)
Real Simple Syndication (RSS)
Regression analysis
Report server
Reporting application
Reporting system
Reporting tools
RFM analysis
RSS feed
RSS reader
Semantic security
Supervised data mining
Support
Unsupervised data mining

▬ Using Your Knowledge

1. Reflect on the differences between reporting systems and data mining systems. What are their similarities and differences? How do their costs differ? What benefits does each offer? How would an organization choose between these two BI tools?

2. Suppose you are a member of the Audubon Society, and the board of the local chapter asks you to help them analyze its member data. The group wants to analyze the demographics of its membership against members' activity, including events attended, classes attended, volunteer activities, and donations. Describe two different reporting applications and one data mining application that they might develop. Be sure to include a specific description of the goals of each system.

3. Suppose you are the director of student activities at your university. Recently, some students have charged that your department misallocates its resources. They claim the allocation is based on outdated student preferences. Funds are given to activities that few students find attractive, and insufficient funds are allocated to new activities in which students do want to participate. Describe how you could use reporting and/or data mining systems to assess this claim.

4. Google *RSS reader* and download an RSS product. Set up feeds to your reader to the five most important business sources you know. Add feeds to your reader about technology and about one of your hobbies. Have at least 15 feeds, total. Run your RSS feeder for 3 days, and list the top five most interesting or informative items your reader made available that you would otherwise not have known about. Document your results by naming your reader, listing your sources, and describing the five most interesting items.

5. Suppose you work at Costco or another major, national, big-box store, and you do a market-basket analysis and identify the 25 pairs of items in the store that have the highest lift and the 25 pairs of items that have the lowest lift. What would you do with this knowledge? Costco (or your big-box store) doesn't have salespeople, so up-selling is not an option. What else might you do with information about these items' lift? Consider advertising, pricing, item location in stores, and any other factor that you might adjust. Do you think the lift calculations are valid for all stores in the United States (or other country)? Why or why not? Are the 50 pairs of products with the highest and lowest lift the best place to focus your attention? What other 50 pairs of products might you want to consider? Explain.

6. Describe a use for RFM analysis for Fox Lake. Consider golf, tennis, the restaurant, or the pro shop as candidates. Which do you think is best suited to RFM? Explain your rationale. For your application, explain what you would do for customers who have the following scores: [1, 1, 1], [3, 1, 1], [1, 4, 1], [3, 3, 1], [1, 1, 3].

7. Describe an application for market-basket analysis for the Fox Lake restaurant. Explain how you would

use the knowledge that two menu items have a lift of 7. Explain how you would use the knowledge that two items have a lift of .003. If they have a lift of 1.03? If they have a lift of 2.1?

8. Neil used data in the FlexTime database to determine that class sizes could not be appreciably increased. Given what you know from this chapter and from the nature of the FlexTime problem, explain why he must have used a reporting application and not a data mining or knowledge management application.

9. Suppose FlexTime is considering investing in the IndoRow system. Describe a potential data mining application that could help FlexTime decide if buying the IndoRow equipment is a good investment.

▰ Collaboration Exercise

Collaborate with students on the following exercise. In particular, consider using Google Docs, Windows Live SkyDrive, Microsoft SharePoint, or some other collaboration tool.

Mary Keeling owns and operates Carbon Creek Gardens, a retailer of trees, garden plants, perennial and annual flowers, and bulbs. "The Gardens," as her customers call it, also sells bags of soil, fertilizer, small garden tools, and garden sculptures. Mary started the business 16 years ago when she bought a section of land that, because of water drainage, was unsuited for residential development. With hard work and perseverance, Mary has created a warm and inviting environment with a unique and carefully selected inventory of plants. The Gardens has become a favorite nursery for serious gardeners in her community.

"The problem," she says, "is that I've grown so large, I've lost track of my customers. The other day, I ran into Tootsie Swan at the grocery store, and I realized I hadn't seen her in ages. I said something like, 'Hi, Tootsie, I haven't seen you for a while,' and that statement unleashed an angry torrent from her. It turns out that she'd been in over a year ago and had wanted to return a plant. One of my part-time employees waited on her and had apparently insulted her, or at least didn't give her the service she wanted. So, she decided not to come back to The Gardens.

"Tootsie was one of my best customers. I'd lost her, and I didn't even know it! That really frustrates me. Is it inevitable that as I get bigger, I lose track of my customers? I don't think so. Somehow, I have to find out when regular customers aren't coming around. Had I known Tootsie had stopped shopping with us, I'd have called her to see what was going on. I need customers like her.

"I've got all sorts of data in my sales database. It seems like the information I need is in there, but how do it get it out?"

In this exercise, you will apply the knowledge of this chapter to Mary Keeling's problem.

1. Mary wants to know when she's lost a customer. One way to help her would be to produce a report, say in PDF format, showing the top 50 customers from the prior year. Mary could print that report or we could place it on a private section of her Web site so that she can download it from wherever she happens to be.

   Periodically—say, once a week—Mary could request a report that shows the top buyers for that week. That report could also be in PDF format, or it could just be produced onscreen. Mary could compare the two reports to determine who is missing. If she wonders whether a customer such as Tootsie has been ordering, she could request a query report on Tootsie's activities.

   Describe the advantages and disadvantages of this solution.

2. Describe the best possible application of an OLAP tool at Carbon Creek. Can it be used to solve the lost-customer problem? Why or why not? What is the best way, if any, for Mary to use OLAP at The Gardens? If none, explain why.

3. Describe the best possible application of decision-tree analysis at Carbon Creek. Can it be used to solve the lost-customer problem? Why or why not? What is the best way, if any, for Mary to use decision-tree analysis at The Gardens? If none, explain why.

4. Describe the best possible application of RFM analysis at Carbon Creek. Can it be used to solve the lost-customer problem? Why or why not? What is the best way, if any, for Mary to use RFM at The Gardens? If none, explain why.

5. Describe the best possible application of market-basket analysis at Carbon Creek. Can it be used to solve the lost-customer problem? Why or why not? What is the best way, if any, for Mary to use market-basket analysis at The Gardens? If none, explain why.

6. Which of the applications of BI tools in this exercise will provide Mary the best value? If you owned Carbon Creek Gardens and you were going to implement just one of these applications, which would you choose? Why?

Case Study

THL

THL, Tourism Holdings Limited, is a New Zealand–based company that owns and operates multiple businesses. In this case, we will examine how THL uses information systems to support vehicle leasing in its four camper-leasing business lines.

Leasing camper vehicles to customers has three fundamental phases:

1. Matching customer requirements with vehicle availability
2. Reserving vehicles and operations support
3. Billing and customer service

Online Reservations Systems

Customers access a Web site for whichever brand of vehicle they wish to rent. On that site, they specify the dates and locations from which they want to rent and return a vehicle. THL information systems access the vehicle inventory to determine which vehicles might be available.

That determination is complex. THL may not have the wanted vehicle in the desired location, but it might have a higher-priced vehicle available and choose to offer the customer a free upgrade. Or, it might have the desired vehicle in a different city and choose to move the vehicle to that location. However, moving the vehicle might impact prior reservations for that vehicle, making such movement infeasible. Finally, this complexity is compounded because certain vehicles are not to be rented from particular locations. (Two-wheel drive standard vehicles cannot be rented for the Australian

outback, for example). And, of course, vehicles undergo both scheduled and unscheduled maintenance.

Pricing is another complicated decision in the reservation process. Like hotels and airlines, THL engages in flex pricing, whereby prices are determined not only by the vehicle and rental period, but also by customer demand.

To accommodate this complexity, THL developed a rule-based availability information system known as Aurora. Business analysts create business rules like those shown in Figure 24. Figure 24 shows an example of rules that block vehicles from rental; Figure 25 shows a screen that is used to set up or modify a rule. All rules are stored in a SQL Server database, a database that also contains all of the vehicle reservation data. Application programs in the Aurora system access and process the business rules when determining vehicle availability. Because rules are set up and managed with easy-to-use interfaces like that in Figure 24, nonprogrammer business analysts are able to change reservation policy without the assistance of technical personnel.

THL also operates information systems for vehicle check-in and customer billing.

The Aurora reservation system off-loads data to a second SQL Server database that operates a Report Server (see Figure 26). By off-loading the data, THL produces numerous sophisticated reports without impacting the performance of the online reservation system.

Reports from the server guide both operational and managerial activities. One report, for example, shows the vehicles that are to be checked out and returned to each rental location. Other reports show which vehicles need to be transferred to other locations, which vehicles

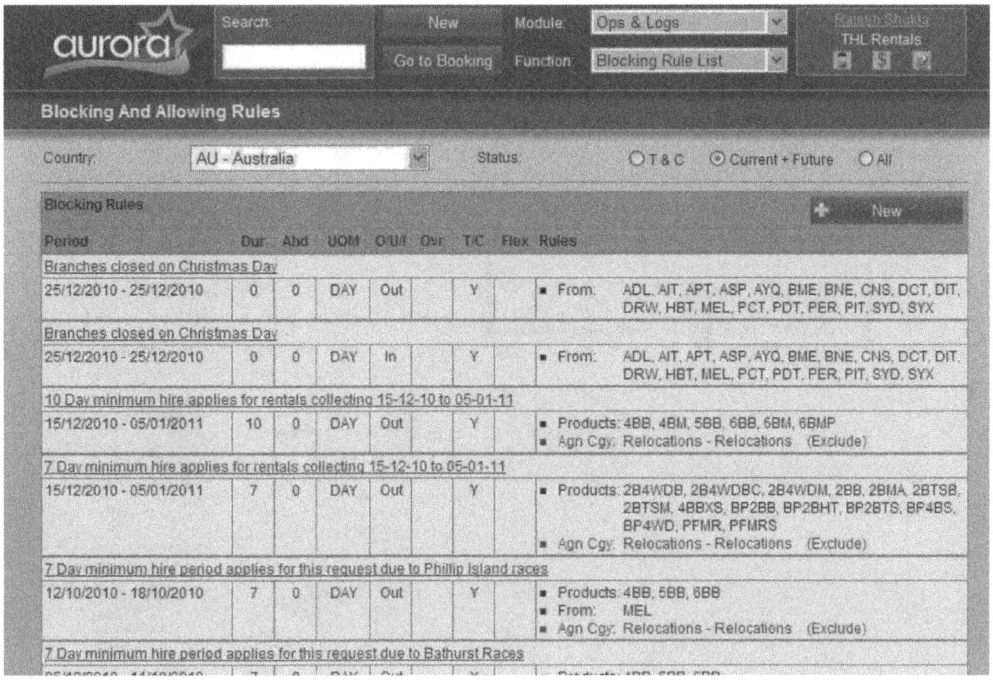

Figure 24
Example Rental Rules

Source: © Tourism Holdings Limited. Used with permission.

Figure 25
Setting Up a Blocking Rule

Source: © Tourism Holdings Limited. Used with permission.

Edit Blocking Rule			
Country:	AU - Australia	Rule Type:	Blocking
Reason / Message:	Branches closed on Christmas Day		
Duration of Booking:	0 *	Book Ahead Period:	0 *
By Date:	◉ Out ○ Use ○ In	Unit of Measure:	Calendar Day
Flags:	☐ Overrideable ☐ Only Flex Bookings	☐ Bypass Availability Check	☑ T&C rule
Period From:	25/12/2010 *	To:	25/12/2010 *

Rule Components: Remove

Type	Items	Excl	Add
■ Products:		☐	(Select)
■ Brands:		☐	(Select)
■ Packages:		☐	▦ ✚
■ Locations From:	☐ ADL ☐ AIT ☐ APT ☐ ASP ☐ AYQ ☐ BME ☐ BNE ☐ CNS ☐ DCT ☐ DIT ☐ DRW ☐ HBT ☐ MEL ☐ PCT ☐ PDT ☐ PER ☐ PIT ☐ SYD ☐ SYX	☐	(Select)
■ Locations To:		☐	(Select)
■ Agent Countries:		☐	(Select)
■ Agent Categories:		☐	(Select)
■ Agents:		☐	▦ ✚

Delete   Save   Back

are to be sent for maintenance, which vehicles are to be retired from the fleet, and so forth.

Business Intelligence Information Systems

"We know our operational data contains a wealth of information about our customers, their rental needs, trends in rental activity and vehicle needs, and other key business drivers," Grant Webster, CEO, stated. "We've already developed numerous OLAP cubes and we're working on other types of business intelligence applications."

As shown in Figure 26 data from the report server is downloaded to a third server that provides OLAP services. Operational data is processed, and OLAP cubes are created on a weekly basis. Figure 27 shows a cube that displays revenue earned from vehicle sales in 2005 (THL is, naturally, reluctant to publish current versions of such private data).

OLAP, which stands for online analytical processing, refers to the production of reports whose structure can be changed dynamically by the user. In Figure 10, the user could, for example, change the brand and geographic market columns, and the totals would be adjusted accordingly. Excel Pivot charts are an example of an OLAP report (or cube, as OLAP

Figure 26
THL Information Systems

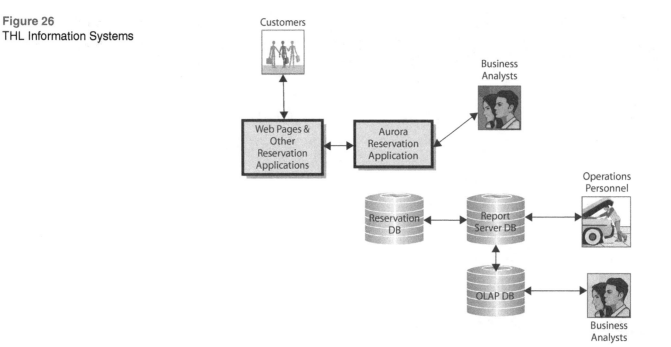

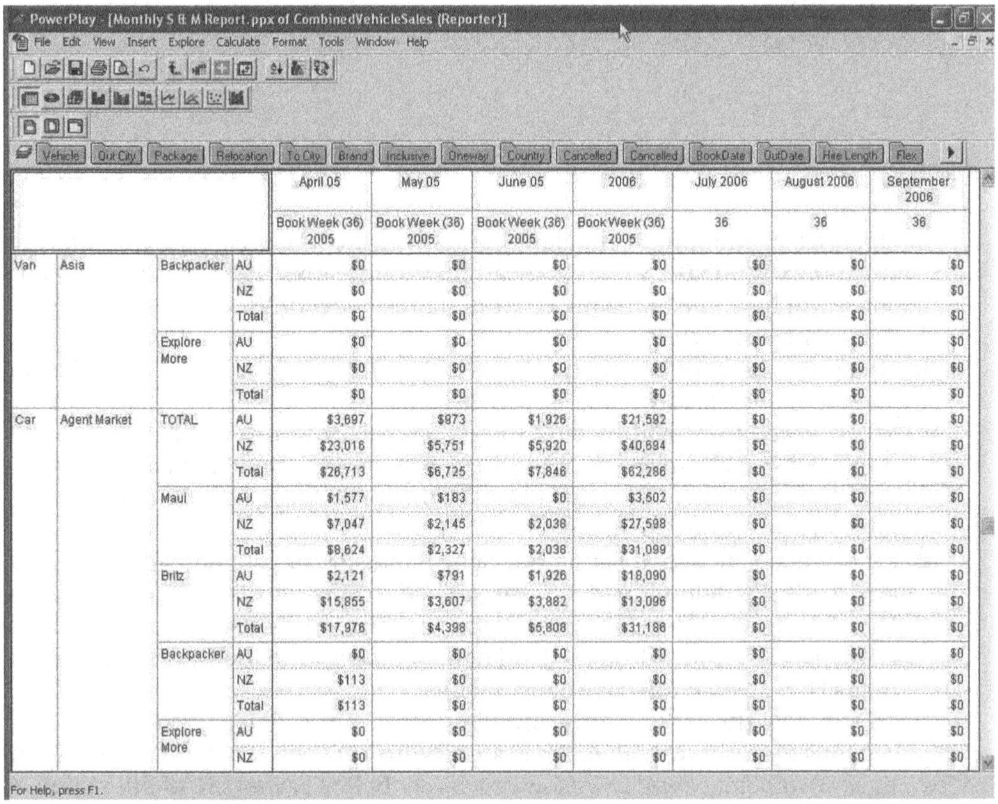

				April 05	May 05	June 05	2006	July 2006	August 2006	September 2006
				Book Week (36) 2005	Book Week (36) 2005	Book Week (36) 2005	Book Week (36) 2005	36	36	36
Van	Asia	Backpacker	AU	$0	$0	$0	$0	$0	$0	$0
			NZ	$0	$0	$0	$0	$0	$0	$0
			Total	$0	$0	$0	$0	$0	$0	$0
		Explore More	AU	$0	$0	$0	$0	$0	$0	$0
			NZ	$0	$0	$0	$0	$0	$0	$0
			Total	$0	$0	$0	$0	$0	$0	$0
Car	Agent Market	TOTAL	AU	$3,697	$973	$1,926	$21,592	$0	$0	$0
			NZ	$23,016	$5,751	$5,920	$40,694	$0	$0	$0
			Total	$26,713	$6,725	$7,846	$62,286	$0	$0	$0
		Maui	AU	$1,577	$183	$0	$3,502	$0	$0	$0
			NZ	$7,047	$2,145	$2,038	$27,598	$0	$0	$0
			Total	$8,624	$2,327	$2,038	$31,099	$0	$0	$0
		Britz	AU	$2,121	$791	$1,926	$18,090	$0	$0	$0
			NZ	$15,855	$3,607	$3,882	$13,096	$0	$0	$0
			Total	$17,976	$4,398	$5,808	$31,186	$0	$0	$0
		Backpacker	AU	$0	$0	$0	$0	$0	$0	$0
			NZ	$113	$0	$0	$0	$0	$0	$0
			Total	$113	$0	$0	$0	$0	$0	$0
		Explore More	AU	$0	$0	$0	$0	$0	$0	$0
			NZ	$0	$0	$0	$0	$0	$0	$0

Figure 27
THL OLAP Report

Source: © Tourism Holdings Limited. Used with permission.

reports are called). The difference is that THL's report server produces reports based on thousands of transactions; such volume would be very difficult to process in Excel.

Questions

1. Considering the rule-based reservation system:
   a. Summarize the benefits of having policy determined by rules rather than by computer code.
   b. What are the consequences of someone entering an incorrect rule? Offer both mundane and drastic examples.
   c. Considering your answer to part b, if you managed the reservation system at THL what process would you use for the modification of rules?
2. Examine the OLAP cube in Figure 27. The values in this report (or cube, as OLAP reports are called) are sums of rental revenue from vehicles.
   a. Using your intuition and business knowledge, what do you think the value $3,697 means? What do $1,587 and $2,121 mean?
   b. State three conclusions that you can make from this data.
   c. The principal advantage of OLAP is that columns and rows can be switched and the report values will be recalculated automatically. Explain what would happen if the user of this report were to switch the first column (geographic area) with the third column (brand). You do not have sufficient data to compute values, but explain in words what will happen.
3. Considering customer reservation data, give an example of the use of each of the following:
   a. Reporting application (other than OLAP)
   b. Market-basket analysis
   c. Unsupervised data mining
   d. Supervised data mining
   e. Rank your answers to parts a–d on the basis of their desirability. Justify your ranking.
4. Suppose that THL decides to start a van rental business in the United States. Suppose that it is considering opening operations in Alaska, California, Arizona, New Mexico, or Florida.
   a. Given the nature of THL's current camper-vehicle rental activities, which of those states do you think would be best? Justify your decision. Consider potential competition, market size, applicability of THL's experience, and other factors you deem relevant.
   b. Summarize THL's competitive strengths for this new operation.
   c. Summarize THL's competitive vulnerabilities for this new operation.
   d. Describe how its reservation system adds value to this new operation.
   e. Summarize the problems that you think THL might have in running a business 7,500 miles (or more) from its headquarters.
5. Name and describe information systems and technologies that THL could use to mitigate the problems in your answer to part e in question 4.

Application Exercises

1.　OLAP cubes are very similar to Microsoft Excel pivot tables.

　　a. Open Excel and import the data in the worksheet named *Vendors* from the Excel file **Ch09Ex01**, which you can find on the text's Web site. The spreadsheet will have the following column names: *VendorName, EmployeeName, Date, Year,* and *Rating*.

　　b. Under the *Insert* ribbon in Excel, click *Pivot Table*. A wizard will open. Select *Excel* and *Pivot table* in the first screen. Click *Next*.

　　c. When asked to provide a data range, drag your mouse over the data you imported so as to select all of the data. Be sure to include the column headings. Excel will fill in the range values in the open dialog box. Place your pivot table in a separate spreadsheet.

　　d. Excel will create a field list on the right-hand side of your spreadsheet. Drag and drop the field named *VendorName* onto the words "Drop Row Fields Here." Drag and drop *EmployeeName* onto the words "Drop Column Fields Here." Now drag and drop the field named *Rating* onto the words "Drop Data Items Here." Voilà! You have a pivot table.

　　e. To see how the table works, drag and drop more fields onto the various sections of your pivot table. For example, drop *Year* on top of *Employee.* Then move *Year* below *Employee.* Now move *Year* below *Vendor.* All of this action is just like an OLAP cube, and, in fact, OLAP cubes are readily displayed in Excel pivot tables. The major difference is that OLAP cubes are usually based on thousands or more rows of data.

2.　It is surprisingly easy to create a market-basket report using table data in Access. To do so, however, you will need to enter SQL expressions into the Access query builder. Here, you can just copy SQL statements to type them in. If you take a database class, you will learn how to code SQL statements like those you will use here.

　　a. Create an Access database with a table named *Order_Data* having columns *OrderNumber, ItemName,* and *Quantity*, with data types Number (*LongInteger*), Text (50), and Number (*LongInteger*), respectively. Define the key as the composite (*OrderNumber, ItemName*).

　　b. Import the data from the Excel file **Ch09Ex02** into the *Order_Data* table.

　　c. Now, to perform the market-basket analysis, you will need to enter several SQL statements into Access. To do so, click the queries tab and select *Create Query* in Design view. Click *Close* when the Show Table dialog box appears. Right-click in the gray section above the grid in the *Select Query* window. Select *SQL View*. Enter the following expression exactly as it appears here:

```
SELECT    T1.ItemName as FirstItem,
          T2.ItemName as SecondItem
FROM      Order_Data T1, Order_Data T2
WHERE     T1.OrderNumber =
          T2.OrderNumber
AND       T1.ItemName <> T2.ItemName;
```

Click the red exclamation point in the toolbar to run the query. Correct any typing mistakes and, once it works, save the query using the name *TwoItemBasket*.

d. Now enter a second SQL statement. Again, click the queries tab and select *Create Query* in Design view. Click *Close* when the Show Table dialog box appears. Right-click in the gray section above the grid in the *Select Query* window. Select *SQL View*. Enter the following expression exactly as it appears here:

SELECT	TwoItemBasket.FirstItem,
	TwoItemBasket.SecondItem,
	Count(*) AS SupportCount
FROM	TwoItemBasket
GROUP BY	TwoItemBasket.FirstItem,
	TwoItemBasket.SecondItem;

Correct any typing mistakes and, once it works, save the query using the name *SupportCount*.

e. Examine the results of the second query and verify that the two query statements have correctly calculated the number of times that two items have appeared together. Explain further calculations you need to make to compute support.

f. Explain the calculations you need to make to compute lift. Although you can make those calculations using SQL, you need more SQL knowledge to do it, and we will skip that here.

g. Explain, in your own words, what the query in part c seems to be doing. What does the query in part d seem to be doing? Again, you will need to take a database class to learn how to code such expressions, but this exercise should give you a sense of the kinds of calculations that are possible with SQL.

Information Systems
Management Opener

Information Systems Management

This part addresses the management of information systems development, resources, and security. Even if you are not an IS major, you need to know about these functions so that you can be a successful and effective consumer of IS professionals' services.

FlexTime and Fox Lake are both small companies with well under $100 million a year in sales. Like most small companies, neither has a formal organization for managing information systems development, resources, and security. However, small organizations are not exempt from these responsibilities, and, in fact, in a small business without professional IS personnel, those responsibilities fall more heavily on business managers like you will be.

If you eventually work for a medium-size or larger organization that does have the support of a professional staff, this part will help you understand the responsibilities and activities of IS professionals, which will enable you to work more effectively with them.

We will examine how Fox Lake could define new business processes and an information system to support those processes. We will also investigate what Fox Lake is and is not doing with regard to the target of is resources. Finally, we will see why Fox Lake's information systems are particularly vulnerable to computer misuse and crime; It,s not going to to be pretty!

Alamy Images

Chapter 8 (original Chapter 10 of "Using MIS, 4/e")

Business Process and Information Systems Development

Business Process and Information Systems Development

"Jeff, we clean the clubhouse restrooms twice a day . . . in the morning before 7 and again just before lunch. We've been doing that for years. Never been a problem." Mike Stone, facilities manager, is defending his department in a meeting with Jeff Lloyd, Fox Lake's general manager, and Anne Foster, manager of the newly formed wedding events department.

"That's just great Mike. Just great." Anne raises her voice, "And what if, like on the PAST THREE SATURDAYS, we have two weddings in the afternoon? Do you think maybe guests at the second wedding would like clean bathrooms?" Anne is incredulous that she has to ask for clean bathrooms, of all things. "It's your friends and family at a wedding . . . at Fox Lake! You would hope the bathrooms will be clean!"

Jeff sits impatiently, he doesn't like the direction of this discussion, but he doesn't know where to take it . . .

Mike continues. "Look, Anne, I can hire staff to clean the bathrooms on whatever schedule you want. I DO have a budget to pay attention to, however, so I'm not going to hire people to clean bathrooms that are already clean because we DIDN'T have two weddings that day."

"Well, Mike, should we talk about our problem with the toilet in the ladies room?"

"What do you mean?"

"I mean for a whole month, we've had a toilet that overflows . . . "

"Mike, is that right?" Jeff jumps in.

"Look. I don't have a plumber on staff. Steve's the weekend manager. He knows we watch our expenses, and he's not going to call a plumber on Saturday, weekend rates and all. So, he's does the right thing. He goes over there and tries to fix it himself."

"Seems like a good response, doesn't it?" Jeff asks, wondering where this one is going.

"I thought so, too. Saves us money and solves the problem. Turns out that plumbing equipment was never designed to have 250 people at an event. It's designed for one or two people from the restaurant, maybe a party of four golfers. Anyway, he fixes the toilet with spare parts and whatnot and, with that heavy use, it breaks again, and Anne comes unglued! Besides, if I had notice, I could bring in some Porta Potties . . . "

"Mike!!! This is a wedding! You're not going to take your bridal gown into a Porta Potty. I CAN'T BELIEVE I'M HAVING THIS DISCUSSION!!!" Anne is stupefied at his comment.

Jeff steps in. "OK, you two. Clearly, we've got some work to do. We're almost at the end of the big wedding season. Take a break and then sit down together and schedule it out. Figure out what it will take to get us through this year. Mike, let me know if you need more money and I'll see what I can come up with. But, I don't mean a lot. Meanwhile, I'll start thinking about a longer-term solution."

Next week, Jeff meets in his office with Laura Shen, who'd been recommended to him as someone who could help solve the wedding events and facilities problems.

"Laura, I don't really know what you do. Margaret Silvester, one of our board members, said you'd helped with some computer problems at her company, and she insisted I meet with you. This doesn't seem like a problem for a computer programmer, though."

"Jeff, I'm not a programmer. I'm what's called a 'business analyst.' I know technology, and while I have written computer programs, that's not what I do. I specialize in understanding business needs, strategies, and goals and helping businesses implement systems to accomplish those needs. Often that involves computer-based systems, but not always."

"Well, what do you know about us?"

"Margaret gave me a quick rundown. You've recently acquired a wedding events business and you've had problems integrating it with the rest of Fox Lake."

"That's about right. But, we didn't acquire a business . . . we hired someone who owned a small business and she hoped to make it bigger working for Fox Lake. I was looking for a source of more revenue."

"So, what's the problem?"

"Facilities, mostly. We had some issues about using membership data for marketing, but not serious ones. The big problems are sharing facilities, timely maintenance, and tracking repairs. And, these wedding events stress us in ways we're not used to. The crew at the restaurant can serve up a few burgers and fries to the club members, but when we start putting high-end caterers into their kitchen space, well, like I said, it's stressful . . . "

"I might be able to help. Did you see this coming when you started wedding events?"

"No, not really. We just thought we could use our buildings for weddings . . . I didn't understand how it would impact everything else."

"Well, let me talk with your key people for a bit, and I'll get back to you with some ideas and a proposal."

Study Questions

Q1 Why do organizations need to manage business processes?

Q2 What are the stages of Business Process Management (BPM)?

Q3 How can BPMN process diagrams help identify and solve process problems?

Q4 Which comes first, business processes or information systems?

Q5 What are systems development activities?

Q6 Why are business processes and systems development difficult and risky?

Q7 What are the keys for successful process and systems development projects?

Q8 2021?

Suppose Fox Lake had hired you instead of Laura. How would you proceed? According to Jeff, "The big problems are sharing facilities, timely maintenance, and tracking repairs." How would you address these problems? What would you advise Fox Lake to do? Would you start by creating a spreadsheet or a database to schedule maintenance? If so, how would Fox Lake use either to solve these problems? Or, would you start by creating some sort of information system that has procedures for scheduling the use of facilities? Or, would you begin with a business process, say the process of planning weddings, and work from there to the need for information systems, and from there to the need for a spreadsheet or a database?

To answer these questions, we will address two major themes in this chapter: business process management and information systems development. The two themes are closely related and overlap in important ways. We begin in Q1 through Q3 by describing the need for process management, the stages in the business process management cycle, and BPMN, a notation used for documenting business processes.

Next, in Q4, we investigate the relationship of processes and systems by asking the question: Which should organizations create first? The response to that question sets up the discussion of systems development activities in Q5 and the challenges and keys to success in development projects in Q6 and Q7. We'll wrap up this chapter with a discussion of how information systems careers are likely to change between now and 2021.

Q1 Why Do Organizations Need to Manage Business Processes?

Here we will define a **business process** as a network of activities, repositories, roles, resources, and data flows that interact to accomplish a business function. *Activities* are collections of related tasks that receive inputs and produce outputs. A *repository* is a collection of something; an inventory is a physical repository and a database is a data repository. The new terms in this definition are **roles**, which are collections of procedures, and **resources**, which are people or computer applications that are assigned to roles. Finally, a **data flow** is the movement of data from one activity or another or from an activity to a repository, or the reverse.

To make this more clear, you can think of roles as job titles. Example roles are *salesperson, credit manager, inventory supervisor,* and the like. Thus, an organization might assign three people (resources) to the salesperson role, or it might create an information system (resource) to perform the credit manager role.

To better understand this definition, consider a simple, but common, example.

A Sample Ordering Business Process

Suppose that you work in sales for a company that sells equipment and supplies to the hotel industry. Your products include hotel furniture, cleaning equipment, and supplies, such as towels and linens and staff uniforms. Processing an order involves the five steps shown in Figure 1. You are one of many people (resources) that perform the salesperson role.

As a salesperson, you do not perform all of the activities shown; rather, you orchestrate their performance. You are the customer's representative within the firm. You ensure that the operations department verifies that the product is available and can be delivered to the customer on the requested schedule. You check with accounting to verify the credit required to process the order, and you check with your boss, a sales manager, to approve any special terms the customer might request (discounts, free shipping, extended return policy, etc.). We will document this process further in Q2.

Why Does This Process Need Management?

When you joined the firm, they taught you to follow this process, and you've been using for it two years. It seems to work, so why does it need to be managed? The fundamental answer to this question is that processes are dynamic and often need to be changed. This need can arise because a process doesn't work well, because of a change in technology, or because of a change in some business fundamental.

Processes That Don't Work Well

The most obvious reason for changing a process is that it doesn't work. The process does not produce the desired result, or it is so confused, with everyone following their own personal way of getting things done, that it is only good fortune when desired outputs are produced, now and then. Businesses with such broken processes cannot survive, and, consequently few processes are such complete failures. More common are processes that work, but not very well.

For example, according to Figure 1, salespeople verify product availability before checking customer credit. If checking availability means nothing more than querying an information system for inventory levels, that sequence makes sense. But suppose that checking availability means that someone in operations needs not only to verify inventory levels, but also to verify that the goods can be shipped to arrive on time. If the order delivery is complex, say the order is for a large number of beds that have to be shipped from three different warehouses, an hour or two of labor may be required to verify shipping schedules.

After verifying shipping, the next step is to verify credit. If it turns out the customer has insufficient credit and the order is refused, the shipping-verification labor will have been wasted. So, it might make sense to check credit before checking availability.

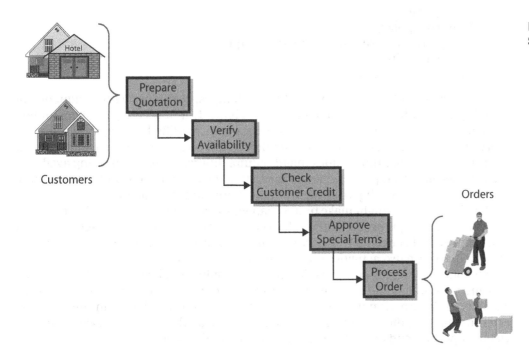

Figure 1
Steps in Processing an Order

Similarly, if the customer's request for special terms is disapproved, the cost of checking availability and credit is wasted. If the customer has requested special terms that are not normally approved, it might make sense to obtain approval of special terms before checking availability or credit. However, your boss might not appreciate being asked to consider special terms for orders in which the items are not available or for customers with bad credit.

Another reason that processes don't work well is that they are misaligned with the organization's goals, objectives, or competitive strategy. If, for example, the vendor has chosen a low-cost strategy, then taking the time to verify shipping dates may be at odds with that competitive strategy. The labor to verify shipping dates will raise sales costs and may prohibit the vendor from providing the lowest possible prices to its customers.

As you can see, it's not easy to determine what process structure is best. The need to monitor process effectiveness and adjust process design, as appropriate, is one reason that processes need to be managed.

Change in Technology

Changing technology is a second reason for managing processes. For example, suppose the equipment supplier in Figure 1 invests in a new information system that enables it to track the location of trucks in real time. Suppose that with this capability the company can provide next-day availability of goods to customers. That capability will be of limited value, however, if the existing credit-checking process requires 2 days. "I can get the goods to you tomorrow, but I can't verify your credit until next Monday" will not be satisfying to either customers or salespeople.

Thus, when new technology changes any of a process's activities in a significant way, the entire process needs to be evaluated. That evaluation is another reason for managing processes.

Change in Business Fundamentals

A third reason for managing business processes is a change in business fundamentals. A substantial change in any of the following factors might result in the need to modify business processes:

- Market (e.g., new customer category, change in customer characteristics)
- Product lines
- Supply chain
- Company policy
- Company organization (e.g., merger, acquisition)
- Internationalization
- Business environment

To understand the implications of such changes, consider just the sequence of verifying availability and checking credit in Figure 1. A new category of customers could mean that the credit-check process needs to be modified; perhaps a certain category of customers is too risky to be extended credit. All sales to such customers must be cash. A change in product lines might require different ways of checking availability. A change in the supply chain might mean that the company no longer stocks some items in inventory but ships directly from the manufacturer instead.

Or, the company might make broad changes to its credit policy. It might, for example, decide to accept more risk and sell to companies with lower credit scores. In this case, approval of special terms becomes more critical than checking credit, and the sequence of those two activities might need to be changed.

Of course, a merger or acquisition will mean substantial change in the organization and its products and markets, as does moving portions of the business offshore or engaging in international commerce. Finally, a substantial change in the business environment, say, the onset of a recession, might mean that credit checking becomes vitally important and needs to be moved to first in this process.

Q2 What Are the Stages in Business Process Management (BPM)?

The factors just discussed will necessitate changes in business processes, whether the organization recognizes that need or not. Organizations can either plan to develop and modify business processes, or they can wait and let the need for change just happen to them. In the latter case, the business will continually be in crisis, dealing with one process emergency after another.

Figure 2 shows the basic activities in **business process management (BPM)**, a cyclical (recurring) process for systematically creating, assessing, and altering business processes. This cycle begins by creating models of business processes. The business users who have expertise and are involved in the particular process (this could be you!) adjust and evaluate those models. Usually teams build an **as-is model** that documents the current situation and then changes that model to make adjustments necessary to solve process problems.

Given the model, the next step is to create system components. Those components have the five elements of every information system, although some are entirely automated (no people and procedures) and some are entirely manual (no hardware or software). Next, needed business processes or changes to existing business processes are implemented.

Well-managed organizations don't stop there. Instead, they create policy, procedures, and committees to continually assess business process effectiveness. The Information Systems Audit and Control Association has created a set of standard practices called **COBIT (Control Objectives for Information and related Technology)** that are often used in the assessment stage of the BPM cycle. Explaining these standards is beyond the scope of this discussion, but you should know that they exist. See *www.isaca.org/cobit* for more information.

When the assessment process indicates that a significant need for change has arisen, the BPM cycle is repeated. Adjusted and new process models are developed, and components are created, implemented, and assessed.

Effective BPM enables organizations to attain continuous process improvement. Like quality improvement, process improvement is never finished. Process effectiveness is constantly monitored, and processes are adjusted as and when required.

Business process management has the same scope as for information systems: functional, cross-functional, and interorganizational. As shown in Figure 3, BPM becomes more difficult as the scope of the underlying processes increases.

Finally, do not assume that business process management applies only to commercial, profit-making organizations. Nonprofit and government organizations

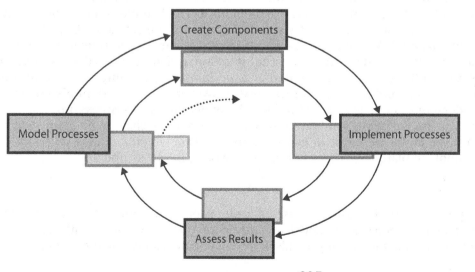

Figure 2
Stages in the BPM Cycle

Scope	Description	Example	BPM Role
Functional	Business process resides within a single business function.	Accounts payable	BPM authority belongs to a single departmental manager who has authority to resolve BPM issues.
Cross-functional	Business process crosses into multiple departments within a single company.	Customer relationship management (CRM); enterprise resource management (ERP)	BPM authority shared across several or many departments. Problem resolution via committee and policy.
Interorganizational	Business process crosses into multiple companies.	Supply chain management (SCM)	BPM authority shared by multiple companies. Problem resolution via negotiation and contract.

Figure 3
Scope of Business Process
Management

have all three types of processes shown in Figure 3, but most of these processes are service-oriented, rather than revenue-oriented. Your state's Department of Labor, for example, has a need to manage its processes, as does the Girl Scouts of America. BPM applies to all types of organizations.

Q3 How Can BPMN Process Diagrams Help Identify and Solve Process Problems?

One of the four stages of BPM, and arguably the most important stage, is to model business processes. It is so important because such models are the blueprint for the new process and system components. If models are incomplete and incorrect, components cannot be created correctly. In this question, you will learn standard notation for creating process documentation.

Need for Standard for Business Processing Notation

As stated, we define a *business process* as a network of activities, repositories, roles, resources, and data flows that interact to accomplish a business function. This definition is commonly accepted, but unfortunately dozens of other definitions are used by other authors, industry analysts, and software products. For example, IBM, a key leader in business process management, has a product called WebSphere Business Modeler that uses a different set of terms. It has activities and resources, but it uses the term *repository* more broadly than we do, and it uses the term *business item* for *data flow*. Other business-modeling software products use still other definitions and terms. These differences and inconsistencies can be problematic, especially when two different organizations with two different sets of definitions must work together. Accordingly, a software-industry standards organization called the **Object Management Group (OMG)** created a standard set of terms and graphical notations for documenting business processes. That standard, called **Business Process Modeling Notation (BPMN)**, is documented at *www.bpmn.org*. A complete description of BPMN is beyond the scope of this text. However, the basic symbols are easy to understand, and they work naturally with our definition of business process. Hence, we will use the BPMN symbols in the illustrations in the chapter. All of the diagrams in this chapter were drawn using Microsoft Visio, which includes several BPMN symbol templates. Figure 4 summarizes the basic BPMN symbols.

Documenting the As-Is Business Order Process

Figure 5 shows the as-is, or existing, order process introduced in Figure 1. First, note that this process is a model, an abstraction that shows the essential elements of the process but omits many details. If it were not an abstraction, the model would be

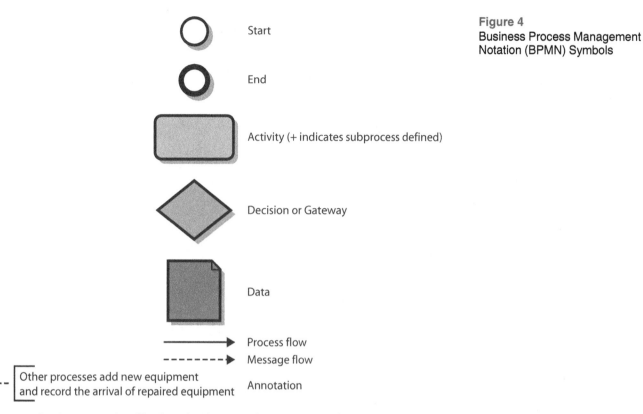

Figure 4
Business Process Management
Notation (BPMN) Symbols

as large as the business itself. This diagram is shown in **swim-lane layout**. In this format, each role in the business process is given its own swim lane. In Figure 5, there are five roles and hence five swim lanes. All activities for a given role are shown in that role's swim lane. Swim-lane layout simplifies process diagrams and draws attention to interactions among components of the diagram.

Two kinds of arrows are shown. Dotted arrows depict the flow of messages and data flows. Solid arrows depict the flow or sequence of the activities in the process. Some sequence flows have data associated with them as well. According to Figure 5, the customer sends an RFQ (request for quotation) to a salesperson (dotted arrow). That salesperson prepares a quotation in the first activity and then (solid arrow) submits the quotation back to the customer. You can follow the rest of the process in this diagram. Allocate inventory means that if the items are available they are allocated to the customer so that they will not be sold to someone else.

Diamonds represent decisions and usually contain a question that can be answered with yes or no. Process arrows labeled Yes and No exit two of the points of the diamond. Three of the activities in the as-is diagram contain a square with a plus (+) sign. This notation means that the activity is considered to be independent of this process and that it is defined in greater detail in another diagram.

For example, the Check Customer Credit subprocess is shown in Figure 6. Note the role named *CRM* in this subprocess. In fact, this role is performed entirely by an information system, although we cannot determine that fact from this diagram. Again, each role is fulfilled by some set of resources, either people or information systems, or both.

Using Process Diagrams to Identify Process Problems

The processes shown in Figures 5 and 6 have problems. Before you continue, examine these figures and see if you can determine what they are.

The problems in these processes involve allocations. The Operations Manager role allocates inventory to the orders as they are processed and the Credit Manager role allocates credit to the customer of orders in process. These allocations are correct as long as the order is accepted. However, if the order is rejected, these allocations are

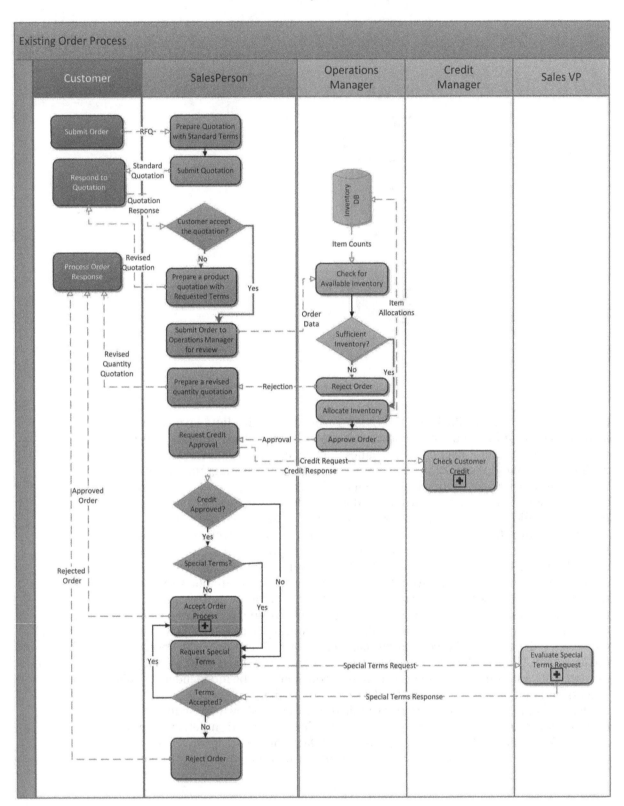

Figure 5
Existing Ordering Process

not freed. Thus, inventory is allocated that will not be ordered, and credit is extended for orders that will not be processed.

One fix (several are possible) is to define an independent process for Reject Order (in Figure 5 that would mean placing a box with a + in the Reject Order activity) and then designing the Reject Order subprocess to free allocations. Creating such a diagram is left as exercise 3 in Using Your Knowledge later in the chapter.

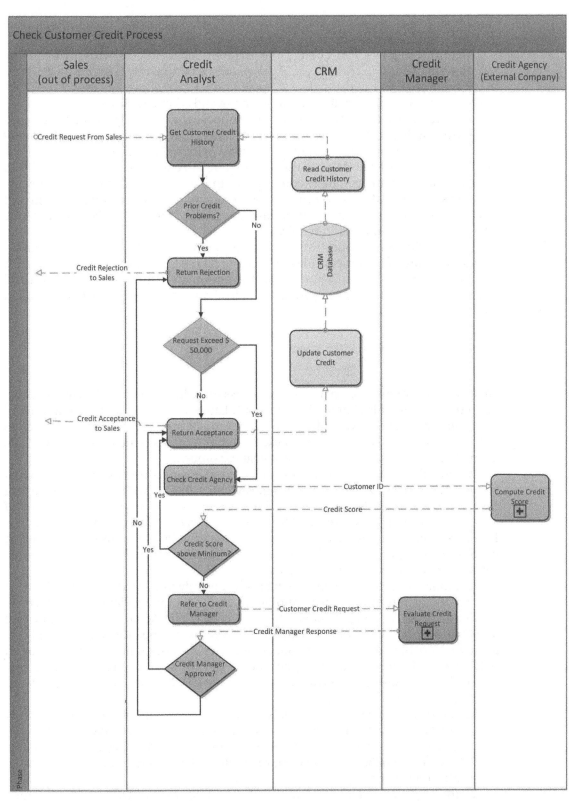

Figure 6
Check Customer Credit
Process

How Can Business Processes Be Improved?

The two major dimensions of business process effectiveness are performance and cost. Process designers can increase the performance of a business process in three fundamental ways. First, they can add more resources to the roles of a given process without changing its structure. This is the *brute-force approach:* add more people, equipment, or systems to the existing way of doing business. Such a change always adds cost; it may be worth doing, however, if the improvement in performance generates sufficient value to justify the cost.

Second, designers can change the *structure* of a process without changing resource allocations. In some cases, if the change is particularly effective it can result in the same or greater performance at no additional cost, or even at less cost. Finally, designers can do both by changing the structure and adding resources.

To better understand these alternatives, suppose the company having the process in Figure 5 finds that its inventory costs are larger than it expects. Investigation of the causes determines that inventory is being held for excessive amounts of time because orders are delayed due to the time required to check the customer's credit. To solve this problem, the company could speed up the process by adding more people resources to the Credit Analyst role shown in Figure 6. Or, the company might add resources by investing in an information system to augment or replace the humans who perform the credit-checking role.

Instead of adding resources, the company could address this problem by changing the structure of the process to check credit before checking inventory availability. Such a change is shown in Figure 7. Another option is for the company to both add resources to the credit-checking process and to change the sequence of inventory and credit checking.

Fox Lake Wedding Planning and Facility Maintenance Processes

To further illustrate the use of business process modeling, consider the Fox Lake scenario that opened this chapter. It ended with Laura, a business analyst, planning to meet with Anne and Mike to determine what might be done to address Fox Lake's problems. Because Fox Lake has no existing maintenance scheduling system, this team of people needed to model a new business process.

Assume that after they met, Laura created the business process model shown in Figure 8. Four roles are shown in vertical swim lanes: The Bride & Family, Wedding Planner, Facilities Application, and Facilities Maintenance. An unknown number of resources will be assigned to each of these roles; many customers will play the Bride & Family role, one or more people will take the Wedding Planner role, some person or computing resource will take the Facilities Application role, and one or more people will take the Facilities Maintenance role.

Examine the exchanges between the Bride & Family role and the Wedding Planner role. Bride & Family provide the requirements that the Wedding Planner uses to create a proposal. Then, Wedding Planner attempts to reserve the facilities. If all facilities are available, the proposal is transformed into bid with costs. If not, the Bride & Family are asked to revise their requirements (smaller number of guests, different date, reception outside, etc.). If the Bride & Family accept the bid and sign the bid, then the facility reservations are confirmed and a deposit is collected. That collection activity is documented as a separate process.

This process model, like all models, is an abstraction. It does not include every detail, but it captures the essence of the process and the need to reserve Fox Lake facilities. It might seem odd to you to formalize the process of planning a wedding in this way, but such formalization is needed to create and implement business processes and related information systems.

By the way, this model is incomplete. Many activities at Fox Lake besides wedding planning need to reserve facilities. Most likely, Laura would document those processes as well, or she might generalize this process into one that would work for all facility users, not just wedding planning. We needn't be concerned with those extensions here, however.

The next step in the BPM process is to create components. That step leads us into the topic of systems development, and we begin by discussing the relationship of business processes and information systems.

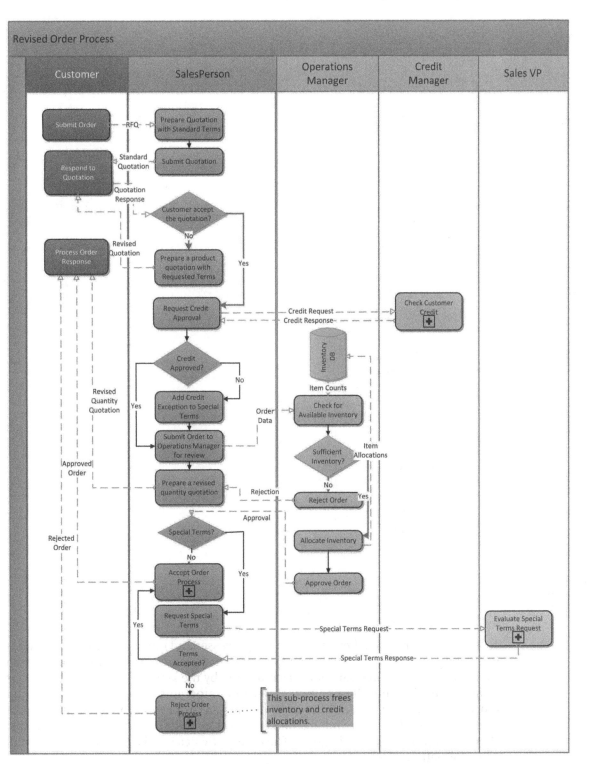

Figure 7
Revised Order Process

Q4 Which Comes First, Business Processes or Information Systems?

This question is surprisingly hard to answer. It's difficult to answer in theory, and it's even more difficult to answer in practice. To understand why, you first need to understand how business processes and information systems relate.

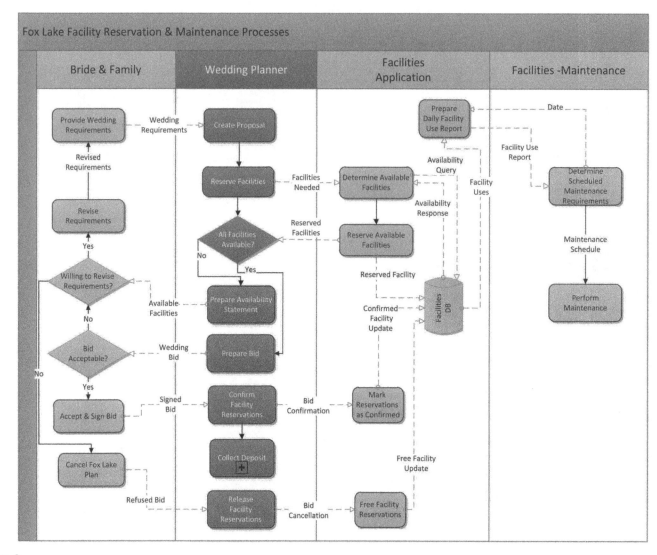

Figure 8
Fox Lake Wedding Planning
and Facilities Maintenance
Processes

How Are Business Processes and Information Systems Related?

To learn the relationship between business processes and information systems, examine Figure 9, which is a color-coded version of Figure 8. Information system elements are shown in bold colors, as indicated by the key. The Facilities database is shown in red, Facilities Reservation application programs are shown in orange, and procedures for using the Facilities Reservation system are shown in blue. This process involves a second, separate billing information system that is processed in the Collect Deposit subprocess shown in green. The other activities in this process are not part of any information system.

We can deduce three important principles from this figure. First, information systems and business processes are not the same thing. Information system elements are embedded within business processes, but there are activities in business processes that are not part of the information system. Second, this business process uses two separate information systems; and, in general, a business process can utilize zero, one, or more information systems.

The third principle is not visible in Figure 9, but we can infer it. The Facilities Reservation information system is likely to be used by other business processes. In fact, the Fox Lake billing process uses this system to bill customers for facility use. In addition, the budgetary process uses the Facility Reservation system to determine

302

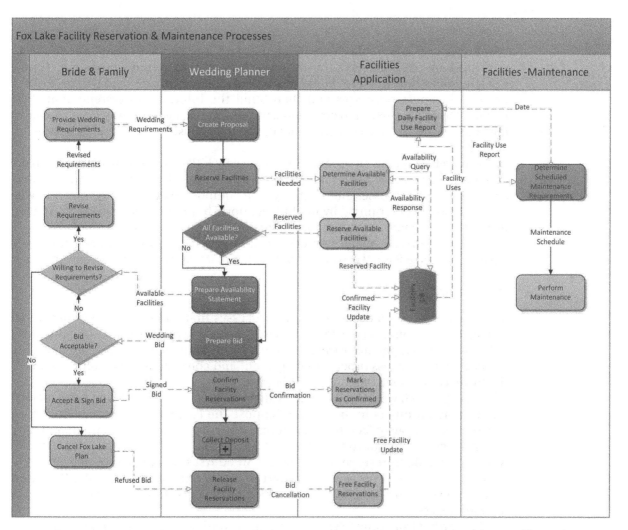

Figure 9
Fox Lake Processes Showing
IS Components

a budget for future facility revenue, and so forth. Thus, a particular information system may be used by one or more business processes.

We can say that the relationship of business processes and information systems is many-to-many, as illustrated in Figure 10. For example, the Wedding Planning process uses two information systems (many), and, at the same time, the Facilities Scheduling system is used in four different business processes (also many).

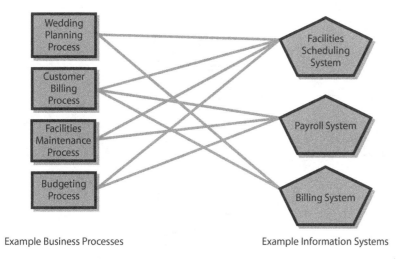

Figure 10

Many-to-Many Relationship of Business Processes and Information Systems

Which Comes First?

Why do we care about this? What difference does it make? The many-to-many relationship between business processes and information systems poses a dilemma when it comes time to build them. Which should we do first? Should we specify one or more business processes and then build the information systems that they require? Or, do we attempt to determine, in the abstract, all of the ways that someone might use an information system, build it, and then construct the business processes around it?

If you reflect on this situation, you can see why ERP systems, which promise to do everything, are both wonderful and terrible. They're wonderful because they include all the business processes and all the system components that an organization will need, at least as determined by the ERP vendor. They're terrible because, to implement ERP, an organization must attempt to do everything at once.

But, for non-ERP business processes and information systems, and for small organizations like Fox Lake, which should come first? Consider the alternatives.

Business Processes First

Suppose we decide to design business processes first and then build information system components as a consequence of that process design. If we take this approach, we'll have a development process that looks like that in Figure 11. The organization will engage in business process management and construct system components in the create components stage of the BPM cycle.

This approach works well for the business processes that are being constructed, but what about others in the future? Suppose the Facilities Reservation system is constructed to reserve facilities like rooms in buildings and the restaurant and that it works well for that purpose. But what if Fox Lake's golf operations department wants to be able to reserve one or both golf courses for special events? The golf course reservation process was not part of the requirements when the Facilities Reservation system was constructed for Wedding Events, and the system won't work for that process.

So, starting from processes and working toward information systems is likely to work well for the business processes under consideration, but will cause problems later, for other processes that use the information systems. So, what if we start with the information system, first?

Figure 11
BPM and Systems
Development

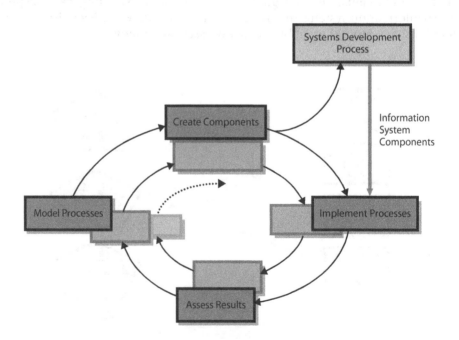

Information System First

To start with systems first, a development team would talk with representative future users of the system and attempt to determine all of the ways that someone at Fox Lake might want to reserve facilities. From those requirements, they would then design components and construct the system.

Systems development is the process of creating and maintaining an information system. The most common technique for developing information systems is the **systems development life cycle (SDLC)**, and it has the five steps shown in Figure 12. A high-level business planning process determines that a system is needed for some function; at Fox Lake that function would be to reserve facilities. Given that system need, the development team would then refine the system definition, determine requirements, design system components, and then implement the system.

This development process makes business processes a poor step-child of the information systems development process. The focus is on hardware, software, data, procedures (for using the system only), and user training. Some aspects of business processes will be constructed as part of the system implementation, but, as you saw in Figure 9, business processes can include many activities that are not part of the information system. Those activities are unlikely to be considered when the system is constructed.

Another Factor: Off-the-Shelf Software

A missing factor in this discussion is off-the-shelf software. Few organizations today can afford to create computer programs and design databases in-house. It is unlikely that Fox Lake, for example, will do so. Instead, most organizations attempt to license software off-the-shelf and adapt it to their needs, or adapt their needs to it.

So, if an organization knows that it will most likely license off-the-shelf software, is it better to design processes first or to develop information systems first? Unfortunately, again, there is no demonstrably correct answer. If an organization starts with business processes first, it is likely to choose a package that will work well for the processes being developed, but that may not work well for other processes that may come along later (like golf operations wanting to reserve golf tee times). However, if it starts with information systems and collects all the requirements, it is likely to find a package that will work better for all users, but, again, business processes will receive short shrift.

And the Answer Is . . .

In theory, it is better to start with business processes. Business processes are closer to the organization's competitive strategy and other goals and

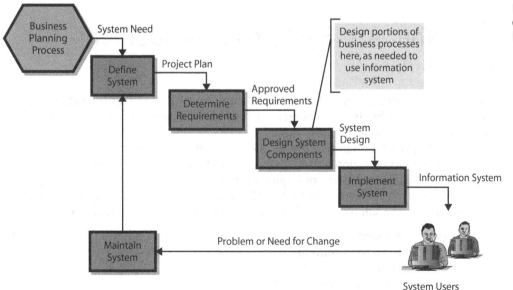

Figure 12
Classic Five-Step Systems Development Life Cycle

objectives. Starting with processes and working toward systems is more likely to result in processes and systems that are aligned with the organization's strategy and direction.

In practice, however, the answer is not clear. Organizations today take both approaches. Sometimes the same organization takes one approach with one set of processes and systems and a second approach with a different set.

The factor that overtakes all is off-the-shelf software. The vendor of the software knows the features that are most commonly needed by its customers. Therefore, if an organization starts with business processes and selects an application that works for those processes, it is likely that the application will also include features and functions that will be needed by other business processes to be designed in the future. At Fox Lake, an application that can be used to reserve buildings and rooms is likely to be adaptable enough to also reserve golf courses and golf facilities.

Most likely, an application software vendor will include procedures for using that software as part of its offering. So, the procedure components in Figure 9 (shown in blue) are most likely part of the package. However, the entire business process in Figure 9 is unlikely to be part of the vendor's package.

Therefore, in most cases, if an organization is likely to license an application from a vendor, it is better to begin with processes. This rule is not ironclad, however. You should expect to find both approaches used in organizations during your career.

Not Possible to Buy Processes or Systems Off-the-Shelf

Before we continue with systems development, do not be misled by the last few paragraphs. It is possible to buy an off-the-shelf computer application that will fulfill the Facilities Application role. Laura, and possibly others, will most likely search for just such an application rather than creating it in-house.

However, it is *not* possible to buy an information system off-the-shelf. The procedures for reserving facilities, confirming reservations, and so on all need to be integrated into Fox Lake's business processes. Employees who fulfill process roles need to be trained on those procedures. The most we can say is that the hardware, software, and database design components can be purchased off-the-shelf. The database data, the procedures, and the people are all provided in-house.

Furthermore, even if the vendor of the application includes business processes as part of the package, as ERP vendors do, those business processes are not yours until you have integrated them into your business and trained your employees.

Keep this in mind when you manage a department that is to receive a new information system or an upgrade. You need to allow time for such integration and training, and you should expect there will be mistakes and problems as the new application is first put into use.

Q5 What Are Systems Development Activities?

As you just learned, systems development can come before business processes or it can be a result of business processes. Given this uncertainty, how can you study systems development activities?

Examine Figure 12 again. It shows the basic phases of the systems development life cycle, the most commonly used process for creating information systems. If we put those phases into the context of Figure 11, we will obtain the diagram in Figure 13. Whether you use the process in Figure 12 (systems first) or the process in Figure 13 (processes first), the same basic activities are involved in creating IS components:

- Define the system.
- Determine the requirements.
- Design system components.
- Implement the system (Figure 12).

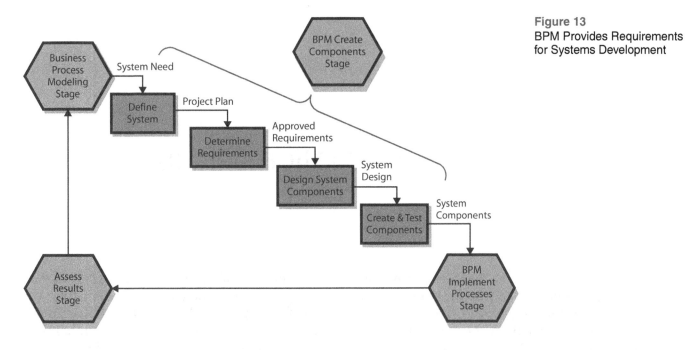

Figure 13
BPM Provides Requirements
for Systems Development

- Create and test components and implement the system (Figure 13).
- Maintain the system (Figure 12).
- Assess process results (Figure 13).

So, if you learn the nature of the work for each of these activities, you will be well prepared to participate as a user, manager, and business professional in development activities regardless of which approach your organization takes. As indicated, there are some important differences in the implementation and maintenance/assess activities, but we can deal with those differences as we go.

So, consider the nature of the work for each of these activities.

Define the System

In response to the need for the new system, the organization will assign a few employees, possibly on a part-time basis, to define the new system, assess its feasibility, and plan the project. In a large organization, someone from the IS department leads the initial team, but the members of that initial team are both users and IS professionals. For an organization like Fox Lake, the team would most likely be led by an outside consultant like Laura.

Define System Goals and Scope

As shown in Figure 14, the first step is to define the goals and scope of the new information system. Is the goal of the new system only to implement the elements

The cost of a project can be determined in a number of ways. For a discussion of a few of the ethical issues relating to cost estimates, see the Ethics Guide in this chapter.

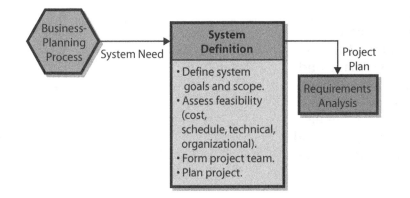

Figure 14
SDLC: System Definition
Phase

Ethics Guide

Estimation Ethics

A *buy-in* occurs when a company agrees to produce a system or product for less than it knows the project will require. Laura could buy-in at Fox Lake if she agreed to build the system for, say, $50,000, when good estimating techniques indicate it will take $75,000. If the contract for the system or product is written for "time and materials," Fox Lake will ultimately pay Laura the $75,000 for the finished system. Or, Fox Lake will cancel the project once the true cost is known. If the contract for the system or product is written for a fixed cost, then Laura will eat the extra costs. She'd use the latter strategy if the contract opens up other business opportunities that are worth the $25,000 loss.

Buy-ins always involve deceit. Most would agree that buying in on a time-and-materials project, planning to stick the customer with the full cost later, is unethical and wrong. Opinions on buying in on a fixed-priced contract vary. You know you'll take a loss, but why? For a favor down the road? Or some other unethical reason? Some would say that because buying in is always deceitful, it should always be avoided. Others say that it is just one of many different business strategies.

What about in-house projects? Do the ethics change if an in-house development team is building a system for use in-house? If team members know there is only $50,000 in the budget, should they start the project if they believe that its true cost is $75,000? If they do start, at some point senior management will either have to admit a mistake and cancel the project or find the additional $25,000. Project sponsors can make all sorts of excuses for such a buy-in. For example, "I know the company needs this system. If management doesn't realize it and fund it appropriately, then we'll just force their hand."

These issues become even stickier if team members disagree about how much the project will cost. Suppose one faction of the team believes the project will cost $35,000, another faction estimates $50,000, and a third thinks $65,000. Can the project sponsors justify taking the average? Or, should they describe the range of estimates?

Other buy-ins are more subtle. Suppose you are a project manager of an exciting new project that is possibly a career-maker for you. You are incredibly busy, working 6 days a week and long hours each day. Your team has developed an estimate for $50,000 for the project. A little voice in the back of your mind says that maybe not all costs for every aspect of the project are included in that estimate. You mean to follow up on that thought, but more pressing matters in your schedule take precedence. Soon you find yourself in front of management, presenting the $50,000 estimate. You probably should have found the time to investigate the estimate, but you didn't. Is your behavior unethical?

Or, suppose you approach a more senior manager with your dilemma. "I think there may be other costs, but I know that $50,000 is all we've got. What should I do?" Suppose the senior manager says something like, "Well, let's go forward. You don't know of anything else, and we can always find more budget elsewhere if we have to." How do you respond?

You can buy in on schedule as well as cost. If the marketing department says, "We have to have the new product for the trade show," do you agree, even if you know it's highly unlikely? What if marketing says, "If we don't have it by then, we should just cancel the project." Suppose it's not impossible to make that schedule, it's just highly unlikely. How do you respond? ■

Discussion Questions

1. Do you agree that buying in on a cost-and-materials project is always unethical? Explain your reasoning. Are there circumstances in which it could be illegal?

2. Suppose you learn through the grapevine that your opponents in a competitive bid are buying in on a time-and-materials contract. Does this change your answer to question 1?

3. Suppose you are a project manager who is preparing a request for proposal on a cost-and-materials systems development project. What can you do to prevent buy-ins?

4. Under what circumstances do you think buying in on a fixed-price contract is ethical? What are the dangers of this strategy?

5. Explain why in-house development projects are always time-and-materials projects.

6. Given your answer to question 5, is buying in on an in-house project always unethical? Under what circumstances do you think it is ethical? Under what circumstances do you think it is justifiable, even if it is unethical?

7. Suppose you ask a senior manager for advice as described in the Guide. Does the manager's response absolve you of guilt? Suppose you ask the manager and then do not follow her guidance. What problems result?

8. Explain how you can buy in on schedule as well as costs.

9. For an in-house project, how do you respond to the marketing manager who says that the project should be cancelled if it will not be ready for the trade show? In your answer, suppose that you disagree with this opinion—suppose you know the system has value regardless of whether it is done by the trade show.

required for the processes in Figure 11? Or, is the new system broader in scope? Should the new system consider unscheduled maintenance as well as scheduled maintenance? Are departments other than wedding planning going to use this new system? Are there other needs for facility use data? Does Jeff, for example, want reports that show the utilization of facilities? These questions are asked and answered as part of the definition phase.

Assess Feasibility

Given the goals and scope of the new system, the next task is to assess feasibility. "Does this project make sense?" The aim here is to eliminate obviously nonsensical projects before forming a project development team and investing significant labor.

Feasibility has four dimensions: **cost**, **schedule**, **technical**, and **organizational feasibility**. Because IS development projects are difficult to budget and schedule, cost and schedule feasibility can be only an approximate, back-of-the-envelope analysis. The purpose is to eliminate any obviously infeasible ideas as soon as possible.

Technical feasibility refers to whether existing information technology is likely to be able to meet the needs of the new system. The new system at Fox Lake is well within the capabilities of existing technology. For more advanced systems, this is not always the case. Between 1995 and 2005, the IRS engaged in a 10-year information systems project disaster when it attempted to use new technology to revamp tax return processing without assessing the technical feasibility. Finally, *organizational feasibility* concerns whether the new system fits within the organization's customs, culture, charter, or legal requirements. At Fox Lake, for example, is a daily maintenance schedule appropriate? Are there union regulations that stipulate that workers need to have advanced notice of hours to be worked? Does the system need to prepare a weekly or monthly schedule to comply with these rules?

Form a Project Team

If the defined project is determined to be feasible, the next step is to form the project team. Normally, the team consists of both IT personnel and user representatives. The project manager and IT personnel can be in-house personnel or outside contractors.

Typical personnel on a development team are a manager (or mangers for larger projects), business analysts, system analysts, programmers, software testers, and users. A **business analyst** is someone who is well versed in Porter's models, organizational strategy, and systems alignment theory, like COBIT, and who also understand the proper role for technology. As shown in Figure 15, business analysts work primarily with business processes as well as with systems development at a high level.

Systems analysts are IS professionals who understand both business and technology. They are active throughout the systems development process and play a key role in moving the project through the systems development process. Systems analysts integrate the work of the programmers, testers, and users. Depending on the nature of the project, the team may also include hardware and communications specialists, database designers and administrators, and other IT specialists. As shown in Figure 15, systems analysts work with process design as well, but their primary focus is information systems development.

The team composition changes over time. During requirements definition, the team will be heavy with business and systems analysts. During design and implementation, it will be heavy with programmers, testers, and database designers. During integrated testing and conversion, the team will be augmented with testers and business users.

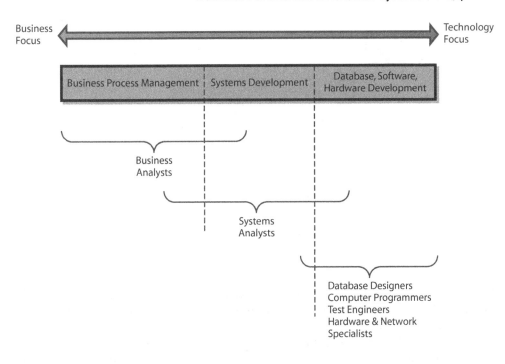

Figure 15
Focus of Personnel Involved
in BPM and Systems
Development

User involvement is critical throughout the system development process. Depending on the size and nature of the project, users are assigned to the project either full or part time. Sometimes users are assigned to review and oversight committees that meet periodically, especially at the completion of project phases and other milestones. Users are involved in many different ways. *The important point is for users to be actively involved in and take ownership of the project throughout the entire development process.*

The first major task for the assembled project team is to plan the project. Members of the project team specify tasks to be accomplished, assign personnel, determine task dependencies, and set schedules. We will discuss this further in Q6.

Determine Requirements

Determining the system's requirements is the most important phase in the systems development process. If the requirements are wrong, the system will be wrong. If the requirements are determined completely and correctly, then design and implementation will be easier and more likely to result in success.

Examples of requirements in Figure 9 are the contents of the Facility Use Report or the fields to be provided in the Facilities Needed data flow. Requirements include not only what is to be produced, but also how frequently and how fast it is to be produced. Some requirements specify the volume of data to be stored and processed.

If you take a course in systems analysis and design, you will spend weeks on techniques for determining requirements. Here, we will just summarize that process. Typically, systems analysts interview users and record the results in some consistent manner. Good interviewing skills are crucial; users are notorious for being unable to describe what they want and need. Users also tend to focus on the tasks they are performing at the time of the interview. Tasks performed at the end of the quarter or end of the year are forgotten if the interview takes place mid-quarter. Seasoned and experienced systems analysts know how to conduct interviews to bring such requirements to light.

As listed in Figure 16, sources of requirements include existing systems as well as the forms, reports, queries, and application features and functions desired in the new system. Security is another important category of requirements.

If the new system involves a new database or substantial changes to an existing database, then the development team will create a data model.

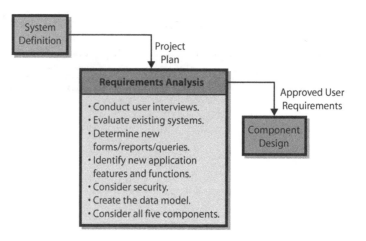

Figure 16
SDLC: Requirements
Analysis Phase

That model must reflect the users' perspective on their business and business activities. Thus, the data model is constructed on the basis of user interviews and must be validated by those users.

Sometimes the requirements determination is so focused on the software and data components that other components are forgotten. Experienced project managers ensure consideration of requirements for all five IS components, not just for software and data. Regarding hardware, the team might ask: Are there special needs or restrictions on hardware? Is there an organizational standard governing what kinds of hardware can, or cannot, be used? Must the new system use existing hardware? What requirements are there for communications and network hardware?

Similarly, the team should consider requirements for procedures and personnel: Do accounting controls require procedures that separate duties and authorities? Are there restrictions that some actions can be taken only by certain departments or specific personnel? Are there policy requirements or union rules that restrict activities to certain categories of employees? Will the system need to interface with information systems from other companies and organizations? In short, requirements need to be considered for all of the components of the new information system.

These questions are examples of the kinds of questions that must be asked and answered during requirements analysis.

Design System Components

Each of the five components is designed in this stage. Typically, the team designs each component by developing alternatives, evaluating each of those alternatives against the requirements, and then selecting from among those alternatives. Accurate requirements are critical here; if they are incomplete or wrong, then they will be poor guides for evaluation.

Figure 17 shows that design tasks pertain to each of the five IS components. For hardware, the team determines specifications for the hardware that they want to acquire. (The team is not designing hardware in the sense of building a CPU or a disk drive.) Program design depends on the source of the programs. For off-the-shelf software, the team must determine candidate products and evaluate them against the requirements. For off-the-shelf with alteration programs, the team identifies products to be acquired off-the-shelf and then determines the alterations required. For custom-developed programs, the team produces design documentation for writing program code.

If the project includes constructing a database, then during this phase database designers convert the data model to a database design. If the project involves off-the-shelf programs, then little database design needs to be done; the programs will have been coded to work with a pre-existing database design.

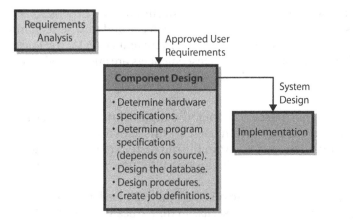

Figure 17
SDLC: Component Design
Phase

Procedure design differs depending on whether the project is part of a BPM process (processes first) or is part of a systems development process (systems first). If the former, then business processes will already be designed, and all that is needed is to create procedures for using the application (like those shown in blue in Figure 9). If the latter, then procedures for using the system need to be developed, and it is possible that business processes that surround the system need to be developed as well.

With regard to people, design involves developing job descriptions for the various roles. These descriptions will detail responsibilities, skills needed, training required, and so forth.

Implementation Activities

The term *implementation* has two meanings for us. It could mean to implement the information systems components, only, or it could mean to implement the information system and the business processes that use the information system. As you read the following task descriptions, keep in mind that the tasks can apply to both interpretations of implementation.

Tasks in the implementation phase are to build and test system components and to convert users to the new system and possibly new business processes (see Figure 18). Developers construct each of the components independently. They obtain, install, and test hardware. They license and install off-the-shelf programs; they write adaptations and custom programs as necessary. They construct a database and fill it with data. They document, review, and test procedures, and they create training programs. Finally, the organization hires and trains needed personnel.

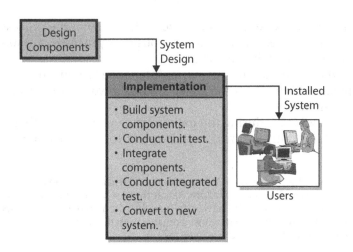

Figure 18
SDLC: Implementation Phase

Testing the system is important, time consuming, and expensive. A **test plan**, which is a formal description of the system's response to use and misuse scenarios, is written. Professional test engineers, called product quality assurance (PQA) test engineers, are hired for this task. Often teams of professional test engineers are augmented by users as well.

System Conversion

Once the system has passed testing, the organization installs the new system. The term **system conversion** is often used for this activity because it implies the process of *converting* business activity from the old system to the new. Again, conversion can be to the new system, only, or it can be to the new system, including new business processes.

Four types of conversion are possible: pilot, phased, parallel, and plunge. Any of the first three can be effective. In most cases, companies should avoid "taking the plunge"!

With **pilot installation**, the organization implements the entire system/business processes on a limited portion of the business. An example would be for Fox Lake to use the new system for a few wedding events. The advantage of pilot implementation is that if the system fails, the failure is contained within a limited boundary.

As the name implies, with **phased installation** the new system/business processes are installed in phases across the organization(s). Once a given piece works, then the organization installs and tests another piece of the system, until the entire system has been installed. Some systems are so tightly integrated that they cannot be installed in phased pieces. Such systems must be installed using one of the other techniques.

With **parallel installation**, the new system/business processes run in parallel with the old one until the new system is tested and fully operational. Parallel installation is expensive, because the organization incurs the costs of running both the existing and new system/business processes. Users must work double-time, if you will, to run both systems. Then, considerable work is needed to reconcile the results of the new with the old.

The final style of conversion is **plunge installation** (sometimes called *direct installation*). With it, the organization shuts off the old system/business processes and starts the new one. If the new system/business processes fail, the organization is in trouble: Nothing can be done until either the new system/business processes are fixed or the old system/business processes are reinstalled. Because of the risk, organizations should avoid this conversion style if possible. The one exception is if the new system is providing a new capability that will not disrupt the operation of the organization if it fails.

Figure 19 summarizes the tasks for each of the five components during the design and implementation phases. Use this figure to test your knowledge of the tasks in each phase.

What Are the Tasks for System Maintenance?

Here, we will consider system maintenance in the sense of the process in Figure 12, only. The tasks that concern maintenance of business processes are subsumed under the assess results phase of the BPM cycle.

With regard to information systems, **maintenance** is a misnomer; the work done during this phase is either to *fix* the system so that it works correctly or to *adapt* it to changes in requirements.

Figure 20 shows tasks during the maintenance phase. First, there needs to be a means for tracking both failures[1] and requests for enhancements to meet new

---

[1]A *failure* is a difference between what the system does and what it is supposed to do. Sometimes you will hear the term *bug* used instead of failure. As a future user, call failures *failures*, because that's what they are. Don't have a *bugs list*, have a *failures list*. Don't have an *unresolved bug*, have an *unresolved failure*. A few months of managing an organization that is coping with a serious failure will show you the importance of this difference in terms.

	Hardware	Software	Data	Procedures	People
Design	Determine hardware specifications.	Select off-the-shelf programs. Design alterations and custom programs as necessary.	Design database and related structures.	Design user and operations procedures.	Develop user and operations job descriptions.
Implementation	Obtain, install, and test hardware.	License and install off-the-shelf programs. Write alterations and custom programs. Test programs.	Create database. Fill with data. Test data.	Document procedures. Create training programs. Review and test procedures.	Hire and train personnel.
	Integrated Test and Conversion				

Unit test each component

Note: Cells shaded tan represent software development.

Figure 19
Design and Implementation for the Five Components

requirements. For small systems, organizations can track failures and enhancements using word-processing documents. As systems become larger, however, and as the number of failure and enhancement requests increases, many organizations find it necessary to develop a tracking database. Such a database contains a description of the failure or enhancement. It also records who reported the problem, who will make the fix or enhancement, what the status of that work is, and whether the fix or enhancement has been tested and verified by the originator.

Typically, IS personnel prioritize system problems according to their severity. They fix high-priority items as soon as possible, and they fix low-priority items as time and resources become available.

Because an enhancement is an adaptation to new requirements, developers usually prioritize enhancement requests separate from failures. The decision to make an enhancement includes a business decision that the enhancement will generate an acceptable rate of return.

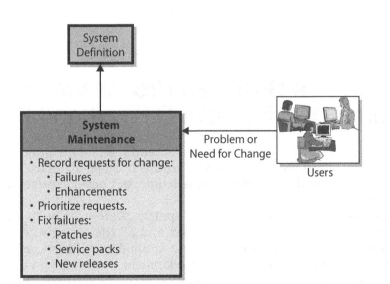

Figure 20
SDLC: System Maintenance Phase

Using MIS InClass *A Group Exercise*

Fox Lake Facilities' Future

Superstock Royalty Free

Suppose that Fox Lake wants to create a facilities reservation system. How should they proceed? As described in Q4, it could model business processes like that in Figure 9 first, and then select an information system. The problem, as described in Q4, is that in the future, if the golf operations, tennis operations, the pro shop, the restaurant, or any other department wants to make a reservation, that system may not have the features and functions needed. They could attempt to model business processes for all of these potential users, and then build the system, but that's a big job.

So, instead, they could begin by asking users in every department about their interest in a reservation system and interviewing users of departments that have such an interest. The advantage there is that they would then need to develop business processes to fit the software, after the fact.

These three scenarios can be summarized as follows:

a. Model business processes for wedding planning and facilities maintenance, similar to that shown in Figure 9. Develop a facility reservation information system that will meet the needs of these departments. Future departments may or may not be able to use the reservation system as built; if not, the system can be altered.

b. Model business processes for every major facility user at Fox Lake. Model processes for wedding events, golf, tennis, the swimming pool, and any other potential facility reservation system user. Develop a facility reservation information system that will meet all of these needs.

c. Identify departments that have a need for a facilities reservation system. Without attempting to specify business processes for these departments, collect requirements for a facilities reservation system. (This alternative amounts to identifying the requirements for the blue, orange, and red elements of Figure 9 for each potential user.)

Fox Lake has to decide. If you were Jeff, what would you do? Form a team, answer the following questions, and make a recommendation to Jeff.

1. List the criteria that you think Fox Lake should use in deciding its development strategy.

2. Score alternatives a–c based on your criteria.

3. Recommend a course of action for Fox Lake to take. Justify your recommendation.

4. Present your recommendation to the rest of the class.

Q6 Why Are Business Processes and Systems Development Difficult and Risky?

Process and systems development is difficult and risky. Many projects are never finished. Of those that are finished, some are 200 or 300 percent over budget. Still other projects finish within budget and schedule, but never satisfactorily accomplish their goals.

User involvement is critical to the system's success, as described in the Guide later in the chapter.

You may be amazed to learn that development failures can be so dramatic. You might suppose that with all the computers and all the systems developed over the years that by now there must be some methodology for successful systems development. In fact, there *are* systems development methodologies that can result in success, and we will discuss the primary one in this chapter. But, even when

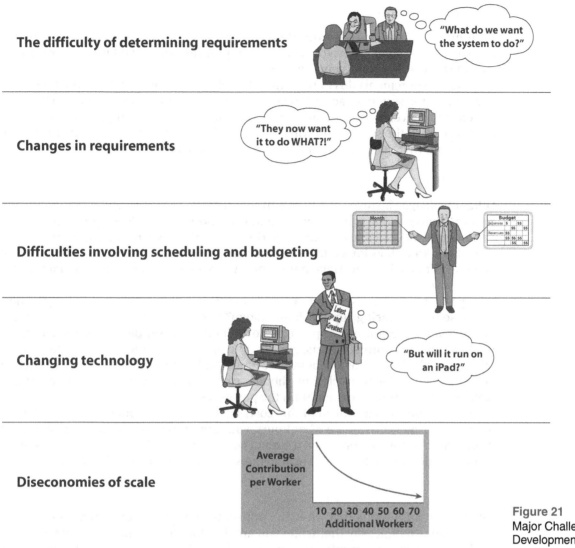

Figure 21
Major Challenges to System
Development

competent people follow this or some other accepted methodology, the risk of failure is still high.

In the following sections, we will discuss the five major challenges to systems development displayed in Figure 21.

The Difficulty of Requirements Determination

First, requirements are difficult to determine. The processes and system diagramed in Figure 11 are a good first start. But, what steps need to be taken to fulfill an activity? What specific data items appear in data flows? What is the specific format of the Reserved Facility report?

The proposed Fox Lake system/processes are simple. Consider, instead, the development of a new interorganizational system to be used by the suppliers of the Boeing 787 airplane. What features and functions should it have? What is to be done if different companies have different ideas about the IS features required? Companies may disagree about the data they are willing to share. How are those differences to be resolved? Hundreds of hours of labor will be required to determine the requirements.

The questions could go on and on. One of the major purposes of the systems development process is to create an environment in which such questions are both asked and answered.

Changes in Requirements

Even more difficult, systems development aims at a moving target. Requirements change as the system is developed, and the bigger the system and the longer the project, the more the requirements change.

When requirements do change, what should the development team do? Stop work and rebuild the system in accordance with the new requirements? If they do that, the system will develop in fits and starts and may never be completed. Or, should the team finish the system, knowing that it will be unsatisfactory the day it is implemented and will, therefore, need immediate maintenance?

Scheduling and Budgeting Difficulties

Other challenges involve scheduling and budgeting. How long will it take to build a system? That question is not easy to answer. Suppose you are developing a new facilities maintenance database at Fox Lake. How long will it take to create the data model? Even if you know how long it takes to create the data model, others may disagree with you and with each other. How many times will you need to rebuild the data model until everyone agrees?

Again, the Fox Lake system is a simple problem. What if you are building the new database for the Boeing supply chain system? How many hours will it take to create the data model, review, and approve it? Consider database applications. How long will it take to build the forms, reports, queries, and application programs? How long will it take to test all of them? What about procedures and people? What procedures need to be developed, and how much time should be set aside to create and document them, develop training programs, and train the personnel?

Further, how much will all of this cost? Labor costs are a direct function of labor hours; if you cannot estimate labor hours, you cannot estimate labor costs. Moreover, if you cannot estimate how much a system costs, then how do you perform a financial analysis to determine if the system generates an appropriate rate of return?

Changing Technology

Yet another challenge is that while the project is underway, technology continues to change. For example, say that while you are developing your facilities maintenance application, Apple, Microsoft, and Google and their business partners all release new versions of their devices and software. You know that with these new devices you can create a better facilities scheduling capability for wedding planners and maintenance workers, but using them means a major change in requirements.

Do you want to stop your development to switch to the new technology? Would it be better to finish developing according to the existing plan? Such decisions are tough. Why build an out-of-date system? But, can you afford to keep changing the project?

Diseconomies of Scale

Unfortunately, as development teams become larger, the average contribution per worker decreases. This is true because as staff size increases, more meetings and other coordinating activities are required to keep everyone in sync. There are economies of scale up to a point, but beyond a workgroup of, say, 20 employees, diseconomies of scale begin to take over.

A famous adage known as **Brooks' Law** points out a related problem: *Adding more people to a late project makes the project later.*[2] Brooks' Law is true not only because a

---

[2]Fred Brooks was a successful executive at IBM in the 1960s. After retiring from IBM, he wrote a classic book on IT project management called *The Mythical Man-Month*. Published by Addison-Wesley in 1975, the book is pertinent today and should be read by every IT or IS project manager. It's an enjoyable book, too.

larger staff requires increased coordination, but also because new people need to be trained. The only people who can train the new employees are the existing team members, who are, thus, taken off productive tasks. The costs of training new people can overwhelm the benefit of their contribution.

In short, managers of software development projects face a dilemma: They can increase work per employee by keeping the team small, but in doing so they extend the project's timeline. Or, they can reduce the project's timeline by adding staff, but because of diseconomies of scale they will have to add 150 or 200 hours of labor to gain 100 hours of work. And, due to Brooks' Law, once the project is late, both choices are bad.

Furthermore, schedules can be compressed only so far. According to one other popular adage, "Nine women cannot make a baby in one month."

Q7 What Are the Keys for Successful Process and Systems Development Projects?

Process and systems development projects, whether they begin with processes and work toward systems or begin with systems and work toward processes, are challenging to manage. In this question we will consider five keys to success:

- Create a work-breakdown structure.
- Estimate time and costs.
- Create a project plan.
- Adjust the plan via trade-offs.
- Manage development challenges.

Create a Work-Breakdown Structure

The key strategy for process and systems development—and, indeed, the key strategy for any project—is to divide and conquer. The project is too large, too complicated, and the duration is too long to attempt to manage it as one piece. Instead, successful project managers break the project into smaller and smaller tasks until each task is small enough to estimate and to manage. Every task should culminate in one or more results called **deliverables**. Examples of deliverables are documents, designs, prototypes, data models, database designs, working data entry screens, and the like. Without a defined deliverable, it is impossible to know if the task was accomplished.

Tasks are interrelated, and to prevent them from becoming a confusing morass project teams create a **work-breakdown structure (WBS)**, which is a hierarchy of the tasks required to complete a project. The WBS for a large project is huge; it might entail hundreds or even thousands of tasks. Figure 22 shows the WBS for the system definition phase for a typical IS project.

In this diagram, the overall task, *System definition,* is divided into *Define goals and scope, Assess feasibility, Plan project,* and *Form project team.* Each of those tasks is broken into smaller tasks until the work has been divided into small tasks that can be managed and estimated.

Estimate Time and Costs

As stated, it is exceedingly difficult to determine duration and labor requirements for many development tasks. Fred Brooks defined software as "logical poetry." Like poetry, software is not made of wood or metal or plastic; it is pure thought-stuff. Some years ago, when I pressed a seasoned software developer for a schedule, he responded by

Figure 22
Example Work-Breakdown
Structure (WBS)

System definition			
1.1	Define goals and scope		
	1.1.1	Define goals	
	1.1.2	Define system boundaries	
	1.1.3	Review results	
	1.1.4	Document results	
1.2	Assess feasibility		
	1.2.1	Cost	
	1.2.2	Schedule	
	1.2.3	Technical	
	1.2.4	Organizational	
	1.2.5	Document feasibility	
	1.2.6	Management review and go/no go decision	
1.3	Plan project		
	1.3.1	Establish milestones	
	1.3.2	Create WBS	
		1.3.2.1	Levels 1 and 2
		1.3.2.2	Levels 3+
	1.3.3	Document WBS	
		1.3.3.1	Create WBS baseline
		1.3.3.2	Input to Project
	1.3.4	Determine resource requirements	
		1.3.4.1	Personnel
		1.3.4.2	Computing
		1.3.4.3	Office space
		1.3.4.4	Travel and Meeting Expense
	1.3.5	Management review	
		1.3.5.1	Prepare presentation
		1.3.5.2	Prepare background documents
		1.3.5.3	Give presentation
		1.3.5.4	Incorporate feedback into plan
		1.3.5.5	Approve project
1.4	Form project team		
	1.4.1	Meet with HR	
	1.4.2	Meet with IT Director	
	1.4.3	Develop job descriptions	
	1.4.4	Meet with available personnel	
	1.4.5	Hire personnel	

asking me, "What would Shakespeare have said if someone asked him how long it would take him to write *Hamlet*?" Another common rejoinder is, "What would a fisherman say if you ask him how long will it take to catch three fish? He doesn't know, and neither do I."

Organizations take three approaches to this challenge. The first is to avoid the major schedule risks and never develop systems and software in-house. Instead, they license packages, such as ERP systems, that include both business processes and information systems components. As stated earlier, even if the vendor provides workable processes, those processes will need to be integrated into the business. However, the schedule risk of integration activities is far less than those for developing processes, programs, databases, and other components.

But what if no suitable package exists? In that case, companies take one of two remaining approaches. They can admit the impossibility of systems development scheduling and plan accordingly. They abandon any confidence in their estimates and invest a certain level of resources into a project, manage it as best they can, and take the schedule that results. Only loose commitments are made regarding the completion date and final system functionality. Project sponsors dislike this approach because they are signing a blank check. But sometimes it is just a matter of admitting the reality that exists: "We don't know, and it's worse to pretend that we do."

The third approach is to attempt to schedule the development project in spite of all the difficulties. Several different estimation techniques can be used. If the project is similar to a past project, the schedule data from that past project can be used for planning. When such similar past projects exist, this technique can produce quality schedule estimates. If there is no such past project, managers can make the best estimates they can. For computer coding, some managers estimate the number of lines of code that will need to be written and apply industry or company averages to estimate the time required. Other coding estimation techniques exist, visit *http://sunset.usc.edu/ csse/research/COCOMOII/cocomo_main.html*. Of course, lines of code and function-point techniques estimate schedules only for software components. The schedules for processes, procedures, databases, and the other components must be estimated using other techniques.

Create a Project Plan

A project plan is a list of WBS tasks, arranged to account for task dependencies, with durations and resources applied. Some tasks cannot be started or finished until other tasks are completed. You can't, for example, put electrical wires in a house until you've built the walls. You can define task dependencies in planning software such as Microsoft Project, and it will arrange the plan accordingly.

Given dependencies, estimates for task duration and resource requirements are then applied to the WBS to form a project plan. Figure 23 shows the WBS as input to Microsoft Project, with task dependencies and durations defined. The display on the right, called a **Gantt chart**, shows tasks, dates, and dependencies.

The user has entered all of the tasks from the WBS and has assigned each task a duration. She has also specified task dependencies, although the means she used are beyond our discussion. The two red arrows emerging from task 4, *Define system boundaries,* indicate that neither the *Review results* task nor the *Assess feasibility* task can begin until *Define system boundaries* is completed. Other task dependencies are also shown; you can learn about them in a project management class.

The **critical path** is the sequence of activities that determine the earliest date by which the project can be completed. Reflect for a moment on that statement: The *earliest date* is the date determined by considering the *longest path* through the network of activities. Paying attention to task dependencies, the planner will compress the tasks as much as possible. Those tasks that cannot be further compressed lie on the critical path. Microsoft Project and other project-planning applications can readily identify critical path tasks.

Figure 23 shows the tasks on the critical path in red. Consider the first part of the WBS. The project planner specified that task 4 cannot begin until 2 days before task 3 starts. (That's the meaning of the red arrow emerging from task 3.) Neither task 5 nor task 8 can begin until task 4 is completed. Task 8 will take longer than tasks 5 and 6, and so task 8—not tasks 5 or 6—is on the critical path. Thus, the critical path to this point is tasks 3, 4, and 8. You can trace the critical path through the rest of the WBS by following the tasks shown in red, though the entire WBS and critical path are not shown.

Figure 23
Gantt Chart of the WBS for the Definition Phase of a Project

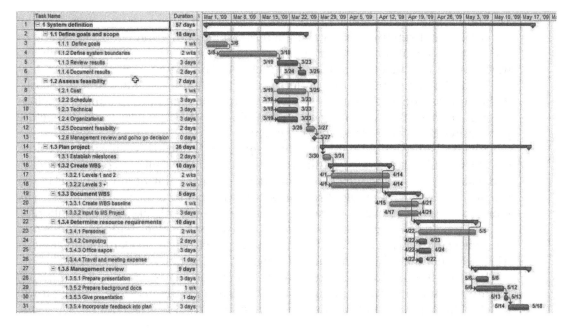

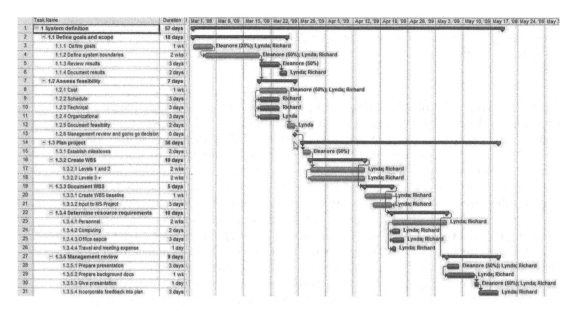

Figure 24
Gantt Chart with Resources
Assigned

*The Guide later in the chapter
states the challenges and
difficulties with project
estimation in the real
world.*

Using Microsoft Project or a similar product, it is possible to assign personnel to tasks and to stipulate the percentage of time that each person devotes to a task. Figure 24 shows a Gantt chart for which this has been done. The notation means that Eleanore works only 25 percent of the time on task 3; Lynda and Richard work full time. Additionally, one can assign costs to personnel and compute a labor budget for each task and for the overall WBS. One can assign resources to tasks and use Microsoft Project to detect and prevent two tasks from using the same resources. Resource costs can be assigned and summed as well.

Managers can use the critical path to perform critical path analysis. First, note that if a task is on the critical path, and if that task runs late, the project will be late. Hence, tasks on the critical path cannot be allowed to run late if the project is to be delivered on time. Second, tasks not on the critical path can run late to the point at which they would become part of the critical path. Hence, up to a point, resources can be taken from noncritical path tasks to shorten tasks on the critical path. **Critical path analysis** is the process by which project managers compress the schedule by moving resources, typically people, from noncritical path tasks onto critical path tasks.

Adjust Plan via Trade-offs

The project plan for the entire project results in a finish date and a total cost. During my career, I've been involved in about a dozen major development projects, and in every one the first response to a completed project plan has been, "Good heavens! No way! We can't wait that long or pay that much!" And my experience is not unusual.

Thus, the first response to a project plan is to attempt to reduce time and costs. Reductions can be made, but not out of thin air. An old adage in planning development projects is, "Believe your first number." Believe what you have estimated before your desires and wishes cloud your judgment.

So, how can schedules and costs be responsibly reduced? By considering trade-offs. A **trade-off** is a balancing of three critical factors: requirements, cost, and time. To understand this balancing challenge, consider the construction of something relatively simple—say, a piece of jewelry like a necklace or the deck on the side of a house. The more elaborate the necklace or the deck, the more time it will take. The less elaborate, the less time it will take. Further, if we embellish the necklace with diamonds and precious gems, it will cost more. Similarly, if we construct the deck from old crates it will be cheaper than if we construct it of clear-grained, prime Port Orford cedar.

We can summarize this situation as shown in Figure 25. We can *trade off* requirements against time and against cost. If we make the necklace simpler, it will take less time. If we eliminate the diamonds and gems, it will be cheaper. The same

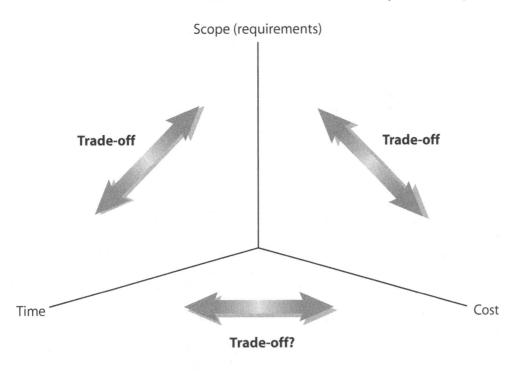

Figure 25
Primary Drivers of Systems
Development

trade-offs exist in the construction of anything: houses, airplane interiors, buildings, ships, furniture, *and* information systems.

The relationship between time and cost is more complicated. Normally, we can reduce time by increasing cost *only to a point*. For example, we can reduce the time it takes to produce a deck by hiring more laborers. At some point, however, there will be so many laborers working on the deck that they will get in one another's way, and the time to finish the deck will actually increase. As discussed earlier, at some point, adding more people creates **diseconomies of scale**, the situation that occurs when adding more resources creates inefficiencies, such as those that occur when adding more people to a late project (recall Brooks' Law).

In some projects, we can reduce costs by increasing time. If, for example, we are required to pay laborers time-and-a-half for overtime, we can reduce costs by eliminating overtime. If finishing the deck—by, say, Friday—requires overtime, then it may be cheaper to avoid overtime by completing the deck sometime next week. This trade-off is not always true, however. Extending the project interval means that we need to pay labor and overhead for a longer period; thus, adding more time can also increase costs.

Consider how these trade-offs pertain to information systems. We specify a set of requirements for the new information system, and we schedule labor over a period of time. Suppose the initial schedule indicates the system will be finished in 3 years. If business requirements necessitate the project be finished in 2 years, we must shorten the schedule. We can proceed in two ways: reduce the requirements or add labor. For the former, we eliminate functions and features. For the latter, we hire more staff or contract with other vendors for development services. Deciding which course to take will be difficult and risky.

Using trade-offs, the WBS plan can be modified to shorten schedules or reduce costs. But they cannot be reduced by management fiat.

Manage Development Challenges

Given the project plan and management's endorsement and approval, the next stage is to do it! The final WBS plan is denoted as the **baseline WBS**. This baseline shows the planned tasks, dependencies, durations, and resource assignments. As the project proceeds, project managers can input actual dates, labor hours, and resource costs.

At any point in time, planning applications can be used to determine whether the project is ahead or behind schedule and how the actual project costs compare to baseline costs.

However, nothing ever goes according to plan, and the larger the project and the longer the development interval, the more things will violate the plan. Four critical factors need to be considered:

1. Coordination
2. Diseconomies of scale
3. Configuration control
4. Unexpected events

Development projects, especially large-scale projects, are usually organized into a variety of development groups that work independently. Coordinating the work of these independent groups can be difficult, particularly if the groups reside in different geographic locations or different countries. An accurate and complete WBS facilitates coordination, but no project ever proceeds exactly in accordance with the WBS. Delays occur, and unknown or unexpected dependencies develop among tasks.

The coordination problem is increased because software is pure thought-stuff. When constructing a new house, electricians install wiring in the walls as they exist; it is impossible to do otherwise. No electrician can install wiring in the wall as designed 6 months ago, before a change. In software, such physical constraints do not exist. It is entirely possible for a team to develop a set of application programs to process a database using an obsolete database design. When the database design was changed, all involved parties should have been notified, but this may not have occurred. Wasted hours, increased cost, and poor morale are the result.

As mentioned in Q6, another problem is diseconomies of scale. The number of possible interactions among team members rises exponentially with the number of team members. Ultimately, no matter how well managed a project is, diseconomies of scale will set in.

As the project proceeds, controlling the configuration of the work product becomes difficult. Consider requirements, for example. The development team produces an initial statement of requirements. Meetings with users produce an adjusted set of requirements. Suppose an event then occurs that necessitates a change to requirements. After deliberation, assume the team decides to ignore a large portion of the requirements changes resulting from the event. At this point, there are four different versions of the requirements. If the changes to requirements are not carefully managed, changes from the four versions will be mixed up, and confusion and disorder will result. No one will know which requirements are the correct, current requirements.

Similar problems occur with designs, program code, database data, and other system components. The term **configuration control** refers to a set of management policies, practices, and tools that developers use to maintain control over the project's resources. Such resources include documents, schedules, designs, program code, test suites, and any other shared resource needed to complete the project. Configuration control is vital; a loss of control over a project's configuration is so expensive and disruptive that it can result in termination for senior project managers.

The last major challenge to large-scale project management is unexpected events. The larger and longer the project, the greater the chance of disruption due to an unanticipated event. Critical people can change companies; even whole teams have been known to pack up and join a competitor. A hurricane may destroy an office; the company may have a bad quarter and freeze hiring just as the project is staffing up; technology will change; competitors may do something that makes the project more (or less) important; or the company may be sold and new management may change requirements and priorities.

Because software is thought-stuff, team morale is crucial. I once managed two strong-headed software developers who engaged in a heated argument over the design of a program feature. The argument ended when one threw a chair at the other. The rest of the team divided its loyalties between the two developers, and work came to a standstill as subgroups sneered and argued with one another when they met in hallways or at the coffee pot. How do you schedule that event into your WBS? As a project manager, you never know what strange event is heading your way. Such unanticipated events make project management challenging, but also incredibly fascinating!

Q8 2021?

Process and systems development will evolve in the next 10 years in three important ways. First, we will see a continuing focus on aligning business processes and information systems with business strategy, goals, and objectives. You and your classmates will be an important factor in that alignment. Unlike earlier generations of business professionals, you are truly computer literate. Although it might seem trivial, your skills with Facebook, Twitter, and foursquare have given you confidence in your ability to master computer-based systems. You also know that such systems can be easy or difficult to use.

Given this background, as future managers in accounting, finance, marketing, operations, and so forth you will be less willing, perhaps unwilling, to compromise. You know that information systems can be constructed to do what you want, and you'll be likely to insist on it.

Second, computer systems will be more easily changed and adapted in the future. Software vendors know that the key to their future growth is not having the single best solution, but rather on having a solution that is readily tailored to their customers' idiosyncrasies. When ERP was new, customers were willing to adapt their business processes to those of the vendors because there was no other choice. But, as indicated by the popularity of ERP industry-specific solution templates, customers want more. They want to be able to do whatever it is they do to gain a competitive advantage over their customers, and adapting their business processes to the same processes used by everyone else isn't going to get them there. So, software vendors will find ways to make their solutions more adaptable, and, as a result, systems and processes will be more agile and better able to adapt to changing needs.

Finally, the next 10 years will see the emergence of new software vendor business models. The Firm, the workout studio in Minneapolis that was the source for the FlexTime case eventually settled on information systems provided by MindBody, Inc. The Firm pays almost nothing in license or usage fees to that vendor. Instead, all of the credit card charges that Firm customers make are processed by MindBody. This processing enables MindBody to earn a small amount on every customer transaction. MindBody supports more than 6,000 studios and trainers in the United States. Its software is a veritable money machine.

A key element of this new business model is the alignment between the goals of workout studios and MindBody, Inc. Both make more money when customers make a purchase. Therefore, MindBody's software includes features and functions that enable studio managers to determine which products, classes, trainers, and even ads and marketing campaigns are the most successful. Furthermore, MindBody has a window on the best practices in the industry. To motivate studios to adapt to new practices that will create more revenue, MindBody provides comparative statistics on any given studio's performance against similar companies in its region.

MindBody's business model is an example of a potentially monumental change in the way that business software is provided. Stay tuned! And, if you can, go to work for a company like MindBody.

Guide

Dealing with Uncertainty

In the mid-1970s, I worked as a database disaster repairman. As an independent consultant, I was called by organizations that licensed the then-new database management systems but had little idea of what to do with them.

One of my memorable clients had converted the company's billing system from an older-technology system to the new world of database processing. Unfortunately, after they cut off the old system, serious flaws were found in the new one, and from mid-November to mid-January the company was unable to send a bill. Of course, customers who do not receive bills do not pay, and my client had a substantial cash-flow problem. Even worse, some of its customers used a calendar-year tax basis and wanted to pay their bills prior to the end of the year. When those customers called to find the amount they owed, accounts receivable clerks had to say, "Well, we don't know. The data's in our computer, but we can't get it out." That was when the company called me for database disaster repair.

The immediate cause of the problem was that the client used the plunge conversion technique. But looking deeper, how did that organization find itself with a new billing system so full of failures?

In this organization, management had little idea about how to communicate with IT, and the IT personnel had no experience in dealing with senior management. They talked past one another.

Fortunately, this client was, in most other respects, a well-managed company. Senior management only needed to learn to manage their IS projects with the same discipline as they managed other departments. So, once we had patched the billing system together to solve the cash-flow problem, the management team began work to implement policies and procedures to instill the following principles:

- Business users, not IS, would take responsibility for the success of new systems.
- Users would actively work with IS personnel throughout systems development, especially during the requirements phase.
- Users would take an active role in project planning, project management, and project reviews.
- No development phase would be considered complete until the work was reviewed and approved by user representatives and management.
- Users would actively test the new system.
- All future systems would be developed in small increments.

I cannot claim that all future development projects at this company proceeded smoothly after the users began to practice these principles. In fact, many users were slow to take on their new responsibilities; in some cases, the users resented the time they were asked to invest in the new practices. Also, some were uncomfortable in these new roles. They wanted to work in their business specialty and not be asked to participate in IS projects about which they knew little. Still others did not take their responsibilities seriously; they would come to meetings ill prepared, not fully engage in the process, or approve work they did not understand.

However, after that billing disaster, senior management understood what needed to be done. They made these practices a priority, and over time user resistance was mostly overcome. When it was not overcome, it was clear to senior management where the true problem lay. ▪

Discussion Questions

1. In general terms, describe how the billing system might have been implemented using pilot conversion. Describe how it might have been implemented using parallel conversion.

2. If you were the billing system project manager, what factors would you consider when deciding the style of conversion to use?

3. If the billing system had been converted using either pilot or parallel, what would have happened?

4. Explain in your own words the benefits that would accrue using the new principles.

5. Summarize the reasons that users resisted these new principles. What could be done to overcome that resistance?

6. Suppose you work in a company where users have little to no active involvement in systems development. Describe likely consequences of this situation. Describe five actions you could take to correct this situation.

Guide

The Real Estimation Process

"I'm a software developer.
I write programs in an object-oriented language called C# (pronounced 'C-sharp'). I'm a skilled object-oriented designer, too. I should be—I've been at it 12 years and worked on major projects for several software companies. For the last 4 years, I've been a team leader. I lived through the heyday of the dot-com era and now work in the development group at an iPad application vendor.

"All of this estimating theory is just that—theory. It's not really the way things work. Sure, I've been on projects in which we tried different estimation techniques. But here's what really happens: You develop an estimate using whatever technique you want. Your estimate goes in with the estimates of all the other team leaders. The project manager sums all those estimates together and produces an overall estimate for the project.

"By the way, in my projects, time has been a much bigger factor than money. At one software company I worked for, you could be 300 percent over your dollar budget and get no more than a slap on the wrist. Be 2 weeks late, however, and you were finished.

"Anyway, the project managers take the projects schedule to senior management for approval, and what happens? Senior management thinks they are negotiating. 'Oh, no,' they say, 'that's way too long. You can surely take a month off that schedule. We'll approve the projects, but we want it done by February 1 instead of March 1.'

"Now, what's their justification? They think that tight schedules make for efficient work. You know that everyone will work extra hard to meet the tighter timeframe. They know Parkinson's Law—

'the time required to perform a task expands to the time available to do it.' So, fearing the possibility of wasting time because of too-lenient schedules, they lop a month off our estimate.

"Estimates are what they are; you can't knock off a month or two without some problem, somewhere. What does happen is that projects get behind, and then management expects us to work longer and longer hours. Like they said in the early years at Microsoft, 'We have

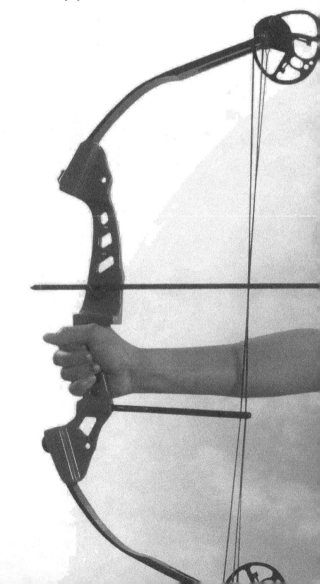

flexible working hours. You can work any 65 hours per week you want.'

"Not that our estimation techniques are all that great, either. Most software developers are optimists. They schedule things as if everything will go as planned, and things seldom do. Also, schedulers usually don't allow for vacations, sick days, trips to the dentist, training on new technology, peer reviews, and all the other things we do in addition to writing software.

"So we start with optimistic schedules on our end, then management negotiates a month or two off, and voilà, we have a late project. After a while, management has been burned by late projects so much that they mentally add the month or even more back onto the official schedule. Then both sides work in a fantasy world, where no one believes the schedule, but everyone pretends they do.

"I like my job. I like software development. Management here is no better or worse than in other places. As long as I have interesting work to do, I'll stay here. But I'm not working myself silly to meet these fantasy deadlines." ■

Discussion Questions

1. What do you think of this developer's attitude? Do you think he's unduly pessimistic or do you think there's merit to what he says?

2. What do you think of his idea that management thinks they're negotiating? Should management negotiate schedules? Why or why not?

3. Suppose a project actually requires 12 months to complete. Which do you think is likely to cost more: (a) having an official schedule of 11 months with at least a 1-month overrun or (b) having an official schedule of 13 months and, following Parkinson's Law, having the project take 13 months?

4. Suppose you are a business manager and an information system is being developed for your use. You review the scheduling documents and see that little time has been allowed for vacations, sick leave, miscellaneous other work, and so forth. What do you do?

5. Describe the intangible costs of having an organizational belief that schedules are always unreasonable.

6. If this developer worked for you, how would you deal with his attitude about scheduling?

7. Do you think there is something different when scheduling information systems development projects than when scheduling other types of projects? What characteristics might make such projects unique? In what ways are they the same as other projects?

8. What do you think managers should do in light of your answer to question 7?

Active Review

Use this Active Review to verify that you understand the ideas and concepts that answer the chapter's study questions.

Q1 Why do organizations need to manage business processes?

Define *business process* using the new definition in this chapter. Define *roles, resources,* and *data flows.* Summarize three reasons that processes need to be changed and give an example of each.

Q2 What are the stages in Business Process Management (BPM)?

Describe the need for BPM and explain why it is a cycle. Name the four stages of the BPM process and summarize the activities in each. Explain the role of COBIT.

Q3 How can BPMN process diagrams help identify and solve process problems?

Explain the need for a process documentation standard. Explain each of the symbols in Figures 5 and 6. Summarize the process problems in these two diagrams and explain how the process in Figure 7 solves those problems. Describe three ways of improving business processes. Explain each of the elements of Figure 8.

Q4 Which comes first, business processes or information systems?

Explain how information systems and business processes differ. Give an example, other than one in this text, of a business process that uses two or more information systems. Give an example, other than one in this text, of an information system that is part of two or more business processes. Explain the problems that occur if we develop business processes first, with IS as a component. Explain the problems that occur if we develop information systems first, with business processes as a component. Explain the differences between Figures 11 and 12. Summarize the issues to address when answering which comes first. Explain why it is not possible to buy processes or systems off-the-shelf.

Q5 What are systems development activities?

Name five basic systems development activities. Explain how they pertain whether developing processes first or information systems first. Describe tasks required for the definition, requirements, and design steps. Explain the role of business analysts and systems analysts. Explain the tasks required to implement and maintain the system and assess the process. Describe four types of process/system conversion. Describe how activities in these last two steps differ depending on whether the processes or systems are developed first.

Q6 Why are business processes and systems development difficult and risky?

Name five major challenges that occur when developing processes and systems. For each, explain how that challenge could arise in the development of the processes and systems to solve the Fox Lake facility reservation problem.

Q7 What are the keys for successful process and systems development projects?

Name five keys for successful development projects. Explain the purpose of a work-breakdown structure. Summarize the difficulties of development estimation and describe three ways of addressing it. Explain the elements in the Gantt chart in Figure 24. Define *critical path,* and explain critical path analysis. Summarize requirements, cost, and schedule trade-offs. List and explain four critical factors for development project management.

Q8 2021?

Name three ways that process and systems development will evolve in the next 10 years. Explain how the computer literacy of you and your classmates contribute to process and systems alignment. Summarize the key to growth for software vendors and explain how that contributes process and system agility. Using the example of MindBody, explain how new business models will enable software to be delivered to customers in innovative ways.

Key Terms and Concepts

As-is model
Baseline WBS
Brooks' Law
Business analyst
Business process
Business process management
    (BPM)
Business Process Modeling
    Notation (BPMN)
COBIT (Control Objectives for
    Information and related
    Technology)
Configuration control
Cost feasibility

Critical path
Critical path analysis
Data flow
Deliverables
Diseconomies of scale
Gantt chart
Maintenance
Object Management
    Group (OMG)
Organizational feasibility
Parallel installation
Phased installation
Pilot installation
Plunge installation

Resources
Roles
Schedule feasibility
Swim-lane layout
System conversion
Systems analysts
Systems development
Systems development life
    cycle (SDLC)
Technical feasibility
Test plan
Trade-off
Work-breakdown structure
    (WBS)

Using Your Knowledge

1. Assume that you are an intern working with Laura and you are present in the initial conversations she has with Fox Lake. Assume that Laura asks you to help her investigate this new system.

   a. Using Figure 13 as a guide, develop a plan for implementing the process in Figure 9. Ignore the Collect Deposit activity. Assume that it has been developed and works.

   b. Specify in detail the tasks to accomplish during the system definition phase.

   c. Write a memo to Laura explaining how you think Fox Lake should proceed.

2. The process documented in Figure 9 does not include unscheduled maintenance. Assume that requests for such maintenance arise during wedding events (they arise from other sources as well, but ignore those sources here) and that they are handled by facilities personnel who are on-call 24 hours a day. Create a process diagram, similar to that in Figure 9, that documents a business process and need for a facilities tracking system.

Assume there will be a Wedding Operations role, and Unscheduled Maintenance Application role, and a Facilities Maintenance Person role. If possible, use Visio to create your diagram, otherwise use PowerPoint.

3. Using your own experience and knowledge, create a process diagram for a Reject Order activity that would fix the allocation problem in Figure 5. Use Figure 6 as an example. Use Visio 2010 and the standard BPMN shapes, if possible. Explain how your process fixes the allocation problem.

4. Search Google or Bing for the phrase "what is a business analyst." Investigate several of the links that you find and answer the following questions:

   a. What are the primary job responsibilities of a business analyst?

   b. What knowledge do business analysts need?

   c. What skills/personal traits do business analysts need?

   d. Would a career as a business analyst be interesting to you? Explain why or why not.

Collaboration Exercise

Collaborate with students on the following exercise. In particular, consider using Google Docs, Windows Live SkyDrive, Microsoft SharePoint, or some other collaboration tool.

Wilma Baker, Jerry Barker, and Chris Bickel met in June 2010 at a convention of resort owners and tourism operators. They sat next to each other by chance while waiting for a presentation; after introducing themselves and laughing at the odd sound of their three names, they were surprised to learn that they managed similar businesses. Wilma Baker lives in Santa Fe, New Mexico, and specializes in renting homes and apartments to visitors to Santa Fe. Jerry Barker lives in Whistler Village, British Columbia, and specializes in renting condos to skiers and other visitors to the Whistler/Blackcomb Resort. Chris Bickel lives in Chatham, Massachusetts, and specializes in renting homes and condos to vacationers to Cape Cod.

The three agreed to have lunch after the presentation. During lunch, they shared frustrations about the difficulty of obtaining new customers, especially in the current economic downturn. Barker was especially concerned about finding customers to fill the facilities that had been constructed to host the Olympics in the prior year.

As the conversation developed, they began to wonder if there was some way to combine forces (i.e., they were seeking a competitive advantage from an alliance). So, they decided to skip one of the next day's presentations and meet to discuss ways to form an alliance. Ideas they wanted to discuss further were sharing customer data, developing a joint reservation service, and exchanging property listings.

As they talked, it became clear they had no interest in merging their businesses; each wanted to stay independent. They also discovered that each was very concerned, even paranoid, about protecting their existing customer base from poaching. Still, the conflict was not as bad as it first seemed. Barker's business was primarily the ski trade, and winter was his busiest season; Bickel's business was mostly Cape Cod vacations, and she was busiest during the summer. Baker's high season was the summer and fall. So, it seemed there was enough difference in their high seasons that they would not necessarily cannibalize their businesses by selling the others' offerings to their own customers.

The question then became how to proceed. Given their desire to protect their own customers, they did not want to develop a common customer database. The best idea seemed to be to share data about properties. That way they could keep control of their customers but still have an opportunity to sell time at the others' properties.

They discussed several alternatives. Each could develop her or his own property database, and the three could then share those databases over the Internet. Or, they could develop a centralized property database that they would all use. Or, they could find some other way to share property listings.

Because we do not know Baker, Barker, and Bickel's detailed requirements, you cannot develop a plan for a specific system. In general, however, they first need to decide how elaborate an information system they want to construct. Consider the following two alternatives:

a. They could build a simple system centered on email. With it, each company sends property descriptions to the others via email. Each independent company then forwards these descriptions to its own customers, also using email. When a customer makes a reservation for a property, that request is then forwarded back to the property manager via email.

b. They could construct a more complex system using a Web-based, shared database that contains data on all their properties and reservations. Because reservations tracking is a common business task, it is likely that they can license an existing application with this capability.

1. Create a process diagram for alternative a, using Figure 8 as a guide. Each company will need to have a role for determining its available properties and sending emails to the other companies that describe them. They will also need to have a role for receiving emails and a role for renting properties to customers. Assume the companies have from three to five agents who can fulfill these roles. Create a role for the email system if you think it is appropriate. Specify roles, activities, repositories, and data flows.

2. Create a process diagram for alternative b, using Figure 8 as a guide. Each company will need to have a role for determining its available properties and adding them to the reservation database. They will also need a role for renting properties that accesses the shared database. Assume the companies have from three to five agents who can fulfill these roles. Create a role for the property database application. Specify roles, activities, repositories, and data flows.

In your answers to 1 and 2, use Microsoft Visio and BPMN templates to construct your diagram. If you don't have those templates, use the cross-functional and basic flowchart templates. If you do not have access to Visio, use PowerPoint instead.

3. Compare and contrast your answers in questions 1 and 2. Which is likely to be more effective in generating rental income? Which is likely to be more expensive to develop? Which is likely to be more expensive to operate?

4. If you were a consultant to Baker, Barker, and Bickel, which alternative would you recommend? Justify your recommendation.

▬ Case Study

Slow Learners, or What?

In 1974, when I was teaching at Colorado State University, we conducted a study of the causes of information systems failures. We interviewed personnel on several dozen projects and collected survey data on another 50 projects. Our analysis of the data revealed that the single most important factor in IS failure was a lack of user involvement. The second major factor was unclear, incomplete, and inconsistent requirements.

At the time, I was a devoted computer programmer and IT techie, and, frankly, I was surprised. I thought that the significant problems would have been technical issues.

I recall one interview in particular. A large sugar producer had attempted to implement a new system for paying sugar-beet farmers. The new system was to be implemented at some 20 different sugar-beet collection sites, which were located in small farming communities, adjacent to rail yards. One of the benefits of the new system was significant cost savings, and a major share of those savings occurred because the new system eliminated the need for local comptrollers. The new system was expected to eliminate the jobs of 20 or so senior people.

The comptrollers, however, had been paying local farmers for decades; they were popular leaders not just within the company, but in their communities as well. They were well liked, highly respected, important people. A system that caused the elimination of their jobs was, using a term from this chapter, *organizationally infeasible*, to say the least.

Nonetheless, the system was constructed, but an IS professional who was involved told me, "Somehow, that new system just never seemed to work. The data were not entered on a timely basis, or they were in error, or incomplete; sometimes the data were not entered at all. Our operations were falling apart during the key harvesting season, and we finally backed off and returned to the old system." Active involvement of system users would have identified this organizational infeasibility long before the system was implemented.

That's ancient history, you say. Maybe, but in 1994 the Standish Group published a now famous study on IS failures. Entitled "The CHAOS Report," the study indicated the leading causes of IS failure are, in descending order: (1) lack of user input, (2) incomplete requirements and specifications, and (3) changing requirements and specifications. That study was completed some 20 years after our study.

In 2004, Professor Joseph Kasser and his students at the University of Maryland analyzed 19 system failures to determine their cause. They then correlated their analysis of the cause with the opinions of the professionals involved in the failures. The correlated results indicated that the first-priority cause of system failure was "Poor requirements"; the second-priority cause was "Failure to communicate with the customer." (Google or Bing "Joseph Kasser" to learn more about this work.)

In 2003, the IRS Oversight Board concluded that the first cause of a massive, expensive failure in the development of a new information system for the IRS was "inadequate business unit ownership and sponsorship of projects. This resulted in unrealistic business cases and continuous project scope 'creep.'"

For over 30 years, studies have consistently shown that leading causes of system failures are a lack of user involvement and incomplete and changing requirements. Yet failures from these very failures continue to mount.

Sources: Standish Group, *www.standishgroup.com*; IRS Oversight Board, "Independent Analysis of IRS Business Systems Modernization, Special Report," December 2003, *http://www.treas.gov/irsob/reports/special_report1203.pdf*.

Questions

1. Using the knowledge you have gained from this chapter, summarize the roles that you think users should take during an information systems development project. What responsibilities do users have? How closely should they work with the IS team? Who is responsible for stating requirements and constraints? Who is responsible for managing requirements?

2. If you ask users why they did not participate in requirements specification, some of the common responses are the following:
   a. "I wasn't asked."
   b. "I didn't have time."
   c. "They were talking about a system that would be here in 18 months, and I'm just worried about getting the order out the door today."
   d. "I didn't know what they wanted."
   e. "I didn't know what they were talking about."
   f. "I didn't work here when they started the project."
   g. "The whole situation has changed since they were here; that was 18 months ago!"

   Comment on each of these statements. What strategies do they suggest to you as a future user and as a future manager of users?

3. If you ask IS professionals why they did not obtain a complete and accurate list of requirements, common responses are:
   a. "It was nearly impossible to get on the users' calendars. They were always too busy."
   b. "The users wouldn't regularly attend our meetings. As a result, one meeting would be dominated by the needs of one group, and another meeting would be dominated by the needs of another group."
   c. "Users didn't take the requirement process seriously. They wouldn't thoroughly review the requirements statements before review meetings."
   d. "Users kept changing. We'd meet with one person one time and another person a second time, and they'd want different things."
   e. "We didn't have enough time."
   f. "The requirements kept changing."

   Comment on each of these statements. What strategies do they suggest to you as a future user and a future manager of users?

4. If it is widely understood that one of the principal causes of IS failures is a lack of user involvement, and if this factor continues to be a problem after 30+ years of experience, does this mean that the problem cannot be solved? For example, everyone knows that you can maximize your gains by buying stocks at their annual low price and selling them at their annual high price, but doing so is very difficult. Is it equally true that although everyone knows that users should be involved in requirements specification, and that requirements should be complete, it just cannot be done? Why or why not?

Application Exercises

1. **A** Do Application Exercise 7-1, if you have not already done so.

   a. Add a Status column to the RESERVATION table, where Status can have values of *Not Confirmed, Confirmed,* or *Cancelled.* Explain why Fox Lake might wish to track cancelled reservations.

   b. Create a data entry form that would be appropriate for the Reserve Facilities activity in Figure 9. Outline procedures required for using that form. Adjust the business process in Figure 9 so that you can reserve one facility at a time.

   c. Create a data entry from that would be appropriate for the Confirm Facility Reservations activity in Figure 9. Outline procedures required for using that form.

   d. Create a data entry from that would be appropriate for the Release Facility Reservations activity in Figure 9. Outline procedures required for using that form.

   e. Create the Daily Facility Use Report in Figure 9. Assume the report has a parameterized query to produce all reservations for a given date.

   f. Input data and test your database. Use the Windows 7 Snipping Tool or some other tool to capture screenshots of your data entry screens and your report. Add them to your procedure outline and turn in the assembled document. (Or, if instructed to do so, turn in your Access database along with your procedure outlines.)

2. Suppose you are given the task of keeping track of the number of labor hours invested in meetings for systems development projects. Assume your company uses the traditional systems-first process illustrated in Figure 12. Further assume that each SDLC step requires two types of meetings: *Working meetings* involve users, business analysts, systems analysts, programmers, and PQA test engineers. *Review meetings* involve all of those people, plus level-1 and level-2 managers of both user departments and the IS department.

   a. Import the data in the Word file **Ch10Ex02** from this text's Web site into a spreadsheet.

   b. Modify your spreadsheet to compute the total labor hours invested in each phase of a project. When a meeting occurs, assume you enter the project phase, the meeting type, the start time, the end time, and the number of each type of personnel attending. Your spreadsheet should calculate the number of labor hours and should add the meeting's hours to the totals for that phase and for the project overall.

   c. Modify your spreadsheet to include the budgeted number (in the source data) of labor hours for each type of employee for each phase. In your spreadsheet, show the difference between the number of hours budgeted and the number actually consumed.

   d. Change your spreadsheet to include the budgeted cost and actual cost of labor. Assume that you enter, once, the average labor cost for each type of employee, as stipulated in the source data.

3. Use Access to develop a failure-tracking database application. Use the data in the Excel file **Ch10Ex03** for this exercise. The data includes columns for the following:

> *FailureNumber*
> *DateReported*
> *FailureDescription*
> *ReportedBy* (the name of the PQA engineer reporting the failure)
> *ReportedBy_email* (the email address of the PQA engineer reporting the failure)
> *FixedBy* (the name of the programmer who is assigned to fix the failure)
> *FixedBy_email* (the email address of the programmer assigned to fix the failure)
> *DateFailureFixed*
> *FixDescription*
> *DateFixVerified*
> *VerifiedBy* (the name of the PQA engineer verifying the fix)
> *VeifiedBy_email* (the email address of the PQA engineer verifying the fix)

a. The data in the spreadsheet are not normalized. Normalize the data by creating a *Failure* table, a *PQA Engineer* table, and a *Programmer* table. Add other appropriate columns to each table. Create appropriate relationships.

b. Create one or more forms that can be used to report a failure, to report a failure fix, and to report a failure verification. Create the form(s) so that the user can just pull down the name of a PQA engineer or programmer from the appropriate table to fill in the *ReportedBy, FixedBy*, and *VerifiedBy* fields.

c. Construct a report that shows all failures sorted by reporting PQA engineer and then by *Date Reported*.

d. Construct a report that shows only fixed and verified failures.

e. Construct a report that shows only fixed but unverified failures.

The International Dimension

The International Dimension
International MIS

The International Dimension

International MIS

Q1 How Does the Global Economy Impact Organizations and Processes?

Businesses compete today in a global market. International business has been sharply increasing since the middle of the twentieth century. After World War II, the Japanese and other Asian economies exploded when those countries began to manufacture and sell goods to the West. The rise of the Japanese auto industry and the semiconductor industry in southeastern Asia greatly expanded international trade. At the same time, the economies of North America and Europe became more closely integrated.

Since then, a number of other factors have caused international business to explode. The fall of the Soviet Union opened the economies of Russia and Eastern Europe to the world market. Even more important, the telecommunications boom during the dot-com heyday caused the world to be encircled many times over by optical fiber that can be used for data and voice communications.

After the dot-com bust, optical fiber was largely underutilized and could be purchased for pennies on the dollar. Plentiful, cheap telecommunications enabled people worldwide to participate in the global economy. Prior to the advent of the Internet, for a young Indian professional to participate in the Western economy, he or she had to migrate to the West—a process that was politicized and limited. Today, that same young Indian professional can sell his or her goods or services over the Internet without leaving home. During this same period, the Chinese economy became more open to the world, and it, too, benefits from plentiful, cheap telecommunications.

Columnist and author Thomas Friedman estimates that from 1991 until 2007, some 3 billion people were added to the world economy.[1] Not all of those people speak English, and not all of them are well enough educated (or equipped) to participate in the world economy. But even if just 10 percent are, then 300 million people were added to the world economy, and even more in the past 3 years!

---

[1]Thomas L. Friedman, *The World Is Flat: A Brief History of the Twenty-First Century 3.0* (New York: Farrar, Strauss and Giroux, 2007).

How Does the Global Economy Change the Competitive Environment?

To understand the impact of globalization, consider each of the elements in Figure ID-1. The enlarged and Internet-supported world economy has altered every one of the five competitive forces. Suppliers have to reach a wider range of customers, and customers have to consider a wider range of vendors. Suppliers and customers benefit not just from the greater size of the economy, but also by the ease with which businesses can learn of each other using tools such as Google and Bing.

Because of the information available on the Internet, customers can more easily learn of substitutions. The Internet has made it easier for new market entrants, although not in all cases. Amazon.com, Yahoo!, and Google, for example, have garnered such a large market share that it would be difficult for any new entrant to challenge them. Still, in other industries, the global economy facilitates new entrants. Finally, the global economy has intensified rivalry by increasing product and vendor choices and by accelerating the flow of information about price, product, availability, and service.

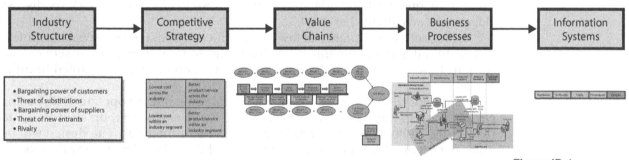

Figure ID-1
Organizational Strategy
Determines Information
Systems

How Does the Global Economy Change Competitive Strategy?

Today's global economy changes thinking about competitive strategies in two major ways. First, the sheer size and complexity of the global economy means that any organization that chooses a strategy allowing it to compete industry-wide is taking a very big bite! Competing in many different countries, with products localized to the language and culture of those countries, is an enormous and expensive task.

For example, to promote Windows worldwide, Microsoft must produce a version of Windows in dozens of different languages. Even in English, Microsoft produces a U.K. version, a U.S. version, an Australian version, and so forth. The problem for Microsoft is even greater, because different countries use different character sets. In some languages, writing flows from left to right. In other languages, it flows from right to left. When Microsoft set out to sell Windows worldwide, it embarked on an enormous project.

The second major way today's world economy changes competitive strategies is that its size, combined with the Internet, enables unprecedented product differentiation. If you choose to produce the world's highest quality and most exotic oatmeal—and if your production costs require you to sell that oatmeal for $350 a pound—your target market might contain only 200 people worldwide. The Internet allows you to find them—and them to find you.

The decision involving a global competitive strategy requires the consideration of these two changing factors.

How Does the Global Economy Change Value Chains and Business Processes?

Because of information systems, any or all of the value chain activities in Figure ID-1 can be performed anywhere in the world. An international company can conduct sales and marketing efforts locally, for every market in which it sells. 3M divisions, for example, sell in the United States with a U.S. sales force, in France with a French sales force, and in Argentina with an Argentinean sales force. Depending on local laws and customs, those sales offices may be owned by 3M, or they may be locally owned entities with which 3M contracts for sales and marketing services. 3M can coordinate all of the sales efforts of these entities using the same CRM system. When 3M managers need to roll up sales totals for a sales projection, they can do so using an integrated, worldwide system.

Manufacturing of a final product is frequently distributed throughout the world. Components of the Boeing 787 are manufactured in Italy, China, England, and numerous other countries and delivered to Washington and South Carolina for final assembly. Each manufacturing facility has its own inbound logistics, manufacturing, and outbound logistics activity, but those activities are linked together via information systems.

For example, Rolls-Royce manufactures an engine and delivers that engine to Boeing via its outbound logistics activity. Boeing receives the engine using its inbound logistics activity. All of this activity is coordinated via shared, interorganizational information systems. Rolls-Royce's CRM is connected with Boeing's supply processes, using techniques such as CRM and enterprise resource planning (ERP). We discuss global supply chains further in Q4.

Because of the abundance of low-cost, well-educated, English-speaking professionals in India, many organizations have chosen to outsource their service and support functions to India. Some accounting functions are outsourced to India as well.

World time differences enable global virtual companies to operate 24/7. Boeing engineers in Los Angeles can develop a design for an engine support strut and send that design to Rolls-Royce in England at the end of their day. The design will be waiting for Rolls-Royce engineers at the start of their day. They review the design, make needed adjustments, and send it back to Boeing in Los Angeles, where the reviewed, adjusted design arrives at the start of the workday in Los Angeles. The ability to work around the clock by moving work into other time zones increases productivity.

Q2 What Are the Characteristics of International IS Components?

To understand the impact of internationalization on information systems, consider the five components. Computer hardware is sold worldwide, and most vendors provide documentation in at least the major languages, so, other than globalized supply chains, internationalization has little impact on that component. The remaining components of an information system, however, are markedly affected.

To begin, consider the user interface for an international information system. Does it include a local-language version of Windows? What about the software application itself? Does an inventory system used worldwide by Boeing suppose that each user speaks English? If so, at what level of proficiency? If not, what languages must the user interface support?

Next, consider the data component. Suppose that the inventory database has a table for parts data and that table contains a column named Remarks. Further suppose Boeing needs to integrate parts data from three different vendors: one in China, one in India, and one in England. What language is to be used for recording remarks? Does someone need to translate all of the remarks into one language? Into three languages?

The human components—procedures and people—are obviously affected by language and culture. As with business processes, information systems procedures need to reflect local cultural values and norms. For systems users, job descriptions and reporting relationships must be appropriate for the setting in which the system is used. We will say more about this in Q5.

What's Required to Localize Software?

The process of making a computer program work in a second language is called **localizing** software. It turns out to be surprisingly hard to do. To localize a document or a Web page, all you need to do is hire a translator to convert your document or page from one language to another. The situation is much more difficult for a computer program, however.

Consider a program you use frequently—say, Microsoft Word—and ask what would need to be done to translate it to a different language. The entire user interface needs to be translated. The menu bar and the commands on the menu bar will need to be translated. It is possible that some of the icons will need to be changed, because some graphic symbols that are harmless in one culture are confusing or offensive in another.

What about an application program like CRM that includes forms, reports, and queries? The labels on each of these will need to be translated. Of course, not all labels translate into words of the same length, and so the forms and reports may need to be redesigned. The questions and prompts for queries, such as "Enter part number for back order," must also be translated.

All of the documentation will need to be translated. That should be just a matter of hiring a translator, except that all of the illustrations in the documentation will need to be redrawn in the second language.

Think, too, about error messages. When someone attempts to order more items than there are in inventory, the application produces an error message. All of those messages will need to be translated. There are other issues as well. Sorting order is one. Spanish uses accents on certain letters, and it turns out that an accented ó will sort after z when you use the computer's default sort ordering. Figure ID-2 summarizes the factors to address when localizing software.

- Translate the user interface, including menu bars and commands.
- Translate, and possibly redesign, labels in forms, reports, and query prompts.
- Translate all documentation and help text.
- Redraw and translate diagrams and examples in help text.
- Translate all error messages.
- Translate text in all message boxes.
- Adjust sorting order for different character set.
- Fix special problems in Asian character sets and in languages that read and write from right to left.

Figure ID-2
Issues to Address with Localizing a Computer Program

Programming techniques can be used to simplify and reduce the cost of localization. However, those techniques must be used in design, long before any code is written. For example, suppose that when a certain condition occurs, the program is to display the message "Insufficient quantity in stock." If the programmer codes all such messages into the computer program, then, to localize that program, the programmer will have to find every such message in the code and then ask a translator to change that code. A preferred technique is to give every error message a unique identifier and to create a separate error file that contains a list of identifiers and their associated text. Then, when an error occurs, program code uses the identifier to obtain the text of the message to be displayed from the error file. During localization, translators simply translate the file of error messages into the second language.

The bottom line for you, as a future manager, is to understand two points: (1) Localizing computer programs is much more difficult, expensive, and time consuming than translating documents. (2) If a computer program is likely to be localized then plan for that localization from the beginning, during design. In addition, when considering the acquisition of a company in a foreign country, be sure to budget time and expense for the localization of information systems.

What Are the Problems and Issues of Global Databases?

A single database reduces data integrity problems and makes it possible to have an integrated view of the customer or the operations of the organization.

International companies that have a single database must, however, declare a single language for the company. Every Remark or Comment or other text field needs to be in single language. If not, the advantages of a single database disappear. This is not a problem for companies that commit to a single company language. For example, Thomas Keidel, former CEO of the Mahr Company (*www.mahr.com*), states, "We standardized on English as the official company language; we use English in our meetings, in our emails, and in other correspondence. We have to do this because we have factories in 14 countries, and it would be impossible to make any decision otherwise. We chose English because it is a language that most business professionals have in common."[2] For a company like this, standardizing on a language for database contents is not a problem.

A single database is not possible, however, for companies that use multiple languages. Such companies often decide to give up on the benefits of a single database to let divisions in different countries use different databases, with data in local languages. For example, an international manufacturer might allow a component manufacturing division in South Korea to have a database in Korean and a final assembly division in Brazil to have a different database in Portuguese. In this scenario, the company needs applications to export and import data among the separated databases.

Besides language, performance is a second issue that confronts global databases. Often, data transmission speeds are too slow to process data from a single geographic location. If so, companies sometimes distribute their database in locations around the world.

Distributed database processing refers to the processing of a single database that resides in multiple locations. If the distributed database contains copies of the same data items, it is called a **replicated database**. If the distributed database does not contain copies of the same data, but rather divides the database into nonoverlapping segments, it is called a **partitioned database**. In most cases, querying either type of distributed database can improve performance without too much development work. However, updating a replicated database so that changes are correctly made to all

---

[2]Private correspondence with the author, May, 2010.

copies of the data is full of challenges that require highly skilled personnel to solve. Still, companies like Amazon.com, which operates call centers in the United States, India, and Ireland, have invested in applications that are able to successfully update distributed databases, worldwide.

Q3 What Are the Challenges of International Cross-Functional Applications?

Functional business processes and applications support particular activities within a single department or business activity. Because the systems operate independently, the organization suffers from islands of automation. Sales and marketing data, for example, are not integrated with operations or manufacturing data.

You learned that many organizations eliminate the problems of information silos by creating cross-functional systems. With international IS, however, such systems may not be worthwhile.

Advantages of Functional Systems

Lack of integration is disadvantageous in many situations, but it has *advantages*, however, for international organizations and international systems. Because an order-processing functional system located in, say, the United States is separate from and independent of the manufacturing systems located in, say, Taiwan, it is unnecessary to accommodate language, business, and cultural differences in a single system. U.S. order-processing systems can operate in English and reflect the practices and culture of the United States. Taiwanese manufacturing information systems can operate in Chinese and reflect the business practices and culture of Taiwan. As long as there is an adequate data interface between the two systems, they can operate independently, sharing data when necessary.

Cross-functional, integrated systems, such as ERP, solve the problems of data isolation by integrating data into a database that provides a comprehensive and organization-wide view. However, as discussed in Q2, that advantage requires that the company standardize on a single language. Otherwise, separated, functional databases are needed.

Problems of Inherent Processes

Processes inherent in ERP and other applications are even more problematic. Each software product assumes that the software will be used by people filling particular roles and performing their actions in a certain way. ERP vendors justify this standardization by saying that their procedures are based on industry-wide best practices and that the organization will benefit by following these standard processes. That statement may be true, but some inherent processes may conflict with cultural norms. If they do, it will be very difficult for management to convince the employees to follow those inherent processes. Or at least it will be difficult in some cultures to do so.

Differences in language, culture, norms, and expectations compound the difficulties of international process management. Just creating an accurate as-is model is difficult and expensive; developing alternative international processes and evaluating them can be incredibly challenging. With cultural differences, it can be difficult just to determine what criteria should be used for evaluating the alternatives, let alone performing the evaluation.

Because of these challenges, in the future it is likely that international business processes will be developed more like interorganizational business processes. A high-level process will be defined to document the service responsibilities of each

343

international unit. Then SOA standards will be used to connect those services into an integrated, cross-functional, international system. Because of encapsulation, the only obligation of an international unit will be to deliver its defined service. One service can be delivered using procedures based on autocratic management policies, and another can be delivered using procedures based on collaborative management policies. The differences will not matter to a SOA-based cross-functional system.

Q4 How Do Interorganizational IS Facilitate Global Supply Chain Management?

A **supply chain** is a network of organizations and facilities that transforms raw materials into products delivered to customers. Figure ID-3 shows a generic supply chain. Customers order from retailers, who in turn order from distributors, who in turn order from manufacturers, who in turn order from suppliers. In addition to the organizations shown here, the supply chain also includes transportation companies, warehouses, and inventories and some means for transmitting messages and information among the organizations involved.

Because of disintermediation, not every supply chain has all of these organizations. Dell, for example, sells directly to the customer. Both the distributor and retailer organizations are omitted from its supply chain. In other supply chains, manufacturers sell directly to retailers and omit the distribution level.

The term *chain* is misleading. *Chain* implies that each organization is connected to just one company up the chain (toward the supplier) and down the chain (toward the customer). That is not the case. Instead, at each level an organization can work with many organizations both up and down the supply chain. Thus, a supply chain is a *network*.

To appreciate the international dimension of a supply chain, consider Figure ID-4. Suppose you decide to take up cross-country skiing. You go to REI (either by visiting one of its stores or its Web site) and purchase skis, bindings, boots, and poles. To fill your order, REI removes those items from its inventory of goods. Those goods have been purchased, in turn, from distributor/importers. According to Figure ID-4, REI purchases the skis, bindings, and poles from one distributor/importer and boots from a second. The distributor/importers, in turn, purchase the required items from the manufacturers, which, in turn, buy raw materials from their suppliers.

In this figure, notice the national flags on the suppliers and manufacturers. For example, the pole manufacturer is located in Brazil and imports plastic from China,

Figure ID-3
Supply Chain Relationships

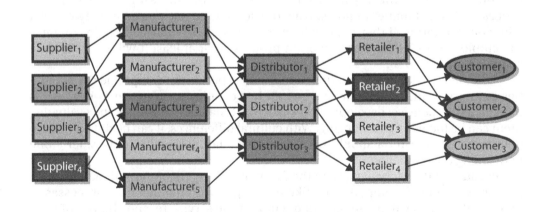

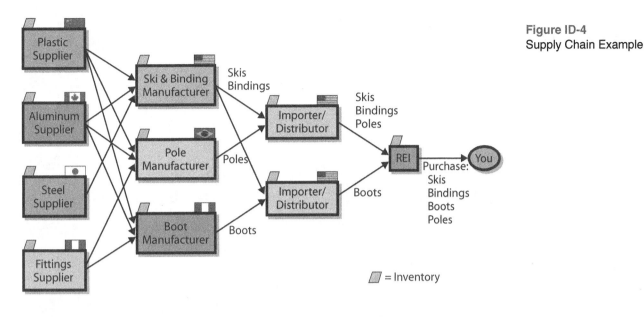

Figure ID-4
Supply Chain Example

aluminum from Canada, and fittings from Italy. The poles are then imported to REI in the United States by Importer/Distributor$_1$.

The only source of revenue in a supply chain is the customer. In the REI example, you spend your money on the ski equipment. From that point all the way back up the supply chain to the raw material suppliers, there is no further injection of cash into the system. The money you spend on the ski equipment is passed back up the supply chain as payments for goods or raw materials. Again, the customer is the only source of revenue.

The Importance of Information in the Supply Chain

During the global economic recession that began with the financial crisis of 2008, the focus of many businesses, worldwide, has been to reduce costs. Supply chain costs have been a primary target for such reductions, especially among companies that have a global supply chain like that in Figure ID-5. For example, Walmart has overhauled its supply chain to eliminate intermediaries, enabling it to buy directly from manufacturers. Walmart's goal is to increase sales and revenues from its private-label goods. At the same time, it also has consolidated purchasing and warehousing into four global merchandizing centers, such as the one near Mexico City that will process goods for emerging markets.[3]

As you'll learn in your production and supply chain courses, many different factors determine the cost and performance of a supply chain. However, information is one of the most important. Consider, for example, inventory management at each the companies in Figure ID-5. How do those companies decide when and how much to purchase? How does the new Walmart processing center in Mexico City determine how many pairs of jeans, ice chests, or bottles of vitamin C to order? How large should the orders be? How frequently should orders be placed? How are those orders tracked? What happens when a shipment disappears? Information is a major factor in making each of those decisions, along with dozens of others. To provide insight into the importance of information, consider just one example, the bullwhip effect.

---

[3]Jim Jubak, "China Feels Global Market Pain," *Jubak's Journal*, August 12, 2010, *http://articles. moneycentral.msn.com/Investing/JubaksJournal/global-markets-pain-moves-to-china.aspx* (accessed August 2010).

Figure ID-5
Example Walmart Supply Chain

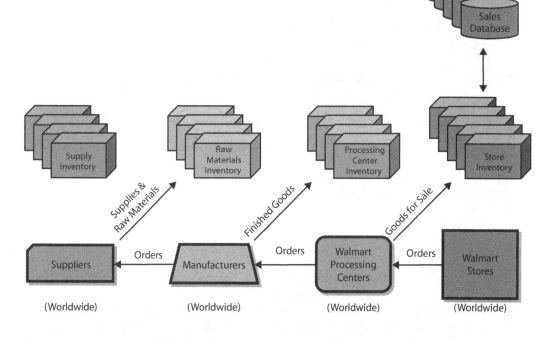

How Can Information Relieve the Bullwhip Effect?

The **bullwhip effect** is a phenomenon in which the variability in the size and timing of orders increases at each stage up the supply chain, from customer to supplier. Figure ID-6 depicts the situation. In a famous study, the bullwhip effect was observed in Procter & Gamble's supply chain for diapers.[4]

Figure ID-6
The Bullwhip Effect

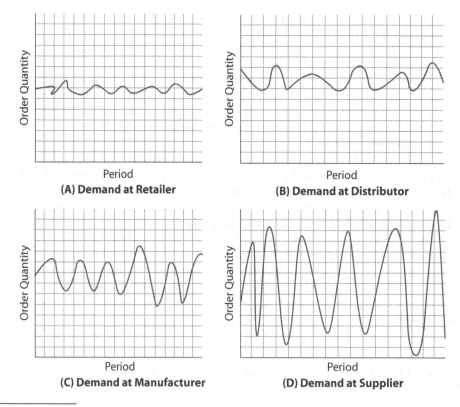

---

[4]Hau L. Lee, V. Padmanabhan, and S. Whang, "The Bullwhip Effect in Supply Chains," *Sloan Management Review*, Spring 1997, pp. 93–102.

Except for random variation, diaper demand is constant. Diaper use is not seasonal; the requirement for diapers does not change with fashion or anything else. The number of babies determines diaper demand, and that number is constant or possibly slowly changing.

Retailers do not order from the distributor with the sale of every diaper package. The retailer waits until the diaper inventory falls below a certain level, called the *reorder quantity*. Then the retailer orders a supply of diapers, perhaps ordering a few more than it expects to sell to ensure that it does not have an outage.

The distributor receives the retailer's orders and follows the same process. It waits until its supply falls below the reorder quantity, and then it reorders from the manufacturer, with perhaps an increased amount to prevent outages. The manufacturer, in turn, uses a similar process with the raw-materials suppliers.

Because of the nature of this process, small changes in demand at the retailer are amplified at each stage of the supply chain. As shown in Figure ID-6, those small changes become quite large variations on the supplier end.

The bullwhip effect is a natural dynamic that occurs because of the multistage nature of the supply chain. It is not related to erratic consumer demand, as the study of diapers indicated. You may have seen a similar effect while driving on the freeway. One car slows down, the car just behind it slows down a bit more abruptly, which causes the third card in line to slow down even more abruptly, and so forth, until the 30th car or so is slamming on its brakes.

The large fluctuations of the bullwhip effect force distributors, manufacturers, and suppliers to carry larger inventories than should be necessary to meet the real consumer demand. Thus, the bullwhip effect reduces the overall profitability of the supply chain.

One way to eliminate the bullwhip effect is to give all participants in the supply chain access to consumer-demand information from the retailer. Each organization can thus plan its inventory or manufacturing based on the true demand (the demand from the only party that introduces money into the system) and not on the observed demand from the next organization up the supply chain. Of course, an *interorganizational information system* is necessary to share such data.

Consider the Walmart example. When Walmart replaces distributors/importers, its supply chain will look like that in Figure ID-7. Along the bottom, each entity orders

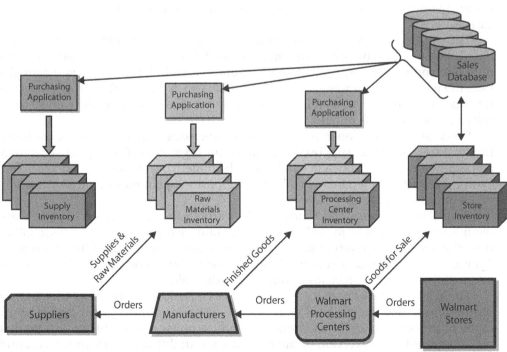

Figure ID-7
Eliminate Bullwhip Effect with True Demand Information

from the entity up the supply chain. Thus, for example, the Walmart processing centers order finished goods from manufacturers. Without knowledge of the true demand, this supply chain is vulnerable to bullwhip effects. However, if each entity can, via an information system, obtain data about the true demand—that is, the demand from the retail customers who are the source of funds for this chain—then each can anticipate orders. The data about true demand will enable each entity to meet order requirements, while maintain a smaller inventory. Eliminating or at least reducing the bullwhip effect are particularly important for international supply chains where logistics costs are high and shipping times are long.

Q5 What Are the Challenges of International IS Management?

Size and complexity make international IT management challenging. International information systems are larger and more complex. Projects to develop them are larger and more complicated to manage. International IT departments are bigger and composed of people from many cultures with many different native languages. International organizations have more IS and IT assets, and those assets are exposed to more risk and greater uncertainty. Because of the complexity of international law, security incidents are more complicated to investigate.

Why Is International IS Development More Challenging?

The factors that affect international information systems development are more challenging than those that affect international software development. If the *system* is truly international, if many people from many different countries will be using the system, then the development project is exceedingly complicated.

To see why, consider the five components. Running hardware in different countries is not a problem, and localizing software is manageable, assuming programs were designed to be localized. Databases pose more difficulties. First, is a single database is to be used, and if so, is it to be distributed? If so, how will updates be processed? Also, what language, currency, and units of measure will be used to store data. If multiple databases are to be used, how are data going to be transported among them. Some of these problems are difficult, but they are solvable with technical solutions.

The same cannot be said for the procedure and people components. An international system is used by people who live and work in cultures that are vastly different from one another. The way that customers are treated in Japan differs substantially from the way that customers are treated in Spain, which differs substantially from the way that customers are treated in the United States. The procedures for using a CRM will be correspondingly different.

Consider the relationship of business processes and information systems. Information systems are supposed to facilitate the organization's competitive strategy and support business processes. But what if the underlying business processes differ? Customer support in Japan and customer support in Spain may involve completely different processes and activities.

Even if the purpose and scope can be defined in some unified way, how are requirements to be determined? Again, if the underlying business processes differ, then the specific requirements for the information system will differ. Managing requirements for a system in one culture is difficult, but managing requirements for international systems can be many times more difficult.

There are two responses to such challenges: (1) either define a set of standard business processes or (2) develop alternative versions of the system that support different processes in different countries. Both responses are problematic. The first response requires conversion of the organization to different work processes, and such conversion can be exceedingly difficult. People resist change, and they will do so with vehemence if the change violates cultural norms.

The second response is easier to implement, but it creates system design challenges. It also means that, in truth, there is not one system, but many.

In spite of the problems, both responses are used. For example, SAP, Oracle, and other ERP vendors define standard business processes via the inherent procedures in their software products. Many organizations attempt to enforce those standard procedures. When it becomes organizationally infeasible to do so, organizations develop exceptions to those inherent procedures and develop programs to handle the exceptions. This choice means high maintenance expense.

What Are the Challenges of International Project Management?

Managing a global IS development project is difficult because of project size and complexity. Requirements are complex, many resources are required, and numerous people are involved. Team members speak different languages, live in different cultures, work in different time zones, and seldom meet face-to-face.

One way to understand how these factors impact global project management is to consider each of the project management knowledge areas as set out by the International Project Management Institute's document, the *PMBOK® Guide* (*www.pmi.org/ Marketplace/Pages/ProductDetail.aspx?GMProduct=00100035801*). Figure ID-8 summarizes challenges for each knowledge area. Project integration is more difficult because international development projects require the complex integration of results from distributed work groups. Also, task dependencies can span teams working in different countries, increasing the difficulty of task management.

The scope and requirements definition for international IS is more difficult, as just discussed. Time management is more difficult because teams in different cultures and countries work at different rates. Some cultures have a 35-hour workweek, and some have a 60-hour workweek. Some cultures expect 6-week vacations, and some expect 2 weeks. Some cultures thrive on efficiency of labor, and others thrive on

Knowledge Areas	Challenge
Project integration	Complex integration of results from distributed work groups. Management of dependencies of tasks from physically and culturally different work groups.
Scope (requirements)	Need to support multiple versions of underlying business processes. Possibly substantial differences in requirements and procedures.
Time	Development rates vary among cultures and countries.
Cost	Cost of development varies widely among countries. Two members performing the same work in different countries may be paid substantially different rates. Moving work among teams may dramatically change costs.
Quality	Quality standards vary among cultures. Different expectations of quality may result in an inconsistent system.
Human resources	Worker expectations differ. Compensation, rewards, work conditions vary widely.
Communications	Geographic, language, and cultural distance among team members impedes effective communication.
Risk	Development risk is higher. Easy to lose control.
Procurement	Complications of international trade.

Figure ID-8
Challenges for International IS Project Management

considerate working relationships. There is no standard rate of development for an international project.

In terms of cost, different countries and cultures pay vastly different labor rates. Using critical path analysis, managers may choose to move a task from one team to another. Doing so, however, may substantially increase costs. Thus, management may choose to accept a delay rather than move work to an available (but more expensive) team. The complex trade-offs that exist between time and cost become even more complex for international projects.

Quality and human resources are also more complicated for international projects. Quality standards vary among countries. The IT industry in some nations, like India, has invested heavily in development techniques that increase program quality. Other countries, like the United States, have been less willing to invest in quality. In any case, the integration of programs of varying quality results in an inconsistent system.

Worker expectations vary among cultures and nations. Compensation, rewards, and worker conditions vary, and these differences can lead to misunderstandings, poor morale, and project delays.

Because of these factors, effective team communication is exceedingly important for international projects, but because of language and culture differences and geographic separation, such communication is difficult. Effective communication is also more expensive. Consider, for example, just the additional expense of maintaining a team portal in three or four languages.

If you consider all of the factors in Figure ID-8, it is easy to understand why project risk is high for international IS development projects. So many things can go wrong. Project integration is complex; requirements are difficult to determine; cost, time, and quality are difficult to manage; worker conditions vary widely; and communication is difficult. Finally, project procurement is complicated by the normal challenges of international commerce.

What Are the Challenges of International IT Management?

The four primary responsibilities of the IT department are: plan, operate, develop, and protect information systems and IT infrastructure. Each of these responsibilities becomes more challenging for international IT organizations.

Regarding planning, the principal task is to align IT and IS resources with the organization's competitive strategy. The task does not change character for international companies; it just becomes more complex and difficult. Multinational organizations and operations are complicated, and the business processes that support their competitive strategies tend also to be complicated. Further, changes in global economic factors can mean dramatic changes in processes and necessitate changes in IS and IT support. Technology adoption can also cause remarkable change. The increasing use of cell phones in developing countries, for example, changes the requirements for local information systems. The rising price of oil will also change international business processes. So planning tasks for international IT are larger and more complex.

Three factors create challenges for international IT operations. First, conducting operations in different countries, cultures, and languages adds complexity. Go to the Web site of any multinational corporation, say *www.3m.com* or *www.dell.com*, and you'll be asked to click on the country in which you reside. When you click, you are likely to be directed to a Web server running in some other country. Those Web servers need to be managed consistently, even though they are operated by people living in different cultures and speaking different languages.

The second operational challenge of international IS is the integration of similar, but different, systems. Consider inventory. A multinational corporation might have dozens of different inventory systems in use throughout the world. To enable the movement of goods, many of these systems need to be coordinated and integrated.

Or consider customer support that operates from three different support centers in three different countries. Each support center may have its own information system, but the data among those systems will need to be exported or otherwise shared. If not, then a customer who contacts one center will be unknown to the others.

The third complication for operations is outsourcing. Many organizations have chosen to outsource customer support, training, logistics, and other backroom activities. International outsourcing is particularly advantageous for customer support and other functions that must be operational 24/7. Many companies outsource logistics to UPS, because doing so offers comprehensive, worldwide shipping and logistical support. The organization's information systems usually need to be integrated with outsource vendors' information systems, and this may need to be done for different systems, all over the world.

The fourth IT department responsibility is protecting IS and IT infrastructure. We consider that function in the next question.

How Does the International Dimension Affect Computer Security Risk Management?

Computer security risk management is more difficult and complicated for international information systems. First, IT assets are subject to more threats. Infrastructure will be located at sites all over the world, and those sites differ in the threats to which they are exposed. Some will be subject to political threats, others to the threat of civil unrest, others to terrorists, and still others will be subject to threats of natural disasters of every conceivable type. Place your data center in Kansas, and it's subject to tornados. Place your data center internationally, and it's potentially subject to typhoons/hurricanes, earthquakes, floods, volcanic eruption, or mudslides. And don't forget epidemics that will affect the data center employees.

Second, the likelihood of a threat is more difficult to estimate for international systems. What is the likelihood that the death of Fidel Castro will cause civil unrest and threaten your data center in Havana? How does an organization assess that risk? What is the likelihood that a computer programmer in India will insert a Trojan horse into code that she writes on an outsourcing contract?

In addition to risk, international information systems are subject to far greater uncertainty. Uncertainty reflects the likelihood that something that "we don't know what we don't know" will cause an adverse outcome. Because of the multitudinous cultures, religions, nations, beliefs, political views, and crazy people in the world, uncertainty about risks to IS and IT infrastructure is high. Again, if you place your data center in Kansas, you have some idea of the magnitude of the uncertainty to which you are exposed, even if you don't know exactly what it is. Place a server in a country on every continent of the world, and you have no idea of the potential risks to which they are exposed.

Regarding safeguards, technical and data safeguards do not change for international information systems. Because of greater complexity, more safeguards or more complex ones may be needed, but technical and data safeguards all work for international systems. Human safeguards are another matter. For example, can an organization depend on the control of separation of duties and authorities in a culture for which graft is an accepted norm? Or, what is the utility of a personal reference in a culture in which it is considered exceedingly rude to talk about someone when they are not present? Because of these differences, human safeguards need to be chosen and evaluated on a culture-by-culture basis.

In short, risk management for both international information systems and IT infrastructure is more complicated, more difficult, and subject to greater uncertainty.

Active Review

Use this Active Review to verify that you understand the ideas and concepts that answer the study questions.

Q1 How does the global economy impact organizations and processes?

Describe how the global economy has changed since the mid-twentieth century. Explain how the dot-com bust influenced the global economy and changed the number of workers worldwide. Summarize the ways in which today's global economy influences the five competitive forces. Explain how the global economy changes the way organizations assess industry structure. How does the global economy change competitive strategy? How do global information systems benefit the value chain? Explain how each primary value chain activity can be performed anywhere in the world.

Q2 What are the characteristics of international IS components?

Explain how internationalization impacts the five components of an IS. What does it mean to localize software? Summarize the work required to localize a computer program. In your own words, explain why it is better to design a program to be localized rather than attempt to adapt an existing single-language program to a second language. Explain the problems of having a single database for an international IS. Define *distributed database, replicated database,* and *partitioned database.* State a source of problems for processing replicated databases.

Q3 What are the challenges of international cross-functional applications?

Summarize the advantages of functional systems for international companies. Summarize the issues of inherent processes for multinational ERP. Explain how SOA services could be used to address the problems of international cross-functional applications.

Q4 How do interorganizational IS facilitate global supply chain management?

Define *supply chain,* and explain why the term *chain* is misleading. Under what circumstances are not all of the organizations in Figure ID-4 not part of the supply chain. Name the only source of revenue in a supply chain. Explain how Walmart is attempting to reduce supply costs. Describe the bullwhip effect, and explain why it adds costs to a supply chain. Explain how the system shown in Figure ID-7 can eliminate the bullwhip effect.

Q5 What are the challenges of international IS management?

State the two characteristics that make international IT management challenging.

Explain the difference between international systems development and international software development. Using the five-component framework, explain why international systems development is more difficult. Give an example of one complication for each knowledge area in Figure ID-8. State the four responsibilities for IT departments. Explain how each of these responsibilities is more challenging for international IT organizations. Describe three factors that create challenges for international IT operations. Explain why international IT assets are subject to more threats. Give three examples. Explain why the likelihood of international threats is more difficult to determine. Describe uncertainty, and explain why it is higher for international IT organizations.

Key Terms and Concepts

Bullwhip effect

Distributed database processing

Localizing

Partitioned database

Replicated database

Supply chain

Using Your Knowledge

1. Suppose that you are about to have a job interview with a multinational company, such as 3M, Starbucks, or Coca-Cola. Further suppose that you wish to demonstrate an awareness of the changes for international commerce that the Internet and modern information technology have made. Using the information in Q1, create a list of three questions that you could ask the interviewer regarding the company's use of IT in its international business.

2. Suppose you work for a business that has $100 million in annual sales that is contemplating acquiring a company in Mexico. Assume you are a junior member of a team that is analyzing the desirability of this acquisition. Your boss, who is not technically savvy, has asked you to prepare a summary of the issues that she should be aware of in the merging of information systems of the two companies. She wants your summary to include a list of questions that she should ask of both your IS department and the IS department personnel in the propsective acquisition. Prepare that summary.

3. Using the information in this module, summarize the strengths and weaknesses of functional systems, CRM, and ERP. How do the advantages and disadvantages of each change in an international setting? For your answer, create a table with strength and weakness columns, and with one row for each of the four systems types.

4. Suppose that you are a junior member of a newly formed, international team that will meet regularly for the next year. You have team members in Europe, North and South America, Japan, Hong Kong, Singapore, Australia, and India. All of your team meetings will be virtual; some will be synchronous, but many will be asynchronous. The team leader has asked you to help prepare the environment for these meetings. In particular, he asked you to summarize the challenges that will occur in conducting these team meetings. He also wants you to assess the strengths and weaknesses of the following collaboration tools: email, Google Docs, Windows Live SkyDrive, Microsoft SharedView, WebEx, and Microsoft SharePoint. Use Figure ID-8, the discussion in Q5 and to prepare your assessment.

Glossary

Glossary

10/100/1000 Ethernet A type of Ethernet that conforms to the IEEE 802.3 protocol and allows for transmission at a rate of 10, 100, or 1,000 Mbps (megabits per second).

32-bit processor Type of addressing used by PCs, as of 2011. Allows for addressing of up to 4 Gigabytes of main memory.

64-bit processor Type of addressing used by power PCs and new servers. Allows for addressing for practically unlimited main memory.

Abstract reasoning The ability to make and manipulate models.

Access A popular personal and small workgroup DBMS product from Microsoft.

Access control list (ACL) A list that encodes the rules stating which packets are to be allowed through a firewall and which are to be prohibited.

Access point (AP) A point in a wireless network that facilitates communication among wireless devices and serves as a point of interconnection between wireless and wired networks. The access point must be able to process messages according to both the 802.3 and 802.11 standards, because it sends and receives wireless traffic using the 802.11 protocol and communicates with wired networks using the 802.3 protocol.

Accurate (information) Information that is based on correct and complete data and that has been processed correctly as expected.

Activity The part of a business process that transforms resources and information of one type into resources and information of another type; can be manual or automated.

AdSense A Web 2.0 product from Google. Google searches an organization's Web site and inserts ads that match content on that site; when users click those ads, Google pays the organization a fee.

Adware Programs installed on the user's computer without the user's knowledge or permission that reside in the background and, unknown to the user, observe the user's actions and keystrokes, modify computer activity, and report the user's activities to sponsoring organizations. Most adware is benign in that it does not perform malicious acts or steal data. It does, however, watch user activity and produce pop-up ads.

AdWords A Web 2.0 advertising product from Google. Vendors agree to pay a certain amount to Google for use of particular search words, which link to the vendor's site.

Alert A form of report, often requested by recipients, that tells them some piece of information, usually time-related, such as notification of the time for a meeting.

Analog signal A wavy signal. A modem converts the computer's digital data into analog signals that can be transmitted over dial-up Internet connections.

Application software Programs that perform a business function. Some application programs are general purpose, such as Excel or Word. Other application programs are specific to a business function, such as accounts payable.

As-is model A model that represents the current situation and processes.

Asymmetric digital subscriber lines (ADSL) DSL lines that have different upload and download speeds.

Asymmetric encryption An encryption method whereby different keys are used to encode and to decode the message; one key encodes the message, and the other key decodes the message. Symmetric encryption is simpler and much faster than asymmetric encryption.

Asynchronous communication Information exchange that occurs when all members of a work team do not meet at the same time, such as those who work different shifts or in different locations.

Attribute (1) A variable that provides properties for an HTML tag. Each attribute has a standard name. For example, the attribute for a hyperlink is *href*, and its value indicates which Web page is to be displayed when the user clicks the link. (2) Characteristics of an entity. Example attributes of *Order* would be *OrderNumber, OrderDate, SubTotal, Tax, Total*, and so forth. Example attributes of *Salesperson* would be *SalespersonName, Email, Phone*, and so forth.

Auction Application that matches buyers and sellers by using an e-commerce version of a standard, competitive-bidding auction process.

Authentication The process whereby an information system approves (authenticates) a user by checking the user's password.

Baseline WBS The final work-breakdown structure that shows the planned tasks, dependencies, durations, and resource assignments.

Beacons Tiny files that gather demographic information; they use a single code to identify users by age, gender, location, likely income, and online activity. Beacons are often image files that install malware code when users open images in junk mail. Most are not malicious and simply verify users' email addresses, activities, and preferences.

Binary digit The means by which computers represent data; also called *bits*. A binary digit is either a zero or a one.

Biometric authentication The use of personal physical characteristics, such as fingerprints, facial features, and retinal scans, to authenticate users.

Bits The means by which computers represent data; also called *binary digit*. A bit is either a zero or a one.

Bluetooth A common wireless protocol designed for transmitting data over short distances, replacing cables.

Bot A computer program that is surreptitiously installed and that takes actions unknown and uncontrolled by the computer's owner or administrator.

Bot herder The individual or organization that controls a botnet.

Botnet A network of bots that is created and managed by the individual or organization that infected the network with the bot program.

Broadband Internet communication lines that have speeds in excess of 256 kbps. DSL and cable modems provide broadband access.

Brooks' Law The famous adage that states: *Adding more people to a late project makes the project later.* Brooks' Law is true not only because a larger staff requires increased coordination, but also because new people need to be trained. The only people who can train the new employees are the existing team members, who are thus taken off productive tasks. The costs of training new people can overwhelm the benefit of their contribution.

Bullwhip effect Phenomenon in which the variability in the size and timing of orders increases at each stage up the supply chain, from customer to supplier.

Bus Means by which the CPU reads instructions and data from main memory and writes data to main memory.

Business analyst A person who understands business strategies, goals, and objectives and who helps businesses develop and manage business processes and information systems.

Business intelligence (BI) Information containing patterns, relationships, and trends.

Business intelligence application Software that uses a tool on a particular type of data for a particular purpose.

Business intelligence application server A computer program that delivers BI (business intelligence) application results in a variety of formats to various devices for consumption by BI users.

Business intelligence system An information system, having all five IS components, that provides the right information, to the right user, at the right time.

Business intelligence tool A computer program that implements a particular BI technique. BI tools include reporting tools, data-mining tools, and knowledge-management tools.

Business process A network of activities, resources, facilities, and information that interact to achieve some business function; sometimes called a *business system*.

Business process management (BPM) A systematic process of modeling, creating, implementing, and assessing business processes.

Business Process Modeling Notation (BPMN) standard set of terms and graphical notations for documenting business processes.

Business process reengineering The activity of altering and designing business processes to fix defective processes, to take advantage of new technology, and to adapt to changes in the business enviornment or business fundamentals.

Business-to-business (B2B) Sales between companies.

Business-to-consumer (B2C) Sales between a supplier and a retail customer (the consumer).

Business-to-government (B2G) Sales between companies and governmental organizations.

Byte(s) (1) A character of data. (2) An 8-bit chunk.

Cable modem A type of modem that provides high-speed data transmission using cable television lines. The cable company installs a fast, high-capacity optical fiber cable to a distribution center in each neighborhood that it serves. At the distribution center, the optical fiber cable connects to regular cable-television cables that run to subscribers' homes or businesses. Cable modems modulate in such a way that their signals do not interfere with TV signals. Like DSL lines, they are always on.

Cache A file on a domain name resolver that stores domain names and IP addresses that have been resolved. Then, when someone else needs to resolve that same domain name, there is no need to go through the entire resolution process. Instead, the resolver can supply the IP address from the local file.

Capital The investment of resources with the expectation of future returns in the marketplace.

Central processing unit (CPU) The CPU selects instructions, processes them, performs arithmetic and logical comparisons, and stores results of operations in memory.

Certificate authority (CA) Trusted, independent third-party company that supplies public keys for encryption.

Channel conflict In e-commerce, a conflict that may result between a manufacturer that wants to sell products directly to consumers and the retailers in the existing sales channels.

Chief information officer (CIO) The title of the principal manager of the IT department. Other common titles are *vice president of information services, director of information services,* and, less commonly, *director of computer services.*

Chief technology officer (CTO) The head of the technology group. The CTO sorts through new ideas and products to identify those that are most relevant to the organization. The CTO's job requires deep knowledge of information technology and the ability to envision how new IT will affect the organization over time.

Clearinghouse Entity that provides goods and services at a stated price, prices and arranges for the delivery of the goods, but never takes title to the goods.

Clickstream data E-commerce data that describes a customer's clicking behavior. Such data includes everything the customer does at the Web site.

Client A computer that provides word processing, spreadsheets, database access, and usually a network connection.

Client hardware Computers and other communication devices (e.g., iPhones, BlackBerries) that users employ to utilize information systems.

Client-server applications Software applications that require code on both the client computer and the server computer. Email is a common example.

Closed source Source code that is highly protected and only available to trusted employees and carefully vetted contractors.

Cloud computing A form of hardware/software outsourcing in which organizations offer flexible plans for customers to lease hardware and software facilities.

Cluster analysis An unsupervised data mining technique whereby statistical techniques are used to identify groups of entities that have similar characteristics. A common use for cluster analysis is to find groups of similar customers in data about customer orders and customer demographics.

COBIT (Control Objectives for Information and related Technology) A set of standard practices, created by the Information Systems Audit and Control Association, that are used in the assessment

stage of the BPM cycle to determine how well an information system complies with an organization's strategy.

Cold sites Remote processing centers that provide office space, but no computer equipment, for use by a company that needs to continue operations after a disaster.

Collaboration The situation in which two or more people work together toward a common goal, result, or product; information systems facilitate collaboration.

Columns Also called *fields,* or groups of bytes. A database table has multiple columns that are used to represent the attributes of an entity. Examples are *PartNumber, EmployeeName,* and *SalesDate.*

Commerce server A computer that operates Web-based programs that display products, support online ordering, record and process payments, and interface with inventory-management applications.

Communication A critical factor in collaboration, consisting of two key elements: (1) the abilities of individuals to share information and receive feedback and (2) the availability of effective systems by which to share information.

Competitive strategy The strategy an organization chooses as the way it will succeed in its industry. According to Porter, there are four fundamental competitive strategies: cost leadership across an industry or within a particular industry segment and product differentiation across an industry or within a particular industry segment.

Computer hardware One of the five fundamental components of an information system.

Computer-based information system An information system that includes a computer.

Computers-in-a-product Computer capabilities embedded within common consumer products.

Conference call A synchronous virtual meeting, in which participants meet at the same time via a voice-communication channel.

Confidence In market-basket terminology, the probability estimate that two items will be purchased together.

Configuration control A set of management policies, practices, and tools that developers use to maintain control over the project's resources.

Content management One of the drivers of collaboration effectiveness, which enables multiple users to contribute to and change documents, schedules, task lists, assignments, and so forth, without one user's work interfering with another's. Content management also enables users to track and report who made what changes, when, and why.

Cookies Data that are stored on the user's computer by a browser. Cookies can be used for authentication, for storing shopping cart contents and user preferences, and for other legitimate purposes. Cookies can also be used to implement spyware.

Cost [of a business process] The cost of the inputs to a business process plus the cost of the activities involved in the process.

Cost feasibility Whether an information system can be developed within budget.

Critical path The sequence of activities that determine the earliest date by which the project can be completed.

Critical path analysis A project management planning process by which tasks and resources are reassigned to tasks so as to reduce the total length of the project's critical path.

Cross-selling The sale of related products; salespeople try to get customers who buy product X to also buy product Y.

Crow's foot A line on an entity-relationship diagram that indicates a 1:N relationship between two entities.

Crow's-foot diagram A type of entity-relationship diagram that uses a crow's foot symbol to designate a 1:N relationship.

Crowdsourcing The process by which organizations use Web 2.0 technologies such as user-generated content to involve their users in the design and marketing of their products.

Curse of dimensionality The more attributes there are, the easier it is to build a data model that fits the sample data but that is worthless as a predictor.

Custom-developed software Tailor-made software.

Customer life cycle Taken as a whole, the processes of marketing, customer acquisition, relationship management, and loss/churn that must be managed by CRM systems.

Customer relationship management (CRM) The set of business processes for attracting, selling, managing, and supporting customers.

Data Recorded facts or figures. One of the five fundamental components of an information system.

Data administration A staff function that pertains to *all* of an organization's data assets. Typical data administration tasks are setting data standards, developing data policies, and providing for data security.

Data aggregators Companies that obtain data from public and private sources and store, integrate, and process it in sophisticated ways.

Data channel Means by which the CPU reads instructions and data from main memory and writes data to main memory.

Data dictionary A file or database that contains data definitions.

Data flow Movement of a data item from one activity to another activity or to or from a repository.

Data integrity problem In a database, the situation that exists when data items disagree with one another. An example is two different names for the same customer.

Data marts Facilities that prepare, store, and manage data for reporting and data mining for specific business functions.

Data mining The application of statistical techniques to find patterns and relationships among data for classification and prediction.

Data mining tools Tools that process data using statistical techniques, many of which are mathematically sophisticated.

Data model A logical representation of the data in a database that describes the data and relationships that will be stored in the database. Akin to a blueprint.

Data standards Definitions, or metadata, for data items shared across the organization. They describe the name, official definition, usage, relationship to other data items, processing restrictions, version, security code, format, and other features of data items that are shared across the organization.

Data warehouses Facilities that prepare, store, and manage data specifically for reporting and data mining.

Database A self-describing collection of integrated records.

Database administration The management, development, operation, and maintenance of the database so as to achieve the organization's objectives. This staff function requires balancing conflicting goals: protecting the database while maximizing its availability for authorized use. In smaller organizations, this function usually is served by a single person. Larger organizations assign several people to an office of database administration.

Database application Forms, reports, queries, and application programs for processing a database. A database can be processed by many different database applications.

Database application system Applications, having the standard five components, that make database data more accessible and useful. Users employ a database application that consists of forms, formatted reports, queries, and application programs. Each of these, in turn, calls on the database management system (DBMS) to process the database tables.

Database management systems (DBMS) A program for creating, processing, and administering a database. A DBMS is a large and complex program that is licensed like an operating system. Microsoft Access and Oracle are example DBMS products.

Database tier In the three-tier architecture, the tier that runs the DBMS and receives and processes SQL requests to retrieve and store data.

DB2 A popular, enterprise-class DBMS product from IBM.

Decision tree A hierarchical arrangement of criteria for classifying customers, items, and other business objects.

Deliverable A task that is one of many measurable or observable steps in a development project.

Denial of service Security problem in which users are not able to access an information system; can be caused by human errors, natural disaster, or malicious activity.

Departmental information system Workgroup information systems that support a particular department.

Desktop virtualization Also called *client virtualization* and *PC virtualization*. The process of storing a user's desktop on a remote server. It enables users to run their desktop from many different client computers.

Digital certificate A document supplied by a certificate authority (CA) that contains, among other data, an entity's name and public key.

Digital divide A divide created between those who have Internet access and those who do not.

Digital signature Encrypted message that uses *hashing* to ensure that plaintext messages are received without alteration.

Digital subscriber line (DSL) A communications line that operates on the same lines as voice telephones, but do so in such a manner that their signals to not interfere with voice telephone service.

Dimension A characteristic of an OLAP measure. Purchase date, customer type, customer location, and sales region are examples of dimensions.

Direct installation See *Plunge installation*.

Dirty data Problematic data. Examples are a value of *B* for customer gender and a value of *213* for customer age. Other examples are a value of *999–999–9999* for

a U.S. phone number, a part color of *gren*, and an email address of WhyMe@GuessWhoIAM-Hah-Hah.org. All these values are problematic when data mining.

Discussion forum A form of asynchronous communication in which one group member posts an entry and other group members respond. A better form of group communication than email, because it is more difficult for the discussion to go off track.

Diseconomy of scale A principle that states as development teams become larger, the average contribution per worker decreases.

Disintermediation Elimination of one or more middle layers in the supply chain.

Distributed database processing A technique for storing database contents on two or more computers. Partitioned databases split the database into pieces that are stored on multiple computers but that do not duplicate any data. Replicated databases duplicate data on two or more computers. Updating replicated databases is challenging.

Domain name The registered, human-friendly valid name in the domain name system (DNS). The process of changing a name into its IP address is called *resolving the domain name*.

Drill down With an OLAP report, to further divide the data into more detail.

Drive-by sniffers People who take computers with wireless connections through an area and search for unprotected wireless networks in an attempt to gain free Internet access or to gather unauthorized data.

DSL (digital subscriber line) modem A device for converting computer signals to the format needed for DSL transmission.

Dual processor A computer with two CPUs.

E-commerce The buying and selling of goods and services over public and private computer networks.

Electronic exchange Site that facilitates the matching of buyers and sellers; the business process is similar to that of a stock exchange. Sellers offer goods at a given price through the electronic exchange, and buyers make offers to purchase over the same exchange. Price matches result in transactions from which the exchange takes a commission.

Email A form of asynchronous communication in which participants send comments and attachments electronically. As a form of group communication, it can be disorganized, disconnected, and easy to hide from.

Email spoofing A synonym for *phishing*. A technique for obtaining unauthorized data that uses pretexting via email. The *phisher* pretends to be a legitimate company and sends email requests for confidential data, such as account numbers, Social Security numbers, account passwords, and so forth. Phishers direct traffic to their sites under the guise of a legitimate business.

Encapsulation (encapsulated) An approach that isolates the logic within that service. No service user knows nor needs to know how the service is performed.

Encryption The process of transforming clear text into coded, unintelligible text for secure storage or communication.

Encryption algorithms Algorithms used to transform clear text into coded, unintelligible text for secure storage or communication. Commonly used methods are DES, 3DES, and AES.

Enterprise 2.0 The application of Web 2.0 technologies, collaboration systems, social networking, and related technologies to facilitate the cooperative work of intellectual workers in organizations.

Enterprise applications IS applications that span more than one department, such as some functional applications, as well as ERP, EAI, and SCM applications.

Enterprise application integration (EAI) The integration of existing systems by providing layers of software that connect applications and their data together.

Enterprise DBMS A product that processes large organizational and workgroup databases. These products support many users, perhaps thousands, and many different database applications. Such DBMS products support 24/7 operations and can manage databases that span dozens of different magnetic disks with hundreds of gigabytes or more of data. IBM's DB2, Microsoft's SQL Server, and Oracle's Oracle are examples of enterprise DBMS products.

Enterprise information system Information systems that support cross-functional processes and activities in multiple departments.

Enterprise resource planning (ERP) applications Cross-functional, enterprise-wide applications that integrate the primary value-chain activities with the functions of human resources and accounting.

Enterprise resource planning (ERP) system An information system based upon ERP technology.

Entity In the E-R data model, a representation of some thing that users want to track. Some entities represent a physical object; others represent a logical construct or transaction.

Entity-relationship (E-R) data model Popular technique for creating a data model whereby developers define the things that will be stored and identify the relationships among them.

Entity-relationship (E-R) diagrams A type of diagram used by database designers to document entities and their relationships to each other.

Ethernet Another name for the IEEE 802.3 protocol, Ethernet is a network protocol that operates at Layers 1 and 2 of the TCP/IP–OSI architecture. Ethernet, the world's most popular LAN protocol, is used on WANs as well.

EVDO A WAN wireless protocol standard.

Exabyte 10^{18} bytes.

Exception alert A message that notifies a system user of an out-of-the-ordinary—exceptional—event.

Experimentation A careful and reasoned analysis of an opportunity, envisioning potential products or solutions or applications of technology, and then developing those ideas that seem to have the most promise, consistent with the resources you have.

Expert system Knowledge-sharing system that is created by interviewing experts in a given business domain and codifying the rules used by those experts.

eXtensible Markup Language (XML) An important document standard that separates document content, structure, and presentation; eliminates problems in HTML. Used for Web Services and many other applications.

Face-to-face (F2F) meetings Meetings that require everyone to be in the same place at the same time.

Fields Also called *columns*; groups of bytes in a database table. A database table has multiple columns that are used to represent the attributes of an entity. Examples are *PartNumber*, *EmployeeName*, and *SalesDate*.

File A group of similar rows or records. In a database, sometimes called a *table*.

File server A computer that stores files.

File Transfer Protocol (FTP) A Layer-5 protocol used to copy files from one computer to another. In interorganizational transaction processing, FTP enables users to exchange large files easily.

Firewall A computing device located between a firm's internal and external networks that prevents unauthorized access to or from the internal network. A firewall can be a special-purpose computer or it can be a program on a general-purpose computer or on a router.

Firmware Computer software that is installed into devices such as printers, print services, and various types of communication devices. The software is coded just like other software, but it is installed into special, programmable memory of the printer or other device.

Five-component framework The five fundamental components of an information system—computer hardware, software, data, procedures, and people—that are present in every information system, from the simplest to the most complex.

Five forces model Model, proposed by Michael Porter, that assesses industry characteristics and profitability by means of five competitive forces—bargaining power of suppliers, threat of substitution, bargaining power of customers, rivalry among firms, and threat of new entrants.

Flash An add-on to browsers that was developed by Adobe and is useful for providing animation, movies, and other advanced graphics within a browser.

Folksonomy A structure of content that emerges from the activity and processing of many users.

Foreign keys A column or group of columns used to represent relationships. Values of the foreign key match values of the primary key in a different (foreign) table.

Form Data entry forms are used to read, insert, modify, and delete database data.

FTP (File Transfer Protocol) A Layer-5 protocol used to copy files from one computer to another. In interorganizational transaction processing, FTP enables users to exchange large files easily.

Functional information system Information systems that support a single business function or process within a department, such as accounts payable or prospect tracking.

Gantt chart A chart that shows tasks, dates, dependencies, and possibly resources.

Gigabyte (GB) 1,024MB.

GNU A set of tools for creating and managing open source software. Originally created to develop an open source Unix-like operating system

GNU General Public License (GPL) Agreement One of the standard license agreements for open source software.

Google Docs A version-management system for sharing documents and spreadsheet data. Documents are stored on a Google server, from which users can access and simultaneously see and edit the documents.

Gramm-Leach-Bliley (GLB) Act Passed by Congress in 1999, this act protects consumer financial data stored by financial institutions, which are defined as banks, securities firms, insurance companies, and organizations that provide financial advice, prepare tax returns, and provide similar financial services.

Granularity The level of detail in data. Customer name and account balance is large-granularity data. Customer name, balance, and the order details and payment history of every customer order is smaller granularity.

Green computing Environmentally conscious computing consisting of three major components: power management, virtualization, and e-waste management.

Grid A network of computers that operates as an integrated whole.

Hacking Occurs when a person gains unauthorized access to a computer system. Although some people hack for the sheer joy of doing it, other hackers invade systems for the malicious purpose of stealing or modifying data.

Hardening A term used to describe server operating systems that have been modified to make it especially difficult for them to be infiltrated by malware.

Hardware Electronic components and related gadgetry that input, process, output, store, and communicate data according to be instructions encoded in computer programs or software.

Hashing A method of mathematically manipulating an electronic message to create a string of bits that characterize the message.

Health Insurance Portability and Accountability Act (HIPAA) The privacy provisions of this 1996 act give individuals the right to access health data created by doctors and other health-care providers. HIPAA also sets rules and limits on who can read and receive a person's health information.

Horizontal-market application Software that provides capabilities common across all organizations and industries; examples include word processors, graphics programs, spreadsheets, and presentation programs.

Host operating system In virtualization, the operating system that hosts the virtual operating systems.

Hot site A remote processing center run by a commercial disaster-recovery service that provides equipment a company would need to continue operations after a disaster.

Href The attribute for a hyperlink.

HSDPA A WAN wireless protocol standard.

HTTPS An indication that a Web browser is using the SSL/TLS protocol to ensure secure communications.

Human capital The investment in human knowledge and skills with the expectation of future returns in the marketplace.

Hyperlink A pointer on a Web page to another Web page. A hyperlink contains the URL of the Web page to access when the user clicks the hyperlink. The URL can reference a page on the Web server that generated the page containing the hyperlink, or it can reference a page on another server.

Hypertext Markup Language (HTML) A language that defines the structure and layout of Web page content. An HTML tag is a notation used to define a data element for display or other purposes.

Hypertext Transfer Protocol (HTTP) A Layer-5 protocol used to process Web pages.

Identification The process whereby an information system identifies a user by requiring the user to sign on with a user name and password.

Identifier An attribute (or group of attributes) whose value is associated with one and only one entity instance.

IEEE 802.3 protocol This standard, also called *Ethernet*, is a network protocol that operates at Layers 1 and 2 of the TCP/IP–OSI architecture. Ethernet, the world's most popular LAN protocol, is used on WANs as well.

IEEE 802.11 protocol A wireless communications standard, widely used today, that enables access within a few hundred feet. The most popular version of this standard is *IEEE 802.11g*, which allows wireless transmissions of up to 54 Mbps.

IEE 802.16 protocol An emerging wireless communications standard, also known as *WiMax*, that enables broadband wireless access for fixed, nomadic, and portable applications. In fixed mode, it enables access across a several-mile or larger region. See also *WiMax*.

If . . . then . . . Format for rules derived from a decision tree (data mining) or by interviewing a human expert (expert systems).

Indexing The most important content function of knowledge management applications, which uses keyword search to determine whether content exists and provides a link to its location.

Industry-specific solutions An ERP template that is designed to serve the needs of companies or organizations in specific industries. Such solutions save time and lower risk. The development of industry-specific solutions spurred ERP growth.

Information (1) Knowledge derived from data, where *data* is defined as recorded facts or figures; (2) data presented in a meaningful context; (3) data processed by summing, ordering, averaging, grouping, comparing, or other similar operations; (4) a difference that makes a difference.

Information silos Islands of automation that work in isolation from one another.

Information system (IS) A group of components that interact to produce information.

Information technology (IT) The products, methods, inventions, and standards that are used for the purpose of producing information.

Inherent processes The procedures that must be followed to effectively use licensed software. For example, the processes inherent in MRP systems assume that certain users will take specified actions in a particular order. In most cases, the organization must conform to the processes inherent in the software.

Input hardware Hardware devices that attach to a computer; includes keyboards, mouse, document scanners, and bar-code (Universal Product Code) scanners.

Instruction set The collection of instructions that a computer can process.

Interenterprise information system Information systems that support processes and activities that span two or more independent organizations.

Internal firewalls A firewall that sits inside the organizational network.

Internet When spelled with a small *i*, as in *internet*, a private network of networks. When spelled with a capital *I*, as in *Internet*, the public internet known as the Internet.

Internet Corporation for Assigned Names and Numbers (ICANN) The organization responsible for managing the assignment of public IP addresses and domain names for use on the Internet. Each public IP address is unique across all computers on the Internet.

Internet Protocol (IP) A Layer-3 protocol. As the name implies, IP is used on the Internet, but it is used on many other internets as well. The chief purpose of IP is to route packets across an internet.

Internet service provider (ISP) An ISP provides users with Internet access. An ISP provides a user with a legitimate Internet address; it serves as the user's gateway to the Internet; and it passes communications back and forth between the user and the Internet. ISPs also pay for the Internet. They collect money from their customers and pay access fees and other charges on the users' behalf.

Intranet A private internet (note small i) used within a corporation or other organization.

Interorganizational information system Information systems that support processes and activities that span two or more independent organizations.

IP address A series of dotted decimals in a format like 192.168.2.28 that identifies a unique device on a network or internet. With the IPv4 standard, IP addresses have 32 bits. With the IPv6 standard, IP addresses have 128 bits. Today, IPv4 is more common, but it will likely be supplanted by IPv6 in the future. With IPv4, the decimal between the dots can never exceed 255.

IP spoofing A type of spoofing whereby an intruder uses another site's IP address as if it were that other site.

IPv4 The most commonly used Internet layer protocol.

IPv6 An Internet layer protocol created to provide for more IP addresses and other benefits.

Islands of automation The structure that results when functional applications work independently in isolation from one another. Usually problematic because data are duplicated, integration is difficult, and results can be inconsistent.

Just-barely-sufficient (information) Information that meets the purpose for which it is generated, but just barely so.

Kerberos A system, developed at MIT, that authenticates users without sending their passwords across a computer network. It uses a complicated system of "tickets" to enable users to obtain services from networks and other servers.

Key (1) A column or group of columns that identifies a unique row in a table. (2) A number used to encrypt data. The encryption algorithm applies the key to the original message to produce the coded message. Decoding (decrypting) a message is similar; a key is applied to the coded message to recover the original text.

Key escrow A control procedure whereby a trusted party is given a copy of a key used to encrypt database data.

Kilobyte (K) 1,024 bytes.

Knowledge management (KM) The process of creating value from intellectual capital and sharing that knowledge with employees, managers, suppliers, customers, and others who need it.

Knowledge management (KM) tools Computer applications used to store employee knowledge and to make that knowledge available to employees, customers, vendors, and others who need it. The source of KM tools is human knowledge, rather than recorded facts and figures.

LAN device A computing device that includes important networking components, including a switch, a router, a DHCP server, and other elements.

Legacy information system An older system that has outdated technologies and techniques but is still used, despite its age.

Library In version-control collaboration systems, a shared directory that allows access to various documents by means of permissions.

License Agreement that stipulates how a program can be used. Most specify the number of computers on which the program can be installed, some specify the number of users that can connect to and use the program remotely. Such agreements also stipulate limitations on the liability of the software vendor for the consequences of errors in the software.

Lift In market-basket terminology, the ratio of confidence to the base probability of buying an item. Lift shows how much the base probability changes when other products are purchased. If the lift is greater than 1, the change is positive; if it is less than 1, the change is negative.

Linkages Process interactions across value chains. Linkages are important sources of efficiencies and are readily supported by information systems.

Linux A version of Unix that was developed by the open source community. The open source community owns Linux, and there is no fee to use it. Linux is a popular operating system for Web servers.

Local area network (LAN) A network that connects computers that reside in a single geographic location on the premises of the company that operates the LAN. The number of connected computers can range from two to several hundred.

Localizing software The process by which computer programs are modified to use different human languages and character sets.

Lost-update problem An issue in multiuser database processing in which two or more users try to make changes to the data but the database cannot make all those changes because it was not designed to process changes from multiple users.

Mac OS An operating system developed by Apple Computer, Inc., for the Macintosh. The current version is Mac OS X. Macintosh computers are used primarily by graphic artists and workers in the arts community. Mac OS was developed for the PowerPC, but as of 2006 runs on Intel processors as well.

Machine code Code that has been compiled from source code and is ready to be processed by a computer.

Main memory A set of cells in which each cell holds a byte of data or instruction; each cell has an address, and the CPU uses the addresses to identify particular data items.

Maintenance In the context of information systems, (1) to fix the system to do what it was supposed to do in the first place or (2) to adapt the system to a change in requirements.

Malware Viruses, worms, Trojan horses, spyware, and adware.

Malware definitions Patterns that exist in malware code. Antimalware vendors update these definitions continuously and incorporate them into their products in order to better fight against malware.

Management information system (MIS) An information system that helps businesses achieve their goals and objectives.

Managerial decision A decision that concerns the allocation and use of resources.

Many-to-many (N:M) relationship Relationships involving two entity types in which an instance of one type can relate to many instances of the second type, and an instance of the second type can relate to many instances of the first. For example, the relationship between Student and Class is N:M. One student may enroll in many classes, and one class may have many students. Contrast with *one-to-many relationships.*

Margin [of a business process] The difference between the value of outputs in a business process and the cost of the process.

Market-basket analysis A data mining technique for determining sales patterns. A market-basket analysis shows the products that customers tend to buy together.

Mashup The combining of output from two or more Web sites into a single user experience.

Maximum cardinality The maximum number of entities that can be involved in a relationship. Common examples of maximum cardinality are 1:N, N:M, and 1:1.

Measure The data item of interest on an OLAP report. It is the item that is to be summed, averaged, or otherwise processed in the OLAP cube. Total sales, average sales, and average cost are examples of measures.

Megabyte (MB) 1,024KB.

Memory swapping The movement of programs and data into and out of memory. If a computer has insufficient memory for its workload, such swapping will degrade system performance.

Merchant companies In e-commerce, companies that take title to the goods they sell. They buy goods and resell them.

Message digest A bit string of a specific, fixed length that is produced by hashing and used to produce digital signatures.

Metadata Data that describe data.

Microblog A Web site on which users can publish their opinions, just like a Web blog, but the opinions are restricted to small amounts of text. Twitter is a microblogging tool.

Microsoft SharePoint A version-control application that includes many collaboration features and functions, including document check-in/checkout, surveys, discussion forums, and workflow.

Minimum cardinality The minimum number of entities that must be involved in a relationship.

Modem Short for *modulator/demodulator*, a modem converts the computer's digital data into signals that can be transmitted over telephone or cable lines.

Modules A suite of applications in an ERP system.

Moore's Law A law, created by Gordon Moore, stating that the number of transistors per square inch on an integrated chip doubles every 18 months. Moore's prediction has proved generally accurate in the 40 years since it was made. Sometimes this law is stated that the performance of a computer doubles every 18 months. Although not strictly true, this version gives the gist of the idea.

Multiparty text chat A synchronous virtual meeting in which participants meet at the same time and communicate by typing comments over a communication network.

Multi-user processing When multiple users process the database at the same time.

My Maps A browser-based mapping system provided by Google that enables users to mash up their content with content provided by others as well as with maps provided by Google.

MySQL A popular open source DBMS product that is license-free for most applications.

Narrowband Internet communication lines that have transmission speeds of 56 kbps or less. A dial-up modem provides narrowband access.

Network A collection of computers that communicate with one another over transmission lines.

Network interface card (NIC) A hardware component on each device on a network (computer, printer, etc.) that connects the device's circuitry to the communications line. The NIC works together with programs in each device to implement Layers 1 and 2 of the TCP/IP–OSI hybrid protocol.

Neural networks A popular supervised data mining technique used to predict values and make classifications, such as "good prospect" or "poor prospect."

Nonmerchant companies E-commerce companies that arrange for the purchase and sale of goods without ever owning or taking title to those goods.

Nonvolatile (memory) Memory that preserves data contents even when not powered (e.g., magnetic and optical disks). With such devices, you can turn the computer off and back on, and the contents will be unchanged.

Normal forms A classification of tables according to their characteristics and the kinds of problems they have.

Normalization The process of converting poorly structured tables into two or more well-structured tables.

Object Management Group (OMG) A software industry standards organization that created a standard set of terms and graphical notations for documenting business processes.

Object-relational database A type of database that stores both OOP objects and relational data. Rarely used in commercial applications.

Off-the-shelf software Software that can be used without having to make any changes.

Off-the-shelf with alterations software Software bought off-the-shelf but altered to fit the organization's specific needs.

Office Web Apps License-free Web application versions of Word, Excel, PowerPoint, and OneNote available on SkyDrive.

OLAP See *Online analytical processing.*

OLAP cube A presentation of an OLAP measure with associated dimensions. The reason for this term is that some products show these displays using three axes, like a cube in geometry. Same as *OLAP report.*

OLAP server Computer server running software that performs OLAP analyses. An OLAP server reads data from an operational database, performs preliminary calculations, and stores the results of those calculations in an OLAP database.

Onboard NIC A built-in network interface card.

One-of-a-kind application Software that is developed for a specific, unique need, usually for a particular company's operations.

One-to-many (1:N) relationship Relationships involving two entity types in which an instance of one type can relate to many instances of the second type, but an instance of the second type can relate to at most one instance of the first. For example, the relationship between *Department* and *Employee* is 1:N. A department may relate to many employees, but an employee relates to at most one department.

Online analytical processing (OLAP) A dynamic type of reporting system that provides the ability to sum, count, average, and perform other simple arithmetic operations on groups of data. Such reports are dynamic because users can change the format of the reports while viewing them.

Open source community A loosely coupled group of programmers who mostly volunteer their time to contribute code to develop and maintain common software. Linux and MySQL are two prominent products developed by such a community.

Operating system (OS) A computer program that controls the computer's resources: It manages the contents of main memory, processes keystrokes and mouse movements, sends signals to the display monitor, reads and writes disk files, and controls the processing of other programs.

Operational decisions Decisions that concern the day-to-day activities of an organization.

Optical fiber cable A type of cable used to connect the computers, printers, switches, and other devices on a LAN. The signals on such cables are light rays, and they are reflected inside the glass core of the optical fiber cable. The core is surrounded by a *cladding* to contain the light signals, and the cladding, in turn, is wrapped with an outer layer to protect it.

Oracle A popular, enterprise-class DBMS product from Oracle Corporation.

Organizational feasibility Whether an information system fits within an organization's customer, culture, or legal requirements.

Output hardware Hardware that displays the results of the computer's processing. Consists of video displays, printers, audio speakers, overhead projectors, and other special-purpose devices, such as large, flatbed plotters.

Outsourcing The process of hiring another organization to perform a service. Outsourcing is done to save costs, to gain expertise, and to free up management time.

Packet A small piece of an electronic message that has been divided into chunks that are sent separately and reassembled at their destination.

Packet-filtering firewall A firewall that examines each packet and determines whether to let the packet pass. To make this decision, it examines the source address, the destination addresses, and other data.

Parallel installation A type of system conversion in which the new system runs in parallel with the old one for a while. Parallel installation is expensive because the organization incurs the costs of running both systems.

Partitioned database A distributed database that is divided into non-overlapping segments and two or more segments are distributed into different geographic locations.

Payload The program codes of a virus that causes unwanted or hurtful actions, such as deleting programs or data, or even worse, modifying data in ways that are undetected by the user.

PC mules Business professionals who carry one or more computing devices wherever they go.

PC virtualization Synonym for *desktop virtualization.*

People As part of the five-component framework, one of the five fundamental components of an information system; includes those who operate and service the computers, those who maintain the data, those who support the networks, and those who use the system.

365

Perimeter firewall A firewall that sits outside the organizational network. It is the first device that Internet traffic encounters.

Permissions In a version-control system, authorizations to access shared documents stored in various directories. Typical permissions are read-only, read-and-edit, and read-edit-and-delete; some directories have no permission—they are off-limits.

Personal DBMS DBMS products designed for smaller, simpler database applications. Such products are used for personal or small workgroup applications that involve fewer than 100 users, and normally fewer than 15. Today, Microsoft Access is the only prominent personal DBMS.

Personal identification number (PIN) A form of authentication whereby the user supplies a number that only he or she knows.

Personal information system Information systems used by a single individual.

Petabyte 10^{15} bytes.

Phased installation A type of system conversion in which the new system is installed in pieces across the organization(s). Once a given piece works, then the organization installs and tests another piece of the system, until the entire system has been installed.

Phisher An individual or organization that spoofs legitimate companies in an attempt to illegally capture personal data, such as credit card numbers, email accounts, and driver's license numbers.

Phishing A technique for obtaining unauthorized data that uses pretexting via email. The *phisher* pretends to be a legitimate company and sends an email requesting confidential data, such as account numbers, Social Security numbers, account passwords, and so forth.

Pilot installation A type of system conversion in which the organization implements the entire system on a limited portion of the business. The advantage of pilot implementation is that if the system fails, the failure is contained within a limited boundary. This reduces exposure of the business and also protects the new system from developing a negative reputation throughout the organization(s).

Plunge installation A type of system conversion in which the organization shuts off the old system and starts the new system. If the new system fails, the organization is in trouble: Nothing can be done until either the new system is fixed or the old system is reinstalled. Because of the risk, organizations should avoid this conversion style if possible. Sometimes called *direct installation*.

Portal server Program similar to a Web server, but with a customizable user interface.

Pre-Internet system Information systems used before widespread commercial use of the Internet. Information systems that were used prior to 1993–1995.

Pretexting A technique for gathering unauthorized information in which someone pretends to be someone else. A common scam involves a telephone caller who pretends to be from a credit card company and claims to be checking the validity of credit card numbers. Phishing is also a form of pretexting.

Price conflict In e-commerce, a conflict that may result when manufacturers offer products at prices lower than those available through existing sales channels.

Price elasticity A measure of the sensitivity in demand to changes in price. It is the ratio of the percentage change in quantity divided by the percentage change in price.

Primary activities In Porter's value chain model, the fundamental activities that create value: inbound logistics, operations, outbound logistics, marketing/sales, and service.

Privacy Act of 1974 Federal law that provides protections to individuals regarding records maintained by the U.S. government.

Private IP address A type of IP address used within private networks and internets. Private IP addresses are assigned and managed by the company that operates the private network or internet.

Probable loss The "bottom line" of risk assessment; the likelihood of loss multiplied by the cost of the loss consequences (both tangible and intangible).

Problem A *perceived* difference between what is and what ought to be.

Problem of the last mile The difficulty involved in getting the capacity of fast optical fiber transmission lines from the street in front of buildings into the homes and smaller businesses located in those buildings. Digging up the street and backyard of every residence and small business to install optical fiber is not affordable; it is hoped that WiMax technology will be able to solve the problem of making the network connections of "the last mile."

Procedures Instructions for humans. One of the five fundamental components of an information system.

Process blueprint In an ERP application, a comprehensive set of inherent processes for all organizational activities, each of which is documented with diagrams that use a set of standardized symbols.

Protocol A standardized means for coordinating an activity between two or more entities.

Public IP address An IP address used on the Internet. Such IP addresses are assigned to major institutions in blocks by the Internet Corporation for Assigned Names and Numbers (ICANN). Each IP address is unique across all computers on the Internet.

Public key/private key A special version of asymmetric encryption that is popular on the Internet. With this method, each site has a public key for encoding messages and a private key for decoding them.

Pull (results) Reports that are produced on request by users.

Push (results) Reports that are published on a scheduled basis to a list of subscribers.

Quad processor A computer with four CPUs.

Query A request for data from a database.

Quick Launch A partial list of resources contained within the site.

RAM Stands for *random access memory*, which is main memory consisting of cells that hold data or instructions. Each cell has an address that the CPU uses to read or write data. Memory locations can be read or written in any order, hence the term *random access*. RAM memory is almost always volatile.

Real Simple Syndication (RSS) A standard for subscribing to content sources; similar to an email system for content.

Record Also called a *row*, a group of columns in a database table.

Regression analysis A type of supervised data mining that estimates the values of parameters in a linear equation. Used to determine the relative influence of variables on an outcome and also to predict future values of that outcome.

Relation The more formal name for a database table.

Relational database Database that carries its data in the form of tables and that represents relationships using foreign keys.

Relationship An association among entities or entity instances in an E-R model or an association among rows of a table in a relational database.

Relevant (information) Information that is appropriate to both the context and the subject.

Remote access system An information system that provides action at a distance, such as telesurgery or telelaw enforcement.

Replicated database Database that is stored and processed in two or more locations. Data are duplicated in all of the replications.

Report A presentation of data in a structured or meaningful context.

Report server A special case of a business intelligence (BI) application server that serves only reports.

Reporting application A business intelligence application that produces information from data by applying reporting tools to that data.

Reporting system A business intelligence system that delivers reports to authorized users at appropriate times.

Reporting tools A type of business intelligence tool, these programs read data from a variety of sources, process that data, format the data into structured reports, and deliver those reports to the users who need them.

Repository A collection of business records, usually implemented as a database.

Resources People or information system applications that are assigned to roles in business processes.

RFM analysis A way of analyzing and ranking customers according to the recency, frequency, and monetary value of their purchases.

Risk The likelihood of an adverse occurrence.

Roles Sets of activities in a business process; resources are assigned to roles.

Router A special-purpose computer that moves network traffic from one node on a network to another.

Row Also called *record*, a group of columns in a database table.

RSS See *Real Simple Syndication*.

RSS feed A data source that transmits using an RSS standard. The output of an RSS feed is consumed by an RSS reader.

RSS reader A program by which users can subscribe to magazines, blogs, Web sites, and other content sources; the reader will periodically check the sources, and, if there has been a change since the last check, it will place a summary of the change and a link to the new content in an inbox.

Safeguard Any action, device, procedure, technique, or other measure that reduces a system's vulnerability to a threat.

Schedule feasibility Whether an information system will be able to be developed on the timetable needed.

Secure Socket Layer (SSL) A protocol that uses both asymmetric and symmetric encryption. SSL is a protocol layer that works between Levels 4 (transport) and 5 (application) of the TCP–OSI protocol architecture. When SSL is in use, the browser address will begin with https://. The most recent version of SSI is called TLS.

Security policy Management's policy for computer security, consisting of a general statement of the organization's security program, issue-specific policy, and system-specific policy.

Security program A systematic plan by which an organization addresses security issues; consists of three components: senior management involvement, safeguards of various kinds, and incident response.

Security threat A challenge to an information system that arises from one of three sources: human error and mistakes, malicious human activity, and natural events and disasters.

Self-efficacy A person's belief that he or she can successfully perform the tasks required in his or her job.

Semantic security Concerns the unintended release of protected information through the release of a combination of reports or documents that are independently not protected.

Server(s) A computer that provides some type of service, such as hosting a database, running a blog, publishing a Web site, or selling goods. Server computers are faster, larger, and more powerful than client computers.

Server farm A large collection of server computers that coordinates the activities of the servers, usually for commercial purposes.

Server hardware Computers that provide communications, database, application, and other computing services to clients; server hardware is selected, operated, and managed by IT professionals.

Server tier In the three-tier architecture, the tier that consists of computers that run Web servers to generate Web pages and other data in response to requests from browsers. Web servers also process application programs.

Server virtualization The process of running two or more operating system instances on the same server. The host operating system runs virtual operating systems as applications.

Service A repeatable task that a business needs to perform.

Service-oriented architecture (SOA) Processing philosophy that advocates that computing systems use a *standard method* to declare the services they provide and the interface by which those services can be requested and used. Web services are an implementation of SOA.

SharedView A Microsoft program that enables one person to share his or her desktop with a small group of others using the Internet. Useful for online meetings.

SharePoint site A workflow site, created in Microsoft's collaboration tool SharePoint, that enables team members to define workflows for their group. The software that runs the site will send emails to team members requesting reviews, create task lists defined for the workflow, check documents in, mark tasks as complete, email the next person in the workflow, and email copies of all correspondence to the workflow leader, who can use this capability to ensure that all teammates perform the work they are requested to do.

Silverlight A browser add-on that was developed by Microsoft to enhance browser features to improve the user interface, include movies, audio, animation and to provide greater programmer control of user activity.

Simple Mail Transfer Protocol (SMTP) A Layer-5 architecture used to send email. Normally used in conjunction with other Layer-5 protocols (POP3, IMAP) for receiving email.

Site license A license purchased by an organization to equip all the computers on a site with certain software.

SLATES Acronym developed by Andrew McAfee that summarizes key characteristics of enterprise 2.0: search, links, author, tagged, extensions, signaled.

Small office/home office (SOHO) A business office with usually fewer than 10 employees often located in the business professional's home.

Smart card A plastic card similar to a credit card that has a microchip. The microchip, which holds much more data than a magnetic strip, is loaded with identifying data. Normally requires a PIN.

Sniffing A technique for intercepting computer communications. With wired networks, sniffing requires a physical connection to the network. With wireless networks, no such connection is required.

SOA Standards Processing standards used to implement service-oriented architecture. They include XML, WSDL, SOAP, and numerous other standards. The particular meaning and function of these standards is unimportant to most business professionals; however, SOA is only possible because such standards exist.

Social capital The investment in social relations with expectation of future returns in the marketplace.

Social CRM CRM that includes social networking elements and gives the customer much more power and control in the customer/vendor relationship.

Social graph A network of relationships, usually among people, but possibly among people and organizations.

Social networking (SN) Connections of people with similar interests. Today, social networks typically are supported by Web 2.0 technology.

Social networking application A computer program that interacts with users and processes information in a social network.

Social networking group An association of social network members related to a particular topic, event, activity, or other collective interest.

Social networking information system An information system that includes features and functions for processing and manipulating a social graph.

Software Instructions for computers. One of the five fundamental components of an information system.

Software as a (free) service (SAAS) (1) Business model whereby companies (such as Google, Amazon.com, and eBay) provide license-free services based on their software, rather than providing software as a product (by means of software-usage licenses). Software as a service is an example of Web 2.0. (2) Business model whereby companies (Microsoft, Oracle) provide paid-for services based on their software. Users need not install software on their computer, but rather pay a fee to use software installed on the seller's servers, somewhere in the cloud.

Source code Computer code as written by humans and that is understandable by humans. Source code must be translated into machine code before it can be processed.

Spoofing When someone pretends to be someone else with the intent of obtaining unauthorized data. If you pretend to be your professor, you are spoofing your professor.

Spyware Programs installed on the user's computer without the user's knowledge or permission that reside in the background and, unknown to the user, observe the user's actions and keystrokes, modify computer activity, and report the user's activities to sponsoring organizations. Malicious spyware captures keystrokes to obtain user names, passwords, account numbers, and other sensitive information. Other spyware is used for marketing analyses, observing what users do, Web sites visited, products examined and purchased, and so forth.

SQL Server A popular enterprise-class DBMS product from Microsoft.

Steering committee A group of senior managers from a company's major business functions that works with the CIO to set the IS priorities and decide among major IS projects and alternatives.

Storage hardware Hardware that saves data and programs. Magnetic disk is by far the most common storage device, although optical disks, such as CDs and DVDs, also are popular.

Stored procedures A computer program stored in the database that is used to enforce business rules.

Strategic decision Decision that concerns broader-scope, organizational issues.

Strength of a relationship To an organization, the likelihood that a person or other organization in a relationship will do something that will benefit the organization.

Strong password A password with the following characteristics: seven or more characters; does not contain the user's user name, real name, or company name; does not contain a complete dictionary word, in any language; is different from the user's previous passwords; and contains both upper- and lowercase letters, numbers, and special characters.

Structured decision A type of decision for which there is a formalized and accepted method for making the decision.

Structured Query Language (SQL) An international standard language for processing database data.

Supervised data mining A form of data mining in which data miners develop a model prior to the analysis and apply statistical techniques to data to estimate values of the parameters of the model.

Supply chain A network of organizations and facilities that transforms raw materials into products delivered to customers.

Support In market-basket terminology, the probability that two items will be purchased together.

Support activities In Porter's value chain model, the activities that contribute indirectly to value creation: procurement, technology, human resources, and the firm's infrastructure.

Swim-lane layout A process diagram layout similar to swim lanes in a swimming pool; each role in the process is shown in its own horizontal rectangle, or lane.

Switch A special-purpose computer that receives and transmits data across a network.

Switching costs Business strategy of locking in customers by making it difficult or expensive to change to another product or supplier.

Symmetric encryption An encryption method whereby the same key is used to encode and to decode the message.

Symmetrical digital subscriber lines (SDSL) DSL lines that have the same upload and download speeds.

Synch The process of synchronizing the data on two or more computers. For example, if you work on your computer at home, when you get to work, you have to synchronize (or synch) your computer at work with any changes you've made on the computer at home.

Synchronous communication Information exchange that occurs when all members of a work team meet at the same time, such as face-to-face meetings or conference calls.

System A group of components that interact to achieve some purpose.

System conversion The process of converting business activity from the old system to the new.

Systems analysts IS professionals who understand both business and technology. They are active throughout the systems development process and play a key role in moving the project from conception to conversion and, ultimately, maintenance. Systems analysts integrate the work of the programmers, testers, and users.

Systems development The process of creating and maintaining information systems. It is sometimes called *systems analysis and design*.

Systems development life cycle (SDLC) The classical process used to develop information systems. These basic tasks of systems development are combined into the following phases: system definition, requirements analysis, component design, implementation, and system maintenance (fix or enhance).

Systems thinking The mental process of making one or more models of the components of a system and connecting the inputs and outputs among those components into a sensible whole, one that explains the phenomenon observed.

Table Also called a *file*, a group of similar rows or records in a database.

Tag In markup languages such as HTML and XML, notation used to define a data element for display or other purposes.

TCP/IP–OSI (protocol) architecture A protocol architecture having five layers that evolved as a hybrid of the TCP/IP and the OSI architecture. This architecture is used on the Internet and on most internets.

Team survey A form of asynchronous communication in which one team member creates a list of questions and other team members respond. Microsoft SharePoint has built-in survey capability.

Technical feasibility Whether existing information technology will be able to meet the needs of a new information system.

Technical safeguard Safeguard that involves the hardware and software components of an information system.

Telediagnosis A remote access system used by health care professionals to provide expertise in rural or remote areas.

Telelaw enforcement A remote access system that provides law enforcement capability.

Telesurgery A remote access system that links surgeons to robotic equipment and patients at a distance.

Terabyte (TB) 1,024GB.

Test plan Groups of sequences of actions that users will take when using the new system.

The Internet The internet that is publicly used throughout the world.

Thick client A software application that requires programs other than just the browser on a user's computer; that is, that requires code on both client and server computers.

Thin client A software application that requires nothing more than a browser and can be run on only the user's computer.

Three-tier architecture Architecture used by most e-commerce server applications. The tiers refer to three different classes of computers. The user tier consists of users' computers that have browsers that request and process Web pages. The server tier consists of computers that run Web servers and in the process generate Web pages and other data in response to requests from browsers. Web servers also process application programs. The third tier is the database tier, which runs the DBMS that processes the database.

Timely (information) Information that is produced in time for its intended use.

Trade-off In project management, a choice among scarce resources such as scope, time, cost, quality, risk, people, and other resources. Managers may need to trade off a delay in the project due date to reduce expense and keep critical employees.

Train the trainer Training sessions in which vendors train the organization's employees, called Super Users, to become in-house trainers in order to improve training quality and reduce training expenses.

Transaction processing system (TPS) An information system that supports operational decision making.

Transmission Control Protocol/Internet Protocol (TCP/IP) architecture A protocol architecture having four layers; forms the basis for the TCP/IP–OSI architecture blend used by the Internet.

Transport Layer Security (TLS) A protocol, using both asymmetric and symmetric encryption, that works between Levels 4 (transport) and 5 (application) of the TCP–OSI protocol architecture. TLS is the new name for a later version of SSL.

Trigger A computer program stored within the database that is executed when certain conditions arise. Primarily used to maintain database consistency.

Trojan horse Virus that masquerades as a useful program or file. A typical Trojan horse appears to be a computer game, an MP3 music file, or some other useful, innocuous program.

Tunnel A virtual, private pathway over a public or shared network from the VPN client to the VPN server.

Twitter A Web 2.0 application that allows users to publish 140-character descriptions of anything.

Uncertainty Those things we don't know.

Unified Modeling Language (UML) A series of diagramming techniques that facilitates OOP development. UML has dozens of different diagrams for all phases of system development. UML does not require or promote any particular development process.

Uniform resource locator (URL) A document's address on the Web. URLs begin on the right with a top-level domain, and, moving left, include a domain name and then are followed by optional data that locates a document within that domain.

Universal Serial Bus (USB) A standard for connecting computers and external devices such as printers, scanners, keyboards, and mice. A USB device is a peripheral device that conforms to the USB standard.

Unix An operating system developed at Bell Labs in the 1970s. It has been the workhorse of the scientific and engineering communities since then.

Unshielded twisted pair (UTP) cable A type of cable used to connect the computers, printers, switches, and other devices on a LAN. A UTP cable has four pairs of twisted wire. A device called an RJ-45 connector is used to connect the UTP cable into NIC devices.

Unstructured decision A type of decision for which there is no agreed-on decision-making method.

Unsupervised data mining A form of data mining whereby the analysts do not create a model or hypothesis before running the analysis. Instead, they apply the data mining technique to the data and observe the results. With this method, analysts create hypotheses after the analysis to explain the patterns found.

User tier In the three-tier architecture, the tier that consists of computers that have browsers that request and process Web pages.

Usurpation Occurs when unauthorized programs invade a computer system and replace legitimate programs. Such unauthorized programs typically shut down the legitimate system and substitute their own processing.

Value According to Porter, the amount of money that a customer is willing to pay for a resource, product, or service.

Value chain A network of value-creating activities.

Value of social capital Value of social network that is determined by the number of relationships in a social network, by the strength of those relationships, and by the resources controlled by those related.

Version control Use of software to control access to and configuration of documents, designs, and other electronic versions of products.

Version management Tracking of changes to documents by means of features and functions that accommodate concurrent work. The means by which version management is done depend on the particular version-management system used; three such systems are wikis, Google Docs, and Windows Live SkyDrive.

Vertical-market application Software that serves the needs of a specific industry. Examples of such programs are those used by dental offices to schedule appointments and bill patients, those used by auto mechanics to keep track of customer data and customers' automobile repairs, and those used by parts warehouses to track inventory, purchases, and sales.

Videoconferencing Technology that combines a conference call with video cameras.

Viral hook An inducement that causes someone to share an ad, link, file, picture, movie, or other resource with friends and associates over the Internet.

Viral marketing A marketing method used in the Web 2.0 world in which *users* spread news about products and services to one another.

Virtual machines A computer program that presents the appearance of an independent operating system within a second host operating system. The host can support mutliple virtual machines, possibly running different operating system programs (Windows, Linux), each of which is assigned assets such as disk space, devices, network connections, over which it has control.

Virtual meeting A meeting in which participants do not meet in the same place and possibly not at the same time.

Virtual private network (VPN) A WAN connection alternative that uses the Internet or a private internet to create the appearance of private point-to-point connections. In the IT world, the term *virtual* means something that appears to exist that does not exist in fact. Here, a VPN uses the public Internet to create the appearance of a private connection.

Virtualization The process by which multiple operating systems share the same computer hardware, usually a server.

Virus A computer program that replicates itself.

Volatile (memory) Data that will be lost when the computer or device is not powered.

Vulnerability An opening or a weakness in a security system. Some vulnerabilities exist because there are no safeguards or because the existing safeguards are ineffective.

WAN wireless A communications system that provides wireless connectivity to a wide area network.

Web The Internet-based network of browsers and servers that process HTTP or HTTPS.

Web 2.0 A loose grouping of capabilities, technologies, business models, and philosophies that characterize new and emerging business uses of the Internet.

WebEx A popular commercial webinar application used in virtual sales presentations.

Web farm A facility that runs multiple Web servers. Work is distributed among the computers in a Web farm so as to maximize throughput.

Web page Document encoded in HTML that is created, transmitted, and consumed using the World Wide Web.

Web server A program that processes the HTTP protocol and transmits Web pages on demand. Web servers also process application programs.

Web storefront In e-commerce, a Web-based application that enables customers to enter and manage their orders.

Webinar A virtual meeting in which attendees view each other on their computer screens.

Wide area network (WAN) A network that connects computers located at different geographic locations.

Wi-Fi Protected Access (WPA and WPA2) An improved wireless security standard developed by the IEEE 802.11 committee to fix the flaws of the Wired Equivalent Privacy (WEP) standard. Only newer wireless hardware uses this technique.

WiMax An emerging technology based on the IEEE 802.16 standard. WiMax is designed to deliver the "last mile" of wireless broadband access and could ultimately replace cable and DSL for fixed applications and replace cell phones for nomadic and portable applications. See also *IEEE 802.16*.

Windows An operating system designed and sold by Microsoft. It is the most widely used operating system.

Windows Live SkyDrive A cloud-based file storage location supported by Microsoft that provides free file storage and Web-based versions of Word, Excel, PowerPoint, and OneNote.

Wired Equivalent Privacy (WEP) A wireless security standard developed by the IEEE 802.11 committee that was insufficiently tested before it was deployed in communications equipment. It has serious flaws.

Wireless NIC (WNIC) Devices that enable wireless networks by communicating with wireless access points. Such devices can be cards that slide into the PCMA slot or they can be built-in, onboard devices. WNICs operate according to the 802.11 protocol.

Work breakdown structure (WBS) A hierarchy of the tasks required to complete a project; for a large project, it might involve hundreds or thousands of tasks.

Workflow A process or procedure by which content is created, edited, used, and disposed.

Workflow control Use of software and information systems to monitor the execution of a work team's processes; ensures that actions are taken at appropriate times and prohibits the skipping of steps or tasks.

Workgroup information system An information system that supports a department or other work team.

Worm A virus that propagates itself using the Internet or some other computer network. Worm code is written specifically to infect another computer as quickly as possible.

Worth-its-cost (information) Information for which there is an appropriate relationship between the cost of the information and its value.

WPA2 See *Wi-Fi Protected Access*.

XML See *eXtensible Markup Language*.

Index